Mementoes of the English Martyrs

and

Confessors for Every Day of the Year

Mementoes of the English Martyrs *and* Confessors for Every Day in the Year

by

Fr. Henry Sebastian Bowden

SOPHIA INSTITUTE PRESS
Manchester, New Hampshire

Bowden's *Mementoes of the English Martyrs and Confessors for Every Day in the Year* was first published in 1910 by Burns and Oates, London. The present edition prefers fidelity to the superb original over modernized diction, and so contains only minimal formatting and editorial changes that do not affect the original content or style. Citations have been added or amended where necessary, and select artwork and poems have been included from the public domain.

Approbations from the original:
Nihil obstat: Gulielmus Canonicus Gildea, D. D., *Censor Deputatus*
Imprimatur: Edmundus Canonicus Surmont, Vicarius Generalis
Westminster, March 17, 1910

Scripture quotations are generally the author's own translations from the Latin Vulgate. Citations have been included that correspond to the Challoner version of the Douay-Rheims Bible, per the imprint of John Murphy Company (Baltimore, 1899).

Cover design by Isabella Fasciano
Front cover art: Historische ornaments, Romanesque, Gothic, Renaissance and Persian, chromolithograph, published 1881 (Getty 1168176925); Beautiful ornate cross (Alamy HAY1BX); 2 blank sheet of an old antique book (Alamy BYRW0R)

Sophia Institute Press
Box 5284, Manchester, NH 03108
1-800-888-9344

www.SophiaInstitute.com

paperback ISBN 978-1-64413-778-9

ebook ISBN 978-1-64413-779-6

Library of Congress Control Number: 2022946401

FIRST EDITION

Laverunt stolas suas,
et dealbaverunt eas in sanguine Agni.

Apocalypse 7:14

Why do I use my paper, ink, and pen?
  Or call my wits to counsel what to say?
Such memories were made for mortal men.
  I speak of saints, whose names cannot decay.

St. Henry Walpole (+1595)

CONTENTS

PUBLISHER'S PREFACE 1

INTRODUCTION 3

JANUARY

✠1. Past and Present (1) — William Blundell, L. 9
2. Past and Present (2) — William Blundell, L. 10
3. Living Stones — Abbot Feckenham, O. S. B. 11
✠4. The Voice of the Preacher — Bl. Thomas Plumtree, Pr. 12
5. Defiling the Sanctuaries — Abbot Feckenham, O. S. B. 13
6. The Prodigal's Return — Fr. John Genings, O. S. F. 14
✠7. Balaam's Ass — Ven. Edward Waterson, Pr. 15
8. The Weak Made Strong — The eleven Marian bishops 16
9. Conversion by Knighthood — Thomas Pounde, S. J. 17
10. The Pilgrimage of Grace (1) — Sir Robert Aske, L. 18
11. The Pilgrimage of Grace (2) — Sir Thomas Percy, L. 19
✠12. The Sin of Ozias (1) — Bp. John White of Winchester 20
13. A Herald of the Truth (2) — Bp. John White of Winchester 21
14. The Oldest Faith — Ven. William Lloyd, Pr. 22
15. Devotion to the Sacraments — Bl. John Fisher, Card. Bp., and Henry VII 23
16. A Boy Orator — Bl. Edmund Campion, S. J. 25
17. Prayer in Suffering — Bl. Edmund Campion, S. J. 26
18. Lifting the Feeble Hands — Bl. Edmund Campion, S. J. 27
19. Before the Sanhedrin — Bl. Edmund Campion, S. J. 28
20. Tribute to Caesar — Bl. Edmund Campion, S. J. 29
✠21. Fortified by Example — Vens. Thomas Reynolds, Pr., and Alban Roe, O. S. B. . 30
✠22. Scruples Cured — Ven. William Pattenson, Pr. 31
23. The Practice of the Law — Ven. Nicholas Woodfen, Pr. 32
✠24. Victims of Perjury — Vens. William Ireland, S. J., and John Grove, L. 33
25. Saul, Otherwise Paul — Ven. Laurence Humphrey, L. 34
26. The Smile of Royalty — Bl. Thomas More, L. 35
27. Mass under Penal Laws — Letter of a missionary priest 36

Key

Abp. (Archbishop)	L. (Layman)	Pr. (Priest)	W. (Widow)
Bp. (Bishop)	O. S. B. (Benedictine)	Prs. (Priests)	✠ — Day of death
Card. (Cardinal)	O. S. F. (Franciscan)	S. J. (Jesuit)	

28. Divine Vengeance on Heresy — Ven. Arthur Bell, O. S. F. 37
29. Supernatural Sympathies — Ven. Edward Stransham, Pr. 38
30. A Talk with a Reformer — Bl. Ralph Sherwin, Pr. 39
31. The Punishment of Achab — Fr. Peto's prophecy 40

FEBRUARY

✠1. Grounds for Faith — Ven. Henry Morse, S. J. 43
2. A Mass of Thanksgiving — Ven. Henry Morse, S. J. 44
✠3. Weep Not for Me — Bl. John Nelson, S. J. 45
4. Gall to Drink — Bl. John Nelson, S. J. 46
5. The Bread of the Strong — Bl. John Nelson, S. J. 47
6. The Sunamitess Rewarded — Margaret Powell, L. 48
✠7. True to a Trust — Bl. Thomas Sherwood, L. 50
8. Prayers with Tears — Bl. John Fisher, Card. Bp. 51
9. The Stones of Israel — Bl. John Fisher, Card. Bp. 52
10. Father of the Poor — Bl. John Fisher, Card. Bp. 53
11. Sorrow Turned to Joy — Ven. George Haydock, Pr.. 54
✠12. A Royal Hypocrite — Ven. George Haydock, Pr. 55
13. Friend of Publicans and Sinners — Ven. James Fenn, Pr. 57
14. Patience in the Apostolate — Ven. John Nutter, Pr. 58
15. Injustice Enthroned — Ven. John Munden, Pr.. 59
16. With the Plague-Stricken — Ven. Henry Morse, S. J. 60
17. From City to City — Ven. Henry Morse, S. J. 61
✠18. Dying Life — Ven. John Pibush, Pr.. 62
19. In the Shadow of Death (1) — Bl. Thomas More, L. 63
20. In the Shadow of Death (2) — Bl. Thomas More, L. 64
✠21. A Martyr Poet — Ven. Robert Southwell, S. J. 65
22. Honey from the Rock — Ven. Robert Southwell, S. J.. 66
23. In the Pit of Misery — Ven. Robert Southwell, S. J. 67
24. More Precious than Life — James, Earl of Derwentwater 68
25. The Changes of Heretics — Bl. Thomas More, L. 69
26. Faith and Loyalty — Ven. Robert Drury, Pr. 70
27. The One Judge — Ven. Mark Barkworth, O. S. B. 71
28. Harboring Priests — Ven. Anne Line, W. 73
29. The Cardinal's Hat — Bl. John Fisher, Card. Bp. 74

MARCH

1. Heavenly Visions — Ven. Stephen Rowsam, Pr. 77
2. Learning to Die — Walter Colman, O. S. F. 78
✠3. The Daily Sacrifice — Bl. Thomas More, L. 79
4. The Vestments of Salvation — Ven. Nicholas Horner, L. 80
5. Filial Reverence — Ven. James Bird, L.. 82
6. The Mother of God — Ven. Henry Heath, O. S. F. 83
✠7. Holy Friendship — Bl. John Larke, Pr. 84

8. In Bonds for Christ (1) — Bl. William Hart, Pr. to the Catholic prisoners (1) . . 85
9. In Bonds for Christ (2) — Bl. William Hart, Pr. to the Catholic prisoners (2) . . 86
10. England's Debt to the Pope — Bl. William Hart, Pr.. 87
✠11. Chains Falling Off — Ven. Thomas Atkinson, Pr. 88
12. A Last Request — Bl. William Hart to the afflicted Catholics (1) 89
13. Stand Fast — Bl. William Hart to the afflicted Catholics (2) 90
14. A Mendicant Lord Chancellor — Bl. Thomas More, L. 91
✠15. The Apostle of Yorkshire — Bl. William Hart, Pr. 92
16. Night turned to Day — Ven. Robert Dalby, Pr.. 94
17. The Motive of a Missioner — Bl. William Hart, Pr. 95
✠18. Christian Modesty — Ven. John Thulis, Pr. 96
19. A Glimpse of Heaven — Ven. Roger Wrenno, L.. 97
20. The Morning Star — Ven. Henry Heath, O. S. F. 98
✠21. Cut Asunder — Ven. Thomas Pilchard, Pr. 99
22. A Catholic's Grave — John Jessop, L.. 100
23. Fruit of Martyrdom — Ven. William Pike, L.. 101
24. The Guardian Angel — Ven. John Hambley, Pr. 102
✠25. The Winepress Alone (1) — Bl. Margaret Clitherow, L. 104
26. Before Herod (2) — Bl. Margaret Clitherow, L. 105
27. A Valiant Woman (3) — Bl. Margaret Clitherow, L.. 106
28. Filial Piety — Bl. Hart to his Protestant mother (1). 107
29. No Comparison — Bl. Hart to his Protestant mother (2) 108
30. Meeting in Heaven — Bl. Hart to his Protestant mother (3) 109
31. Jesus Dulcis Memoria — Ven. Henry Heath, O. S. F. 110

APRIL

1. Love of the Seminary — Ven. Thomas Maxfield, Pr. 113
✠2. False Brethren — Bl. John Payne, Pr. 114
3. Avoidance of Scandal — Abp. Nicholas Heath of York 115
4. The Last of His Line — Bp. Thomas Goldwell of St. Asaph 116
5. Strength in Union — Ven. Henry Walpole, S.J.. 117
6. The Song of the Spirit — Ven. Henry Walpole, S.J. .118
✠7. Under the Shadow of the Most High — Ven. Henry Walpole, S.J. 119
8. Devotion to St. Winefride — Ven. Edward Oldcorne, S.J. 120
9. Life in Religion — Ven. Henry Heath, O. S. F., to a nun. 121
10. Virgo Potens — Ven. Henry Heath, O. S. F. 122
✠11. Lost and Found — Ven. George Gervase, O. S. B. 123
12. Tormenting Ministers — Ven. George Gervase, O. S. B. 124
✠13. A Fruitful Old Age — Ven. John Lockwood, Pr. 125
14. A Cry for Relief (1) — William Blundell, L. 126
15. A Cry for Relief (2) — William Blundell, L. 128
16. Awaiting Sentence — Ven. Henry Heath, O. S. F. 130
17. Prayer for England — Ven. Henry Heath, O. S. F. 131
18. The Bride of St. Francis — Ven. Henry Heath, O. S. F. 133

19. Good Books — Ven. James Duckett, L. 134
✠20. Penitent and Martyr — Ven. James Bell, Pr. 135
✠21. Devotion to the Priesthood — Ven. Thomas Tichborne, Pr. 136
22. An Unexpected Cure — Ven. Robert Watkinson, Pr. 137
23. Ten Just Men — Bl. John Fisher, Card. Bp. 138
24. Always the Same — Bl. John Fisher, Card. Bp. 139
25. One in Life and Death — Vens. Robert Anderton and William Marsden, Prs. . 140
✠26. A Cheerful Giver — Ven. Edward Morgan, Pr. 141
27. Light and Darkness — Ven. Francis Page, S.J. 142
28. Love, Earthly and Heavenly — Ven. Francis Page, S.J. 143
29. In the Waves — Vens. Robert Anderton and William Marsden, Prs. 144
30. The Pharisees Silenced — Ven. Robert Anderton, Pr. 145

MAY

1. The Witness of Tradition — Bl. Richard Reynolds, Bridgettine. 147
2. Mass of the Holy Ghost — Bl. John Houghton, Carthusian 148
✠3. The Seal of Confession — Fr. Henry Garnet, S.J. 149
✠4. Holy Wrath — Bl. John Haile, Pr. 150
5. The Voice of the Bridegroom — Bls. Houghton, Lawrence, and Webster, Carthusians 151
6. A Model of the Flock — Bl. Richard Reynolds, Bridgettine 152
7. Holy Fear — Bl. Thomas Cottam, Pr. 153
8. A Garment of Camel's Hair — Bl. Thomas Cottam, Pr. 154
✠9. A Joyful Countenance — Bl. Thomas Pickering, O. S. B. 155
10. The True Plotters — Bl. Richard Newport, Pr. 156
✠11. A Violated Cloister — Bls. John Rochester and John Walworth, Carthusians . 157
12. Called by Name — Bl. John Stone, Augustinian 158
13. A Royal Penitent — Catherine of Aragon to Bl. John Forest, O. S. F. (1) 159
14. One Only Gospel — Bl. John Forest, O. S. F., to Queen Catherine (2) 160
15. Points in Controversy — Bl. Richard Thirkell, Pr. 162
16. The Confession of an Apostate — Nichols to Bl. Luke Kirby, Pr. 163
17. Devotion to Relics — Mary Hutton, L. 164
18. The Mother of the Machabees — Bl. Margaret Pole, W. 166
✠19. Come Quickly — Ven. Peter Wright, S.J. 167
20. Prayers in Latin — Bl. Robert Johnson, Pr. 169
21. Hung on Presumption — Ven. William Scot, O. S. B. 170
✠22. A Living Holocaust — Bl. John Forest, O. S. F. 171
23. Patience under Calumny — Bl. Lawrence Richardson, Pr. 172
24. A Catholic Cavalier — William Blundell, L. 173
25. Refusing a Challenge — William Blundell, L. 174
26. Praise and Thanksgiving — Bl. John Shert, Pr. 175
27. Father Forgive Them — Bl. Thomas Cottam, Pr. 176
28. The Snares of the Pharisees — Bl. Thomas Ford, Pr. 177
✠29. Holy Mass and Martyrdom — Bl. Richard Thirkell, Pr. 178

✠30. Love of the Cross — Bl. William Filbie, Pr. 179
31. Wisdom in Speech — Bl. Luke Kirby, Pr. 180

JUNE

1. Reparation (1) — Bl. John Storey, L. 183
2. Reparation (2) — Bl. John Storey, L. 184
✠3. Dignity of the Priesthood — Ven. Francis Ingleby, Pr. 185
4. Wisdom of the Ancients — Bp. David Poole of Peterborough 186
✠5. The House of My God — Fr. John Gray, O. S. F. 187
6. A Boon of the Penal Laws — William Blundell, L. 188
7. A Priest to the Rescue — Bl. Richard Thirkell, Pr. 189
8. Our Lady of Ipswich — Bl. Thomas More, L. 190
9. The End and the Means — Ven. William Harcourt, S.J. 191
10. "Possumus" (We Can) — Ven. Thomas Whitebread, S.J. 192
11. An Unjust Judgment — Ven. Thomas Whitebread, S.J. 193
12. Love's Servile Lot — Ven. Robert Southwell, S.J. 194
✠13. Yea, Yea, and No, No — Bl. Thomas Woodhouse, S.J. 195
14. The Learning of the Simple — Ven. John Rigby, L. 196
15. A Bribe Rejected — Five Jesuit martyrs 197
16. A Puritan Conscience — Ven. John Southworth, Pr. 198
17. The Commission to Preach — Ven. John Southworth, Pr. 199
18. Looking on Jesus — Ven. John Southworth, Pr. 200
✠19. The Whims of a King — Bl. Sebastian Newdigate, Carthusian 201
✠20. Leave to Lie — Ven. Thomas Whitebread, S.J., on the scaffold 202
✠21. Fetters Unloosed — Ven. John Rigby, L. 203
22. Ascending the Steps — Bl. John Fisher, Card. Bp. 204
23. Learning for Life — Bl. John Fisher, Card. Bp. 205
24. The Wedding Garment — Bl. John Fisher, Card. Bp. 206
25. A Martyr's Sleep — Bl. John Fisher, Card. Bp. 207
26. The Bones of Elias — Bl. John Fisher, Card. Bp. 208
27. Feeding the Hungry — Margaret Clement, L. 209
✠28. A Dangerous Seducer — Ven. John Southworth, Pr. 210
29. St. Peter's Remorse — Ven. Robert Southwell, S.J. 211
✠30. A Good Day — Ven. Philip Powell, O. S. B. 212

JULY

✠1. The Fruits of the Spirit — Ven. Oliver Plunket, Abp. 215
✠2. Prayer without Ceasing — Ven. Monford Scott, Pr. 216
3. Tyburn in Gala — Ven. Thomas Maxfield, Pr. 217
✠4. A Man of God — Ven. John Cornelius, S.J. 219
✠5. The Last First — Ven. George Nichols, Pr. 220
✠6. The Privileges of Martyrdom — Bl. Thomas More, L. 221
✠7. The Spouse of the Canticles — Ven. Roger Dicconson, Pr., and companions . . 222
✠8. The Shield of Faith — Bl. Adrian Fortescue, L. 223

9. Introducer to Christ — Ven. Ralph Milner, L. 224
10. The Winding-Sheet — Bl. Thomas More, L. 225
11. "For My Sake and the Gospel" — Ven. Ralph Milner, L. 226
✠12. Apostolic Charity — Ven. John Buckley, O. S. F. 227
✠13. Pilate's Wife — Ven. Thomas Tunstall, Pr. 228
✠14. The Law Eternal — Ven. Richard Langhorne, L. 229
15. No Compromise — Bl. Thomas More, L. 230
✠16. The Continuity Theory — Ven. John Sugar, Pr. 231
17. Zeal for Martyrdom — Ven. Robert Grissold, L. 232
18. His Father's Son — Ven. William Davies, Pr. 233
✠19. "Bones Thou Hast Humbled" — Ven. Anthony Brookby, O. S. F. 234
20. No Priest, No Religion — Ven. William Plessington, Pr. 235
21. The Three Children in the Furnace — Ven. William Davies, Pr., and companions . 236
22. Always Ready — Ven. Philip Evans, S. J. 237
23. A Fall and a Rising — Ven. Richard Sympson, Pr. 238
✠24. Another Judas — Ven. John Bost, Pr. 239
25. The Seed of the Church — Ven. John Ingram, Pr. 240
26. A Brother in Need — Ven. George Swallowell, L. 242
✠27. Voices from Heaven — Ven. Robert Sutton, Pr. 243
✠28. A Client of St. Anne — Ven. William Ward, O. F. S. 244
✠29. A Burning Heart — Ven. William Ward, O. F. S. 245
✠30. At Last — Bl. Thomas Abel, Pr. 246
✠31. Shod for the Gospel — Bl. Everard Hanse, Pr. 247

AUGUST

1. Peter Repentant — John Thomas, L. 249
2. Casting Out Fear — Ven. Thomas Whitaker, Pr. 250
✠3. The Baptist and Herod — Ven. Thomas Belchiam, O. S. F. 251
4. Hermit and Martyr — Ven. Nicholas Postgate, Pr. 252
5. The Wings of a Dove — Ven. Nicholas Postgate, Pr. 253
6. Twice Hanged — Ven. John Woodcock, O. S. F. 254
✠7. A Public Confession — Ven. Edward Bamber, Pr. 255
✠8. A Champion of the Pope — Bl. John Felton, L. 256
✠9. Poison Detected — Ven. Thomas Palasor, Pr. 257
10. Forward to the Mark — Ven. John Woodcock, O. S. F. 258
11. The Northern Rising — Letter of St. Pius V. 259
12. The Abomination of Desolation — Bl. Thomas Percy, L. 260
13. Cleansing the Temple — Bl. Thomas Percy, L. 261
14. Absolved from Afar — Ven. Hugh Green, Pr. 262
15. The Four Last Things — Ven. Hugh Green, Pr., on the scaffold. 263
16. Four Things More — Ven. Hugh Green, Pr., on the scaffold. 264
17. A Hunted Life — Ven. Thomas Holford, Pr. 265
18. The Eternal Priesthood — Ven. Roger Cadwallador, Pr. 266
✠19. A Lamentation Fulfilled — Ven. Hugh Green, Pr. 267

20. Thirty Pieces of Silver — Bl. Thomas Percy, L. 268
21. The Friday Abstinence — Bl. Thomas Percy, L. 269
✠22. The Holy House of Loreto — Bl. William Lacy, Pr. 270
23. The Crown of Dignity — Ven. John Kemble, Pr. 271
24. A Voluntary Offering — Ven. John Wall, O. S. F. 272
25. Reproached for Christ — Ven. Charles Baker, S. J. 273
✠26. Cheerful in Adversity — Bp. Thomas Thirlby of Ely. 274
✠27. Glorifying God — Ven. Roger Cadwallador, Pr. 275
✠28. Striking Their Breasts — Ven. Edmund Arrowsmith, S. J. 276
✠29. Murder for Example — Ven. Richard Herst, L. 277
✠30. Visiting the Prisoners — Ven. Margaret Ward, L. 278
✠31. The Tabernacle of Kore — Ven. Thomas Felton, O. F. M. 279

SEPTEMBER

1. A Life-Offering for the People — Ven. John Goodman, Pr. 281
2. Time and Eternity — Bl. Thomas More, L. 282
3. How Long, O Lord? — Bl. Thomas Abel, Pr., to Bl. John Forest, O. S. F. 283
4. Perseverance — Bl. John Forest to Bl. Thomas Abel. 284
5. Faithful in the End — Bp. Edmund Bonner of London. 285
6. An Easter Offering — Ven. Edward Barlow, O. S. B. 286
✠7. The Contemplative Way — Ven. John Duckett, Pr. 287
8. Holy Rivalry — Vens. Ralph Corby, S. J., and John Duckett, Pr. 288
9. The Kiss of Peace — Vens. Ralph Corby, S. J., and John Duckett, Pr. 289
10. Pressed Out of Measure — Bp. Gilbert Bourne of Bath and Wells 290
11. Hereditary Champion of England — Robert Dymoke, L. 291
12. A Martyr's Maxims (1) — Bl. Adrian Fortescue, L. 292
13. A Martyr's Maxims (2) — Bl. Adrian Fortescue, L. 293
14. Separated unto the Gospel — Ven. Edward Barlow, O. S. B. 294
15. The Primitive Church — Ven. Edward Barlow, O. S. B. 295
16. Horror of Scandal — Ven. Edward Barlow, O. S. B. 296
17. Romans the Only Priests — Ven. Edward Barlow, O. S. B. 297
18. Stronger than Death — Ven. Richard Herst, L. 298
19. Prayers for the Dead — Ven. Richard Herst, L. 299
20. To Save Others — Ven. John Duckett, Pr. 300
21. A Holy Youth — Ven. Edmund Arrowsmith, S. J. 301
22. Lowly, but Bold — Ven. Edmund Arrowsmith, S. J. 302
23. The Narrow Way — Ven. John Wall, O. S. F. 303
24. A Martyr's Legacies — Bl. Everard Hanse, Pr. 304
25. A Reprover of Sin — Ven. Oliver Plunket, Abp., on the scaffold 305
26. A Fair Trial — Ven. Oliver Plunket, Abp. 306
✠27. A Peacemaker — Bp. Thomas Watson of Lincoln 307
28. Petition for Readmission — Ven. John Woodcock, O. S. F. 308
✠29. Love of Parents — Ven. William Spenser, Pr. 309
30. Little Bells of Gold — Ven. Roger Cadwallador, Pr. 310

OCTOBER

✠1. A True Israelite — Ven. John Robinson, Pr. 313
2. The Unity of Christendom — Bl. Thomas More, L. 314
3. An Advocate of Christ — Ven. Philip Powell, O. S. B. 315
4. The Final Judgment — Bl. Edmund Campion, S.J. 316
5. A Mother's Sacrifice — Ven. William Hartley, Pr. 317
6. The Catholic Association — George Gilbert, S.J. 318
7. Poverty Preferred — Bp. Edmund Bonner of London 319
✠8. Casting Out Devils — Ven. Richard Dibdale, Pr. 320
9. Our Captain Christ (1) — Bl. Richard Thirkell to the Catholic prisoners (1). 321
10. Our Captain Christ (2) — Bl. Richard Thirkell to the Catholic prisoners (2). 322
11. The Image of Christ — Ven. Thomas Bullaker, O. S. F. 323
✠12. Fire from Heaven — Ven. Thomas Bullaker, O. S. F. 324
13. The Last Gloria — Ven. Thomas Bullaker, O. S. F. 325
14. The Dwellers of Capharnaum — Ven. Thomas Bullaker, O. S. F. 326
15. A Prophecy Fulfilled — Ven. Thomas Bullaker, O. S. F. 327
✠16. Father of Many Sons — William Allen, Card. 328
17. On Attendance at Protestant Services — William Allen, Card. 329
18. An Apostate Land — William Allen, Card. 330
✠19. From Prison to Paradise — Ven. Philip Howard, L. 331
20. The Hatred of Herodias (1) — Ven. Philip Howard, L. 333
21. The Hatred of Herodias (2) — Ven. Philip Howard, L. 334
22. A Filial Appeal — Ven. Robert Southwell, S.J., to his Protestant father (1) . . 335
23. The Strictness of the Reckoning — Ven. Robert Southwell, S.J., to his Protestant father (2) 336
24. And Then the Judgment — Ven. Robert Southwell, S.J., to his Protestant father (3) 337
25. Our Home in Heaven — Ven. Robert Southwell, S.J., to his Protestant father (4) 338
26. Wisdom Learnt in Chains — Bl. Richard Thirkell, Pr. 339
27. A Worm and No Man — Bl. Alexander Briant, S.J. 340
28. The More Excellent Way — Bl. Alexander Briant, S.J. 341
29. With Arms Outstretched — Ven. Henry Heath, O. S. F. 342
✠30. The Voice of the People — Ven. John Slade, L. 343
31. Thirst for Martyrdom — Ven. Henry Heath, O. S. F. 344

NOVEMBER

1. Upon the Image of Death — Ven. Robert Southwell, S.J. 347
✠2. The Waters of Mara — Ven. John Bodey, L. 348
3. A Vision in the Night — Ven. John Bodey, L. 349
4. Masses for the Dead — Ven. John Cornelius, S.J. 350
5. The Blackfriars Collapse — Robert Drury, S.J. 351
6. The Vow of Religion — Ven. John Cornelius, S.J., to a nun 352
7. God's Ways Not Ours — Ven. Edmund Genings, Pr. 354

8. Faith and Loyalty — Bl. Edward Powell, Pr. 355
✠9. The Last Mass — Ven. George Nappier, Pr. 357
10. Unseen in the Midst of Them — Ven. George Nappier, Pr. 358
11. A Blessed Lot — Ven. Peter Wright, S.J., on the scaffold 359
12. Called to Account — Bl. Edmund Campion, S.J. to Protestant Bp. Cheney . . 360
13. Need of Contrition — Ven. John Almond, Pr. 361
14. Guardian of the Sanctuary — Bl. Hugh Faringdon, O.S.B. 362
✠15. The Watchman on the Walls — Bl. Richard Whiting, O.S.B. 363
✠16. Devotion to St. Jerome — Ven. Edward Osbaldeston, Pr. 364
17. Strong in Hope — Bp. Ralph Bayne of Lichfield 365
18. The Passion Foretold — Bl. Edmund Campion, S.J. 366
19. False Witnesses — Bl. Edmund Campion, S.J. 367
20. Lifelong Repentance — Bp. Cuthbert Tunstall of Durham 368
21. Shedding Innocent Blood — Bl. Edmund Campion, S.J. 369
22. Willing Sacrifices — Ven. Robert Southwell, S.J. 370
✠23. Wasted Away — Bp. Richard Pate of Worcester 371
24. Alone with God — Bl. Thomas More, L. 372
25. A Daughter's Farewell — Bl. Thomas More, L. 373
✠26. The House of Zaccheus — Ven. Marmaduke Bowes, L. 374
27. Wolves in Sheep's Clothing — Ven. George Errington, L., and companions . . 375
28. The Martyrs' Shrines — Bl. James Thompson, Pr. 377
✠29. Firstfruits — Bl. Cuthbert Mayne, Pr. 378
✠30. Satan Thwarted — Ven. Alexander Crowe, Pr. 379

DECEMBER

✠1. A Sight to God and Man — Bl. Edmund Campion, S.J. 381
2. Keeper of the Vineyard — Bl. John Beche, O.S.B. 382
3. The Cross and the Crown — Bl. Alexander Briant, S.J. 383
4. Painless Torment — Bl. Alexander Briant, S.J. 384
✠5. Blood for Blood — Ven. John Almond, Pr. 385
6. Flores Martyrum — Ven. John Almond, Pr. 386
7. Faith and Works — Ven. John Almond, Pr. 387
8. The Sleep of the Just — Bl. Ralph Sherwin, Pr. 388
9. Malchus's Ear — Ven. John Mason, L. 389
✠10. The Sweat of the Passion — Ven. Eustace White, Pr. 390
✠11. The Office of Our Lady — Ven. Arthur Bell, O.S.F. 391
✠12. All Things to All Men — Ven. Thomas Holland, S.J. 392
13. Invocation of the Saints — Ven. Edmund Genings, Pr. 393
14. The Fool's Robe — Ven. Edmund Genings, Pr. 394
15. Not in the Judgment Hall — Ven. Edmund Genings, Pr. 395
16. A Mighty Hunter — Ven. Swithin Wells, L. 396
17. In Bonds, but Free — Ven. Swithin Wells, L. 397
18. The Good Thief — Ven. John Roberts, O.S.B. 398
19. The Last Supper — Ven. John Roberts, O.S.B. 399

20. The Mission to Teach — Ven. John Roberts, O. S. B. 400
21. Priest, Not Traitor — Ven. John Roberts, O. S. B. 401
22. The Rights of the Church — Ven. John Roberts, O. S. B. 402
23. Freemen Born — Ven. Edmund Genings and companions 403
✠24. A Priest's Epitaph at Douay — George Muscot, Pr. 404
25. The Burning Babe — Ven. Robert Southwell, S. J. 405
26. Fit for War and Comely — Bl. Alexander Briant, S. J. 406
27. Black but Beautiful — Bl. Alexander Briant, S. J. 407
28. Graven in God's Hands — Bl. Ralph Sherwin, Pr. 408
✠29. The Witness of a Good Conscience — William Howard, Viscount 410
30. A Persecutor Penitent — Ven. John Almond, Pr. 411
31. Sorrow to Life — Bp. Owen Oglethorpe of Carlisle 412

APPENDIX: SELECT POETRY OF THE MARTYRS 415

INDEX OF NAMES 429

PUBLISHER'S

PREFACE

FR. HENRY Sebastian Bowden (1836–1920) was a priest of the London Oratory in the later years of the Oxford Movement, and an outstanding pupil of the celebrated John Henry Cardinal Newman and Fr. Ronald Knox. Serving as Superior of the Oratory in his turn, Fr. Bowden was known to combine insightful scholarship and devotion with a pastoral wisdom and cheer that endeared him to all; including the libertine celebrity Oscar Wilde, whose deathbed request for absolution and entry into the Church was largely due to the good priest's earlier influence. Regarded in life as the most effective preacher in London, a friend described Fr. Bowden in *The Times,* shortly after his death: "He was always a priest, but he was a soldier-priest, a scholar, and a high-spirited English gentleman."[1]

Having converted from Anglicanism at a young age, Fr. Bowden was well aware that he owed a great debt to the historic witness and supernatural merits of the English martyrs, in whose honor he composed the present work: *Mementoes of the English Martyrs and Confessors.* First published in 1910, he wrote it as "a daily remembrance of our forefathers in the Faith," and a means of instilling greater piety and zeal in those at risk of neglecting the heroic legacy bequeathed to them. The inspiration of such daily reminders likewise resounds in our own time, when Catholic doctrine and worship are again facing government censorship and restriction in many lands.

In addition to a fresh typesetting and more readable layout, this edition of Fr. Bowden's book benefits from the addition of several missing source citations, a small appendix of poetry by some of the martyrs themselves, and

[1] Fathers of the Oratory, *Spiritual Teaching of Father Sebastian Bowden* (New York: P.J. Kenedy and Sons, 1921), xi.

a series of stunning engravings by McFarlane and Erskine, remastered from an 1878 printing of Bp. Richard Challoner's celebrated *Memoirs of Missionary Priests,* the most important early compendium on the subject. Apart from an update to the capitalization standard and certain name spellings, no changes have been made to the body text apart from correcting original errors; for this reason, it is worth noting that many of the individuals recalled here as "Venerable" or "Blessed" are now honored as canonized saints in the universal Church, which we have footnoted as appropriate.

Fr. Bowden's *Mementoes,* here republished more than a century after the original, holds another important lesson for today's reader: the common traits discernible in the lives of the martyrs — their divine courage, their profound reverence for the sacred, their heartfelt charity toward others — often appear as the crowning of what was otherwise a very *ordinary* Christian life, patterned on a simple yet daily fidelity to grace. This insight colored Fr. Bowden's priestly ministry, as may be found expressed in one of his posthumous works:

> Seek union with God in whatever is your special work and rule of life, taking it all as done for Him, and remembering that the only one thing to live for is the doing of His will. Life, really, only consists of this. Every human being on this earth must settle for himself the *details* of his own particular life and the duty of every day, and be responsible to God for it; but whatever our own particular work is, it is always the discipline for our soul. So if, after all your efforts, however hard, you have to give up — if schemes fail, and it all comes to nothing — then it must be for you, "*Fiat!* — as He wills!" But it has been, no matter how unsuccessful, *your* way of coming nearer to Him: and this is the only thing that matters.[2]

May the English martyrs and confessors inspire us to this same daily *Fiat,* come what may — and in the words of the author: "May we learn to set a higher value on the Faith as we realize the cost of its inheritance."

[2] Ibid., 66–67.

Introduction

As a daily remembrance of our forefathers in the Faith, these selections have been made from the records of their lives and times, and also from their writings. While the fullest and most important biographies are naturally predominant, the list is, it is hoped, fairly representative. In these pages are included not only those whom the Church has declared to be "Venerable" or "Blessed," but also various others of either sex, conspicuous as witnesses to the Faith, or for their zeal in its behalf. Such characteristic incidents have also been added as may fill up the portraiture of the period.

The claims of the martyrs on our devotion need hardly be expressed. If the apostle of every country is specially venerated as the means by which the Faith was first received, what honor is due to this goodly company of our own race and speech which at so great a cost preserved the Faith for us? Its members are our patrons, then, by the double tie of nature and grace. "Look," says the prophet, "to the rock whence you are hewn, to the hole of the pit whence you were dug out" (Is 51:1). And our forefathers in the Faith are indeed "exceedingly honorable." Fisher, the "saintly cardinal"; More, the illustrious chancellor; Campion, the "golden-mouthed"; Southwell, the priest poet; Margaret Pole, the last of the Plantagenets; Margaret Clitherow, in the "winepress alone"; Ralph Milner, the sturdy yeoman; Philip Howard, the victim of Herodias; Swithin Wells, a "hunter before the Lord"; Horner, the tailor, with his vestments of salvation; Mason, the serving-man; Plunket, last in time, not least in dignity or holiness. All these high or humble, with the sons of Sts. Augustine, Benedict, Bridget, Bruno, Francis, Ignatius, and the crowd of secular priests, bear the same palm and shine with the same aureole, for they confessed *una voce* the same Faith and sealed it with their blood, and for this land of ours. But for their willing sacrifices, this country might have been as frozen in heresy as Norway or Sweden and other northern lands.

The period dealt with is full of instruction. It opens with the greed, lust, and despotism of Henry VIII, triumphant in the suppression of the monasteries, the divorce of Catherine, and the Oath of Supremacy. We note next the beginning of the new religion, the brief restoration of the Faith under Mary, then Protestantism established in blood under Elizabeth. Amidst the later persecutions, none appear more malicious than that of the Commonwealth; for the Puritans, like the Nonconformists of today, proclaimed liberty of conscience, and with that cry on their lips put Catholics to death solely for their faith. In contrast with the false brethren and apostates, with the time-servers and the traitors of every kind — alas, too often found — and against the growing domination of heretics and tyrants, the martyrs stand out as the champions of faith and freedom, and of freedom for the Faith.

Considering the ubiquity and cunning of both private informers and government spies, it may seem strange how the missionaries found even a temporary shelter on landing in England, but this was supplied to them by the Catholic laity without thought of personal risk. Harboring priests was always regarded as felony and often punished by death, yet the cottages and shops of the poorer classes and the country houses of the gentry were ever open to the missioner. Without the welcome hospitality and services of the laity, the work of the apostolate would have been practically impossible.

It is curious to note how the fire of persecution strengthened men's souls. "In Henry VIII's time," writes a missionary priest, "the whole kingdom, with all its bishops and learned men, abjured the Faith at the word of the tyrant. But now in his daughter's time, boys and women boldly profess the Faith before the judge, and refuse to make the slightest concession even at the risk of death." It must be remembered, however, that many took the oath under Henry without realizing the nature or consequences of their act. For, save in the matter of the King's Supremacy, a tenet which was differently interpreted, the Faith was left intact. Under Elizabeth, however, Protestantism undisguised was introduced, and the whole Marian episcopacy, with one exception, died in prison rather than conform.

The bishops then suffered for their religion alone, and their civil loyalty was never questioned. The martyrs, however, were tried and condemned on the charge of treason—treason, meaning any resistance to the Crown or State in the matter of religion—and for their resistance, that is, for their faith, they died. Those, like Bls. Felton, Storey, Woodhouse, who refused to acknowledge Elizabeth as queen, because deposed by the pope, won their crowns not as rebels or conspirators, but as champions of the pope's authority, refusing the

Oath of Supremacy, on declining by apostasy to save their lives. Loyalty to the lawful authority of the Crown was ever a first principle with Catholics. The "Pilgrimage of Grace" and the "Northern Rising," both undertaken to restore the old religion, were heralded by explicit declarations of loyalty to the reigning monarchs. Revolution was scouted as the offspring and badge of heresy. Thus Bl. Edward Powell challenged the apostate Barnes to show that the ancient creed had ever produced sedition or rebellion. In the Armada crisis, Catholics, grievously as they had suffered, came forward, with a Howard at their head, to defend throne and country. Under Charles I, thirty years later, Catholics formed a fourth or even a third of the Royalist Army. When, then, Gregory XIII in 1580 exempted Catholics from the obligation of the bull of excommunication, we find priests and laity alike declaring Elizabeth *de juro et de facto* their Queen, for, apart from the bull, she was the rightful successor to Mary, and in possession. The loyalty of the martyrs was indeed emphatic and outspoken. "God bless and save her," "Preserve her from her enemies," was their constant prayer on the scaffold. Ven. R. Drury and the twelve other appellant priests declared in their testimonial that they were as ready to shed their blood in defense of Queen and country as they would be in behalf of the lawful authority of the Church. Yet, notwithstanding all this, for priest or layman, high or low, recusancy was treason, treason meant death, and the appellants suffered with the rest.

The Church then was in the catacombs. Her sanctuaries violated, her liturgy and solemn Offices silenced, the Holy Sacrifice offered only in secret and at the risk of life. Still her divine notes shone clearly in the darkness. Though black, she was beautiful. The penalty of joining her communion was probably death, yet out of 265 declared "Blessed" or "Venerable" from Elizabeth till Charles II, 1577 to 1681, fifty were converts from Conformity or Protestantism. Of these fifty, thirty were of the University of Oxford, nine from that of Cambridge. Amongst them fellows of colleges like Campion and Hartley (St. John's), Sherwin (Exeter), Munden (New), Forde (Trinity), Richardson (Brasenose), Pilchard (Balliol); noted schoolmasters like Shert and Cottam; holders of rich benefices like Sutton, vicar of Lutterworth, Hanse, promoted to a wealthy living by the University of Cambridge; librarians, Heath, Corpus Christi, Cambridge, men known for scholarship, learning, and position, and held in such account by the enemies of the Faith, that honors, preferments, even bishoprics were offered them as a bribe for apostasy. It seemed the hour of antichrist, and the whole world seated in wickedness, yet the hand of the Lord was not shortened that it could not save, nor His ear heavy that it could not hear.

Even in these short extracts some of the martyrs' characteristics are clearly apparent. The grace of their bearing in youth: Briant, the beautiful Oxford boy; their dignity in venerable old age: Lockwood, fourscore and seven, apologizing for his slowness in mounting the ladder; their bright and cheerful courage: Cadwallador, the clatter of his fetters, his "little bells of gold"; their ready wit: Anderton, Pope Joan, and Queen Elizabeth; their silence under torture when speech meant not apostasy, but only danger to a friend: Sherwin and Briant; their accurately theological replies to their tormentors: Almond, Roberts, Plessington, Barlow; the hidden heroism of the devout women: Margaret Ward. Then the matchless melody and stateliness of their diction: what classic examples may be met with in More's prayer in the Tower; Campion's defense on his trial; or as a tribute of filial piety, Hart's letters to his Protestant mother; or his clarion call, "Stand fast!" to the Catholic prisoners; or the sacred verses of Southwell, the first religious poet of his time; while the ditties of William Blundell present a striking instance of rugged but devotional phrase. But perhaps the most prominent trait of the martyrs is their candor and simplicity, the utter absence of mannerism or affectation in life or death; and this stands out in strong contrast with the pretentious cant of the ministers their tormentors, and the inane but virulent pomposity of their judges the pseudo-bishops.

As regards their spiritual life, their fasts and penances, their disciplines and hairshirts, their unwearied prayers reveal their training for the conflict, while their forgiveness of their persecutors under the bitter tortures shows whose disciples they were. Their genuine Catholicism, their instinctive love of their Faith is seen in their attachment to the Church's language, their prayers in Latin, and their refusal to pray with heretics or to ask for their prayers. "We are not of your faith," said Bl. Kirby, "To pray with you would be to dishonor God." How truly they suffered for the Faith may be gathered from the fact that under Henry VIII the Oath of Supremacy would have saved their lives, while under Elizabeth and after, the rack, the rope, the knife need never have been theirs had they consented to go but once to the Protestant church, or had accused themselves of treason which they had never committed. May we learn to set a higher value on the Faith as we realize the cost of its inheritance, and may we grasp the truth that faith is to be preserved for ourselves and our children, not by concession or compromise, not by crying peace when there is no peace, or declaring our professed enemies our surest friends, but by its steadfast and outspoken defense at the sacrifice of every temporal interest, and, if need be, of life itself.

With regard to the plan of the following pages: the day of death is marked by a cross. When several martyrdoms take place on the same day, or several pages are allotted to the same individual, all but the "crossed" name are distributed as vacancies occur. The consequent separation of names from their proper days, or the dispersion of extracts belonging to the same individual or the inversion of their natural sequence is doubtless inconvenient, but it was of the first importance to keep the day of the death with the facts and details of martyrdom on its proper date when the feast of the martyr may be observed. Moreover, it must be remembered that the mementoes are not biographical memoirs, but short extracts or paragraphs, each complete and distinct in itself and telling its own tale.

The compiler begs to express his sincere thanks to their authors or possessors for leave to use the following works: Rev. Dom. Bede Camm, O. S. B., *The Lives of the English Martyrs*; the Very Rev. Fr. Stebbing, provincial of the Redemptorists, Fr. Bridgett's Works; the Rev. John Pollen, S. J., *The Acts of the Martyrs*; the Rev. E. G. Phillipps, Ushaw College, *The Extinction of the Ancient Hierarchy*; Francis Blundell, Esq., of Crosby, the *Ditties of W. Blundell*, and the *Cavalier's Note-Book*. Challoner's *Missionary Priests* has been taken as a textbook, and much use has been made of the *Records of the English Catholics*, the *Douay Diary*, the *Life and Letters of Cardinal Allen*, and of Mrs. Hope's *Franciscan Martyrs*.

Grateful thanks are also due to the Very Rev. Canon Gildea, D. D., the *censor deputatus*, and to Rev. Fr. Christie and Brother Vincent Hayles of the Oratory, London, for much valuable assistance.

January

PAST AND PRESENT (1)

✠ William Blundell, L., 1600

The time hath been we had one faith,
And strode aright one ancient path;
The time is now that each man may
See new Religions coin'd each day.

Sweet Jesu, with thy mother mild.
Sweet Virgin mother, with thy child,
Angels and Saints of each degree,
Redress our country's misery.

The time hath been priests did accord
In exposition of God's word;
The time is now, like shipman's hose,
It's turn'd by each fond preacher's glose.

The time hath been that sheep obeyed
Their pastors, doing as they said;
The time is now that sheep will preach,
And th' ancient pastors seem to teach.

The time hath been the prelate's door
Was seldom shut against the poor;
The time is now, so wives go fine,
They take not thought the beggar kine.

The time hath been men did believe
God's sacraments his grace did give;
The time is now men say they are
Uncertain signs and tokens bare.

January 2

PAST AND PRESENT (2)

William Blundell, L., 1600

The time hath been men would live chaste,
And so could maid that vows had past;
The time is now that gift has gone,
New gospellers such gifts have none.

Sweet Jesu, with thy mother mild,
Sweet Virgin mother, with thy child;
Angels and Saints of each degree
Redress our country's misery.

The time hath been that Saints could see,
Could hear and help our misery;
The time is now that fiends alone
Have leave to range — saints must be gone.

The time hath been fear made us quake
To sin, lest God should us forsake;
The time is now the vilest knave
Is sure (he'll say) God will him save.

The time hath been to fast and pray,
And do almsdeeds was thought the way;
The time is now, men say indeed,
Such stuff with God hath little meed.

The time hath been, within this land,
One's word as good as was his bond;
The time is now, all men may see,
New faiths have killed old honesty.

January 3

LIVING STONES

Abbot Feckenham, O. S. B., 1585

John Howman was born at Feckenham in Worcestershire, and is known by the name of his birthplace. As a Benedictine monk he became chaplain to Bishop Bonner, and was imprisoned in the reign of Edward VI for his defense of the Faith. Under Mary, he became dean of St. Paul's, and, later, abbot of the restored Abbey of Westminster. In spite of its late dissolution, he received the Queen on St. Thomas's Eve, December 20, 1556, with twenty-eight other monks, all men of mature age, the youngest being upwards of forty, and all pious and learned. Some three years later, when he met Elizabeth for the opening of her first Parliament at the abbey door, he in his pontifical robes and his monks in procession with their lighted candles, the Queen cried out, "Away with these lights! We see very well." The litany was sung in English, and Dr. Cox, a married priest and bitter heretic, preached against the Catholic religion and the monks, and urged the Queen to destroy them. The abbot then knew that his fate was sealed. On July 12, 1559, Feckenham and his monks were ejected for refusing to take the Oath of Supremacy. He was imprisoned, and died at Wisbeach, 1585. His abbey was destroyed, but the stones live.

"Be ye also as living stones built up, a spiritual house, a holy priesthood, to offer up spiritual sacrifices, acceptable to God" (1 Pt 2:5).

January 4

THE VOICE OF THE PREACHER

✠ Bl. Thomas Plumtree, Pr., 1572

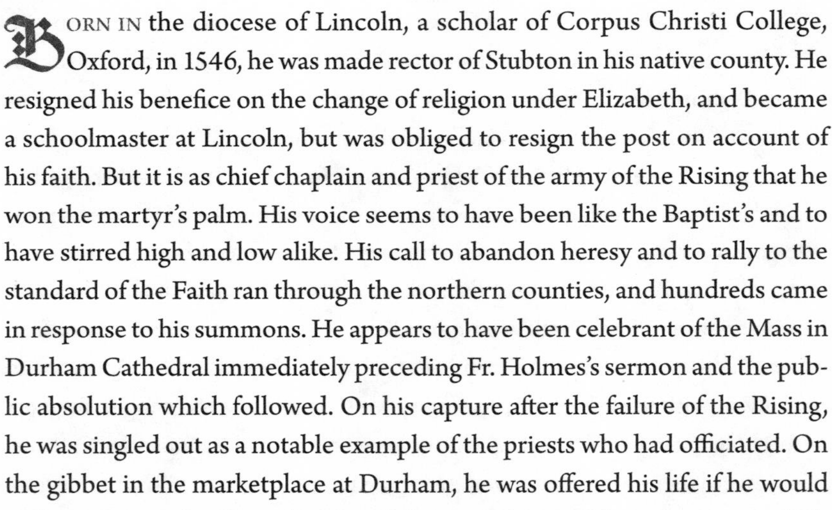

Born in the diocese of Lincoln, a scholar of Corpus Christi College, Oxford, in 1546, he was made rector of Stubton in his native county. He resigned his benefice on the change of religion under Elizabeth, and became a schoolmaster at Lincoln, but was obliged to resign the post on account of his faith. But it is as chief chaplain and priest of the army of the Rising that he won the martyr's palm. His voice seems to have been like the Baptist's and to have stirred high and low alike. His call to abandon heresy and to rally to the standard of the Faith ran through the northern counties, and hundreds came in response to his summons. He appears to have been celebrant of the Mass in Durham Cathedral immediately preceding Fr. Holmes's sermon and the public absolution which followed. On his capture after the failure of the Rising, he was singled out as a notable example of the priests who had officiated. On the gibbet in the marketplace at Durham, he was offered his life if he would embrace heresy, but he refused, and dying to this world received eternal life from Christ. He suffered January 4, 1572, and was buried in the marketplace.

"Wherein I labor even unto bands. . . . but the word of God is not bound" (2 Tm 2:9).

January 5

DEFILING THE SANCTUARIES

Abbot Feckenham, O. S. B., 1585

SPEECH IN the House of Lords: "My good Lords, when in Queen Mary's days your honor do know right well how the people of this realm did live in order and under law. There was no spoiling of churches, pulling down of altars, and most blasphemous treading down of the Sacrament under their feet, and hanging up the knave of clubs in the place thereof. There was no knocking or cutting of the face and legs of the crucifix, and of the image of Christ. There was no open flesh-eating or shambles-keeping in the Lent and days prohibited. The subjects of this realm, and especially such as were of the honorable council in Queen Mary's days, knew the way to church or chapel, and to begin their daily work by calling for help and grace by humble prayer. But now since the coming of our most sovereign and dear lady Queen Elizabeth, by the only preachers and scaffold-players of this new religion all things are changed and turned upside down. Obedience is gone; humility and meekness clean abolished; virtuous, chaste, and straight living abandoned."

"Her priests have despised My law and have defiled My sanctuaries.... Her princes in the midst of her are like wolves ravening the prey, to shed blood and destroy souls" (Ez 22:26–27).

January 6

THE PRODIGAL'S RETURN

Fr. John Genings, O. S. F., 1660

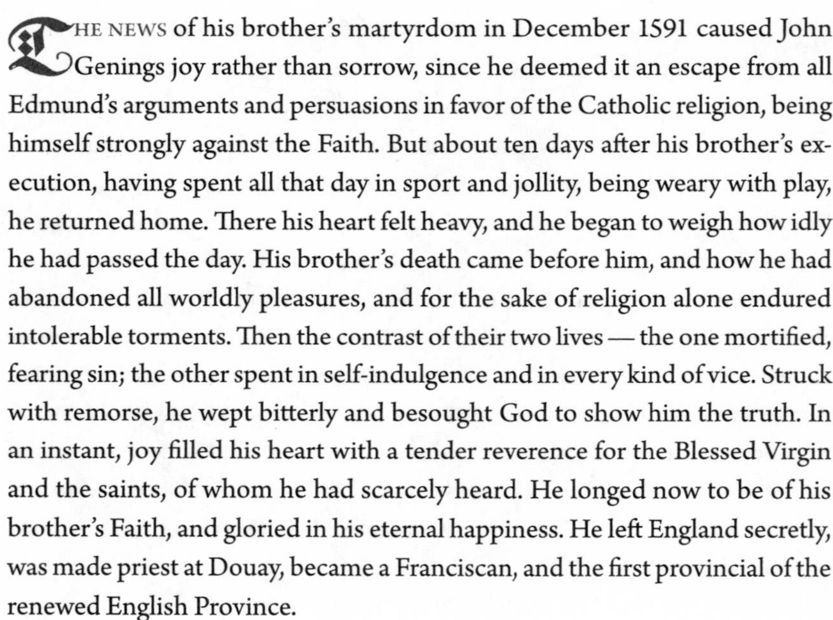

The news of his brother's martyrdom in December 1591 caused John Genings joy rather than sorrow, since he deemed it an escape from all Edmund's arguments and persuasions in favor of the Catholic religion, being himself strongly against the Faith. But about ten days after his brother's execution, having spent all that day in sport and jollity, being weary with play, he returned home. There his heart felt heavy, and he began to weigh how idly he had passed the day. His brother's death came before him, and how he had abandoned all worldly pleasures, and for the sake of religion alone endured intolerable torments. Then the contrast of their two lives — the one mortified, fearing sin; the other spent in self-indulgence and in every kind of vice. Struck with remorse, he wept bitterly and besought God to show him the truth. In an instant, joy filled his heart with a tender reverence for the Blessed Virgin and the saints, of whom he had scarcely heard. He longed now to be of his brother's Faith, and gloried in his eternal happiness. He left England secretly, was made priest at Douay, became a Franciscan, and the first provincial of the renewed English Province.

"I will arise and go to my father and say to him: Father, I have sinned against heaven and before thee" (Lk 15:18).

January 7

BALAAM'S ASS

✠ Ven. Edward Waterson, Pr., 1593

He was born in London and brought up in the Protestant religion. In company with certain merchants, he traveled to Turkey to see the East, and there a rich Turk, taking a fancy to him, offered him his daughter in marriage if he would renounce Christianity. Waterson, however, refused the proposal with horror, and taking Rome on his way homewards was instructed and reconciled to the Church. He was then admitted as a student at Rheims, and though he had but little learning, his zeal mastered all difficulties, and he was ordained priest in mid-Lent 1592 and sent to England. Shortly after his arrival he was apprehended and condemned on account of his priesthood. Catholic eyewitnesses relate that, as he was being drawn to his execution, the hurdle suddenly stood still, and the officers in vain flogged the horses to move it. Fresh animals were secured, but they broke the traces, and the hurdle remained fixed. Waterson had therefore to be led on foot to the gallows; there the ladder shook violently of itself till the martyr, by the sign of the cross, made it still, and ascending won his crown.

"And when the ass saw the angel standing, she fell under the feet of the rider: who, being angry, beat her sides more vehemently with a staff" (Nm 22:27).

* *Waterson was beatified by Pope Pius XI on 15 December 1929.*

January 8

THE WEAK MADE STRONG

The eleven Marian bishops

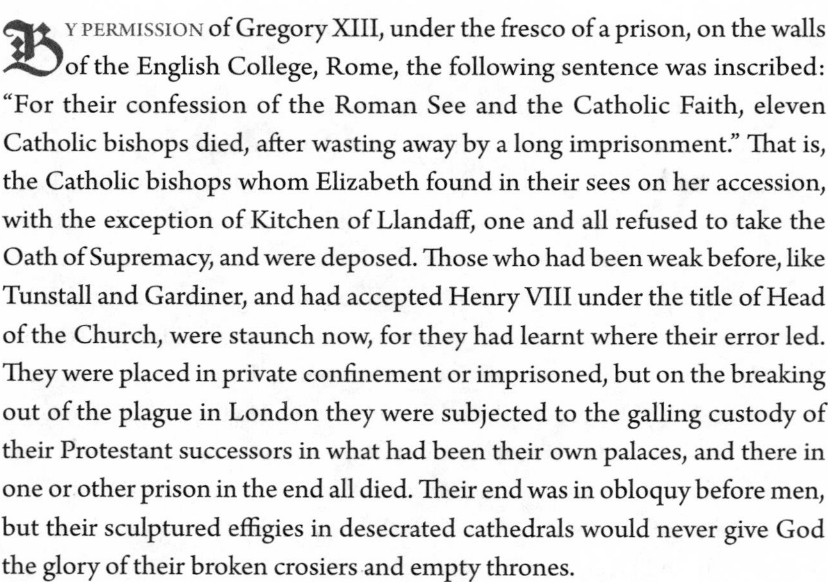

By permission of Gregory XIII, under the fresco of a prison, on the walls of the English College, Rome, the following sentence was inscribed: "For their confession of the Roman See and the Catholic Faith, eleven Catholic bishops died, after wasting away by a long imprisonment." That is, the Catholic bishops whom Elizabeth found in their sees on her accession, with the exception of Kitchen of Llandaff, one and all refused to take the Oath of Supremacy, and were deposed. Those who had been weak before, like Tunstall and Gardiner, and had accepted Henry VIII under the title of Head of the Church, were staunch now, for they had learnt where their error led. They were placed in private confinement or imprisoned, but on the breaking out of the plague in London they were subjected to the galling custody of their Protestant successors in what had been their own palaces, and there in one or other prison in the end all died. Their end was in obloquy before men, but their sculptured effigies in desecrated cathedrals would never give God the glory of their broken crosiers and empty thrones.

"They recovered strength from weakness, and became valiant in war.... They had trials of mockeries and stripes, moreover also of bands and prisons.... being approved by the testimony of their faith" (Heb 11:34, 36, 39).

January 9

CONVERSION BY KNIGHTHOOD

Thomas Pounde, S. J., 1615

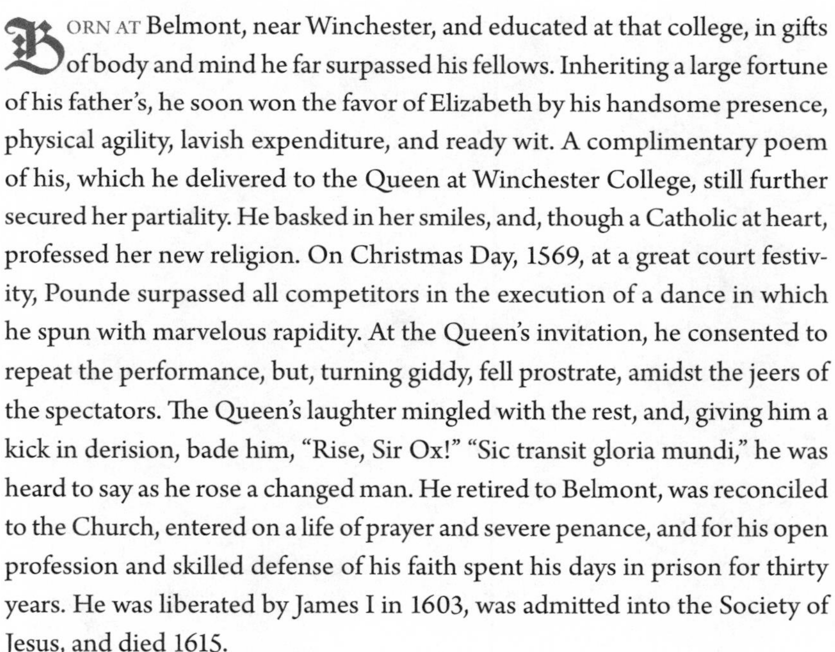

Born at Belmont, near Winchester, and educated at that college, in gifts of body and mind he far surpassed his fellows. Inheriting a large fortune of his father's, he soon won the favor of Elizabeth by his handsome presence, physical agility, lavish expenditure, and ready wit. A complimentary poem of his, which he delivered to the Queen at Winchester College, still further secured her partiality. He basked in her smiles, and, though a Catholic at heart, professed her new religion. On Christmas Day, 1569, at a great court festivity, Pounde surpassed all competitors in the execution of a dance in which he spun with marvelous rapidity. At the Queen's invitation, he consented to repeat the performance, but, turning giddy, fell prostrate, amidst the jeers of the spectators. The Queen's laughter mingled with the rest, and, giving him a kick in derision, bade him, "Rise, Sir Ox!" "Sic transit gloria mundi," he was heard to say as he rose a changed man. He retired to Belmont, was reconciled to the Church, entered on a life of prayer and severe penance, and for his open profession and skilled defense of his faith spent his days in prison for thirty years. He was liberated by James I in 1603, was admitted into the Society of Jesus, and died 1615.

"O ye sons of men, how long will you be dull of heart? Why do you love vanity, and seek after lying?" (Ps 4:3).

January 10

THE PILGRIMAGE OF GRACE (1)

Sir Robert Aske, L., 1537

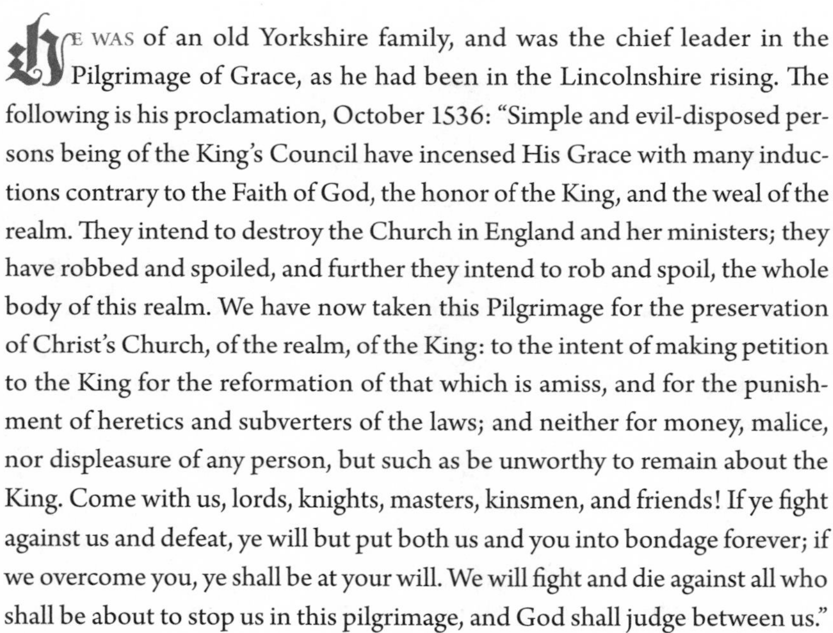

He was of an old Yorkshire family, and was the chief leader in the Pilgrimage of Grace, as he had been in the Lincolnshire rising. The following is his proclamation, October 1536: "Simple and evil-disposed persons being of the King's Council have incensed His Grace with many inductions contrary to the Faith of God, the honor of the King, and the weal of the realm. They intend to destroy the Church in England and her ministers; they have robbed and spoiled, and further they intend to rob and spoil, the whole body of this realm. We have now taken this Pilgrimage for the preservation of Christ's Church, of the realm, of the King: to the intent of making petition to the King for the reformation of that which is amiss, and for the punishment of heretics and subverters of the laws; and neither for money, malice, nor displeasure of any person, but such as be unworthy to remain about the King. Come with us, lords, knights, masters, kinsmen, and friends! If ye fight against us and defeat, ye will but put both us and you into bondage forever; if we overcome you, ye shall be at your will. We will fight and die against all who shall be about to stop us in this pilgrimage, and God shall judge between us."

"What wouldest thou ask of us? We are ready to die rather than transgress the laws of God received from our fathers" (2 Mc 7:2).

January 11

THE PILGRIMAGE OF GRACE (2)

Sir Thomas Percy, L., 1536

IN OCTOBER 1536, from the Scottish Borders to the Humber, the good staunch Catholics of the North flocked to the banners of the Pilgrimage of Grace. Second in command under Aske, leading the vanguard of six thousand men under the banner of St. Cuthbert, rode Sir Thomas Percy, brother of the Earl of Northumberland. They marched, some forty thousand strong, into Yorkshire, and Henry quailed before the pilgrims, though his forces were large. By deceitfully promising the redress of their grievances, he cajoled them into dispersing and returning home. But in the next spring, on their reassembling, he dispatched more numerous troops to the Duke of Norfolk, his lieutenant, who succeeded in securing their leaders. Sir Thomas, though he surrendered, was taken to Westminster, tried, and hanged with, amongst other supposed leaders, the abbot of Jervaulx and the Dominican friar John Pickering. They suffered "because, as false traitors, they conspired to deprive the King of his royal dignity, namely, of being on earth the Supreme Head of the Church in England."

Thus, though not among the beatified, they died for the Faith.

"For whom do you stay? I will not obey the commandment of the king, but the commandment of God which was given by Moses" (2 Mc 7:30).

January 12

THE SIN OF OZIAS

✠ Bp. John White of Winchester, 1560 (1)

He was warden of Winchester School in 1551, when the second master perverted to Calvinism; the head boy, Joliffe, and many of the scholars were infected by the heresy. It was the year of the sweating sickness. Joliffe and his followers were seized with the malady and died. Then the warden, by his powerful exhortations, brought the school to penance, and renewed the faith of the boys — some two hundred strong. For his resistance to Edward VI's innovations, he was committed to the Tower. Promoted by Mary to the See of Winchester, at her funeral sermon he said, "She found the realm poisoned with heresy and purged it, and, remembering herself to be a member of Christ's Church, she refused to write herself head thereof, which title no prince fifteen hundred years after Christ usurped, and was herself by her learning able to render the cause why. She could say that after Zacharias was dead, Ozias the prince took on him the priest's office, which prospered not with him because it was not his vocation, but God struck him therefore with leprosy on his forehead. She would say, 'How can I, being a woman, be Head of the Church, who by the Scriptures am forbidden to speak in the Church.' "

"And Ozias the king was a leper to the day of his death ... for which he had been cast out of the house of the Lord" (2 Par 26:21).

January 13

A HERALD OF THE TRUTH

Bp. John White of Winchester, 1560 (2)

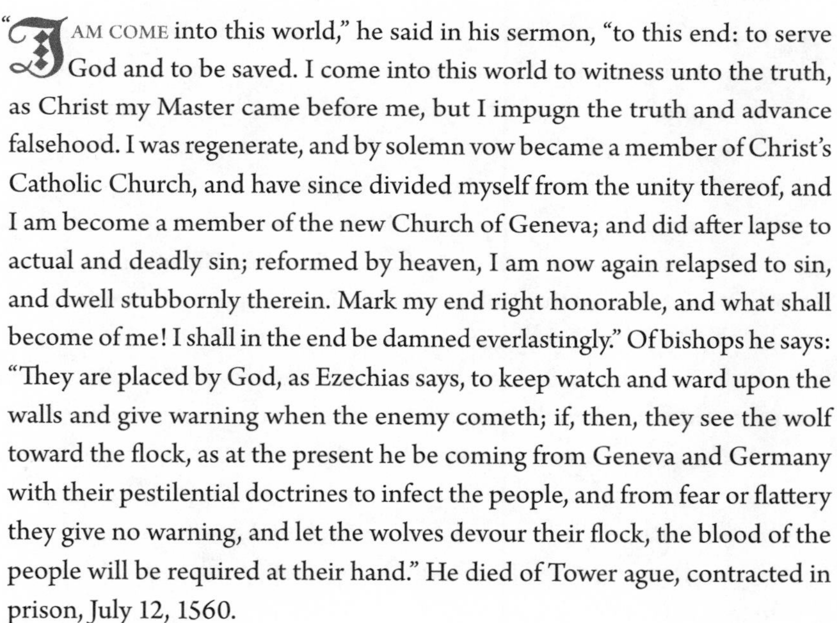

"I AM COME into this world," he said in his sermon, "to this end: to serve God and to be saved. I come into this world to witness unto the truth, as Christ my Master came before me, but I impugn the truth and advance falsehood. I was regenerate, and by solemn vow became a member of Christ's Catholic Church, and have since divided myself from the unity thereof, and I am become a member of the new Church of Geneva; and did after lapse to actual and deadly sin; reformed by heaven, I am now again relapsed to sin, and dwell stubbornly therein. Mark my end right honorable, and what shall become of me! I shall in the end be damned everlastingly." Of bishops he says: "They are placed by God, as Ezechias says, to keep watch and ward upon the walls and give warning when the enemy cometh; if, then, they see the wolf toward the flock, as at the present he be coming from Geneva and Germany with their pestilential doctrines to infect the people, and from fear or flattery they give no warning, and let the wolves devour their flock, the blood of the people will be required at their hand." He died of Tower ague, contracted in prison, July 12, 1560.

"I am come into the world that I should give testimony of the truth" (Jn 18:37).

January 14

THE OLDEST FAITH

Ven. William Lloyd, Pr., 1679

Born in Carmarthenshire, he became a convert, was ordained at Lisbon, and returned to the English mission. In spite of continuous illness, he toiled for souls till his arrest for the Oates Plot, for which he was condemned, but died in prison at Brecknock six days before the date appointed for his execution in 1679. He left a speech for his execution, of which a portion is here summarized: "The Faith in which I leave this world is that in which the apostles lived and died after having received the Holy Ghost, and I do renounce all errors against that Faith. Without faith no one can please God, and without pleasing God no one can be saved, and seeing there is no faith save that which Christ taught to His apostles, it behooveth every man to find out that Faith and to live and die in it, though they lose the world thereby, for it means being saved or damned forever. Now that apostolic Faith must be the oldest, for it was planted by our Savior Himself, which He promised should last forever, and against which the gates of hell should never prevail. For this reason, I made choice of the holy, Catholic, apostolic Faith and Roman religion to live and die in."

"Built on the foundation of the prophets and apostles, Jesus Christ Himself being the chief cornerstone" (Eph 2:20).

January 15

DEVOTION TO THE SACRAMENTS

Bl. John Fisher, Card. Bp., and Henry VII, 1509

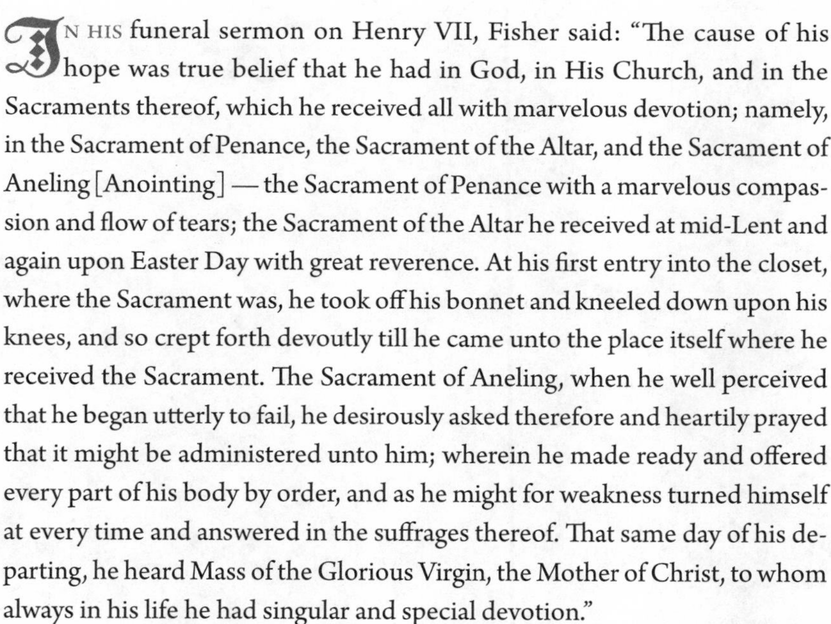

IN HIS funeral sermon on Henry VII, Fisher said: "The cause of his hope was true belief that he had in God, in His Church, and in the Sacraments thereof, which he received all with marvelous devotion; namely, in the Sacrament of Penance, the Sacrament of the Altar, and the Sacrament of Aneling [Anointing] — the Sacrament of Penance with a marvelous compassion and flow of tears; the Sacrament of the Altar he received at mid-Lent and again upon Easter Day with great reverence. At his first entry into the closet, where the Sacrament was, he took off his bonnet and kneeled down upon his knees, and so crept forth devoutly till he came unto the place itself where he received the Sacrament. The Sacrament of Aneling, when he well perceived that he began utterly to fail, he desirously asked therefore and heartily prayed that it might be administered unto him; wherein he made ready and offered every part of his body by order, and as he might for weakness turned himself at every time and answered in the suffrages thereof. That same day of his departing, he heard Mass of the Glorious Virgin, the Mother of Christ, to whom always in his life he had singular and special devotion."

"If thou didst know the gift of God" (Jn 4:10).

* *Fisher was canonized by Pope Pius XI on 19 May 1935.*

EDMUND CAMPION

"On his way to London"

January 16

A BOY ORATOR

Bl. Edmund Campion, S.J., 1581

Born 1540, of Catholic parents in London, he was educated at Christ's Hospital, Newgate, and for his proved ability was given a scholarship by Sir John White in his new foundation of St. John's College, Oxford. But he was famous for his gift of eloquence from his earliest youth. As a bluecoat boy of thirteen years of age, he made an oration to Queen Mary on her accession, opposite St. Paul's, on behalf of the London scholars, and his modest grace charmed no less than his eloquence. At Oxford, his oratorical preeminence was attested by the various addresses he was chosen to deliver, but the growing convictions of the truth of Catholicism drove him from the university in 1569 on the completion of the proctorship. After a visit to Ireland, he was reconciled to the Church, repaired to Douay, and, there to wipe out by penance the "mark of the beast," as he called his Anglican deaconship, he entered the Society of Jesus in Rome, 1573; and after seven years in Prague, he landed at Dover, 1580. For thirteen months he preached, as occasion permitted, twice and thrice a day throughout England, and his fervent eloquence won innumerable souls. After continuous hairbreadth escapes, he was arrested at Dame Yates house at Lyford, July 11, 1581, and taken to the Tower.

> *"And thou, child, shalt be called the prophet of the Highest: for thou shalt go before the face of the Lord to prepare His ways"* (Lk 1:76).

* *Campion was canonized by Pope Paul VI on 25 October 1970.*

January 17

PRAYER IN SUFFERING

Bl. Edmund Campion, S.J., 1581

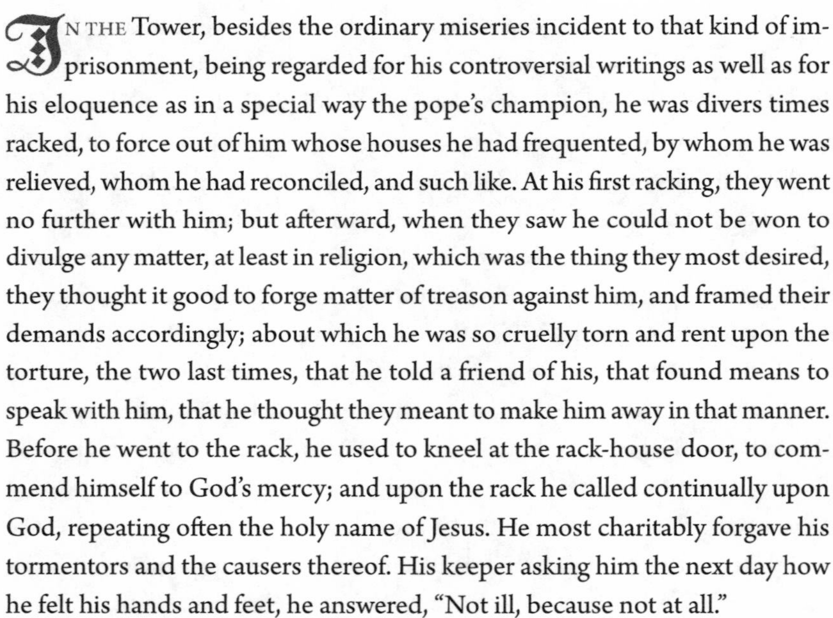

In the Tower, besides the ordinary miseries incident to that kind of imprisonment, being regarded for his controversial writings as well as for his eloquence as in a special way the pope's champion, he was divers times racked, to force out of him whose houses he had frequented, by whom he was relieved, whom he had reconciled, and such like. At his first racking, they went no further with him; but afterward, when they saw he could not be won to divulge any matter, at least in religion, which was the thing they most desired, they thought it good to forge matter of treason against him, and framed their demands accordingly; about which he was so cruelly torn and rent upon the torture, the two last times, that he told a friend of his, that found means to speak with him, that he thought they meant to make him away in that manner. Before he went to the rack, he used to kneel at the rack-house door, to commend himself to God's mercy; and upon the rack he called continually upon God, repeating often the holy name of Jesus. He most charitably forgave his tormentors and the causers thereof. His keeper asking him the next day how he felt his hands and feet, he answered, "Not ill, because not at all."

"When I am weak, then am I powerful" (2 Cor 12:10).

January 18

LIFTING THE FEEBLE HANDS

Bl. Edmund Campion, S.J., 1581

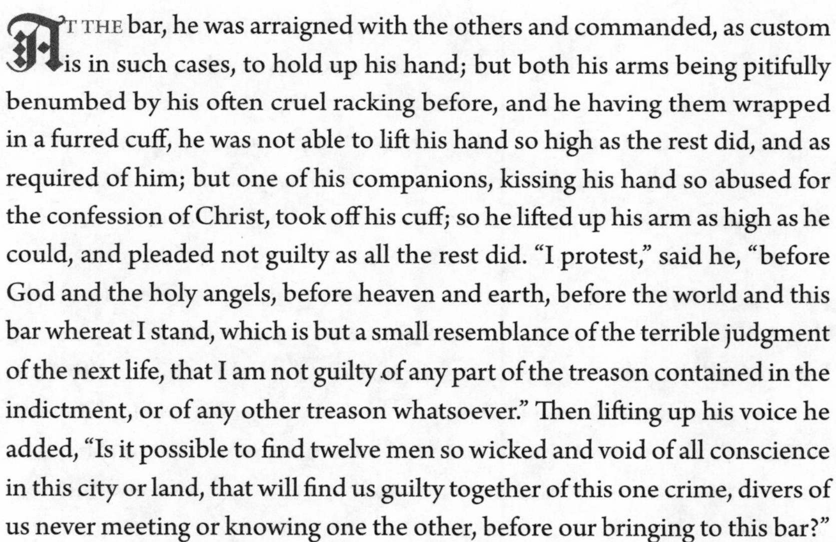

At the bar, he was arraigned with the others and commanded, as custom is in such cases, to hold up his hand; but both his arms being pitifully benumbed by his often cruel racking before, and he having them wrapped in a furred cuff, he was not able to lift his hand so high as the rest did, and as required of him; but one of his companions, kissing his hand so abused for the confession of Christ, took off his cuff; so he lifted up his arm as high as he could, and pleaded not guilty as all the rest did. "I protest," said he, "before God and the holy angels, before heaven and earth, before the world and this bar whereat I stand, which is but a small resemblance of the terrible judgment of the next life, that I am not guilty of any part of the treason contained in the indictment, or of any other treason whatsoever." Then lifting up his voice he added, "Is it possible to find twelve men so wicked and void of all conscience in this city or land, that will find us guilty together of this one crime, divers of us never meeting or knowing one the other, before our bringing to this bar?"

"Therefore, lift up the hands which hang down and the feeble knees" (Heb 12:12).

January 19

BEFORE THE SANHEDRIN

Bl. Edmund Campion, S.J., 1581

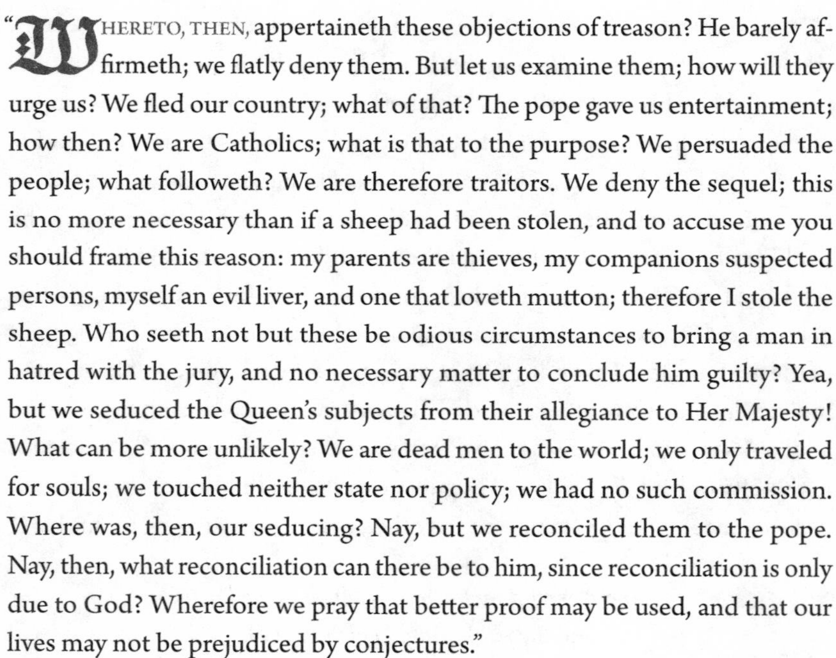

“WHERETO, THEN, appertaineth these objections of treason? He barely affirmeth; we flatly deny them. But let us examine them; how will they urge us? We fled our country; what of that? The pope gave us entertainment; how then? We are Catholics; what is that to the purpose? We persuaded the people; what followeth? We are therefore traitors. We deny the sequel; this is no more necessary than if a sheep had been stolen, and to accuse me you should frame this reason: my parents are thieves, my companions suspected persons, myself an evil liver, and one that loveth mutton; therefore I stole the sheep. Who seeth not but these be odious circumstances to bring a man in hatred with the jury, and no necessary matter to conclude him guilty? Yea, but we seduced the Queen’s subjects from their allegiance to Her Majesty! What can be more unlikely? We are dead men to the world; we only traveled for souls; we touched neither state nor policy; we had no such commission. Where was, then, our seducing? Nay, but we reconciled them to the pope. Nay, then, what reconciliation can there be to him, since reconciliation is only due to God? Wherefore we pray that better proof may be used, and that our lives may not be prejudiced by conjectures.”

“Jesus answered him: If I have spoken evil, bear witness of the evil, but if well, why smitest thou Me?” (Jn 18:23).

January 20

TRIBUTE TO CAESAR

Bl. Edmund Campion, S. J., 1581

"Her Majesty herself and the commissioners as well urged me on the point of supremacy, and as to whether the pope might lawfully excommunicate her! I acknowledged Her Highness as my governess and sovereign; I acknowledged Her Majesty *de facto et de jure* to be Queen; I confessed an obedience due to the Crown as my temporal head and primate. This I said then; so I say now. I will willingly pay to Her Majesty what is hers, yet I must pay to God what is His. As to whether the excommunication, admitting that it were of effect, would discharge me of my allegiance, I said this was a dangerous question, and they that demanded this demanded my blood. If I would admit the pope's authority and then he should excommunicate her, I would then do as God would give me grace; but I never admitted any such matter, neither ought I to be wrested with any such suppositions. To conclude. They are not matters of fact; they be not in the trial of the country; the jury ought not to take any notice of them; for though they are doubtless very discreet men, and trained in debates pertinent to their own calling, yet they are laymen, they are temporal, and unfit judges to decide so deep a question."

"Render therefore to Caesar the things that are Caesar's; and to God the things that are God's" (Mt 22:21).

January 21

FORTIFIED BY EXAMPLE

✠ Ven. Thomas Reynolds, Pr., and Ven. Alban Roe, O. S. B., 1641

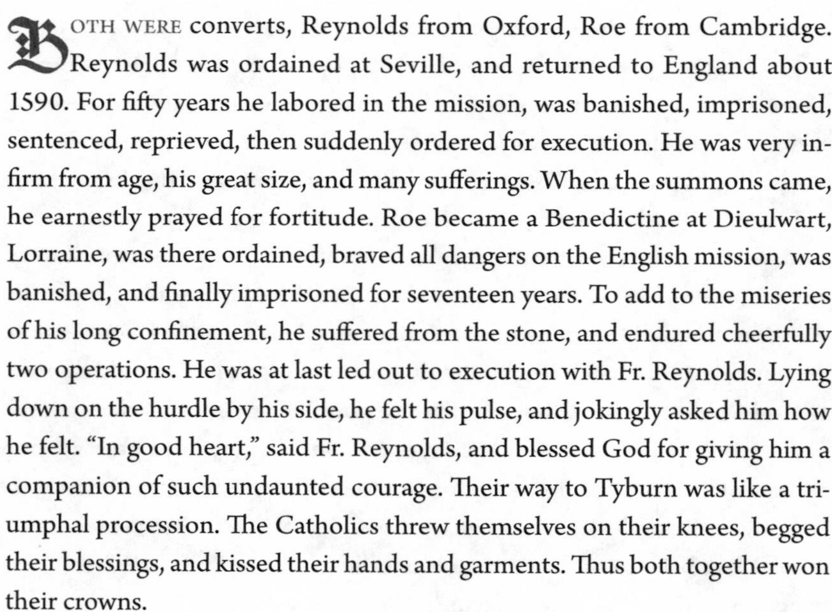

Both were converts, Reynolds from Oxford, Roe from Cambridge. Reynolds was ordained at Seville, and returned to England about 1590. For fifty years he labored in the mission, was banished, imprisoned, sentenced, reprieved, then suddenly ordered for execution. He was very infirm from age, his great size, and many sufferings. When the summons came, he earnestly prayed for fortitude. Roe became a Benedictine at Dieulwart, Lorraine, was there ordained, braved all dangers on the English mission, was banished, and finally imprisoned for seventeen years. To add to the miseries of his long confinement, he suffered from the stone, and endured cheerfully two operations. He was at last led out to execution with Fr. Reynolds. Lying down on the hurdle by his side, he felt his pulse, and jokingly asked him how he felt. "In good heart," said Fr. Reynolds, and blessed God for giving him a companion of such undaunted courage. Their way to Tyburn was like a triumphal procession. The Catholics threw themselves on their knees, begged their blessings, and kissed their hands and garments. Thus both together won their crowns.

"A brother helped by a brother is like a strong city" (Prv 18:19).

* *Reynolds was beatified by Pope Pius XI on 15 December 1929; Roe was canonized by Pope Paul VI on 25 October 1970.*

January 22

SCRUPLES CURED

✠ Ven. William Pattenson, Pr., 1592

BORN IN the county of Durham, he entered Douay College, was ordained priest in 1587, and went upon the English mission in 1589. After two years' work, he came up to London to consult some fellow priests, and so rid himself of certain scruples of conscience with which he was much troubled. He stayed in London at Mr. Laurence Mompesson's house (a Catholic gentleman) in Clerkenwell, where was in hiding another priest, Mr. James Young. On the Third Sunday of Advent, after both had said Mass, the pursuivant suddenly entered the house. Mr. Young escaped through the hiding place, but Mr. Pattenson was caught in attempting to follow him. He was tried at the Old Bailey and condemned. The night before his execution, he was put down into the condemned hole with seven malefactors. In his zeal for their salvation all his own troubles, interior scruples, and fear of impending death vanished; he gave himself up entirely to their conversion, and spoke with such effect that six out of the seven were reconciled by him, and died the next morning professing the Catholic Faith. The persecutors were so enraged at the conversion of these men, that they caused the martyr to be cut down immediately, so that he was alive and conscious while being cut open.

"According to the multitude of my sorrows in my heart, Thy consolations have given joy to my soul" (Ps 93:19).

* *Pattenson was beatified by Pope Pius XI on 15 December 1929.*

January 23

THE PRACTICE OF THE LAW

Ven. Nicolas Woodfen, Pr., 1586

HIS TRUE name was Nicolas Wheeler. He was born at Leominster, Herefordshire, and in the school of that town he was esteemed highly for his abilities. He performed his priest's studies at Douay and Rheims, and was ordained at the latter town, March 25, 1581. He was sent on the English mission the following June, and arrived in London in a state of great necessity, having, as he said, no money to buy food and scarce clothes for his back. A fellow priest, Fr. Davis, whose address he found, supplied his immediate needs and introduced him to Catholics, and, by the help of Mr. Francis Brown, Lord Montague's brother, a lodging was found for him at a haberdasher's in Fleet Street. There, disguised as a lawyer, he labored with great profit among the members of the Inns of Court, for he had a handsome presence, affable and courteous manners, and great power of attraction. But Morris, the pursuivant, found him out and forced him to flee. He was again nearly caught with Fr. Davis in his next hiding place at Sir T. Tresham's house at Hoxton, but his hour was not yet come. The third time, however, he fell into the pursuivant's hands he was tried, sentenced, and suffered with great constancy at Tyburn, January 21, 1586.

"For all the law is fulfilled in one word: Thou shalt love thy neighbor as thyself" (Gal 5:14).

* *Woodfen was beatified by Pope John Paul II on 22 November 1987.*

January 24

VICTIMS OF PERJURY

✠ Vens. William Ireland, S. J., and John Grove, L., 1679

IRELAND WAS of gentle birth. His uncle was killed in the King's service and his relations assisted Charles II to escape after his defeat at Worcester. Educated at St. Omers, he entered the Society of Jesus, went on the English mission in 1677, and was apprehended as a conspirator in the pretended Oates Plot. Oates swore that he had been present with Ireland at a meeting held in August to kill the King. Ireland proved by the evidence of above forty witnesses, many of them of note, that he was in the country when Oates swore he was in London at the time named, yet he was condemned to death. Ireland said he pardoned all who had a hand in his death, that if he were guilty of treason he would be bound then to declare it, or the name of any accomplice, even of his own father. "As for ourselves," he said, "we would beg a thousand pardons both of God and man; but, seeing that we cannot be believed, we must commit ourselves to the mercy of Almighty God, and hope to find pardon through Christ."

After begging the prayers of all Catholics, he was executed at Tyburn, with John Grove, a Catholic layman, whose innocence was likewise fully proved, January 14, 1679. The cheerful patience and constancy of both martyrs astonished the beholders.

"A false witness shall not be unpunished: and he that speaketh lies shall perish" (Prv 19:9).

* *Ireland and Grove were beatified by Pope Pius XI on 15 December 1929.*

January 25

SAUL, OTHERWISE PAUL

Ven. Lawrence Humphrey, L., 1591

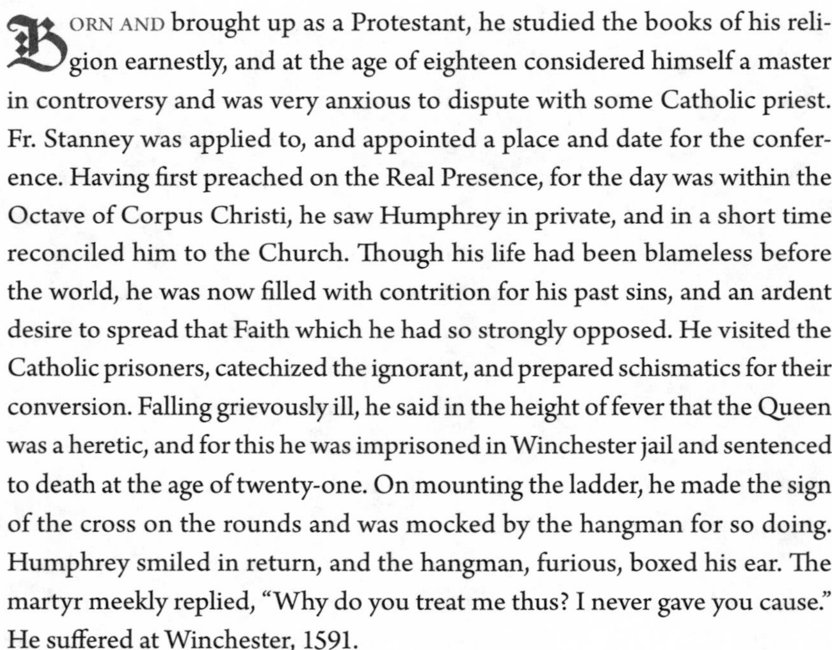

Born and brought up as a Protestant, he studied the books of his religion earnestly, and at the age of eighteen considered himself a master in controversy and was very anxious to dispute with some Catholic priest. Fr. Stanney was applied to, and appointed a place and date for the conference. Having first preached on the Real Presence, for the day was within the Octave of Corpus Christi, he saw Humphrey in private, and in a short time reconciled him to the Church. Though his life had been blameless before the world, he was now filled with contrition for his past sins, and an ardent desire to spread that Faith which he had so strongly opposed. He visited the Catholic prisoners, catechized the ignorant, and prepared schismatics for their conversion. Falling grievously ill, he said in the height of fever that the Queen was a heretic, and for this he was imprisoned in Winchester jail and sentenced to death at the age of twenty-one. On mounting the ladder, he made the sign of the cross on the rounds and was mocked by the hangman for so doing. Humphrey smiled in return, and the hangman, furious, boxed his ear. The martyr meekly replied, "Why do you treat me thus? I never gave you cause." He suffered at Winchester, 1591.

"I will show him how great things he must suffer for My name's sake" (Acts 9:16).

* *Humphrey was beatified by Pope Pius XI on 15 December 1929.*

January 26

THE SMILE OF ROYALTY

Bl. Thomas More, L., 1535

HENRY VIII took such pleasure in More's company that he would sometimes upon the sudden come to his house at Chelsea to be merry with him; whither on a time unlooked for, he came to dinner, and after dinner, in a fair garden of his, walked with him by the space of an hour holding his arms about his neck. Of all of which favors he made no more account than a deep wise man should do. Wherefore, when that after the King's departure his son-in-law, Mr. William Roper, rejoicingly came unto him saying these words, "Sir, how happy are you whom the King hath so familiarly entertained, as I have never seen him do to any other except Cardinal Wolsey, whom I have seen His Grace walk withal arm in arm," Sir Thomas More answered in this sort: "I thank our Lord, son, I find His Grace my very good Lord indeed, and I believe he doth as singularly favor me as he doth any subject within this realm. Howbeit, Son Roper, I have no cause to be proud thereof, for if my head could win him one castle in France, it should not fail to serve his turn."

"It is good to trust in the Lord, rather than
to trust in princes" (Ps 117:9).

* *More was canonized by Pope Pius XI on 19 May 1935.*

January 27

MASS UNDER PENAL LAWS

Letter of a missionary priest

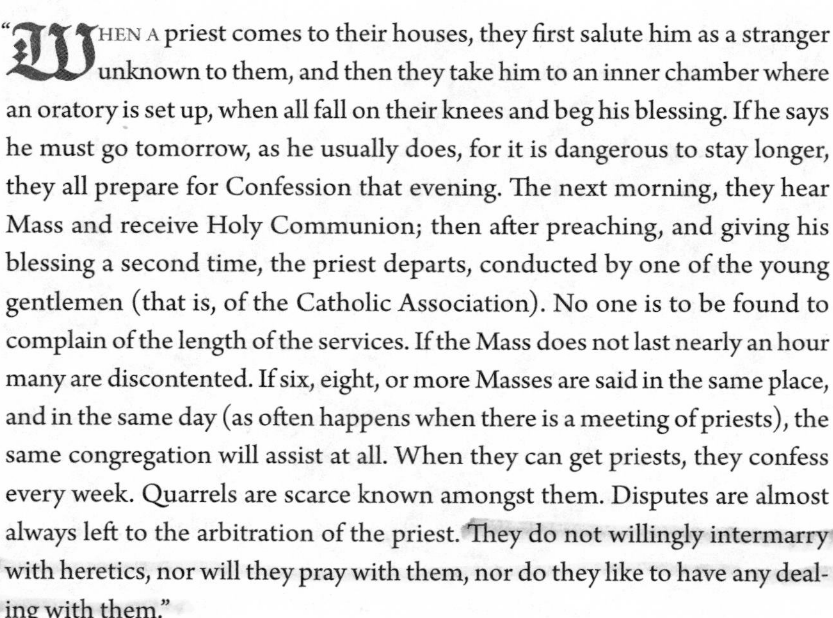

"When a priest comes to their houses, they first salute him as a stranger unknown to them, and then they take him to an inner chamber where an oratory is set up, when all fall on their knees and beg his blessing. If he says he must go tomorrow, as he usually does, for it is dangerous to stay longer, they all prepare for Confession that evening. The next morning, they hear Mass and receive Holy Communion; then after preaching, and giving his blessing a second time, the priest departs, conducted by one of the young gentlemen (that is, of the Catholic Association). No one is to be found to complain of the length of the services. If the Mass does not last nearly an hour many are discontented. If six, eight, or more Masses are said in the same place, and in the same day (as often happens when there is a meeting of priests), the same congregation will assist at all. When they can get priests, they confess every week. Quarrels are scarce known amongst them. Disputes are almost always left to the arbitration of the priest. They do not willingly intermarry with heretics, nor will they pray with them, nor do they like to have any dealing with them."

"Thou hast prepared a table before me against them that afflict me. Thou hast anointed my head with oil; and my chalice which inebreateth me, how goodly is it" (Ps 22:5).

January 28

DIVINE VENGEANCE ON HERESY

Ven. Arthur Bell, O. S. F., 1643, on the scaffold

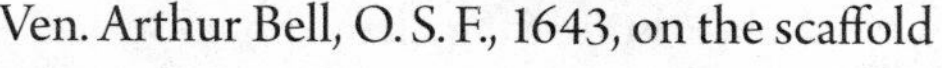

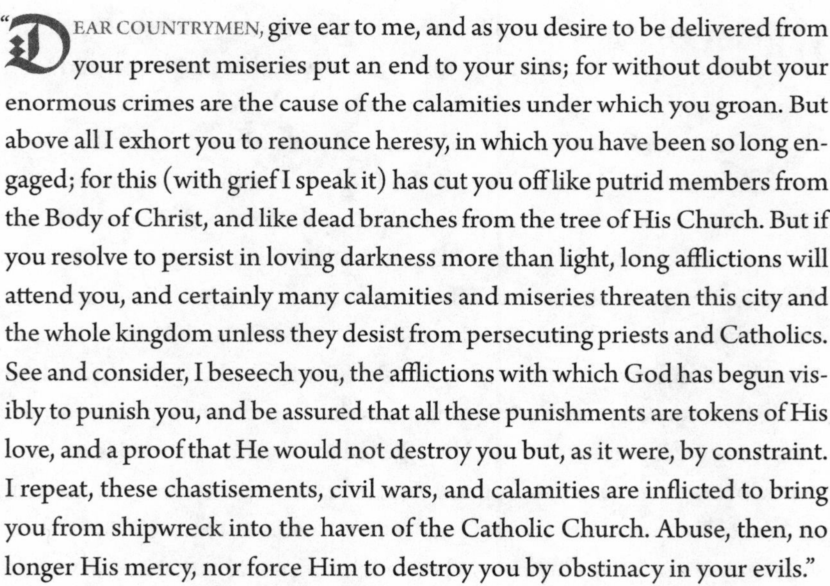

"Dear countrymen, give ear to me, and as you desire to be delivered from your present miseries put an end to your sins; for without doubt your enormous crimes are the cause of the calamities under which you groan. But above all I exhort you to renounce heresy, in which you have been so long engaged; for this (with grief I speak it) has cut you off like putrid members from the Body of Christ, and like dead branches from the tree of His Church. But if you resolve to persist in loving darkness more than light, long afflictions will attend you, and certainly many calamities and miseries threaten this city and the whole kingdom unless they desist from persecuting priests and Catholics. See and consider, I beseech you, the afflictions with which God has begun visibly to punish you, and be assured that all these punishments are tokens of His love, and a proof that He would not destroy you but, as it were, by constraint. I repeat, these chastisements, civil wars, and calamities are inflicted to bring you from shipwreck into the haven of the Catholic Church. Abuse, then, no longer His mercy, nor force Him to destroy you by obstinacy in your evils."

"Know thou and see that it is an evil and a bitter thing to have left the Lord thy God" (Jer 2:19).

* *Bell was beatified by Pope John Paul II on 22 November 1987.*

January 29

SUPERNATURAL SYMPATHIES

Ven. Edward Stransham, Pr., 1586

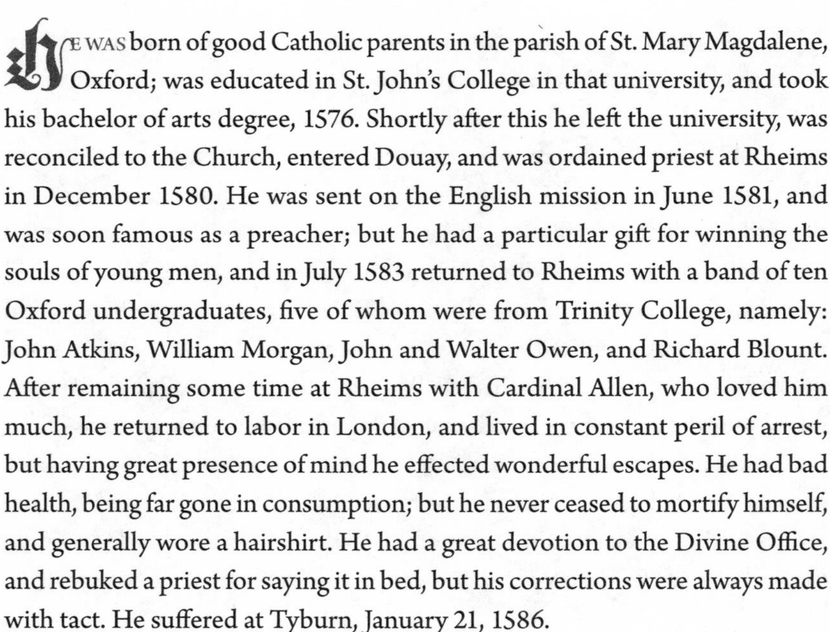

HE WAS born of good Catholic parents in the parish of St. Mary Magdalene, Oxford; was educated in St. John's College in that university, and took his bachelor of arts degree, 1576. Shortly after this he left the university, was reconciled to the Church, entered Douay, and was ordained priest at Rheims in December 1580. He was sent on the English mission in June 1581, and was soon famous as a preacher; but he had a particular gift for winning the souls of young men, and in July 1583 returned to Rheims with a band of ten Oxford undergraduates, five of whom were from Trinity College, namely: John Atkins, William Morgan, John and Walter Owen, and Richard Blount. After remaining some time at Rheims with Cardinal Allen, who loved him much, he returned to labor in London, and lived in constant peril of arrest, but having great presence of mind he effected wonderful escapes. He had bad health, being far gone in consumption; but he never ceased to mortify himself, and generally wore a hairshirt. He had a great devotion to the Divine Office, and rebuked a priest for saying it in bed, but his corrections were always made with tact. He suffered at Tyburn, January 21, 1586.

"I became all things to all men, that I might save all" (1 Cor 9:22).

* *Stransham was beatified by Pope Pius XI on 15 December 1929.*

January 30

A TALK WITH A REFORMER

Bl. Ralph Sherwin, Pr., Dec. 1

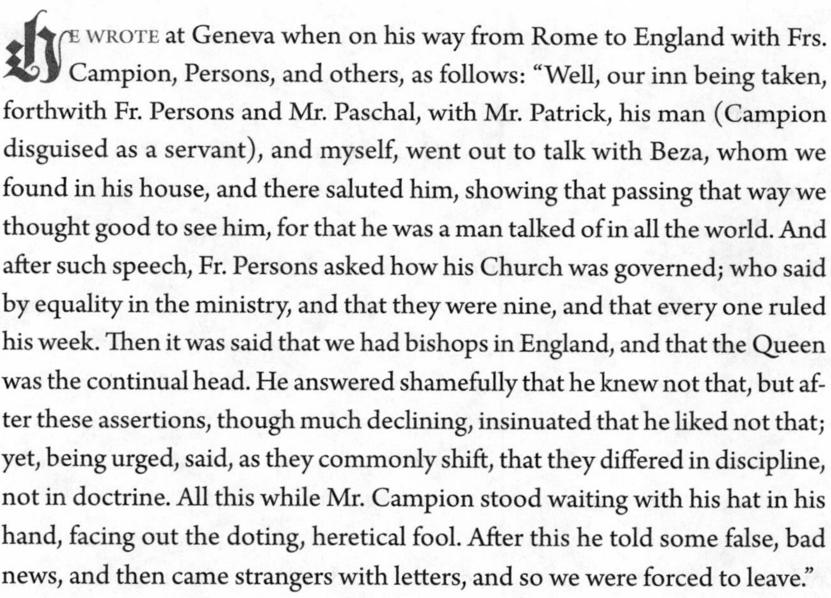

He wrote at Geneva when on his way from Rome to England with Frs. Campion, Persons, and others, as follows: "Well, our inn being taken, forthwith Fr. Persons and Mr. Paschal, with Mr. Patrick, his man (Campion disguised as a servant), and myself, went out to talk with Beza, whom we found in his house, and there saluted him, showing that passing that way we thought good to see him, for that he was a man talked of in all the world. And after such speech, Fr. Persons asked how his Church was governed; who said by equality in the ministry, and that they were nine, and that every one ruled his week. Then it was said that we had bishops in England, and that the Queen was the continual head. He answered shamefully that he knew not that, but after these assertions, though much declining, insinuated that he liked not that; yet, being urged, said, as they commonly shift, that they differed in discipline, not in doctrine. All this while Mr. Campion stood waiting with his hat in his hand, facing out the doting, heretical fool. After this he told some false, bad news, and then came strangers with letters, and so we were forced to leave."

"A man that is a heretic . . . avoid: Knowing that he that is such an one is subverted and sinneth, being condemned by his own judgment" (Ti 3:10–11).

* *Sherwin was canonized by Pope Paul VI on 25 October 1970.*

January 31

THE PUNISHMENT OF ACHAB

Fr. Peto's prophecy

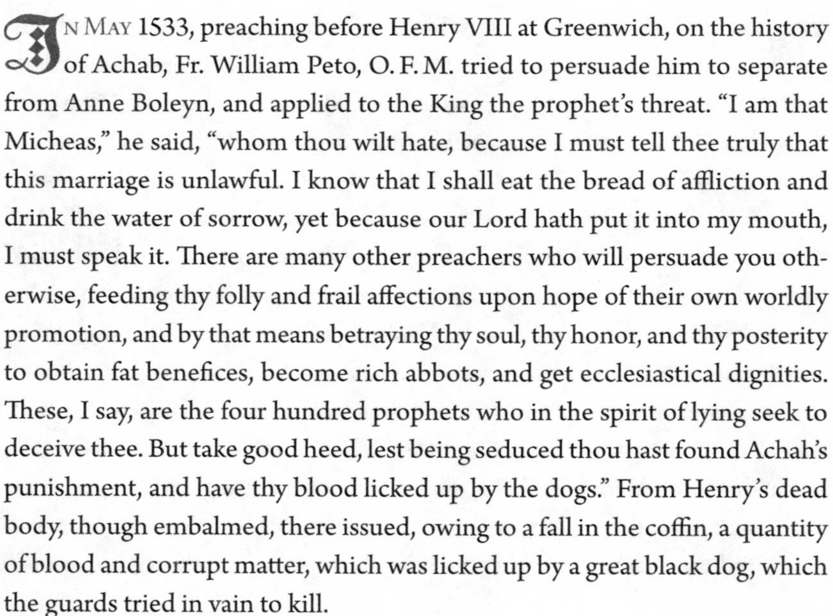

In May 1533, preaching before Henry VIII at Greenwich, on the history of Achab, Fr. William Peto, O. F. M. tried to persuade him to separate from Anne Boleyn, and applied to the King the prophet's threat. "I am that Micheas," he said, "whom thou wilt hate, because I must tell thee truly that this marriage is unlawful. I know that I shall eat the bread of affliction and drink the water of sorrow, yet because our Lord hath put it into my mouth, I must speak it. There are many other preachers who will persuade you otherwise, feeding thy folly and frail affections upon hope of their own worldly promotion, and by that means betraying thy soul, thy honor, and thy posterity to obtain fat benefices, become rich abbots, and get ecclesiastical dignities. These, I say, are the four hundred prophets who in the spirit of lying seek to deceive thee. But take good heed, lest being seduced thou hast found Achah's punishment, and have thy blood licked up by the dogs." From Henry's dead body, though embalmed, there issued, owing to a fall in the coffin, a quantity of blood and corrupt matter, which was licked up by a great black dog, which the guards tried in vain to kill.

"Where the dogs licked the blood of Naboth shall the dogs lick thy blood, even thine" (3 Kgs 21:19).

February

February 1

GROUNDS FOR FAITH

✠ Ven. Henry Morse, S.J., 1645

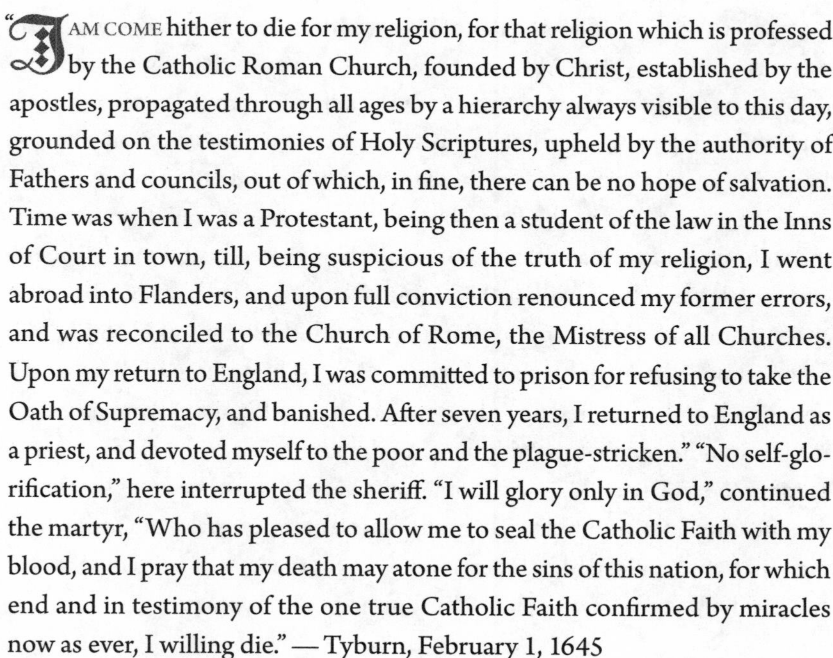

"I AM COME hither to die for my religion, for that religion which is professed by the Catholic Roman Church, founded by Christ, established by the apostles, propagated through all ages by a hierarchy always visible to this day, grounded on the testimonies of Holy Scriptures, upheld by the authority of Fathers and councils, out of which, in fine, there can be no hope of salvation. Time was when I was a Protestant, being then a student of the law in the Inns of Court in town, till, being suspicious of the truth of my religion, I went abroad into Flanders, and upon full conviction renounced my former errors, and was reconciled to the Church of Rome, the Mistress of all Churches. Upon my return to England, I was committed to prison for refusing to take the Oath of Supremacy, and banished. After seven years, I returned to England as a priest, and devoted myself to the poor and the plague-stricken." "No self-glorification," here interrupted the sheriff. "I will glory only in God," continued the martyr, "Who has pleased to allow me to seal the Catholic Faith with my blood, and I pray that my death may atone for the sins of this nation, for which end and in testimony of the one true Catholic Faith confirmed by miracles now as ever, I willing die." — Tyburn, February 1, 1645

"Thy testimonies, O Lord, are made exceedingly credible" (Ps 92:5).

* *Morse was canonized by Pope Paul VI on 25 October 1970.*

February 2

A MASS OF THANKSGIVING

Ven. Henry Morse, S.J., 1645

On February 1, 1645, the day of his execution, he celebrated, early in the morning, a Votive Mass of the Blessed Trinity in thanksgiving for the great favor God was pleased to do him in calling him to the crown of martyrdom, having first, according to custom, recited the Litanies of our Blessed Lady and of All the Saints, for the conversion of England. After which he made an exhortation to the Catholics who were present, and, having rested for an hour, said the canonical hours, and then visited his fellow prisoners, and took leave of them with a cheerfulness that was extraordinary. The little space that remained he employed in prayer with a religious of his order, till, being admonished that his time was come, he cast himself on his knees, and, with hands and eyes lifted up to heaven, gave hearty thanks to Almighty God for His infinite mercy toward him, and offered himself without reserve as a sacrifice to His Divine Majesty. "Come, my sweetest Jesus," said he, "that I may now be inseparably united to Thee in time and eternity: welcome ropes, hurdles, gibbets, knives, and butchery, welcome for the love of Jesus my Savior." At nine, he was drawn on a sledge by four horses to Tyburn.

"What shall I render to the Lord, for all the things that He hath rendered to me? I will take the chalice of salvation, and call upon the name of the Lord" (Ps 115:12–13).

February 3

WEEP NOT FOR ME

✠ Bl. John Nelson, S. J., 1578

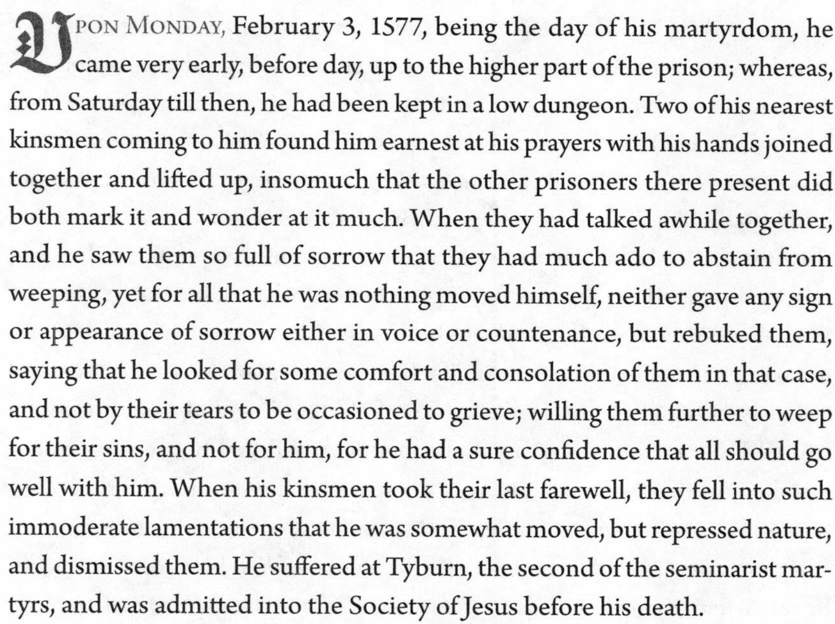

UPON MONDAY, February 3, 1577, being the day of his martyrdom, he came very early, before day, up to the higher part of the prison; whereas, from Saturday till then, he had been kept in a low dungeon. Two of his nearest kinsmen coming to him found him earnest at his prayers with his hands joined together and lifted up, insomuch that the other prisoners there present did both mark it and wonder at it much. When they had talked awhile together, and he saw them so full of sorrow that they had much ado to abstain from weeping, yet for all that he was nothing moved himself, neither gave any sign or appearance of sorrow either in voice or countenance, but rebuked them, saying that he looked for some comfort and consolation of them in that case, and not by their tears to be occasioned to grieve; willing them further to weep for their sins, and not for him, for he had a sure confidence that all should go well with him. When his kinsmen took their last farewell, they fell into such immoderate lamentations that he was somewhat moved, but repressed nature, and dismissed them. He suffered at Tyburn, the second of the seminarist martyrs, and was admitted into the Society of Jesus before his death.

"But Jesus turning to them said: Daughters of Jerusalem, weep not for Me, but for your children" (Lk 23:28).

February 4

GALL TO DRINK

Bl. John Nelson, S.J., 1578

Born, in 1534, of an ancient Yorkshire family, he was nearly forty years of age when he went to the newly–established college at Douay and was ordained, and of his four brothers two followed his example. He returned to England 1577, and after a year's ministry was called upon to exorcise a possessed person. The evil spirit, when it was cast out, told him that it would cost him his life. He was apprehended, Sunday, December 1, as he was saying the next day's Matins. He refused to take the Oath of Supremacy, declared repeatedly that the pope was the Supreme Head of the Church and that the new religion set up in England was both schismatical and heretical as a voluntary departure from Catholic unity. For this statement he was condemned as guilty of high treason. He had always held that England would never be restored to the Church save by bloodshedding, and that his own life would be taken for that cause. He received his sentence therefore with great calmness and prepared himself for death. He was confined in a filthy underground dungeon infested with vermin. The jailer's wife offered him some wine, but he refused it, saying he would prefer water or rather vinegar and gall, to more closely follow his Lord.

"And they gave Him wine mingled with gall. And when He had tasted, He would not drink" (Mt 27:34).

February 5

THE BREAD OF THE STRONG

Bl. John Nelson, S.J., 1578

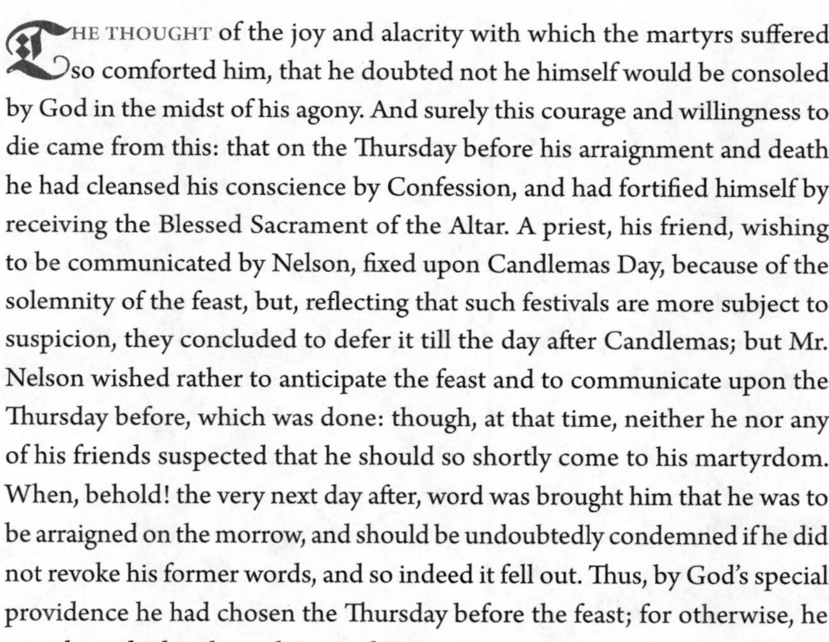

THE THOUGHT of the joy and alacrity with which the martyrs suffered so comforted him, that he doubted not he himself would be consoled by God in the midst of his agony. And surely this courage and willingness to die came from this: that on the Thursday before his arraignment and death he had cleansed his conscience by Confession, and had fortified himself by receiving the Blessed Sacrament of the Altar. A priest, his friend, wishing to be communicated by Nelson, fixed upon Candlemas Day, because of the solemnity of the feast, but, reflecting that such festivals are more subject to suspicion, they concluded to defer it till the day after Candlemas; but Mr. Nelson wished rather to anticipate the feast and to communicate upon the Thursday before, which was done: though, at that time, neither he nor any of his friends suspected that he should so shortly come to his martyrdom. When, behold! the very next day after, word was brought him that he was to be arraigned on the morrow, and should be undoubtedly condemned if he did not revoke his former words, and so indeed it fell out. Thus, by God's special providence he had chosen the Thursday before the feast; for otherwise, he must have died without the sacred Viaticum.

"And he walked in the strength of that food to Horeb the Mount of God" (3 Kgs 19:8).

February 6

THE SUNAMITESS REWARDED

Margaret Powell, L., 1642

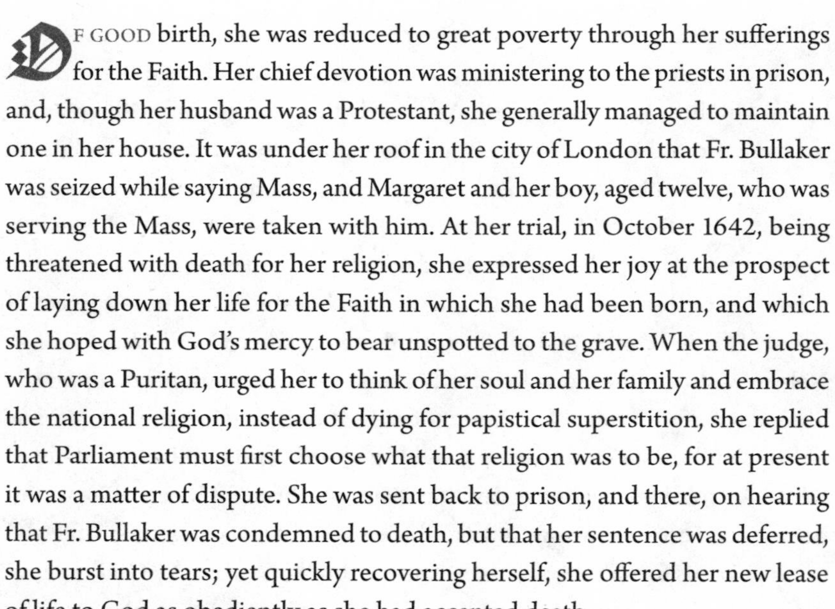

OF GOOD birth, she was reduced to great poverty through her sufferings for the Faith. Her chief devotion was ministering to the priests in prison, and, though her husband was a Protestant, she generally managed to maintain one in her house. It was under her roof in the city of London that Fr. Bullaker was seized while saying Mass, and Margaret and her boy, aged twelve, who was serving the Mass, were taken with him. At her trial, in October 1642, being threatened with death for her religion, she expressed her joy at the prospect of laying down her life for the Faith in which she had been born, and which she hoped with God's mercy to bear unspotted to the grave. When the judge, who was a Puritan, urged her to think of her soul and her family and embrace the national religion, instead of dying for papistical superstition, she replied that Parliament must first choose what that religion was to be, for at present it was a matter of dispute. She was sent back to prison, and there, on hearing that Fr. Bullaker was condemned to death, but that her sentence was deferred, she burst into tears; yet quickly recovering herself, she offered her new lease of life to God as obediently as she had accepted death.

"Now there was a great woman there who detained him [Eliseus] to eat bread: and as he often passed that way, he turned into her house to eat bread" (4 Kgs 4:8).

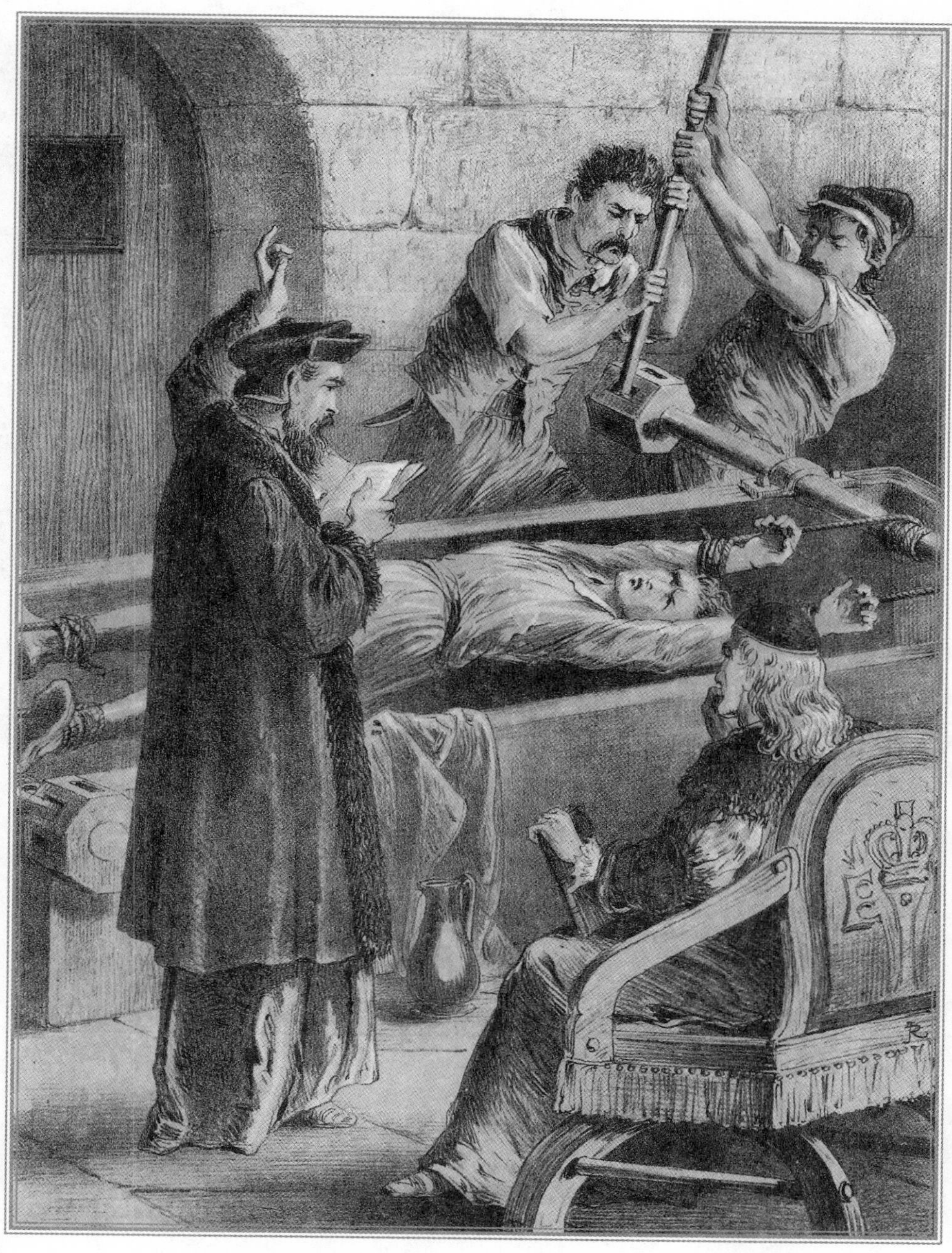

THOMAS SHERWOOD
"In the Tower he was most cruelly racked"

February 7

TRUE TO A TRUST

✠ Bl. Thomas Sherwood, L., 1578

HIS PARENTS both suffered much for the Faith. His mother was a sister of Mr. Francis Tregian, in whose house Bl. Cuthbert Mayne was taken. Their son Thomas, one of fourteen children, followed his father's trade of draper, intending however to cross to Douay and become a priest. One day when walking in the streets of London he was seized on the cry of "Stop the traitor!" raised by a youth, Martin Tregony, a virulent papist-hunter. His mother, Lady Tregony, was a pious Catholic, and Sherwood frequently visited her, and Martin suspected him of assisting in having Mass said in her house. At his condemnation, Sherwood declared that the pope and not the Queen was the Head of the Church in England, and was then most cruelly racked to discover where he had heard Mass. He could not be induced, however, to betray or bring any man into danger. After this, he was cast into a filthy, dark dungeon, swarming with loathsome and ferocious rats, and only left it twice during three months to be again tortured on the rack. He had lost the use of his limbs, was starving, and searched with pain, but no compromising words passed his lips. He was executed at Tyburn, February 7, 1578, aged twenty-seven.

"Keep that which is committed to thy trust" (1 Tm 6:20).

February 8

PRAYERS WITH TEARS

Bl. John Fisher, Card. Bp., 1535

"He never omitted so much as one Collect of his daily service, which he used commonly to say to himself alone, without the help of any chaplain, not in such speed or hasty manner to be at an end, as many will do, but in most reverent and devout manner, so distinctly and tractably pronouncing every word, that he seemed a very devourer of heavenly food, never satiated nor filled therewith. Insomuch that talking on a time with a Carthusian monk, who much commended his zeal and diligent pains in compiling his book against Luther, he answered again, saying that he wished that time of writing had been spent in prayer, thinking that prayer would have done more good and was of more merit.

"And to help this devotion, he caused a great hole to be digged through the wall of his church at Rochester, whereby he might the more commodiously have prospect into the church at Mass and Evensong times. When he himself used to say Mass, as many times he used to do, if he was not letted by some urgent and great cause, ye might then perceive in him such earnest devotion that many times the tears would fall from his cheeks."

"With a strong cry and tears, offering up prayers" (Heb 5:7).

February 9

THE STONES OF ISRAEL

Bl. John Fisher, Card. Bp., 1535

After reminding our Lord of His promise that the Gospel should be preached throughout the world as a testimony to all nations, he recalls how the apostles were but soft and yielding clay till they were baked hard by the fire of the Holy Ghost, and then offered a prayer to be fulfilled in himself. "So, good Lord, do now in like manner again with Thy Church Militant, change and make the soft and slippery earth into hard stones. Set in Thy Church strong and mighty pillars, that may suffer and endure great labors — watching, poverty, thirst, hunger, cold, and heat — which also shall not fear the threatenings of princes, persecution, neither death, but always persuade and think with themselves to suffer, with a good will, slanders, shame, and all kinds of torments for the glory and laud of Thy holy name. By this manner, good Lord, the truth of Thy Gospel shall be preached throughout the world.... Oh! if it would please our Lord God to show this great goodness and mercy in our days, the memorial of His so doing ought, of very right, to be left in perpetual writing, never to be forgotten of all our posterity, that every generation might love and worship Him time without end."

"His bow rested upon the strong, and the bands of his arms and his hands were loosed, by the hands of the mighty one of Jacob: thence he came forth a pastor, the stone of Israel" (Gn 49:24).

February 10

FATHER OF THE POOR

Bl. John Fisher, Card. Bp., 1535

To poor sick persons he was a physician, to the lame he was a staff, to poor widows an advocate, to orphans a tutor, and to poor travelers a host. Wheresoever he lay, either at Rochester or elsewhere, his order was to inquire where any poor sick folks lay near him, which after he once knew, he would diligently visit them. And when he saw any of them likely to die, he would preach to them, teaching them the way to die, with such godly persuasions that for the most part he never departed till the sick persons were well satisfied and contented with death. Many times it was his chance to come to such poor houses as, for want of chimneys, were unbearable for the smoke, yet himself would there sit three or four hours together when none of his servants were able to abide in the house. And in some other poor houses where stairs were wanting, he would never disdain to climb up a ladder for such a good purpose. And when he had given them such ghostly comfort as he thought expedient for their souls, he would at his departure leave behind him his charitable alms, giving charge to his steward daily to prepare meat for them if they were poor.

"Because I had delivered the poor man that cried out; and the fatherless, that had no helper. The blessing of him that was ready to perish came upon me, and I comforted the heart of the widow" (Jb 29:12–13).

February 11

SORROW TURNED TO JOY

Ven. George Haydock, Pr., 1584

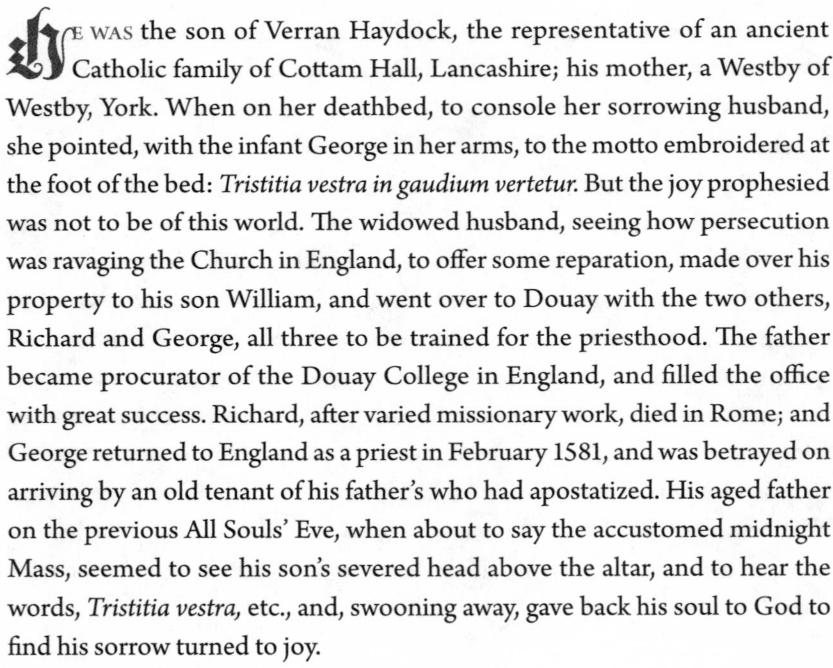

He was the son of Verran Haydock, the representative of an ancient Catholic family of Cottam Hall, Lancashire; his mother, a Westby of Westby, York. When on her deathbed, to console her sorrowing husband, she pointed, with the infant George in her arms, to the motto embroidered at the foot of the bed: *Tristitia vestra in gaudium vertetur.* But the joy prophesied was not to be of this world. The widowed husband, seeing how persecution was ravaging the Church in England, to offer some reparation, made over his property to his son William, and went over to Douay with the two others, Richard and George, all three to be trained for the priesthood. The father became procurator of the Douay College in England, and filled the office with great success. Richard, after varied missionary work, died in Rome; and George returned to England as a priest in February 1581, and was betrayed on arriving by an old tenant of his father's who had apostatized. His aged father on the previous All Souls' Eve, when about to say the accustomed midnight Mass, seemed to see his son's severed head above the altar, and to hear the words, *Tristitia vestra,* etc., and, swooning away, gave back his soul to God to find his sorrow turned to joy.

"Your sorrow shall be turned into joy" (Jn 16:20).

* *Haydock was beatified by Pope John Paul II on 22 November 1987.*

February 12

A ROYAL HYPOCRITE

✠ Ven. George Haydock, Pr., 1584

ARRESTED AS a priest in February 1582 in St. Paul's Churchyard, he was confined in the Tower, where he was robbed of all his money, and suffered much from the hardships of his imprisonment, and from a lingering disease that he had contracted in Italy. On February 7, 1583, he was sentenced to death for having been made priest by the pope's authority beyond the seas. He attributed this happy event to the prayers of St. Dorothy, virgin and martyr, whose day it was, and he marked it in the calendar of his breviary, which he left to Dr. Creagh, archbishop of Armagh, then a prisoner in the Tower. But to his sorrow he heard that the Queen had changed her mind, and that he was not to suffer. His confessor, however, a man of great experience, encouraged him by the assurance that these rumors were industriously spread abroad only to represent the Queen as averse from these cruelties, and to remove any odium from her, as if they were extorted from her against her inclinations. The falseness of the Queen's reported leniency was proved by the event. Fr. Haydock, without a sign of any pardon, was hung at Tyburn, and the whole butchery performed February 12, 1584.

"They spoke indeed peacefully to me; and speaking in anger of the earth they devised guile" (Ps 34:20).

JAMES FENN
"It was a moving spectacle"

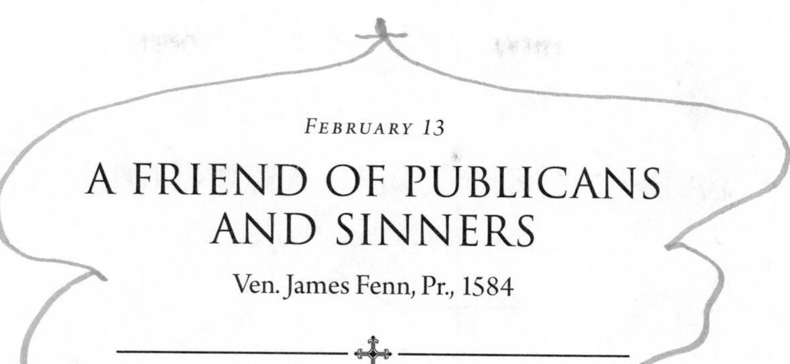

February 13

A FRIEND OF PUBLICANS AND SINNERS

Ven. James Fenn, Pr., 1584

ORDAINED PRIEST when a widower of mature age, he labored first in his own county, Somersetshire. He was soon apprehended, and to complete his disgrace was exposed to the people, chained and fettered, on a market day. Removed to the Marshalsea, where his priesthood was unknown, he spent his time in strengthening the Catholics, administering the Sacraments and reconciling Protestants to the Church. The main objects of his charity, however, were the criminals and pirates under sentence of death. These he visited and exhorted with great affection to make good use of the time by repenting of their sins and seeking pardon through the power Christ had left with His Church. Many responded to his call; among them one noted pirate, till then in despair at the load of his sins, cast himself at his feet and desired to be reconciled. This was done, and so staunch was this convert that he absolutely refused the prayers and communion of the Protestant minister, and on the scaffold publicly professed his faith. As Fr. Fenn was being laid on the hurdle his little daughter Frances came weeping to take leave of him. The good man lifted his pinioned hands as far as he could and gave her his blessing, and was drawn to Tyburn, February 12, 1584.

"Behold a glutton and a wine bibber, the friend of publicans and sinners" (Lk 7:34).

* *Fenn was beatified by Pope Pius XI on 15 December 1929.*

February 14

PATIENCE IN THE APOSTOLATE

Ven. John Nutter, Pr., 1584

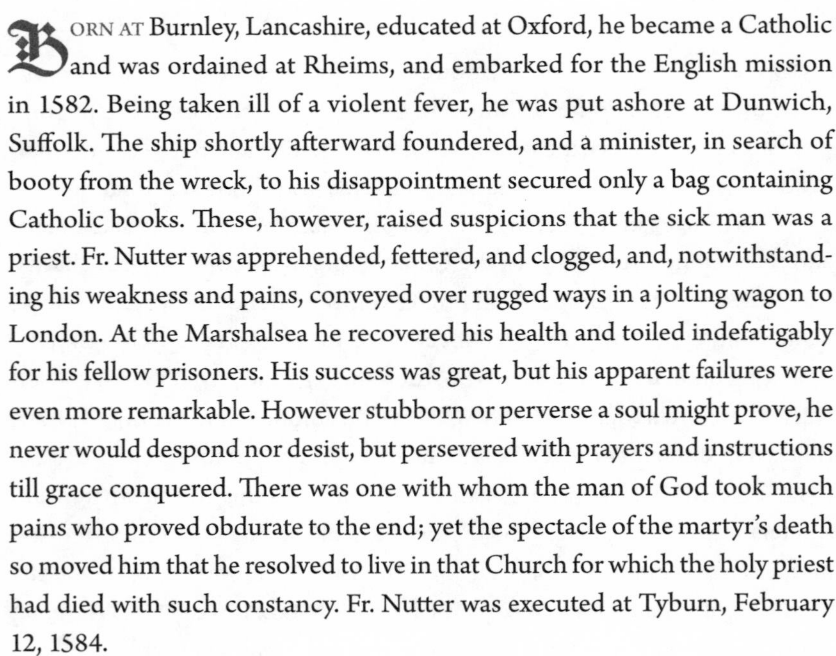

BORN AT Burnley, Lancashire, educated at Oxford, he became a Catholic and was ordained at Rheims, and embarked for the English mission in 1582. Being taken ill of a violent fever, he was put ashore at Dunwich, Suffolk. The ship shortly afterward foundered, and a minister, in search of booty from the wreck, to his disappointment secured only a bag containing Catholic books. These, however, raised suspicions that the sick man was a priest. Fr. Nutter was apprehended, fettered, and clogged, and, notwithstanding his weakness and pains, conveyed over rugged ways in a jolting wagon to London. At the Marshalsea he recovered his health and toiled indefatigably for his fellow prisoners. His success was great, but his apparent failures were even more remarkable. However stubborn or perverse a soul might prove, he never would despond nor desist, but persevered with prayers and instructions till grace conquered. There was one with whom the man of God took much pains who proved obdurate to the end; yet the spectacle of the martyr's death so moved him that he resolved to live in that Church for which the holy priest had died with such constancy. Fr. Nutter was executed at Tyburn, February 12, 1584.

"Thou, O man of God ... pursue justice, charity, patience.... Fight the good fight" (1 Tm 6:11–12).

* *Nutter was beatified by Pope Pius XI on 15 December 1929.*

February 15

INJUSTICE ENTHRONED

Ven. John Munden, Pr., 1584

HE WAS born at Maperton, in Dorsetshire, was educated at Oxford, and became a fellow of New College, 1562. The fact of his being a Catholic, however, getting known, he was deprived of his fellowship in 1566, went abroad to Rheims and to Rome, and returned a priest to England in 1582. About the end of February that year, as he was going up from Winchester to London, he was met on Hounslow Heath by a lawyer, named Hammond, who, knowing him to be a priest, delivered him to the justices of Staines, who sent him to Sir Francis Walsingham, the secretary of state. The secretary inveighed against the seminarists, the Rheims translations of the New Testament, and questioned him, among other matters, as to whether the Queen was sovereign both *de jure* and *de facto*. To this, on Munden replying that he did not rightly understand these terms, Walsingham gave him a stunning blow on his head. He was then examined by Popham, the attorney general, who accused him of having led an immoral life in his own country, and loaded him with fresh insults. After a twelvemonth's imprisonment, he suffered with Frs. Haydock, Fenn, Hemerford, and Nutter. Being the last, he helped them by his prayers on earth as they him by theirs in heaven. — February 12, 1584

"He that justifieth the wicked, and he that condemneth the just, both are an abomination before God" (Prv 17:15).

* *Munden was beatified by Pope Pius XI on 15 December 1929.*

February 16

WITH THE PLAGUE-STRICKEN

Ven. Henry Morse, S.J., 1645

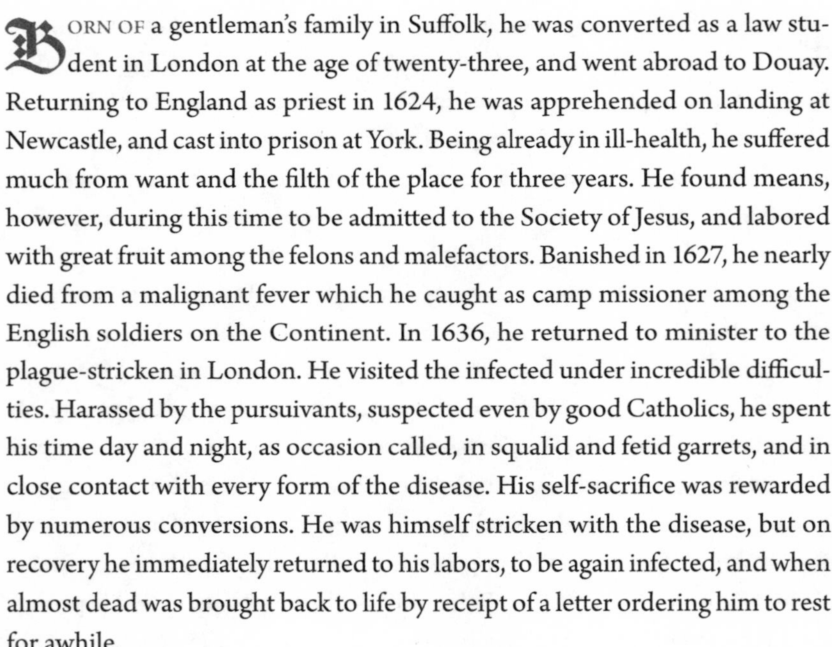

Born of a gentleman's family in Suffolk, he was converted as a law student in London at the age of twenty-three, and went abroad to Douay. Returning to England as priest in 1624, he was apprehended on landing at Newcastle, and cast into prison at York. Being already in ill-health, he suffered much from want and the filth of the place for three years. He found means, however, during this time to be admitted to the Society of Jesus, and labored with great fruit among the felons and malefactors. Banished in 1627, he nearly died from a malignant fever which he caught as camp missioner among the English soldiers on the Continent. In 1636, he returned to minister to the plague-stricken in London. He visited the infected under incredible difficulties. Harassed by the pursuivants, suspected even by good Catholics, he spent his time day and night, as occasion called, in squalid and fetid garrets, and in close contact with every form of the disease. His self-sacrifice was rewarded by numerous conversions. He was himself stricken with the disease, but on recovery he immediately returned to his labors, to be again infected, and when almost dead was brought back to life by receipt of a letter ordering him to rest for awhile.

"The blind see, the lame walk, the lepers are cleansed, . . . the poor have the gospel preached to them. And blessed is he who is not scandalized in Me" (Mt 11:5–6).

February 17

FROM CITY TO CITY

Ven. Henry Morse, S.J., 1645

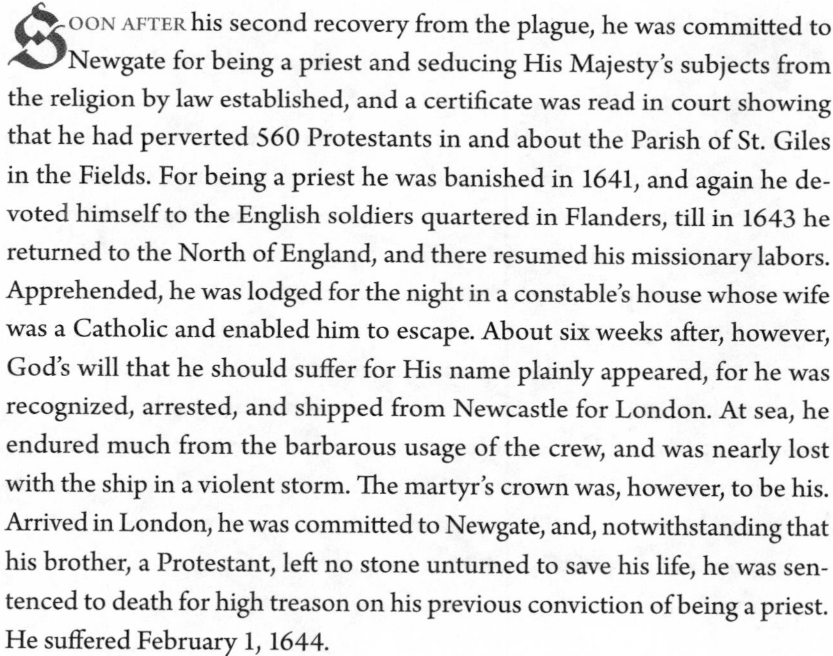

SOON AFTER his second recovery from the plague, he was committed to Newgate for being a priest and seducing His Majesty's subjects from the religion by law established, and a certificate was read in court showing that he had perverted 560 Protestants in and about the Parish of St. Giles in the Fields. For being a priest he was banished in 1641, and again he devoted himself to the English soldiers quartered in Flanders, till in 1643 he returned to the North of England, and there resumed his missionary labors. Apprehended, he was lodged for the night in a constable's house whose wife was a Catholic and enabled him to escape. About six weeks after, however, God's will that he should suffer for His name plainly appeared, for he was recognized, arrested, and shipped from Newcastle for London. At sea, he endured much from the barbarous usage of the crew, and was nearly lost with the ship in a violent storm. The martyr's crown was, however, to be his. Arrived in London, he was committed to Newgate, and, notwithstanding that his brother, a Protestant, left no stone unturned to save his life, he was sentenced to death for high treason on his previous conviction of being a priest. He suffered February 1, 1644.

"And when they shall persecute in one city,
flee into another" (Mt 10:23).

February 18

A DYING LIFE

✠ Ven. John Pibush, Pr., 1601

BORN AT Thirsk in Yorkshire, he made his studies at Rheims, was ordained priest in 1587, and sent to the English mission in 1589. His work lay in Gloucestershire, and after a year's labors he was apprehended at Moreton le Marsh and committed to Gloucester jail. Some of the felons confined there having managed to break a passage through the walls, Pibush, like the other prisoners, made his escape. He was apprehended, however, the next day, sent up to London, tried, and condemned on account of his priesthood. For seven years his execution was postponed, and during the whole of that period he was kept in the Queen's Bench huddled up with the other prisoners, some of them the worst of criminals. Through the miseries of his imprisonment, he contracted a grievous infirmity, so that he was sometimes for hours without sense or movement. His worst sufferings, however, were from the brutality and blasphemies of his fellow prisoners. His patience touched their hearts at last, and his jailer gave him a separate cell, in which at times he said Mass to the great comfort of his soul. He was executed at St. Thomas Waterings, February 18, 1601.

"Why do you persecute me as God, and glut yourselves with my flesh? For I know that my Redeemer liveth.... and that in my flesh I shall see my God" (Jb 19:22, 25–26).

* *Pibush was beatified by Pope Pius XI on 15 December 1929.*

February 19

IN THE SHADOW OF DEATH (1)

Bl. Thomas More, L., 1535

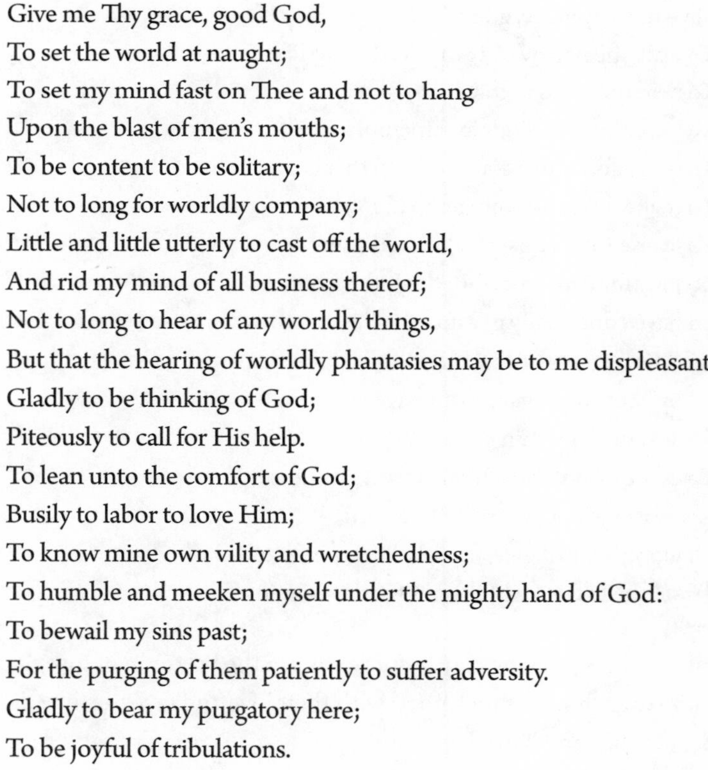

Give me Thy grace, good God,
To set the world at naught;
To set my mind fast on Thee and not to hang
Upon the blast of men's mouths;
To be content to be solitary;
Not to long for worldly company;
Little and little utterly to cast off the world,
And rid my mind of all business thereof;
Not to long to hear of any worldly things,
But that the hearing of worldly phantasies may be to me displeasant.
Gladly to be thinking of God;
Piteously to call for His help.
To lean unto the comfort of God;
Busily to labor to love Him;
To know mine own vility and wretchedness;
To humble and meeken myself under the mighty hand of God:
To bewail my sins past;
For the purging of them patiently to suffer adversity.
Gladly to bear my purgatory here;
To be joyful of tribulations.

"To enlighten them that sit in darkness and in the shadow of death" (Lk 1:79).

February 20

IN THE SHADOW OF DEATH (2)

Bl. Thomas More, L., 1535

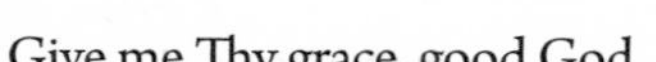

Give me Thy grace, good God,
To walk the narrow way that leadeth to life;
To bear the cross with Christ;
To have the last things in remembrance;
To have afore mine eye my death that is ever at hand.
To make death no stranger to me,
To foresee and consider the everlasting fire of hell.
To pray for pardon before the Judge come;
To have continually in mind the Passion that Christ suffered for me.
For His benefits uncessantly to give Him thanks.
To buy the time again that I have lost.
To abstain from vain confabulations.
To eschew light foolish mirth and gladness.
Recreations not necessary to cut off;
Of worldly substance, friends, liberty, life, and all,
To set the loss at right naught for the winning of Christ.

To think my worst enemies my best friends, for the brethren of Joseph could never have done him so much good with their love and favor as they did him with their malice and hatred.

"To direct our feet into the way of peace" (Lk 1:79).

February 21

A MARTYR POET

✠ Ven. Robert Southwell, S.J., 1595

OF AN old Norfolk family, he was stolen by a gipsy as an infant, but the theft was speedily discovered, and Southwell proved his gratitude to his rescuer by seeking out and converting the woman who detected the theft when he returned to England as a Jesuit priest in 1584. He labored on the mission with great success, in which his mastery of the English tongue stood him in good service. His poems, in their directness and force, their antitheses, and terseness, in beauty of conception and fidelity of expression, rank with those of the finest Elizabethan sonneteers. His lyre, however, was tuned to no mere amorous strains, but to show how "virtue and verse suit together." The divine beauty of Jesus and Mary, the operations of grace, the deformity of sin, the nature of contrition, contempt of the world, the brevity of life, all these are told with a charm and a grace in verses now little, alas! known, and are set forth with equal power in his letters. He was shamefully betrayed by a woman, once his penitent, was ten times tortured, and, after three years' confinement in the Tower in a filthy hole, was brought out, covered with vermin, at the age of thirty-three to receive his martyr's crown.

"The mercies of the Lord I will sing forever" (Ps 88:2).

* *Southwell was canonized by Pope Paul VI on 25 October 1970.*

February 22

HONEY FROM THE ROCK

Ven. Robert Southwell, S.J., 1595

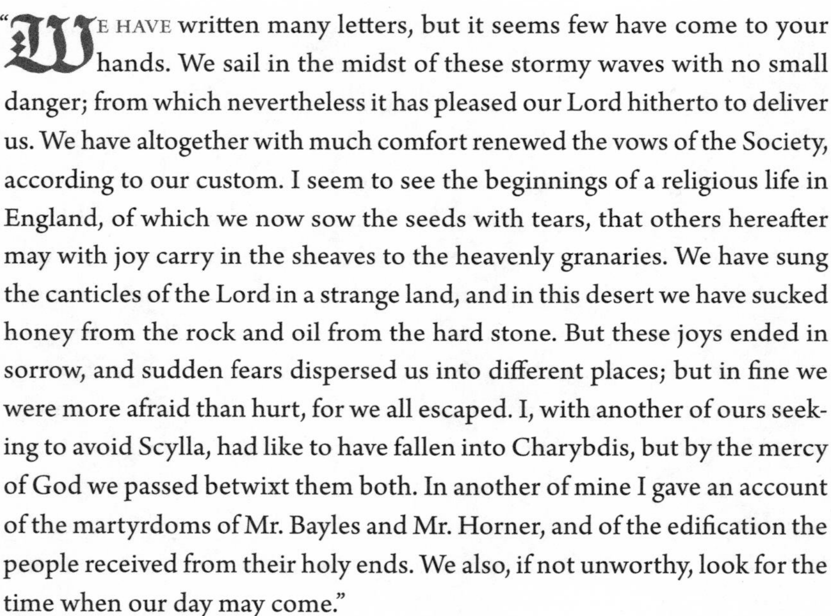

“We have written many letters, but it seems few have come to your hands. We sail in the midst of these stormy waves with no small danger; from which nevertheless it has pleased our Lord hitherto to deliver us. We have altogether with much comfort renewed the vows of the Society, according to our custom. I seem to see the beginnings of a religious life in England, of which we now sow the seeds with tears, that others hereafter may with joy carry in the sheaves to the heavenly granaries. We have sung the canticles of the Lord in a strange land, and in this desert we have sucked honey from the rock and oil from the hard stone. But these joys ended in sorrow, and sudden fears dispersed us into different places; but in fine we were more afraid than hurt, for we all escaped. I, with another of ours seeking to avoid Scylla, had like to have fallen into Charybdis, but by the mercy of God we passed betwixt them both. In another of mine I gave an account of the martyrdoms of Mr. Bayles and Mr. Horner, and of the edification the people received from their holy ends. We also, if not unworthy, look for the time when our day may come.”

“He set him upon high land . . . that he might suck honey out of the rock and oil out of the hardest stone” (Dt 32:13).

February 23

IN THE PIT OF MISERY

Ven. Southwell on his fellow Catholics

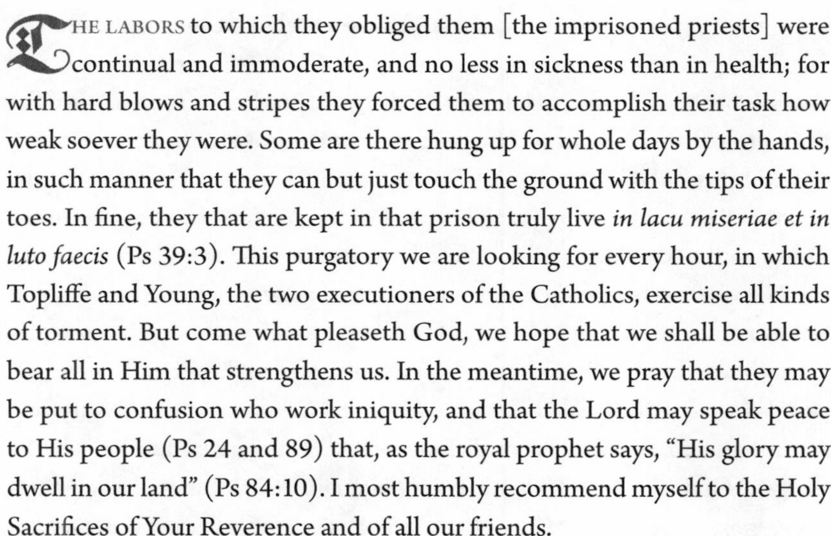

THE LABORS to which they obliged them [the imprisoned priests] were continual and immoderate, and no less in sickness than in health; for with hard blows and stripes they forced them to accomplish their task how weak soever they were. Some are there hung up for whole days by the hands, in such manner that they can but just touch the ground with the tips of their toes. In fine, they that are kept in that prison truly live *in lacu miseriae et in luto faecis* (Ps 39:3). This purgatory we are looking for every hour, in which Topliffe and Young, the two executioners of the Catholics, exercise all kinds of torment. But come what pleaseth God, we hope that we shall be able to bear all in Him that strengthens us. In the meantime, we pray that they may be put to confusion who work iniquity, and that the Lord may speak peace to His people (Ps 24 and 89) that, as the royal prophet says, "His glory may dwell in our land" (Ps 84:10). I most humbly recommend myself to the Holy Sacrifices of Your Reverence and of all our friends.

"My flesh is clothed with rottenness and the filth of dust;
my skin is withered and drawn together" (Jb 7:5).

February 24

MORE PRECIOUS THAN LIFE

James, Earl of Derwentwater, 1716

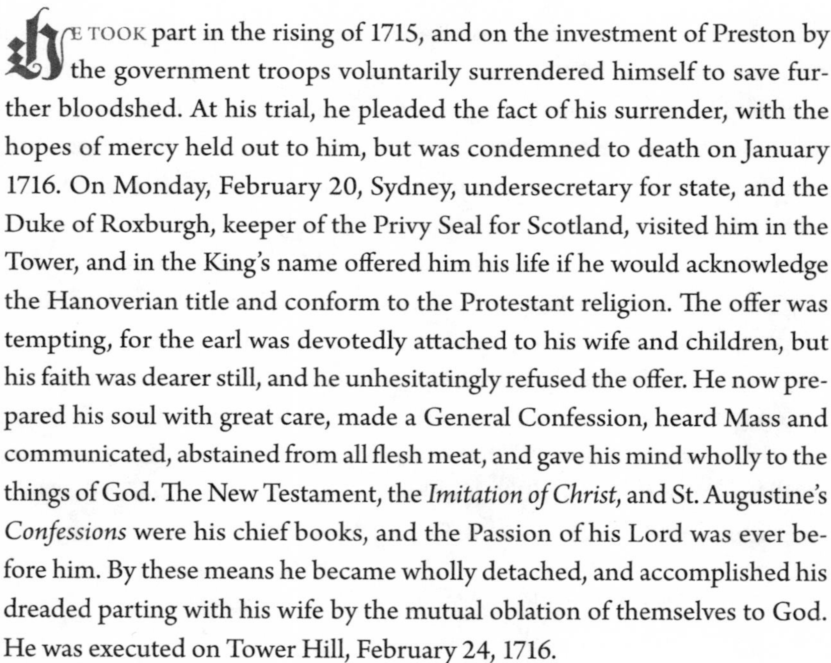

HE TOOK part in the rising of 1715, and on the investment of Preston by the government troops voluntarily surrendered himself to save further bloodshed. At his trial, he pleaded the fact of his surrender, with the hopes of mercy held out to him, but was condemned to death on January 1716. On Monday, February 20, Sydney, undersecretary for state, and the Duke of Roxburgh, keeper of the Privy Seal for Scotland, visited him in the Tower, and in the King's name offered him his life if he would acknowledge the Hanoverian title and conform to the Protestant religion. The offer was tempting, for the earl was devotedly attached to his wife and children, but his faith was dearer still, and he unhesitatingly refused the offer. He now prepared his soul with great care, made a General Confession, heard Mass and communicated, abstained from all flesh meat, and gave his mind wholly to the things of God. The New Testament, the *Imitation of Christ*, and St. Augustine's *Confessions* were his chief books, and the Passion of his Lord was ever before him. By these means he became wholly detached, and accomplished his dreaded parting with his wife by the mutual oblation of themselves to God. He was executed on Tower Hill, February 24, 1716.

"But I fear none of these things, neither do I count my life more precious than myself, so that I may consummate my course" (Acts 20:24).

February 25

THE CHANGES OF HERETICS

Bl. Thomas More, L., 1535

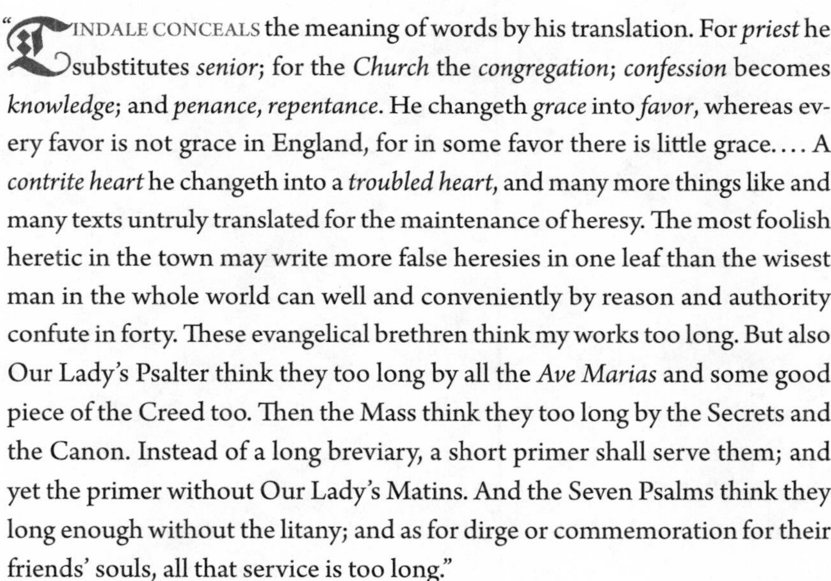

"Tindale conceals the meaning of words by his translation. For *priest* he substitutes *senior*; for the *Church* the *congregation*; *confession* becomes *knowledge*; and *penance*, *repentance*. He changeth *grace* into *favor*, whereas every favor is not grace in England, for in some favor there is little grace.... A *contrite heart* he changeth into a *troubled heart*, and many more things like and many texts untruly translated for the maintenance of heresy. The most foolish heretic in the town may write more false heresies in one leaf than the wisest man in the whole world can well and conveniently by reason and authority confute in forty. These evangelical brethren think my works too long. But also Our Lady's Psalter think they too long by all the *Ave Marias* and some good piece of the Creed too. Then the Mass think they too long by the Secrets and the Canon. Instead of a long breviary, a short primer shall serve them; and yet the primer without Our Lady's Matins. And the Seven Psalms think they long enough without the litany; and as for dirge or commemoration for their friends' souls, all that service is too long."

"Keep that which is committed to thy trust, avoiding the profane novelties of words and appositions of knowledge falsely so called" (1 Tm 6:20).

February 26

FAITH AND LOYALTY

Ven. Robert Drury, Pr., 1607

BORN OF a gentleman's family in Buckinghamshire, he followed his studies at Rheims and Valladolid, at the college lately founded by Philip II for the English clergy. There he was ordained, and sent on the English mission in 1593. His work lay in and about London, and his zeal and learning were alike edifying. In 1601, Elizabeth set forth a proclamation on November 7, that she would be willing to show some favor to such of the clergy as would assure her of their allegiance to her as their lawful Queen. On this, Drury, with thirteen others of the most earnest of the secular clergy, drew up a declaration affirming their loyalty to the Queen, while at the same time they acknowledged the supreme spiritual authority of the Bishop of Rome, as successor of St. Peter, which they believed to be wholly compatible with their civil allegiance; and they further declared their readiness to shed their blood for the Queen or the Church if the rights of either were attacked. This declaration does not seem to have lessened the persecutions, though the subscribers themselves were left unmolested. A new oath, however, was framed under James I, abjuring the pope's power, and on Drury refusing to take this as against his conscience, he was executed at Tyburn, February 26, 1607.

"I will speak of Thy testimonies before kings, and will not be ashamed" (Ps 118:46).

* *Drury was beatified by Pope John Paul II on 22 November 1987.*

February 27

THE ONE JUDGE

Ven. Mark Barkworth, O. S. B., 1601

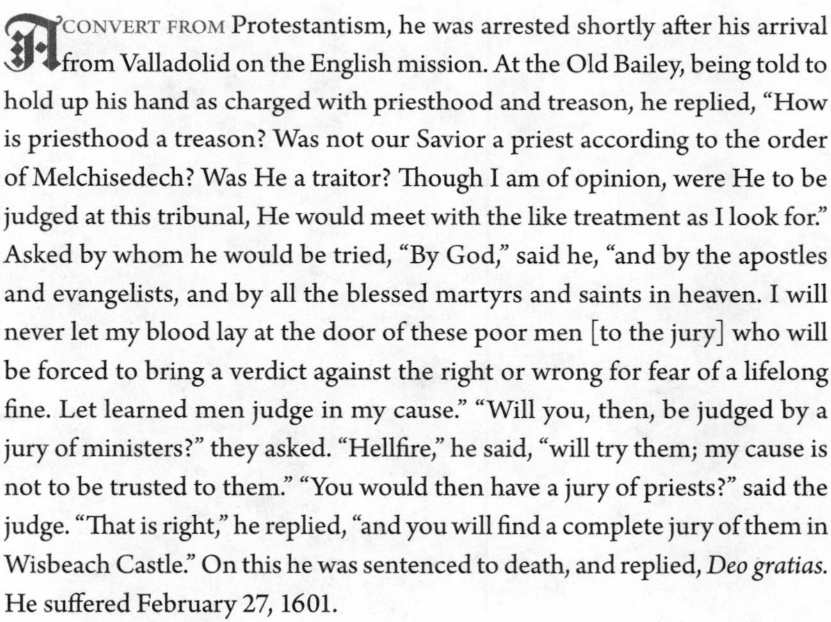

A CONVERT FROM Protestantism, he was arrested shortly after his arrival from Valladolid on the English mission. At the Old Bailey, being told to hold up his hand as charged with priesthood and treason, he replied, "How is priesthood a treason? Was not our Savior a priest according to the order of Melchisedech? Was He a traitor? Though I am of opinion, were He to be judged at this tribunal, He would meet with the like treatment as I look for." Asked by whom he would be tried, "By God," said he, "and by the apostles and evangelists, and by all the blessed martyrs and saints in heaven. I will never let my blood lay at the door of these poor men [to the jury] who will be forced to bring a verdict against the right or wrong for fear of a lifelong fine. Let learned men judge in my cause." "Will you, then, be judged by a jury of ministers?" they asked. "Hellfire," he said, "will try them; my cause is not to be trusted to them." "You would then have a jury of priests?" said the judge. "That is right," he replied, "and you will find a complete jury of them in Wisbeach Castle." On this he was sentenced to death, and replied, *Deo gratias.* He suffered February 27, 1601.

"But to me it is a very small thing to be judged by you or by man's day" (1 Cor 4:3).

* *Barkworth was beatified by Pope Pius XI on 15 December 1929.*

ANNE LINE
"She declared to the standers by with a loud voice"

FEBRUARY 28

HARBORING PRIESTS

Ven. Anne Line, W., 1601

A DEVOUT widow gentlewoman, she suffered continuous ill-health, but her soul was strong. She received the Blessed Sacrament at least weekly, and always with abundance of tears. Her one desire was to win the palm of martyrdom, and she feared much but she would be deprived of it, as very few of her sex had then suffered. The assurance of a former confessor of hers, Bl. Thompson, himself a martyr, and a vision she had of our Lord on the Cross, bid her hope that her desire would be obtained, and she was not deceived. On Candlemas Day, 1601, her house was beset by pursuivants at the very time Mass was beginning, but, as the doors were strongly barred, the priest, Mr. Page, managed to escape, and the house was searched in vain. Mrs. Line, however, was arrested and carried in a chair to the Old Bailey, for she was too weak to walk, and there sentenced to death. At Tyburn, she declared, "I am sentenced to death for harboring a Catholic priest, and so far I am from repenting that I wish I could have entertained a thousand." She suffered February 27, 1601, before the two priests, Bls. Barkworth and Filcock; and the former blessed her dead body, saying they would quickly follow her.

"He that receiveth a prophet in the name of a prophet, shall receive the reward of a prophet" (Mt 10:41).

* *Line was canonized by Pope Paul VI on 25 October 1970.*

February 29

THE CARDINAL'S HAT

Bl. John Fisher, Card. Bp., 1535

ON HEARING news of his promotion to the sacred purple, from personal humility and contempt of honor, he remarked that, if the cardinal's hat were laid at his feet, he would not stoop to pick it up; yet that he held the dignities of the Church in due reverence the following dialogue shows.

"My Lord of Rochester," said Cromwell, "if the pope should now send you a cardinal's hat, what would you do? Would you take it?"

"Sir," said he, "I know myself so far unworthy of any such dignity, that I think of nothing less than such matters; but if he do send it me, assure yourself I will work with it by all the means I can to benefit the Church of Christ, and in that respect I will receive it on my knees." The King's rage was uncontrollable. When he heard of this answer of the servant of God, he said to Cromwell: "Yea, is he yet so lusty? Well, let the pope send him a hat when he will; but I will so provide that whensoever it cometh he shall wear it on his shoulders, for head shall he have none to set it on." And so was his death decreed.

"Thou hast set on his head a crown of precious stones" (Ps 20:4).

March

March 1

HEAVENLY VISIONS

Ven. Stephen Rowsam, Pr., 1587

BORN IN Staffordshire, as a commoner at Oriel College and again when a minister at the Church of St. Mary's, Oxford, he is said to have had divers strange visions, and to have beheld a bright crown over his head, which he showed to his companions. Being converted, he went to Rheims, was ordained priest, and was again favored with supernatural visions and voices. Once when saying Mass, a large spider covered with dirt fell from the roof into the chalice after Consecration, but he consumed it from reverence to the Precious Blood. He arrived in England in 1583, and was arrested the same year and cast into the "Little Ease" in the Tower. During the eighteen months of imprisonment in this wretched hole, he was consoled by many heavenly visitations, and birds would circle round him and sing as he knelt in prayer. In 1585, he was banished, but his zeal for the Faith soon brought him back to England, where he was again arrested, thrust into Gloucester jail, and condemned. On his way back to the prison after the sentence, he was pelted and covered with filth by some youths on a dunghill. On the morning of his martyrdom, he celebrated Mass, and, going forth, completed his thanksgiving by the sacrifice of his life. — March 1587

"I will pour out My spirit upon all flesh: ... and your young men shall see visions, and your old men shall dream dreams" (Jl 2:28).

* *Rowsam was beatified by Pope John Paul II on 22 November 1987.*

March 2

LEARNING TO DIE

Walter Colman, O. S. F., 1645

After leading for some years a worldly life, he entered the novitiate of the Recollects at Douay about 1628. Born a poet, he wrote verses as a help to his devotions on the Duel of Death. His novice master, to mortify him, ordered him to throw his composition into the fire, and he instantly obeyed. On landing as a priest in England, he was seized and racked, and having no shirt, for by the rule the Franciscan habit must be worn next the skin, suspicions were aroused, but he calmed them by attributing his needy apparel to his extreme poverty. On refusing to take the Oath of Allegiance, he was, however, imprisoned. Released through his friends' generosity, he began his missionary labors. Disguised as a cavalier, his wit, brilliant talents, and polished manners made him generally popular, and aided his work for souls. But the secret of his power lay under his gay exterior, in his complete detachment from earthly things, and his constant thought of death. He was many times arrested, and at length condemned, but he was left chained, insulted, often beaten, to drag out three or four years in a filthy prison till he learnt in practice the study of his life — how to die. — Newgate, 1645

"In the morning thou shalt say: Who will grant me evening? and at evening: Who will grant me morning?" (Dt 28:67).

March 3

THE DAILY SACRIFICE

✠ Bl. Thomas More, L., 1535

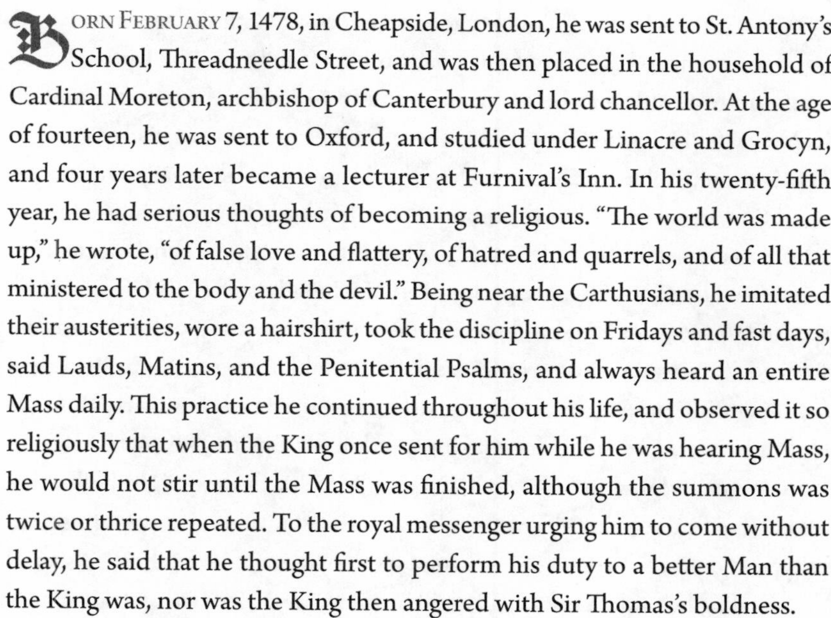

Born February 7, 1478, in Cheapside, London, he was sent to St. Antony's School, Threadneedle Street, and was then placed in the household of Cardinal Moreton, archbishop of Canterbury and lord chancellor. At the age of fourteen, he was sent to Oxford, and studied under Linacre and Grocyn, and four years later became a lecturer at Furnival's Inn. In his twenty-fifth year, he had serious thoughts of becoming a religious. "The world was made up," he wrote, "of false love and flattery, of hatred and quarrels, and of all that ministered to the body and the devil." Being near the Carthusians, he imitated their austerities, wore a hairshirt, took the discipline on Fridays and fast days, said Lauds, Matins, and the Penitential Psalms, and always heard an entire Mass daily. This practice he continued throughout his life, and observed it so religiously that when the King once sent for him while he was hearing Mass, he would not stir until the Mass was finished, although the summons was twice or thrice repeated. To the royal messenger urging him to come without delay, he said that he thought first to perform his duty to a better Man than the King was, nor was the King then angered with Sir Thomas's boldness.

"His sacrifices were consumed by fire every day" (Ecclus 45:17).

March 4

THE VESTMENTS OF SALVATION

Ven. Nicholas Horner, L., 1590

A NATIVE OF York, a tailor by trade and a zealous Catholic, he endeavored, according to his ability, to persuade others to embrace the Faith. Having come up to London to be cured of a wound in his leg, he was committed to Newgate for harboring priests. There the heavy fetter on his leg and the deprivation of all medical aid rendered an amputation necessary. During the operation, he sat upon a form, unbound, in silence, a priest the while (Hewett, who was afterward himself a martyr) holding his head, and he was further comforted by such a vivid apprehension of Christ bearing His Cross that he seemed to see it on His shoulders. Freed at the earnest suit of his friends, he worked at his trade at some lodgings at Smithfield. Again cast into Bridewell for harboring priests, he was hung up by the wrists till he nearly died. At length condemned solely for making a jerkin for a priest, he was hanged in front of his lodging in Smithfield, March 3, 1590. On the night before his execution, finding himself overwhelmed with anguish, he betook himself to prayer, and perceived a bright crown of glory hanging over his head. Assured of its reality, he said: "O Lord, Thy will be mine," and died with extraordinary signs of joy.

"He hath clothed me with the garments of salvation" (Is 61:10).

* *Horner was beatified by Pope John Paul II on 22 November 1987.*

JAMES BIRD

"His father one day passing by, and viewing the face of his son"

March 5

FILIAL REVERENCE

Ven. James Bird, L., 1593

BORN AT Winchester of a gentleman's family and brought up a Protestant, he became a Catholic and went to study at Rheims. On his return, he was apprehended and charged with being reconciled to the Roman Church, and maintaining the pope under Christ to be the Head of the Church. Brought to the bar, he acknowledged the indictment and received sentence of death as for high treason, though both life and liberty were offered him if he would but once go to the Protestant church. When his father solicited him to save his life by complying, he modestly answered that, as he had always been obedient to him, so he would obey him now could he do so without offending God. After a long imprisonment, he was hanged and quartered at Winchester, March 25, 1593. He suffered with wonderful constancy and cheerfulness, being but nineteen years old. His head was set upon a pole upon one of the gates of the city. His father, one day passing by, thought that the head bowing down made him a reverence, and cried out: "Oh, Jemmy my son, ever obedient in life, even when dead thou payest reverence to thy father. How far from thy heart was all treason or other wickedness."

"Honor thy father in work and word, and all patience, that a blessing may come upon thee from him" (Ecclus 3:9–10).

* *Bird was beatified by Pope Pius XI on 15 December 1929.*

March 6

THE MOTHER OF GOD

Ven. Henry Heath, O. S. F., 1643

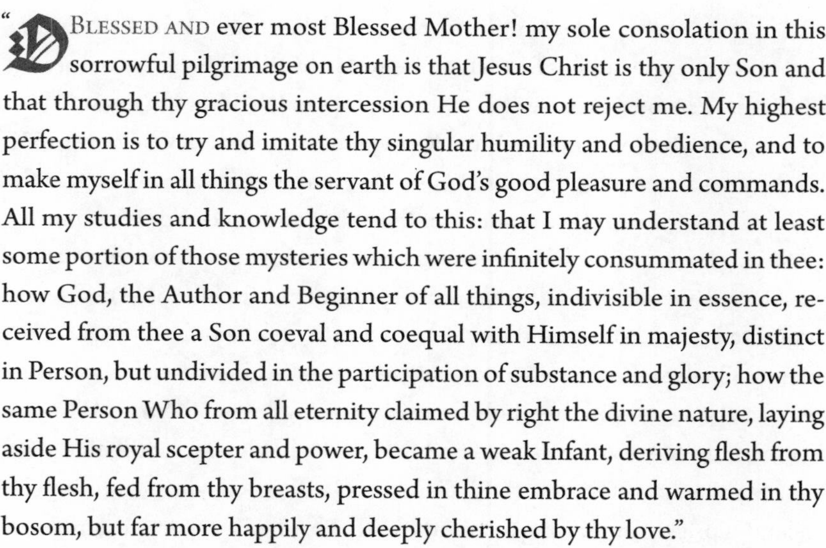

"O Blessed and ever most Blessed Mother! my sole consolation in this sorrowful pilgrimage on earth is that Jesus Christ is thy only Son and that through thy gracious intercession He does not reject me. My highest perfection is to try and imitate thy singular humility and obedience, and to make myself in all things the servant of God's good pleasure and commands. All my studies and knowledge tend to this: that I may understand at least some portion of those mysteries which were infinitely consummated in thee: how God, the Author and Beginner of all things, indivisible in essence, received from thee a Son coeval and coequal with Himself in majesty, distinct in Person, but undivided in the participation of substance and glory; how the same Person Who from all eternity claimed by right the divine nature, laying aside His royal scepter and power, became a weak Infant, deriving flesh from thy flesh, fed from thy breasts, pressed in thine embrace and warmed in thy bosom, but far more happily and deeply cherished by thy love."

"Blessed is the womb that bore Thee and the paps that gave Thee suck" (Lk 11:27).

* *Heath was beatified by Pope John Paul II on 22 November 1987.*

March 7

HOLY FRIENDSHIP

✠ Bl. John Larke, Pr., 1544

IN 1504, he was presented to the small Rectory of St. Ethelburga, Bishopsgate, a benefice which he retained till a few years before his death. In 1526, he was presented to the Rectory of Woodford in Essex, which he resigned when Sir Thomas More appointed him to that of Chelsea in 1531. Sir Thomas was at that time lord chancellor, and in that capacity he had the right of appointment by a grant from the abbot and canons of Westminster. Little as is known of the life and ministry of the future martyr, the patronage of the blessed Thomas is a sufficient proof of his merits, for he would never have promoted one whom he did not feel was worthy of the office. It was Larke's Mass at Chelsea that More served daily, and priest and server held each other in mutual esteem, and their holy friendship strengthened them for the coming sacrifice. More was martyred on July 6, 1535, but it was not till nine years later that Larke was tried with Bl. Germain Gardiner, a layman, and Bl. John Ireland, a priest, for refusing to take the oath. Fortified by More's example, he stood firm in the hour of trial, and suffered at Tyburn, March 7, 1544.

"For she is an infinite treasure to men: which they that use, become the friends of God, being commended for the gift of discipline" (Ws 7:14).

March 8

IN BONDS FOR CHRIST (1)

Bl. William Hart, Pr. to the Catholic prisoners

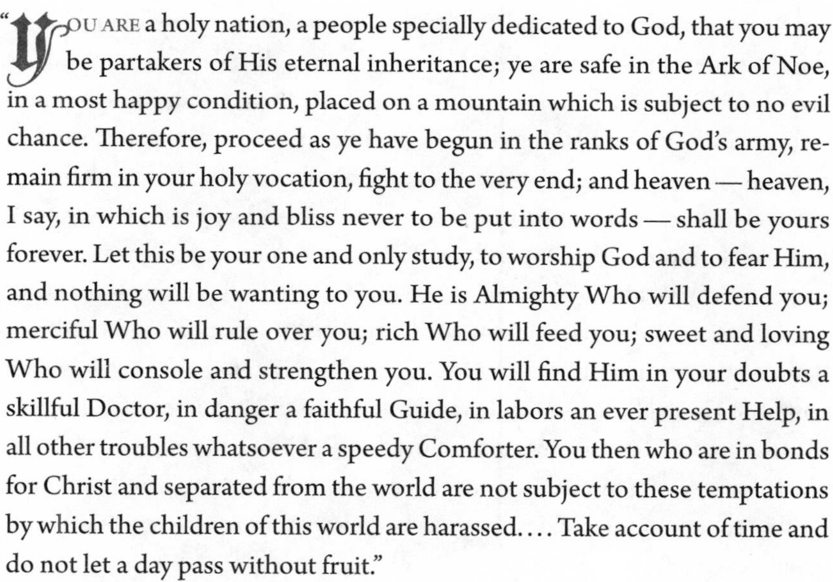

"YOU ARE a holy nation, a people specially dedicated to God, that you may be partakers of His eternal inheritance; ye are safe in the Ark of Noe, in a most happy condition, placed on a mountain which is subject to no evil chance. Therefore, proceed as ye have begun in the ranks of God's army, remain firm in your holy vocation, fight to the very end; and heaven — heaven, I say, in which is joy and bliss never to be put into words — shall be yours forever. Let this be your one and only study, to worship God and to fear Him, and nothing will be wanting to you. He is Almighty Who will defend you; merciful Who will rule over you; rich Who will feed you; sweet and loving Who will console and strengthen you. You will find Him in your doubts a skillful Doctor, in danger a faithful Guide, in labors an ever present Help, in all other troubles whatsoever a speedy Comforter. You then who are in bonds for Christ and separated from the world are not subject to these temptations by which the children of this world are harassed.... Take account of time and do not let a day pass without fruit."

"We are the sons of God. And if sons, heirs also ... and joint heirs with Christ: yet so, if we suffer with Him, we may also be glorified with Him" (Rom 8:16–17).

March 9

IN BONDS FOR CHRIST (2)

Bl. William Hart, Pr. to the Catholic prisoners

"Let all your thoughts and meditations be on heaven and heavenly things. Let your prayers be ardent, but your actions discreet and well considered; bear trials with patience. I pray you, for Christ's sake, that you so live and so bear yourselves in all things that the enemies of the Faith may be forced to account you, not as relaxed, but as modest and religious. But before all things, carefully preserve the unity of the spirit in the bond of peace, loving each other with fraternal charity; let there be no dissensions among you, no discords; for thus will God embrace you with His love, and the angels proclaim your praises. And I beseech you, for Christ's sake, most beloved brethren, daily, nay, every hour, to pray for me, a wretched sinner, that I may finish my course to God's glory, and I will pray for you here and in heaven, if God grant me that grace. Farewell, my most beloved sons, I beseech you to pardon me whatsoever wrong by chance or negligence I may have done you. This I have written to you in the greatest haste, when almost overcome with sleep and greatly wearied."

"Above all things have charity, which is the bond of perfection" (Col 3:14).

March 10

ENGLAND'S DEBT TO THE POPE

Bl. William Hart, Pr., 1583

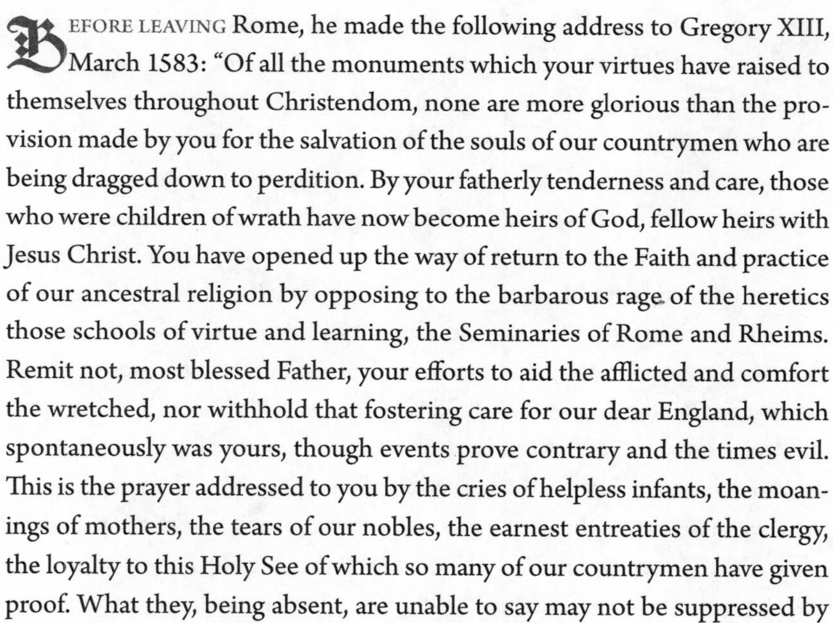

BEFORE LEAVING Rome, he made the following address to Gregory XIII, March 1583: "Of all the monuments which your virtues have raised to themselves throughout Christendom, none are more glorious than the provision made by you for the salvation of the souls of our countrymen who are being dragged down to perdition. By your fatherly tenderness and care, those who were children of wrath have now become heirs of God, fellow heirs with Jesus Christ. You have opened up the way of return to the Faith and practice of our ancestral religion by opposing to the barbarous rage of the heretics those schools of virtue and learning, the Seminaries of Rome and Rheims. Remit not, most blessed Father, your efforts to aid the afflicted and comfort the wretched, nor withhold that fostering care for our dear England, which spontaneously was yours, though events prove contrary and the times evil. This is the prayer addressed to you by the cries of helpless infants, the moanings of mothers, the tears of our nobles, the earnest entreaties of the clergy, the loyalty to this Holy See of which so many of our countrymen have given proof. What they, being absent, are unable to say may not be suppressed by us who are privileged to behold your fatherly countenance."

"Feed My lambs. . . . Feed My sheep" (Jn 21:15–17).

March 11

CHAINS FALLING OFF

✠ Ven. Thomas Atkinson, Pr., 1616

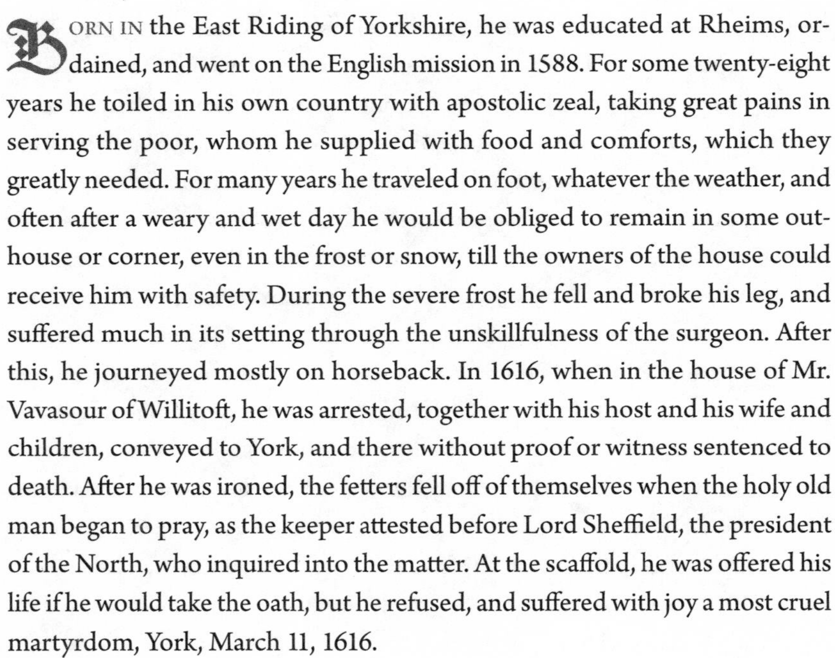

Born in the East Riding of Yorkshire, he was educated at Rheims, ordained, and went on the English mission in 1588. For some twenty-eight years he toiled in his own country with apostolic zeal, taking great pains in serving the poor, whom he supplied with food and comforts, which they greatly needed. For many years he traveled on foot, whatever the weather, and often after a weary and wet day he would be obliged to remain in some outhouse or corner, even in the frost or snow, till the owners of the house could receive him with safety. During the severe frost he fell and broke his leg, and suffered much in its setting through the unskillfulness of the surgeon. After this, he journeyed mostly on horseback. In 1616, when in the house of Mr. Vavasour of Willitoft, he was arrested, together with his host and his wife and children, conveyed to York, and there without proof or witness sentenced to death. After he was ironed, the fetters fell off of themselves when the holy old man began to pray, as the keeper attested before Lord Sheffield, the president of the North, who inquired into the matter. At the scaffold, he was offered his life if he would take the oath, but he refused, and suffered with joy a most cruel martyrdom, York, March 11, 1616.

"And the angel striking Peter on the side, raised him up, saying: Arise quickly. And the chains fell off from his hands" (Acts 12:7).

* *Atkinson was beatified by Pope John Paul II on 22 November 1987.*

March 12

A LAST REQUEST

Bl. William Hart to the afflicted Catholics (1)

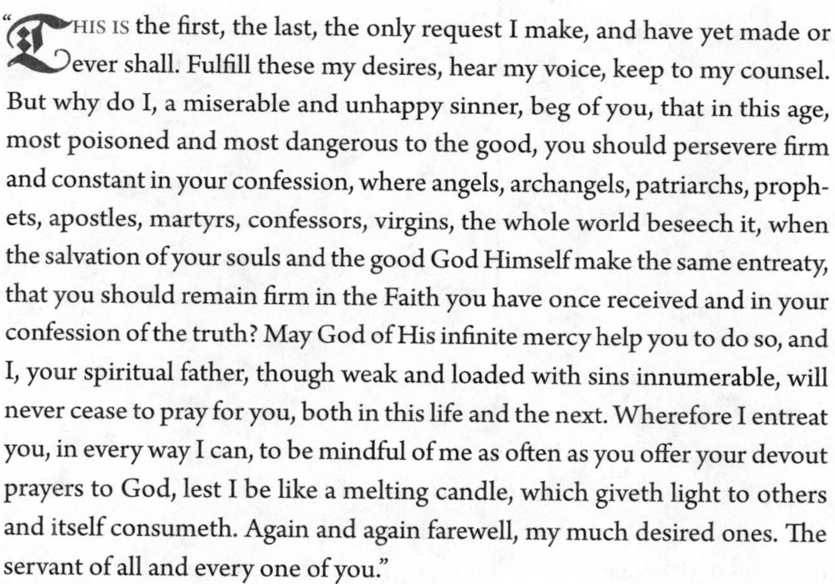

"This is the first, the last, the only request I make, and have yet made or ever shall. Fulfill these my desires, hear my voice, keep to my counsel. But why do I, a miserable and unhappy sinner, beg of you, that in this age, most poisoned and most dangerous to the good, you should persevere firm and constant in your confession, where angels, archangels, patriarchs, prophets, apostles, martyrs, confessors, virgins, the whole world beseech it, when the salvation of your souls and the good God Himself make the same entreaty, that you should remain firm in the Faith you have once received and in your confession of the truth? May God of His infinite mercy help you to do so, and I, your spiritual father, though weak and loaded with sins innumerable, will never cease to pray for you, both in this life and the next. Wherefore I entreat you, in every way I can, to be mindful of me as often as you offer your devout prayers to God, lest I be like a melting candle, which giveth light to others and itself consumeth. Again and again farewell, my much desired ones. The servant of all and every one of you."

"Lest perhaps when I have preached to others, I myself should become a castaway" (1 Cor 9:27).

March 13

STAND FAST

Bl. William Hart to the afflicted Catholics (2)

"STAND FAST, brethren, stand steadfast, I say, in that Faith which Christ planted, the apostles preached, the martyrs confirmed, the whole world approved and embraced. Stand firm in that Faith which, as it is the oldest, is also the truest and most sure, and which is most in harmony with the Holy Scriptures and with all antiquity. Stand constant in that Faith which has a worship worthy of all honor and reverence, Sacraments most holy, abounding in spiritual consolation. For if ye have remained constant in this Faith, that is, in the Catholic Church, in the Ark of Noe, in the House of Rahab, with what joy and consolation of the soul will ye not be flooded: yours will be the Sacrament of Penance for the cleansing of your souls; yours the Sacrament of the Body and Blood of our Savior for the refreshing of your souls; you will be partakers of all the satisfaction and merits of Christ, of the fellowship of the saints, of the suffrages, prayers, fasts, and almsdeeds of all the just whom the Catholic Church throughout the world holds in her bosom. O blessed they, yea, and thrice blessed, who in this deplorable world stand firm in the Faith of Christ."

"The devil . . . goeth about seeking whom he may devour. Whom resist ye, strong in faith" (1 Pt 5:8–9).

March 14

A MENDICANT LORD CHANCELLOR

Bl. Thomas More, L., 1535

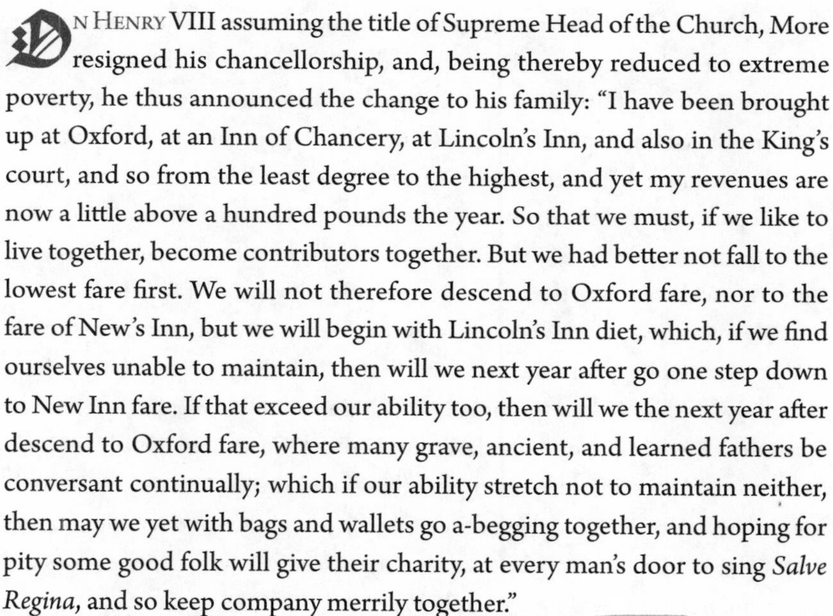

On Henry VIII assuming the title of Supreme Head of the Church, More resigned his chancellorship, and, being thereby reduced to extreme poverty, he thus announced the change to his family: "I have been brought up at Oxford, at an Inn of Chancery, at Lincoln's Inn, and also in the King's court, and so from the least degree to the highest, and yet my revenues are now a little above a hundred pounds the year. So that we must, if we like to live together, become contributors together. But we had better not fall to the lowest fare first. We will not therefore descend to Oxford fare, nor to the fare of New's Inn, but we will begin with Lincoln's Inn diet, which, if we find ourselves unable to maintain, then will we next year after go one step down to New Inn fare. If that exceed our ability too, then will we the next year after descend to Oxford fare, where many grave, ancient, and learned fathers be conversant continually; which if our ability stretch not to maintain neither, then may we yet with bags and wallets go a-begging together, and hoping for pity some good folk will give their charity, at every man's door to sing *Salve Regina*, and so keep company merrily together."

"As having nothing and possessing all things" (2 Cor 6:10).

March 15

THE APOSTLE OF YORKSHIRE

✠ Bl. William Hart, Pr., 1583

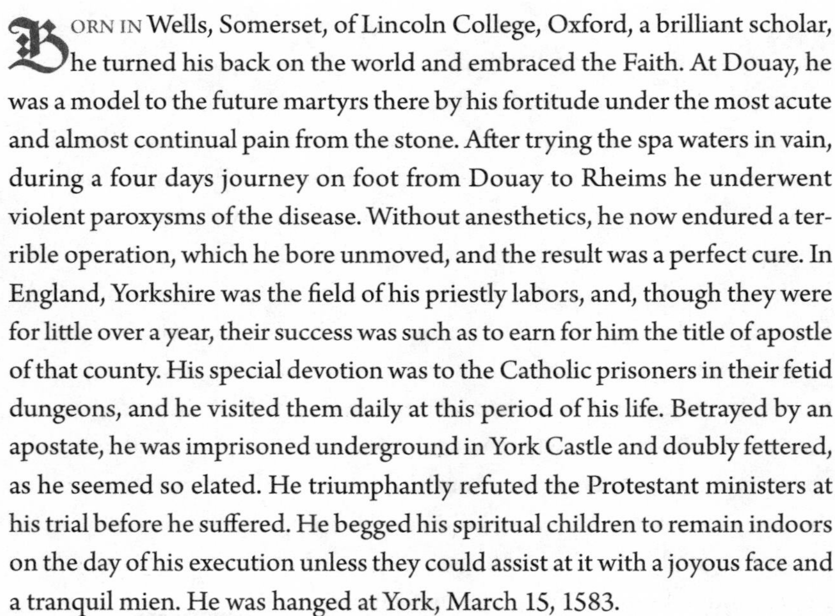

Born in Wells, Somerset, of Lincoln College, Oxford, a brilliant scholar, he turned his back on the world and embraced the Faith. At Douay, he was a model to the future martyrs there by his fortitude under the most acute and almost continual pain from the stone. After trying the spa waters in vain, during a four days journey on foot from Douay to Rheims he underwent violent paroxysms of the disease. Without anesthetics, he now endured a terrible operation, which he bore unmoved, and the result was a perfect cure. In England, Yorkshire was the field of his priestly labors, and, though they were for little over a year, their success was such as to earn for him the title of apostle of that county. His special devotion was to the Catholic prisoners in their fetid dungeons, and he visited them daily at this period of his life. Betrayed by an apostate, he was imprisoned underground in York Castle and doubly fettered, as he seemed so elated. He triumphantly refuted the Protestant ministers at his trial before he suffered. He begged his spiritual children to remain indoors on the day of his execution unless they could assist at it with a joyous face and a tranquil mien. He was hanged at York, March 15, 1583.

"Be ye steadfast, immovable, always abounding in the work of the Lord, knowing that your labor is not in vain" (1 Cor 15:58).

JOHN AMIAS & ROBERT DALBY
"At the place of execution"

March 16

NIGHT TURNED TO DAY

Ven. Robert Dalby, Pr., 1589

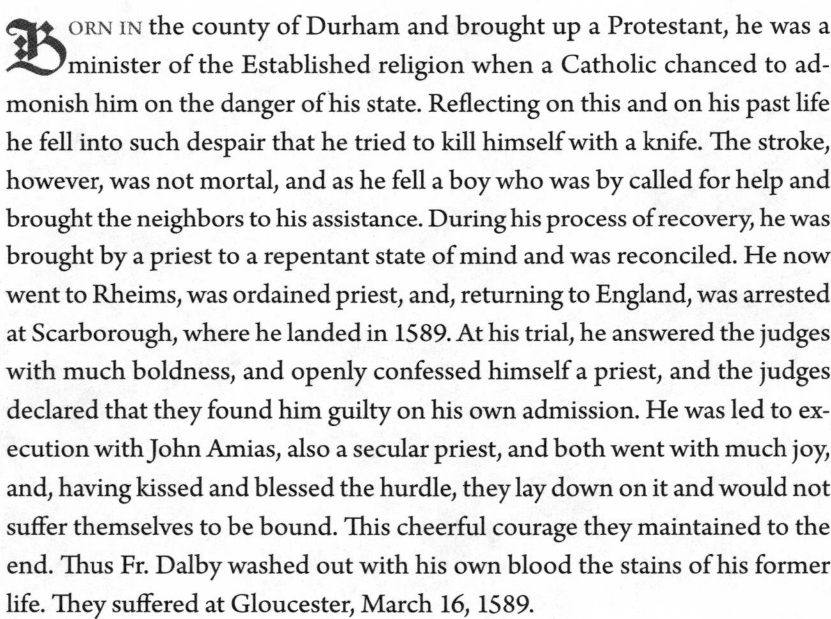

Born in the county of Durham and brought up a Protestant, he was a minister of the Established religion when a Catholic chanced to admonish him on the danger of his state. Reflecting on this and on his past life he fell into such despair that he tried to kill himself with a knife. The stroke, however, was not mortal, and as he fell a boy who was by called for help and brought the neighbors to his assistance. During his process of recovery, he was brought by a priest to a repentant state of mind and was reconciled. He now went to Rheims, was ordained priest, and, returning to England, was arrested at Scarborough, where he landed in 1589. At his trial, he answered the judges with much boldness, and openly confessed himself a priest, and the judges declared that they found him guilty on his own admission. He was led to execution with John Amias, also a secular priest, and both went with much joy, and, having kissed and blessed the hurdle, they lay down on it and would not suffer themselves to be bound. This cheerful courage they maintained to the end. Thus Fr. Dalby washed out with his own blood the stains of his former life. They suffered at Gloucester, March 16, 1589.

"They have turned night into day, and after darkness I hope for light again" (Jb 17:12).

* *Dalby was beatified by Pope Pius XI on 15 December 1929.*

March 17

THE MOTIVE OF A MISSIONER

Bl. William Hart, Pr., 1583

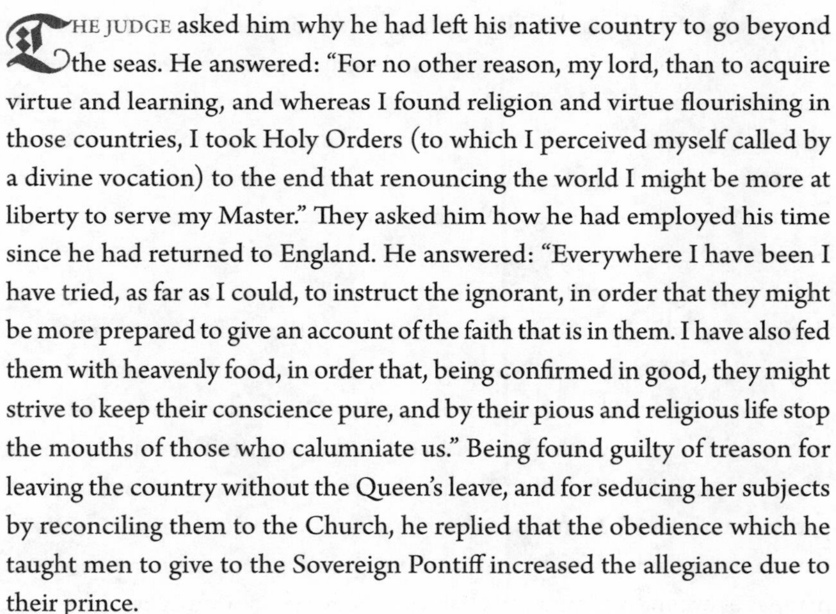

The judge asked him why he had left his native country to go beyond the seas. He answered: "For no other reason, my lord, than to acquire virtue and learning, and whereas I found religion and virtue flourishing in those countries, I took Holy Orders (to which I perceived myself called by a divine vocation) to the end that renouncing the world I might be more at liberty to serve my Master." They asked him how he had employed his time since he had returned to England. He answered: "Everywhere I have been I have tried, as far as I could, to instruct the ignorant, in order that they might be more prepared to give an account of the faith that is in them. I have also fed them with heavenly food, in order that, being confirmed in good, they might strive to keep their conscience pure, and by their pious and religious life stop the mouths of those who calumniate us." Being found guilty of treason for leaving the country without the Queen's leave, and for seducing her subjects by reconciling them to the Church, he replied that the obedience which he taught men to give to the Sovereign Pontiff increased the allegiance due to their prince.

"In all things let us exhibit ourselves as the ministers of God . . . in charity unfeigned, in the word of truth" (2 Cor 6:4, 6–7).

March 18

CHRISTIAN MODESTY

✠ Ven. John Thulis, Pr., 1616

BORN AT Up-Holland in Lancashire, he studied at Rheims and was ordained priest at Rome. Soon after his return to England he was arrested and imprisoned at Wisbeach, whence he escaped or was released, for he subsequently labored as a missioner in his own county and was there arrested by order of Lord Derby and cast into Lancaster jail. In the same prison with him was a weaver by trade, Roger Wrenno, a zealous and devout soul. Together before the Lent assizes in 1616 they found the means of escape about five in the evening, and walked fast the whole night for, as they thought, some thirty miles, when on the sun rising they found themselves again under the very walls of Lancaster jail. Nothing daunted, they saw in this mishap God's will for their martyrdom. Arrested again, they were both offered their lives if they would take the Oath of Allegiance, but they steadfastly refused. Special efforts were made on behalf of Thulis, who was much loved for his marvelous patience and charity. In many sicknesses, when nigh to death, in controversies with ministers, under insults and calumny, he had never lost his gentleness of manner or evenness of mind. His last words to his fellow priests in prison were an exhortation to mutual charity. He suffered at Lancaster, March 18, 1616.

"Let your modesty be known before all men" (Phil 4:5).

* *Thulis was beatified by Pope John Paul II on 22 November 1987.*

March 19

A GLIMPSE OF HEAVEN

Ven. Roger Wrenno, L., 1616

WRENNO, A weaver, was condemned with Ven. Thulis for assisting priests. After he was turned off the ladder, the rope broke with the weight of his body, and he fell down to the ground. After a short space he came perfectly to himself, and, going upon his knees, began to pray very devoutly, his eyes and hands lifted up to heaven. Upon this the minister Lee came to him and extolled the mercies of God in his regard and likewise the King's clemency, who would give him his life if he would but take the oath. The good man at this arose, saying, "I am the same man I was, and in the same mind; use your pleasure with me," and with that he ran to the ladder, and went up it as fast as he could. "How now," says the sheriff, "what does the man mean, that he is in such haste?" "Oh!" says the good man, "if you had seen that which I have just now seen you would be as much in haste to die as I now am." And so the executioner, putting a stronger rope about his neck, turned the ladder, and quickly sent him to see the good things of which before he had had a glimpse. He suffered at Lancaster, March 18, 1616.

"I believe to see the good things of the Lord in the land of the living" (Ps 26:13).

* *Wrenno was beatified by Pope John Paul II on 22 November 1987.*

March 20

THE MORNING STAR

Ven. Henry Heath, O. S. F., 1643

Born at Peterborough, 1600, a Protestant, educated at Corpus Christi College, Cambridge; as librarian of that college he studied religious questions. In comparing the Patristic quotations of the Protestant Whitaker with those of the Catholic Bellarmine, he found the latter so much more true and correct that he was drawn to the Faith. He now exposed the errors of Protestantism with such publicity and force that the college authorities resolved on his expulsion and imprisonment. He fled therefore to the Spanish embassy in London, then the asylum of distressed Catholics, but was refused admittance. He next applied to Mr. George Jerningham, a well-known Catholic, who, taking him for a spy, rejected him with bitter reproaches. Thus, destitute of friends and repulsed on all sides, he bethought him of the devotion of Catholics to our Blessed Lady, in whom he had hitherto but little faith. Turning to her as the Morning Star of the wanderer and the hope of the afflicted, he besought her to take pity on him, and vowed in return to devote himself to her service. When on a sudden the same Mr. Jerningham, who had rejected him, came up and accosted him with kindness, took him to a priest, Fr. Muscot, who confessed him and reconciled him to the Church.

"As a shining light goeth forward and increaseth even to perfect day" (Prv 4:18).

March 21

CUT ASUNDER

✠ Ven. Thomas Pilchard, Pr., 1587

A fellow of Balliol, he was made priest at Rheims and returned to England in 1583. He was of most gentle, courteous manners and an indefatigable missioner. His work lay in the western counties, and, when apprehended, he was cast into Dorchester jail. There he converted many of his fellow prisoners, and from all parts his counsel was sought. At length he was tried and sentenced to death. Sentences of this sort were, however, rare in Dorchester, and an executioner could hardly be found until at length a cook, or rather a butcher, was hired at a great cost. But after the rope was cut and the priest, being still alive, stood on his feet under the scaffold, the fellow held back struck with fear. At length, compelled by the officials to finish his work, he drove his knife, hardly knowing what he did, into the body of the priest, and leaving it there he again hung back horror-stricken amidst the groans of the spectators. This lasted so long that Mr. Pilchard, coming completely to himself, naked and horribly wounded, inclining his head to the sheriff, said: "Is this, then, your justice, Mr. sheriff?" At last, he was brutally dispatched. He suffered at Dorchester, March 21, 1587.

"They were stoned, they were cut asunder, they were tempted, they were put to death by the sword" (Heb 11:37).

* *Pilchard was beatified by Pope John Paul II on 22 November 1987.*

March 22

A CATHOLIC'S GRAVE

John Jessop, L., (ca. 1587)

HE WAS Ven. Pilchard's faithful and loving companion, and before and after his imprisonment his chief instrument in saving souls. He was with Pilchard when the latter was captured in Fleet Street, and, being unable to conceal his grief, and known to be Pilchard's companion elsewhere, he was apprehended and suffered to linger in prison, and at length died, either from grief or the filth of the place, though he was a man in the flower of his age, being less than forty years old. In his will he gave special directions that his body should not be buried in a graveyard, but as closely as possible to the body of Pilchard in the fields by the place of his execution. When his friends and his wife asked him to consult in this matter the honor of his family, and not to make light of consecrated ground, he replied that all graveyards were now profaned by the bodies of heretics, and that he felt assured the blood and members of so great a martyr would abundantly sanctify the place he had chosen. This was shown by the fact that till Pilchard's limbs were taken down from the walls, where they had been hung, the whole surrounding country was swept with the most terrific storms and lightnings.

"Behold, I will open your graves and will bring you out of your sepulchres, O My people: and will bring you into the land of Israel" (Ez 37:12).

March 23

FRUIT OF MARTYRDOM

Ven. William Pike, L., 1591

HE WAS born at Parley, near Christchurch, Hampshire, and became a joiner by trade in the town of Dorchester. He was put on his trial for having spoken in prison too freely in favor of the Catholic religion. The "bloody" question about the pope's supremacy was put to him, and he frankly confessed that he maintained the authority of the Roman See, and he was condemned to die a traitor's death. When they asked him, as is their wont, whether to save his life and family he would recant, he boldly replied that it did not become a son of Mr. Pilchard to do so. "Did that traitor, then, pervert you?" asked the judge. "That holy priest of God and true martyr of Christ," he replied, "taught me the truth of the Catholic Faith." Asked when he first met him, "It was on a journey," said he, "returning from this city." He was hanged at Dorchester in 1591, and cut down alive. Being a very able, strong man, when the executioners came to throw him on the block to quarter him, he stood upon his feet, on which the sheriff's men overmastering him threw him down and pinned his hands fast to the ground with their halberts, and so the butchery was performed.

"Unless the grain of wheat falling into the ground die, itself remaineth alone. But if it die it bringeth forth much fruit" (Jn 12:24–25).

* *Pike was beatified by Pope John Paul II on 22 November 1987.*

March 24

THE GUARDIAN ANGEL

Ven. John Hambley, Pr., 1587

A NATIVE OF Somersetshire, he arrived from Douay on the English mission in 1585. Arrested, he spent two years in prison and was then condemned. In terror at his death sentence, he promised to yield to what the judges required, which was practically tantamount to denying the Faith. Great hereat was the jubilation of the heretics, and not least that of the judge. But whilst the priest was standing between the constables, like the rest of the condemned, there came up to him (for the assizes were held in booths in the open) a certain unknown man, who, after placing some letters in his hand, at once withdrew, no one preventing him, which in itself was a kind of miracle. Mr. Hambley read and reread them, until at length he broke into tears and gave signs of being strongly moved, but refused to give the contents of the letters or the name of the bearer. The next morning, before the judge, he expressed his shame for his promise of conformity, was sentenced, and bravely won his martyr's crown. Although these letters, doubtless, restored him to a right mind, yet neither the writer nor the bearer have ever been discovered, and many believed that they were brought by his guardian angel. He suffered at Salisbury about Easter, 1587.

"He hath given His angels charge over thee, to guard thee in all thy ways" (Ps 90:11).

* *Hambley was beatified by Pope John Paul II on 22 November 1987.*

MARGARET CLITHEROW
"Pressed to death at York"

March 25

THE WINEPRESS ALONE (1)

✠ Bl. Margaret Clitherow, L., 1586

Forbidden to see husband or child, pestered by successive ministers, and herself charged with gross immorality, Margaret learnt at length, on March 24, that she was to die on the morrow, that year Good Friday. She had prepared herself for this by fasting and prayer, but she begged for a maid to be with her during the night, for "though death is my comfort," she said, "the flesh is frail," but, as no one could be admitted, the keeper's wife sat with her for a while. The first hours of the night Margaret passed on her knees in prayer, clothed in a linen habit made by herself for her passion. At three, she rose and laid herself flat on the stones for a quarter of an hour, then rested on her bed. At eight, the sheriffs called, and with them she walked barefoot, going along through the crowd to the Tolbooth. There, turning from the ministers, she knelt and prayed by herself. Forced to undress, she laid herself on the ground clothed only in the linen habit, her face covered with a handkerchief, her hands outstretched and bound as if on a cross. The weighted door was laid on her; at the first crushing pain she cried, "Jesu, mercy," and after a quarter of an hour passed to her God.

"I have trodden the winepress alone" (Is 63:3).

* *Clitherow was canonized by Pope Paul VI on 25 October 1970.*

March 26

BEFORE HEROD (2)

Bl. Margaret Clitherow, L., 1586

On March 10, 1586, when she had been at liberty some eighteen months, her husband was summoned before the council at York, and in his absence his house was searched. The priest there in hiding escaped, but Margaret and her children were taken prisoners. Enraged at their failure, the searchers stripped a Flemish boy of twelve years, staying in the house, and threatened him with rods till he showed them the priest's chamber, and where the church stuff was kept. At her trial, lest her children might be forced by evidence to be guilty of her blood, she refused to plead, giving as a reason however that she had committed no offense. Two chalices were therefore produced and religious pictures, and two ruffians clad themselves in the priestly vestments and began playing the fool, pulling and hauling themselves before the judges, while one, holding up a piece of bread, said to the martyr, "Behold the God in Whom thou believest." At her second examination she again refused to plead, saying that there was no evidence against her save that of children, whom you can make say anything for a rod or an apple. The judge urged her to demand a jury, but in vain, and on her refusal she was sentenced to be pressed to death.

"Herod questioned Him in many words, but Jesus answered him nothing" (Lk 23:9).

March 27

A VALIANT WOMAN (3)

Bl. Margaret Clitherow, L., 1586

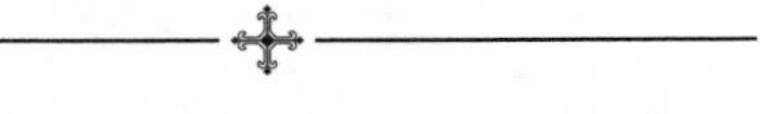

Wife of John Clitherow, sometime sheriff of York, she was thirty years of age, and already married, when a growing dissatisfaction with the Protestant religion led her, after due inquiry, to embrace the Faith. During the following twelve years of her Catholic life, her house was a refuge for priests, whom she received at her own peril and unknown to her husband. With this help she brought up her children in the Faith and her eldest son for the priesthood. She managed to hear Mass almost daily, communicated twice a week, and fasted rigorously. For her persistent recusancy she was repeatedly cast into prison, even for two years together and more, but her sufferings only increased her fervor. Were it not, she said, for her husband and child, she would rather stay there always, apart from the world with God. Still, when at liberty, she was most attentive to the care of her house, and with her servant took part herself in the humblest menial work. She was exposed to much ill-usage even from Catholics, who misjudged and censured her, but her constancy and patience never failed. Her husband said she had only two faults, fasting too much and refusing to go to church.

"Her children rose up and called her blessed: her husband, and he praised her. Many daughters have gathered together riches: thou hast surpassed them all" (Prv 31:28–29).

March 28

FILIAL PIETY

Bl. Hart to his Protestant mother (1)

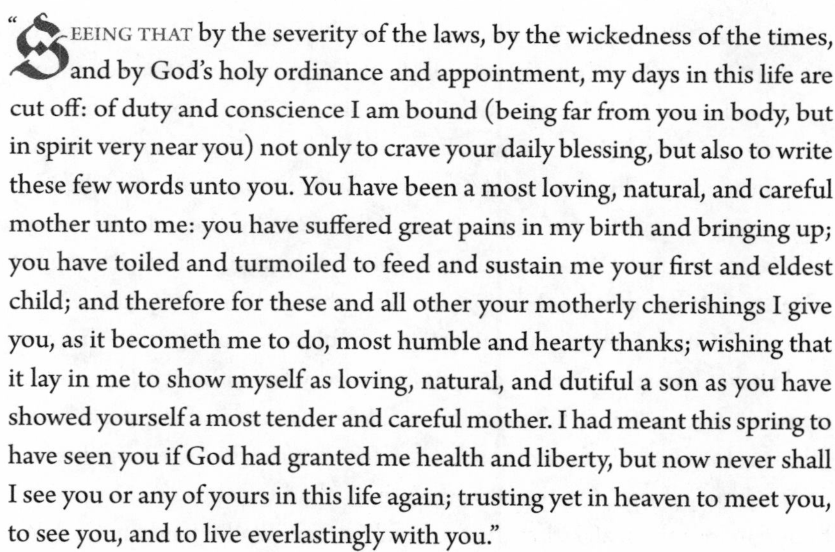

"Seeing that by the severity of the laws, by the wickedness of the times, and by God's holy ordinance and appointment, my days in this life are cut off: of duty and conscience I am bound (being far from you in body, but in spirit very near you) not only to crave your daily blessing, but also to write these few words unto you. You have been a most loving, natural, and careful mother unto me: you have suffered great pains in my birth and bringing up; you have toiled and turmoiled to feed and sustain me your first and eldest child; and therefore for these and all other your motherly cherishings I give you, as it becometh me to do, most humble and hearty thanks; wishing that it lay in me to show myself as loving, natural, and dutiful a son as you have showed yourself a most tender and careful mother. I had meant this spring to have seen you if God had granted me health and liberty, but now never shall I see you or any of yours in this life again; trusting yet in heaven to meet you, to see you, and to live everlastingly with you."

"Forget not the groanings of thy mother" (Ecclus 7:29).

March 29

NO COMPARISON

Bl. Hart to his Protestant mother (2)

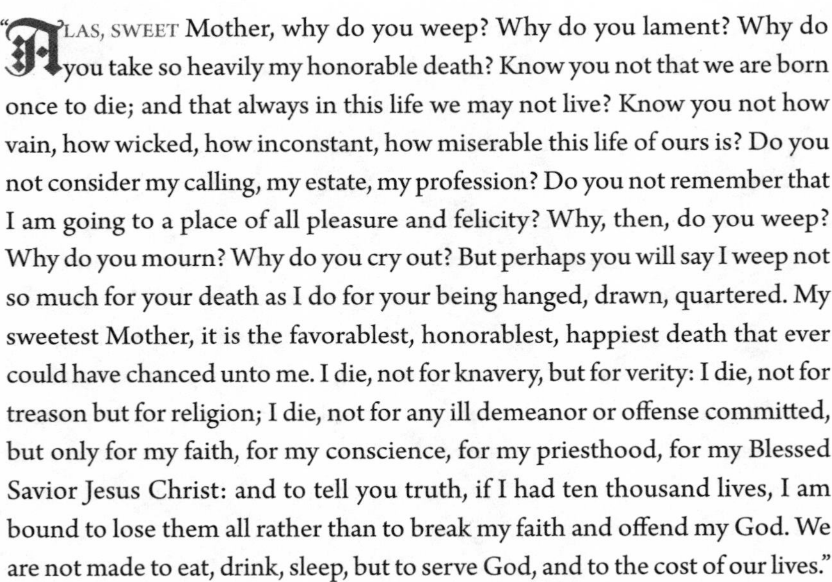

"ALAS, SWEET Mother, why do you weep? Why do you lament? Why do you take so heavily my honorable death? Know you not that we are born once to die; and that always in this life we may not live? Know you not how vain, how wicked, how inconstant, how miserable this life of ours is? Do you not consider my calling, my estate, my profession? Do you not remember that I am going to a place of all pleasure and felicity? Why, then, do you weep? Why do you mourn? Why do you cry out? But perhaps you will say I weep not so much for your death as I do for your being hanged, drawn, quartered. My sweetest Mother, it is the favorablest, honorablest, happiest death that ever could have chanced unto me. I die, not for knavery, but for verity: I die, not for treason but for religion; I die, not for any ill demeanor or offense committed, but only for my faith, for my conscience, for my priesthood, for my Blessed Savior Jesus Christ: and to tell you truth, if I had ten thousand lives, I am bound to lose them all rather than to break my faith and offend my God. We are not made to eat, drink, sleep, but to serve God, and to the cost of our lives."

"For I reckon that the sufferings of this time are not worthy to be compared with the glory to come" (Rom 8:18).

March 30

MEETING IN HEAVEN

Bl. Hart to his Protestant mother (3)

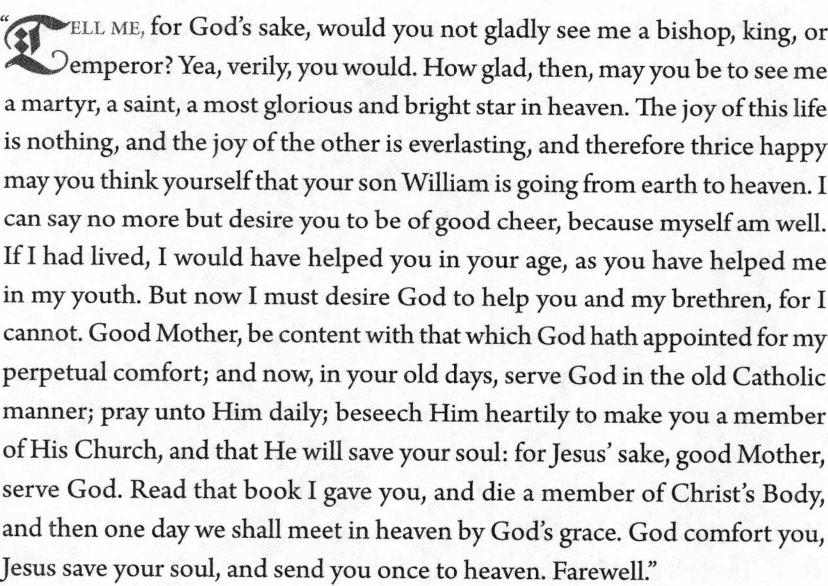

"TELL ME, for God's sake, would you not gladly see me a bishop, king, or emperor? Yea, verily, you would. How glad, then, may you be to see me a martyr, a saint, a most glorious and bright star in heaven. The joy of this life is nothing, and the joy of the other is everlasting, and therefore thrice happy may you think yourself that your son William is going from earth to heaven. I can say no more but desire you to be of good cheer, because myself am well. If I had lived, I would have helped you in your age, as you have helped me in my youth. But now I must desire God to help you and my brethren, for I cannot. Good Mother, be content with that which God hath appointed for my perpetual comfort; and now, in your old days, serve God in the old Catholic manner; pray unto Him daily; beseech Him heartily to make you a member of His Church, and that He will save your soul: for Jesus' sake, good Mother, serve God. Read that book I gave you, and die a member of Christ's Body, and then one day we shall meet in heaven by God's grace. God comfort you, Jesus save your soul, and send you once to heaven. Farewell."

"As one whom the mother caresseth, so will I comfort you, and you shall be comforted in Jerusalem" (Is 66:13).

March 31

JESUS DULCIS MEMORIA

Ven. Henry Heath, O. S. F., 1643

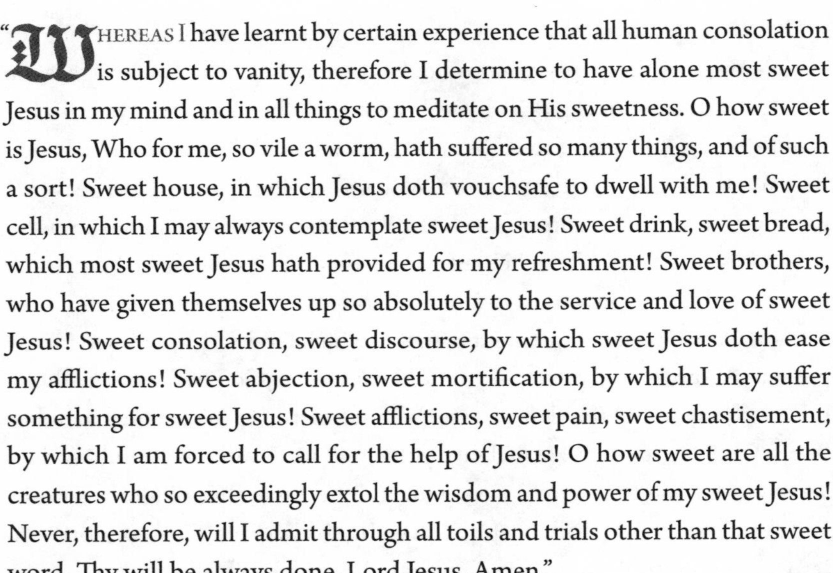

"Whereas I have learnt by certain experience that all human consolation is subject to vanity, therefore I determine to have alone most sweet Jesus in my mind and in all things to meditate on His sweetness. O how sweet is Jesus, Who for me, so vile a worm, hath suffered so many things, and of such a sort! Sweet house, in which Jesus doth vouchsafe to dwell with me! Sweet cell, in which I may always contemplate sweet Jesus! Sweet drink, sweet bread, which most sweet Jesus hath provided for my refreshment! Sweet brothers, who have given themselves up so absolutely to the service and love of sweet Jesus! Sweet consolation, sweet discourse, by which sweet Jesus doth ease my afflictions! Sweet abjection, sweet mortification, by which I may suffer something for sweet Jesus! Sweet afflictions, sweet pain, sweet chastisement, by which I am forced to call for the help of Jesus! O how sweet are all the creatures who so exceedingly extol the wisdom and power of my sweet Jesus! Never, therefore, will I admit through all toils and trials other than that sweet word. Thy will be always done, Lord Jesus. Amen."

"Taste and see how sweet the Lord is" (Ps 33:9).

April

April 1

LOVE OF THE SEMINARY

Ven. Thomas Maxfield, Pr., 1616

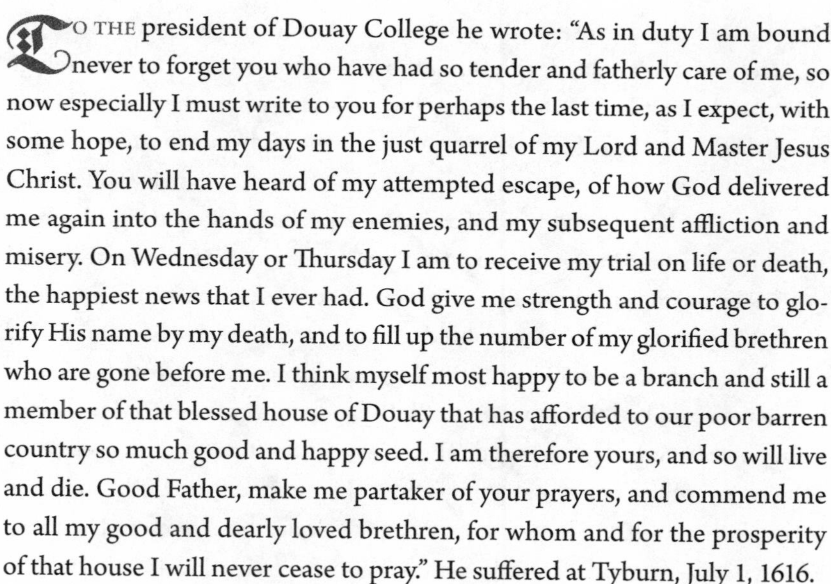

TO THE president of Douay College he wrote: "As in duty I am bound never to forget you who have had so tender and fatherly care of me, so now especially I must write to you for perhaps the last time, as I expect, with some hope, to end my days in the just quarrel of my Lord and Master Jesus Christ. You will have heard of my attempted escape, of how God delivered me again into the hands of my enemies, and my subsequent affliction and misery. On Wednesday or Thursday I am to receive my trial on life or death, the happiest news that I ever had. God give me strength and courage to glorify His name by my death, and to fill up the number of my glorified brethren who are gone before me. I think myself most happy to be a branch and still a member of that blessed house of Douay that has afforded to our poor barren country so much good and happy seed. I am therefore yours, and so will live and die. Good Father, make me partaker of your prayers, and commend me to all my good and dearly loved brethren, for whom and for the prosperity of that house I will never cease to pray." He suffered at Tyburn, July 1, 1616.

"Who maketh the barren woman to dwell in a house,
the joyful mother of children" (Ps 112:9).

* *Maxfield was beatified by Pope Pius XI on 15 December 1929.*

April 2

FALSE BRETHREN

✠ Bl. John Payne, Pr., 1582

Born in the diocese of Peterborough, he entered Douay in 1574, and returned to England with Bl. Cuthbert Mayne in 1576. His chief refuge in England was at Lady Petre's house at Ingatestone, where the priests' hiding place, discovered in 1855, proved to be under the bedroom floor, measuring fourteen feet by two feet, one inch in breadth and ten feet in height. He wrote to Douay that both the number of converts, especially among the gentlemen, and their constancy under persecution were alike amazing. He was arrested in 1579 by means of "Judas" Eliot. This man had been employed in positions of trust in several Catholic households, to their great loss. He had embezzled monies of Lady Petre, and had enticed a young woman away from the Roper household, and had then applied to Bl. Payne to marry them, and on his refusal determined to be avenged. The charge of theft and murder was now hanging over him, but by betraying a priest he escaped from both, and filled his pockets as well. On his perjured evidence alone, though refuted in court, Fr. Payne was sentenced and hung at Chelmsford, April 2, 1582. The holy name *Jesus* was on his lips as he died.

"If my enemy had reviled me, I would have borne it. . . .
But thou a man of one mind with me, . . . in the house
of God we walked with consent" (Ps 54:13–15).

* *Payne was canonized by Pope Paul VI on 25 October 1970.*

April 3

AVOIDANCE OF SCANDAL

Abp. Nicholas Heath of York, 1579

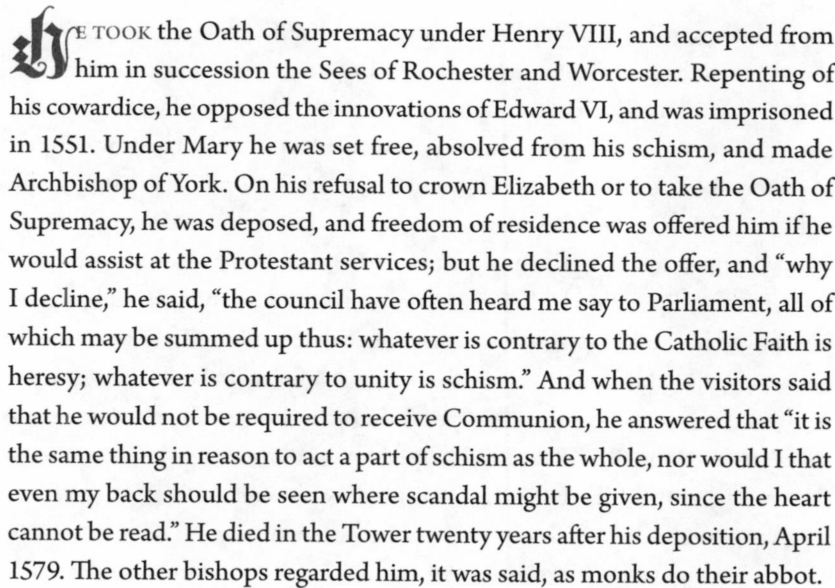

HE TOOK the Oath of Supremacy under Henry VIII, and accepted from him in succession the Sees of Rochester and Worcester. Repenting of his cowardice, he opposed the innovations of Edward VI, and was imprisoned in 1551. Under Mary he was set free, absolved from his schism, and made Archbishop of York. On his refusal to crown Elizabeth or to take the Oath of Supremacy, he was deposed, and freedom of residence was offered him if he would assist at the Protestant services; but he declined the offer, and "why I decline," he said, "the council have often heard me say to Parliament, all of which may be summed up thus: whatever is contrary to the Catholic Faith is heresy; whatever is contrary to unity is schism." And when the visitors said that he would not be required to receive Communion, he answered that "it is the same thing in reason to act a part of schism as the whole, nor would I that even my back should be seen where scandal might be given, since the heart cannot be read." He died in the Tower twenty years after his deposition, April 1579. The other bishops regarded him, it was said, as monks do their abbot.

"Whoever shall scandalize one of these little ones that believe in Me, it were better for him that a millstone were hanged round his neck and he were cast into the sea" (Mk 9:41).

April 4

THE LAST OF HIS LINE

Bp. Thomas Goldwell of St. Asaph, 1585

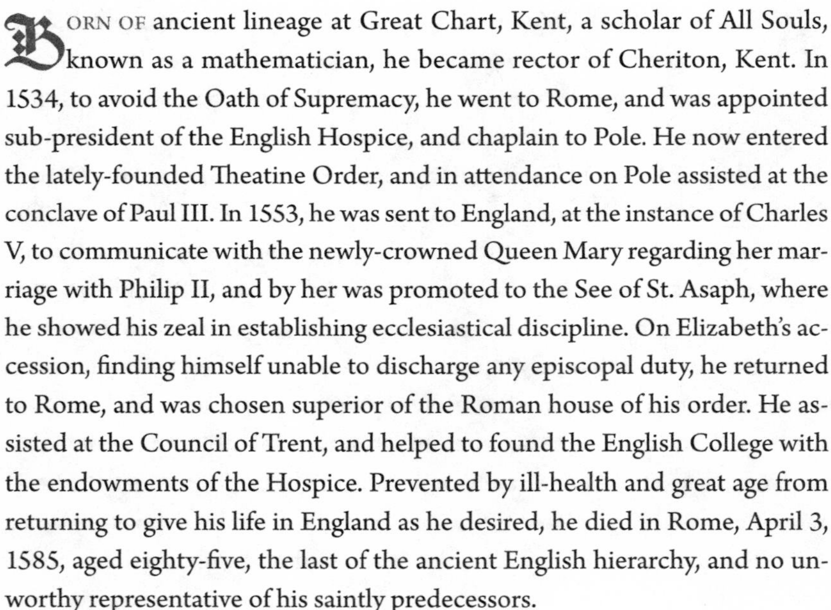

Born of ancient lineage at Great Chart, Kent, a scholar of All Souls, known as a mathematician, he became rector of Cheriton, Kent. In 1534, to avoid the Oath of Supremacy, he went to Rome, and was appointed sub-president of the English Hospice, and chaplain to Pole. He now entered the lately-founded Theatine Order, and in attendance on Pole assisted at the conclave of Paul III. In 1553, he was sent to England, at the instance of Charles V, to communicate with the newly-crowned Queen Mary regarding her marriage with Philip II, and by her was promoted to the See of St. Asaph, where he showed his zeal in establishing ecclesiastical discipline. On Elizabeth's accession, finding himself unable to discharge any episcopal duty, he returned to Rome, and was chosen superior of the Roman house of his order. He assisted at the Council of Trent, and helped to found the English College with the endowments of the Hospice. Prevented by ill-health and great age from returning to give his life in England as he desired, he died in Rome, April 3, 1585, aged eighty-five, the last of the ancient English hierarchy, and no unworthy representative of his saintly predecessors.

"Abide in Me, and I in you. As the branch cannot bear fruit of itself, unless it abide in the vine, so neither can you, unless you abide in Me" (*Jn* 15:4).

April 5

STRENGTH IN UNION

Ven. Henry Walpole, S.J., 1595

"I AM MUCH astonished that so vile a creature as I am should be so near, as they tell me, to the crown of martyrdom: but this I know for certain, that the blood of my most Blessed Savior and Redeemer and His most sweet love is able to make me worthy of it, *omnia possum in eo qui me comfortat* (Phil 4:13). Your Reverence, most loving Father, is engaged in the midst of the battle. I sit here an idle spectator of the field; yet King David has appointed an equal portion for us both, and love, charity, and union, which unites us together in Jesus Christ our Lord, makes us mutually partakers of another's merits, and what can be more closely united than we two, who, as Your Reverence sees, *simul segregati sumus in hoc ministerium*. About mid-Lent I hope my lot will be decided, as then the assizes will be held. Meanwhile I have leisure to prepare myself, and I beg Your Reverence to join your holy prayers with my poor ones, and I trust that our Lord may grant me, not regarding my many imperfections, but the fervent labors, prayers, and holy sacrifices of so many fathers, and my brothers His servants, to glorify Him in life or death."

"That you stand fast in one spirit, with one mind laboring together for the faith of the gospel" (Phil 1:27).

* *Walpole was canonized by Pope Paul VI on 25 October 1970.*

April 6

THE SONG OF THE SPIRIT

Ven. Henry Walpole, S.J., 1595

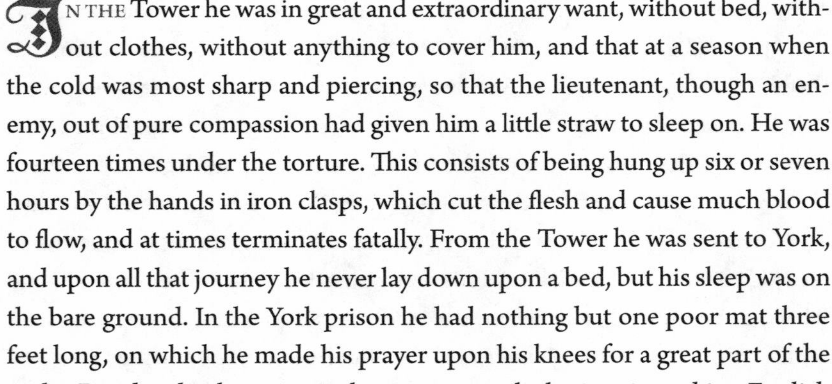

IN THE Tower he was in great and extraordinary want, without bed, without clothes, without anything to cover him, and that at a season when the cold was most sharp and piercing, so that the lieutenant, though an enemy, out of pure compassion had given him a little straw to sleep on. He was fourteen times under the torture. This consists of being hung up six or seven hours by the hands in iron clasps, which cut the flesh and cause much blood to flow, and at times terminates fatally. From the Tower he was sent to York, and upon all that journey he never lay down upon a bed, but his sleep was on the bare ground. In the York prison he had nothing but one poor mat three feet long, on which he made his prayer upon his knees for a great part of the night. Besides this long prayer he spent not a little time in making English verses, for which he had a particular talent and grace; for, before he left the kingdom, he had made a poem on the martyrdom of Fr. Campion, for which the publisher was condemned to lose his ears and to pass the remainder of his days in prison, and there, after nine years, he made a pious end.

"I will pray with the spirit, I will pray also with the understanding; I will sing with the spirit, I will sing also with the understanding" (1 Cor 14:15).

April 7

UNDER THE SHADOW OF THE MOST HIGH

✠ Ven. Henry Walpole, S.J., 1595

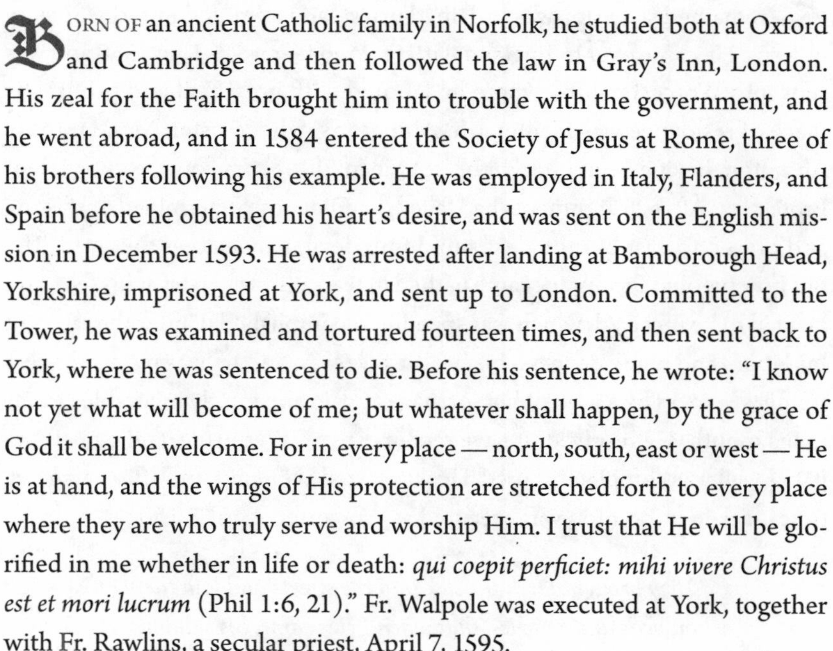

Born of an ancient Catholic family in Norfolk, he studied both at Oxford and Cambridge and then followed the law in Gray's Inn, London. His zeal for the Faith brought him into trouble with the government, and he went abroad, and in 1584 entered the Society of Jesus at Rome, three of his brothers following his example. He was employed in Italy, Flanders, and Spain before he obtained his heart's desire, and was sent on the English mission in December 1593. He was arrested after landing at Bamborough Head, Yorkshire, imprisoned at York, and sent up to London. Committed to the Tower, he was examined and tortured fourteen times, and then sent back to York, where he was sentenced to die. Before his sentence, he wrote: "I know not yet what will become of me; but whatever shall happen, by the grace of God it shall be welcome. For in every place — north, south, east or west — He is at hand, and the wings of His protection are stretched forth to every place where they are who truly serve and worship Him. I trust that He will be glorified in me whether in life or death: *qui coepit perficiet: mihi vivere Christus est et mori lucrum* (Phil 1:6, 21)." Fr. Walpole was executed at York, together with Fr. Rawlins, a secular priest, April 7, 1595.

"Who dwells under the shadow of the Most High shall abide under the protection of the God of heaven" (Ps 90:1).

April 8

DEVOTION TO ST. WINEFRIDE

Ven. Edward Oldcorne, S. J., 1606

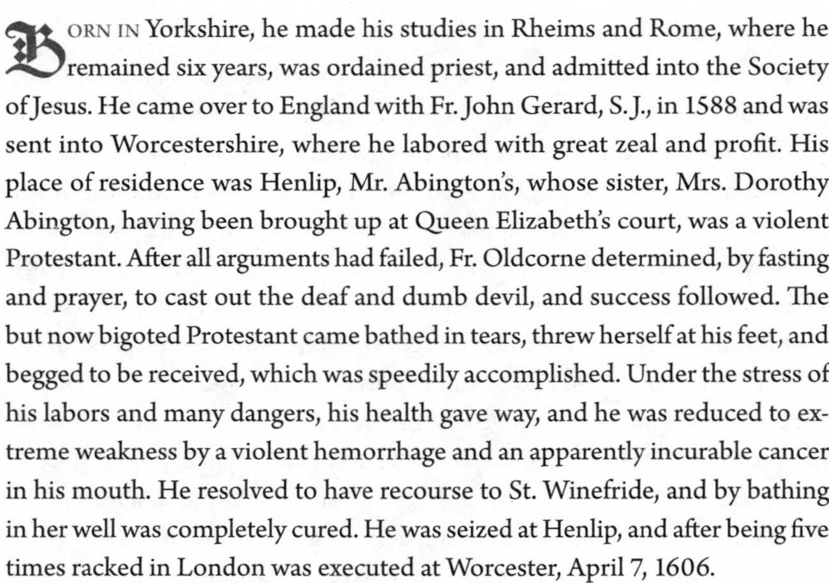

Born in Yorkshire, he made his studies in Rheims and Rome, where he remained six years, was ordained priest, and admitted into the Society of Jesus. He came over to England with Fr. John Gerard, S. J., in 1588 and was sent into Worcestershire, where he labored with great zeal and profit. His place of residence was Henlip, Mr. Abington's, whose sister, Mrs. Dorothy Abington, having been brought up at Queen Elizabeth's court, was a violent Protestant. After all arguments had failed, Fr. Oldcorne determined, by fasting and prayer, to cast out the deaf and dumb devil, and success followed. The but now bigoted Protestant came bathed in tears, threw herself at his feet, and begged to be received, which was speedily accomplished. Under the stress of his labors and many dangers, his health gave way, and he was reduced to extreme weakness by a violent hemorrhage and an apparently incurable cancer in his mouth. He resolved to have recourse to St. Winefride, and by bathing in her well was completely cured. He was seized at Henlip, and after being five times racked in London was executed at Worcester, April 7, 1606.

"They brought forth the sick into the streets and laid them on beds and couches, that when Peter came, his shadow at the least might overshadow them, that they might be delivered from their infirmities" (Acts 5:15).

* *Oldcorne was beatified by Pope Pius XI on 15 December 1929.*

"Mementoes of the English Martyrs and Confessors"

April 9

LIFE IN RELIGION

Ven. Henry Heath, O. S. F., to a nun

"The very house and walls of thy enclosure cannot but put thee in mind where and how thou hast lived these many years, as if thou hadst been long already dead and buried in thy habit from the world. How sweetly now canst thou say to thyself, 'O happy time, O blessed years, that I have now passed in my Redeemer's service! O blessed prison! O happy chains and bonds of my vows which I have borne for sweet Jesus! Here I have daily carried my cross, which has taught me the way of true humility and patience. Here have I been broken of my own proper will and judgment, which would have hindered me from being wholly resigned and obedient to the will of God. Here have I been trained up in virtue, in the fear of God, in the way to heaven. Here I sweetly sing the praises of my Redeemer. Here have I followed Him through every step of His Passion. Here have I spent many a groan to come to Jesus when He has hid Himself from me. And now my whole pilgrimage is to be ended! Now I go to my sweet Beloved, no more trouble or temptation, never to be separated from Him.' "

"My Beloved to me and I to Him" (Cant 2:16).

For Every Day in the Year
Fr Henry Sebastian Bowden
Sophia Pub

April 10

VIRGO POTENS

Ven. Henry Heath, O. S. F., 1643

FR. HEATH'S own conversion was a remarkable effect of Mary's intercession, but more striking yet was that of his aged father. A bigoted Protestant, he seemed proof alike against arguments and prayers, and was now on the brink of the grave. To our Lady Fr. Heath turned, beseeching her aid for his father in his extreme peril, when suddenly the old man, now fourscore, crossed the sea, arrived at Douay, and was reconciled to the Church. Again, during Fr. Heath's guardianship, when his community was dying of want and disease, through our Lady's prayers the sick recovered and their needs were relieved. And now, to obtain the superior's consent to his going to England, he started on a pilgrimage to her shrine at Montaigu in Brabant. At Ghent he found his petition refused, but still completed his pilgrimage, and on the way back the same superior who refused now granted his request. From that time till his death, Fr. Heath seemed a changed man. His anxieties and fears were succeeded by a holy calm, and supernatural joy manifested itself in his whole conduct, but especially at Mass. He constantly extolled the glory of the martyrs, as if he had already a foretaste of their reward. Thus did our Lady answer his prayers.

"He Who is mighty hath done great things for me, and holy is His name" (Lk 1:49).

April 11

LOST AND FOUND

✠ Ven. George Gervase, O. S. B., 1608

He was born at Bosham in Sussex. His father belonged to a noted family in that county, and his mother was of the ancient stock of the Shelleys. He was left an orphan when he was twelve years of age, and not long after was kidnapped by a pirate (probably a lieutenant of Drake, who was then buccaneering on the Spanish Main), and was taken to the West Indies with two of his brothers, and, considering his surroundings, the lawlessness, plunder, and bloodshed of a pirate's life, it is not surprising to learn that he quite lost his religion. At length, he found means of returning to England, and went over to Flanders, where his eldest brother Henry was staying, both for conscience's sake and to enjoy the free practice of his religion. By his example, George was reconciled to the Catholic Faith, entered Douay, was ordained priest 1603, and entered on the English mission 1604. After two years, he was apprehended and banished. His brother had provided a comfortable home for him at Lille, but his zeal for souls drew him again to England, where he was shortly apprehended, and, refusing to take the Oath of Allegiance, was condemned. He suffered at Tyburn, April 11, 1608, aged thirty-seven, having been admitted to the Benedictine Order.

"My father and mother have left me, but the Lord hath taken me up" (Ps 26:10).

* *Gervase was beatified by Pope Pius XI on 15 December 1929.*

April 12

TORMENTING MINISTERS

Ven. George Gervase, O. S. B., 1608

"Urged at his examination as to whether the pope could depose princes, he demurred, saying it was a hard question, and at last replied, 'Yes, and also all the princes of the world'; and on his trial answered, 'What I have said my blood is ready to answer.' After his condemnation, the bishop sent seven ministers on the Sunday morning before his execution to deal with him; one was Dr. Morton, whom I saw. They all tormented him according to their diversities of spirits, but, as the keeper said, he remained a most obstinate papist. This much I will adjoin of my own knowledge (he being dearest unto me), that since the first persecution in England, never any priest for the space of two or three days ever had more affliction amongst ministers, and that by means of the bishop. The whole Sunday night before his death he was accompanied by five ministers. On the hurdle he lifted up his bound hands, signing to me to pray for him. At the gallows, at the minister's final importunities, he said: 'Tut, tut, look to thyself, poor man.' He was cruelly butchered, but now enjoyeth all felicity, being most devout to our Blessed Lady." Written by one who was present.

"They surrounded me like bees, and they burned like fire among thorns" (Ps 117:12).

April 13

A FRUITFUL OLD AGE

✠ Ven. John Lockwood, Pr., 1642

Of a good Yorkshire Catholic family, he gave up his estate, became a priest, and labored for forty-four years as a missioner in his own county. He was imprisoned, banished, retaken, condemned to death, reprieved, escaped, or obtained his liberty, and was finally apprehended at the house of Mrs. Catenby, a Catholic widow, where he had lived some years. He was cultivating his little garden when he was seized, and, being too weak to walk or ride, he was laid across the horse and thus conveyed to York. There he was sentenced to death with Mr. Catherick, a fellow priest. Mr. Catherick was to suffer first, but, showing signs of fear, Fr. Lockwood claimed as senior the privilege of taking precedence. He then earnestly prayed for their mutual perseverance, and beginning with much difficulty to climb the ladder, he begged the sheriff to have patience, as it was a piece of hard service for an old man fourscore and seven. At length, with the help of two men, whom he paid for their pains, he reached the top, and asking Fr. Catherick with a smile how he did, the latter replied: "In good heart, blessed be God; your good example has strengthened me." So both won their crown. — April 13, 1642

"They that are planted in the house of the Lord shall flourish in the courts of the house of our God. They shall still increase in a fruitful old age" (Ps 91:14–15).

* *Lockwood was beatified by Pope Pius XI on 15 December 1929.*

April 14

A CRY FOR RELIEF (1)

William Blundell, L., 1600

We Catholics, tormented sore
With heresy's foul railing tongue,
With prisons, tortures, loss of goods,
Of land, yea, lives, even thieves among,
Do crave, with heart surcharged with grief,
Of Thee, sweet Jesu, some relief.

We crave relief in this distress,
We seek some ease of this annoy;
Yet are we well content with all,
So Thee in end we may enjoy;
Ourselves to Thee we do resign
Relieve us, Lord, our cause is Thine.

Our cause is Thine, and Thine are we,
Who from Thy truth refuse to slide:
Our faith Thy truth, true faith the cause
For which these garboyles we abide;
True faith, I say, as plain appears
To all who shut not eyes and ears.

To all who shut not eyes and ears
'Gainst fathers, scriptures, Church, and thee,
Who built Thy Church, as doctors all
With scriptures plainly do agree,
Not, soon to fall, upon the sand,
But on a Rock still sure to stand.

Still sure to stand, yea, on a hill,
For all her friends and foes to see,
Her friends to foster and defend,
Her foes to vanquish gloriously;
From age to age this hath she done,
Thus shall she do in time to come.

April 15

A CRY FOR RELIEF (2)

William Blundell, L., 1600

In time to come, as heretofore,
Most certainly she shall prevail
'Gainst all the force and sleighty wiles,
Wherewith hell-gates may her assail;
Who shoot against this brazen wall
With their fond bolts themselves will gall.

Themselves to gall they will be sure,
Who strive to ruinate Thy house,
And to withdraw Thy children dear
From soft lap of Thy dearest spouse,
Thy children whom, with streams of blood,
Thou bought, sweet Lord, upon the Rood.

Upon the Rood Thou bought our souls
With price more worth than all Thou bought,
Yet doth the fiend our foes so blind,
Both souls and price they set at naught;
They reckon not enough their ill,
Except with theirs our souls they spill.

Our souls to spill they think full soon
Or else our bodies to enthrall;
Or, at the least, to wantful state,
Through hard pursuits, to bring us all;
Come quickly, therefore, Lord Jesus,
And judge this cause twixt them and us.

Give judgment, Lord, twixt them and us,
The balance yet let pity hold:
Let mercy measure their offense,
And grace reduce them to Thy fold,
That we, all children of Thy spouse,
May live as brethren in Thy house.

April 16

AWAITING SENTENCE

Ven. Henry Heath, O. S. F., 1643

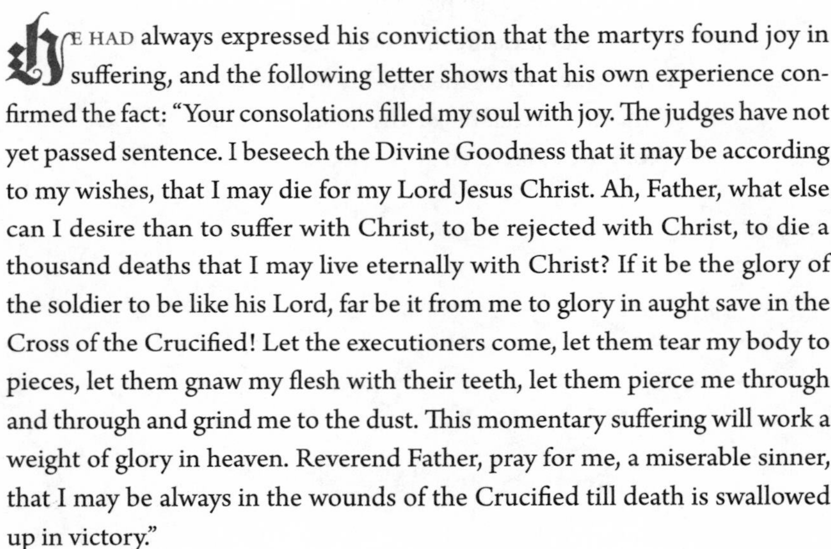

HE HAD always expressed his conviction that the martyrs found joy in suffering, and the following letter shows that his own experience confirmed the fact: "Your consolations filled my soul with joy. The judges have not yet passed sentence. I beseech the Divine Goodness that it may be according to my wishes, that I may die for my Lord Jesus Christ. Ah, Father, what else can I desire than to suffer with Christ, to be rejected with Christ, to die a thousand deaths that I may live eternally with Christ? If it be the glory of the soldier to be like his Lord, far be it from me to glory in aught save in the Cross of the Crucified! Let the executioners come, let them tear my body to pieces, let them gnaw my flesh with their teeth, let them pierce me through and through and grind me to the dust. This momentary suffering will work a weight of glory in heaven. Reverend Father, pray for me, a miserable sinner, that I may be always in the wounds of the Crucified till death is swallowed up in victory."

"For me, to live is Christ, and to die is gain" (Phil 1:21).

April 17

PRAYER FOR ENGLAND

Ven. Henry Heath, O. S. F., 1643

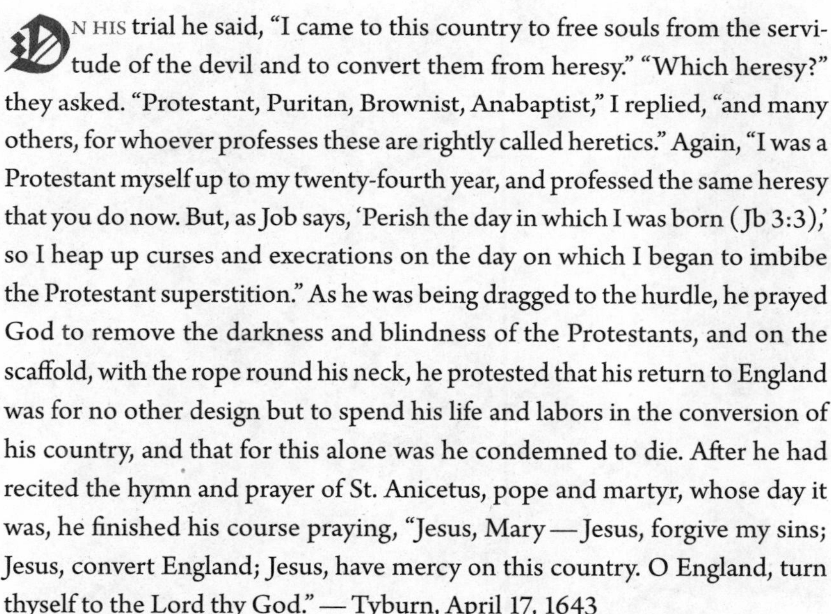

In his trial he said, "I came to this country to free souls from the servitude of the devil and to convert them from heresy." "Which heresy?" they asked. "Protestant, Puritan, Brownist, Anabaptist," I replied, "and many others, for whoever professes these are rightly called heretics." Again, "I was a Protestant myself up to my twenty-fourth year, and professed the same heresy that you do now. But, as Job says, 'Perish the day in which I was born (Jb 3:3),' so I heap up curses and execrations on the day on which I began to imbibe the Protestant superstition." As he was being dragged to the hurdle, he prayed God to remove the darkness and blindness of the Protestants, and on the scaffold, with the rope round his neck, he protested that his return to England was for no other design but to spend his life and labors in the conversion of his country, and that for this alone was he condemned to die. After he had recited the hymn and prayer of St. Anicetus, pope and martyr, whose day it was, he finished his course praying, "Jesus, Mary — Jesus, forgive my sins; Jesus, convert England; Jesus, have mercy on this country. O England, turn thyself to the Lord thy God." — Tyburn, April 17, 1643

"Convert us, O Lord, to Thee and we shall be converted;
renew our days as from the beginning" (Lam 5:21).

HENRY HEATH

"Taking him to be a shoplifter calls the watch"

April 18

THE BRIDE OF ST. FRANCIS

Ven. Henry Heath, O. S. F., 1643

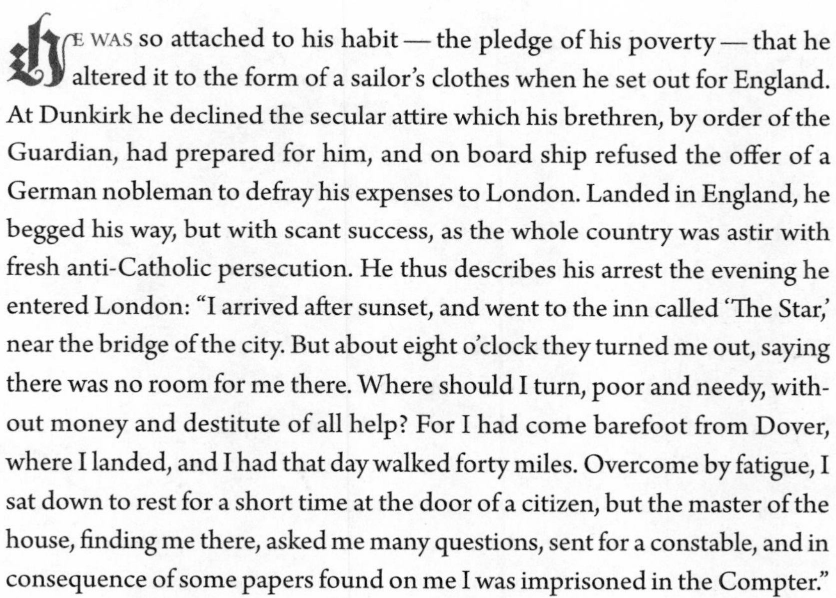

HE WAS so attached to his habit — the pledge of his poverty — that he altered it to the form of a sailor's clothes when he set out for England. At Dunkirk he declined the secular attire which his brethren, by order of the Guardian, had prepared for him, and on board ship refused the offer of a German nobleman to defray his expenses to London. Landed in England, he begged his way, but with scant success, as the whole country was astir with fresh anti-Catholic persecution. He thus describes his arrest the evening he entered London: "I arrived after sunset, and went to the inn called 'The Star,' near the bridge of the city. But about eight o'clock they turned me out, saying there was no room for me there. Where should I turn, poor and needy, without money and destitute of all help? For I had come barefoot from Dover, where I landed, and I had that day walked forty miles. Overcome by fatigue, I sat down to rest for a short time at the door of a citizen, but the master of the house, finding me there, asked me many questions, sent for a constable, and in consequence of some papers found on me I was imprisoned in the Compter."

"The foxes have holes, and the birds of the air nests, but the Son of Man hath not where to lay His head" (Mt 8:20).

April 19

GOOD BOOKS

Ven. James Duckett, L., 1602

Brought up as a Protestant, he was apprenticed to a Catholic bookseller, Peter Mason. After reading "The Foundation of the Catholic Religion," Duckett ceased to attend the Protestant church, and was committed to Bridewell for his persistent refusal to go there. Being freed by his master's means, he was a second time apprehended and sent to the Compter. Again freed, he found means of being reconciled, and after a while married a good Catholic widow, Anne Cooper. They supported themselves by making priests' vestments, altar necessaries, and publishing Catholic books. On these being discovered, his house was searched, and he was imprisoned for two years in Newgate. Discharged on his wife's petition, she being in labor, he was again imprisoned for having bound certain Latin and English primers, and was again sent to the leads, Newgate. While in prison he printed other Catholic books, and was cast into Limbo, a dark dungeon traversed by the city sewer with its poisonous filth. Freed yet once more, he was again apprehended and hanged with his betrayer, whom he forgave and kissed on the scaffold. Of his twelve years of married life, nine were passed in prison. He suffered at Tyburn, April 19, 1602.

"They that instruct many to justice shall shine as stars for all eternity" (Dn 12:3).

* *Duckett was beatified by Pope Pius XI on 15 December 1929.*

April 20

PENITENT AND MARTYR

✠ Ven. James Bell, Pr., 1584

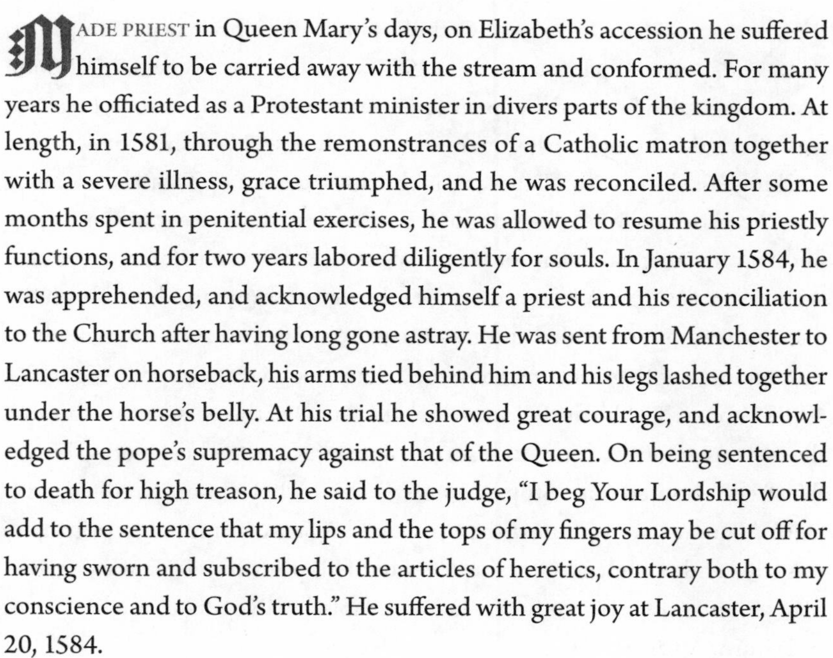

MADE PRIEST in Queen Mary's days, on Elizabeth's accession he suffered himself to be carried away with the stream and conformed. For many years he officiated as a Protestant minister in divers parts of the kingdom. At length, in 1581, through the remonstrances of a Catholic matron together with a severe illness, grace triumphed, and he was reconciled. After some months spent in penitential exercises, he was allowed to resume his priestly functions, and for two years labored diligently for souls. In January 1584, he was apprehended, and acknowledged himself a priest and his reconciliation to the Church after having long gone astray. He was sent from Manchester to Lancaster on horseback, his arms tied behind him and his legs lashed together under the horse's belly. At his trial he showed great courage, and acknowledged the pope's supremacy against that of the Queen. On being sentenced to death for high treason, he said to the judge, "I beg Your Lordship would add to the sentence that my lips and the tops of my fingers may be cut off for having sworn and subscribed to the articles of heretics, contrary both to my conscience and to God's truth." He suffered with great joy at Lancaster, April 20, 1584.

"I saw his ways, and I healed him and brought him back, and restored comforts to him and to them that mourn for him" (Is 57:18).

* *Bell was beatified by Pope Pius XI on 15 December 1929.*

April 21

DEVOTION TO THE PRIESTHOOD

✠ Ven. Thomas Tichborne, Pr., 1602

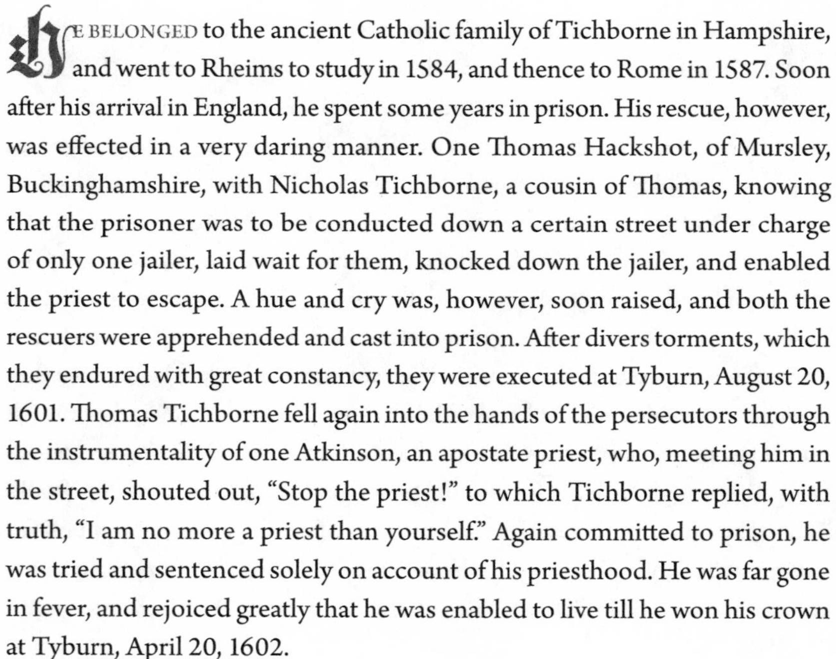

HE BELONGED to the ancient Catholic family of Tichborne in Hampshire, and went to Rheims to study in 1584, and thence to Rome in 1587. Soon after his arrival in England, he spent some years in prison. His rescue, however, was effected in a very daring manner. One Thomas Hackshot, of Mursley, Buckinghamshire, with Nicholas Tichborne, a cousin of Thomas, knowing that the prisoner was to be conducted down a certain street under charge of only one jailer, laid wait for them, knocked down the jailer, and enabled the priest to escape. A hue and cry was, however, soon raised, and both the rescuers were apprehended and cast into prison. After divers torments, which they endured with great constancy, they were executed at Tyburn, August 20, 1601. Thomas Tichborne fell again into the hands of the persecutors through the instrumentality of one Atkinson, an apostate priest, who, meeting him in the street, shouted out, "Stop the priest!" to which Tichborne replied, with truth, "I am no more a priest than yourself." Again committed to prison, he was tried and sentenced solely on account of his priesthood. He was far gone in fever, and rejoiced greatly that he was enabled to live till he won his crown at Tyburn, April 20, 1602.

"For every high priest taken from among men is ordained for men in the things that may appertain to God, that he may offer up gifts and sacrifices for sins" (Heb 5:1).

April 22

AN UNEXPECTED CURE

Ven. Robert Watkinson, Pr., 1602

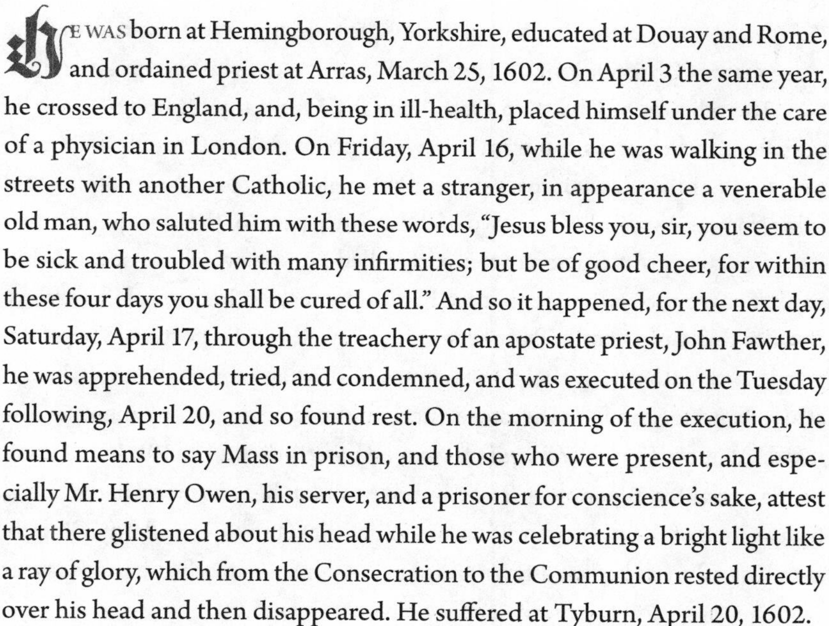

HE WAS born at Hemingborough, Yorkshire, educated at Douay and Rome, and ordained priest at Arras, March 25, 1602. On April 3 the same year, he crossed to England, and, being in ill-health, placed himself under the care of a physician in London. On Friday, April 16, while he was walking in the streets with another Catholic, he met a stranger, in appearance a venerable old man, who saluted him with these words, "Jesus bless you, sir, you seem to be sick and troubled with many infirmities; but be of good cheer, for within these four days you shall be cured of all." And so it happened, for the next day, Saturday, April 17, through the treachery of an apostate priest, John Fawther, he was apprehended, tried, and condemned, and was executed on the Tuesday following, April 20, and so found rest. On the morning of the execution, he found means to say Mass in prison, and those who were present, and especially Mr. Henry Owen, his server, and a prisoner for conscience's sake, attest that there glistened about his head while he was celebrating a bright light like a ray of glory, which from the Consecration to the Communion rested directly over his head and then disappeared. He suffered at Tyburn, April 20, 1602.

"Come to Me all you that labor and are burdened,
and I will refresh you" (Mt 11:28).

* *Watkinson was beatified by Pope Pius XI on 15 December 1929.*

April 23

TEN JUST MEN

Bl. John Fisher, Card. Bp., 1535

✣

PREACHING ON the Penitential Psalms, he was led to review and bewail the state of Christendom, and unconsciously sketches his own position in it. "The religion of Christian Faith," he says, "is greatly diminished; we be very few; and whereas sometime we were spread almost through the world, now we be thrust down into a very straight angle or corner. Our enemies held away from us Asia and Africa, two of the greatest parts of the world. Also, they hold from us a great portion of this part, called Europe, which we now inhabit, so that scant the sixth part that we had in possession before is left unto us. Besides this, our enemies daily lay await to have this little portion. Therefore, good Lord, without Thy help, the name of Christian men shall utterly be destroyed and fordone.... Therefore, merciful Lord, exercise Thy mercy, show it indeed upon Thy Church, *quia tempus est miserendi ejus* (Ps 101:14). If there be many righteous people in Thy Church Militant, hear us, wretched sinners, for the love of them; be merciful unto Zion, that is to say, to all Thy Church. If in Thy Church be but a few righteous persons, so much the more is our wretchedness, and the more need we have of Thy mercy."

"And Abraham said: What if ten [just men] be found there? And He said: I will not destroy it for the sake of ten" (Gn 18:32).

April 24

ALWAYS THE SAME

Bl. John Fisher, Card. Bp., 1535

Being after his condemnation the space of four days in his prison, he occupied himself in continual prayer most fervently; and although he looked daily for death, yet could ye not have perceived him one whit dismayed or disquieted thereat, neither in word nor countenance, but still continued his former trade of constancy and patience, and that rather with a more joyful cheer and free mind than ever he had done before, which appeared well by this chance. A false report of his execution having been fixed for a certain day, the cook brought him no dinner, and on the bishop asking the reason, the cook replied that he thought the bishop would be already dead, and that therefore it would be vain to dress anything for him. "Well," said the bishop merrily to him again, "for all that report thou seest me yet alive, and therefore whatsoever news thou shalt hear of me hereafter, let me no more lack my dinner, but make it ready as thou art wont to do; and if thou see me dead, when thou comest, then eat it thyself. But I promise thee, if I be alive, I mind, by God's grace, to eat never a bit the less."

"Whether you eat or drink, or whatsoever else you do, do all to the glory of God" (1 Cor 10:31).

April 25

ONE IN LIFE AND DEATH

Vens.. Robert Anderton and Vens.. William Marsden, Prs., 1586

THE JUDGE, Anderson, in the Isle of Wight, though he consented to the prisoners being found guilty of high treason, would not pronounce sentence of death without the authority of the Queen, saying that this was her wish in the case of seminarists. On March 10, 1586, they were therefore sent to the Marshalsea, London, and were examined by two of the Privy Council, who soon managed to extract treasonable matter from them. They were asked if they would keep the promise they had made never to try to persuade anybody in the matter of religion. They denied ever having made such a promise; and Anderton said that as he regarded every one outside the unity of the Church of Rome in danger of damnation, he would be bound to endeavor to reclaim them; and Marsden affirmed that to persuade the people of the truth of Catholicism was the one subject for which he had come to the country. The Queen, therefore, the Proclamation said, could only let the law take its course. They were sent back to the island, and there "on some high ground in sight of the moaning sea," the scaffold was erected, and refusing for the last time pardon as the price of apostasy, they together won their crown, April 25, 1586.

"Who then shall separate us from the love of Christ?" (Rom 8:35).

* *Anderton and Marsden were beatified by Pope Pius XI on 15 December 1929.*

April 26

A CHEERFUL GIVER

✠ Ven. Edward Morgan, Pr., 1642

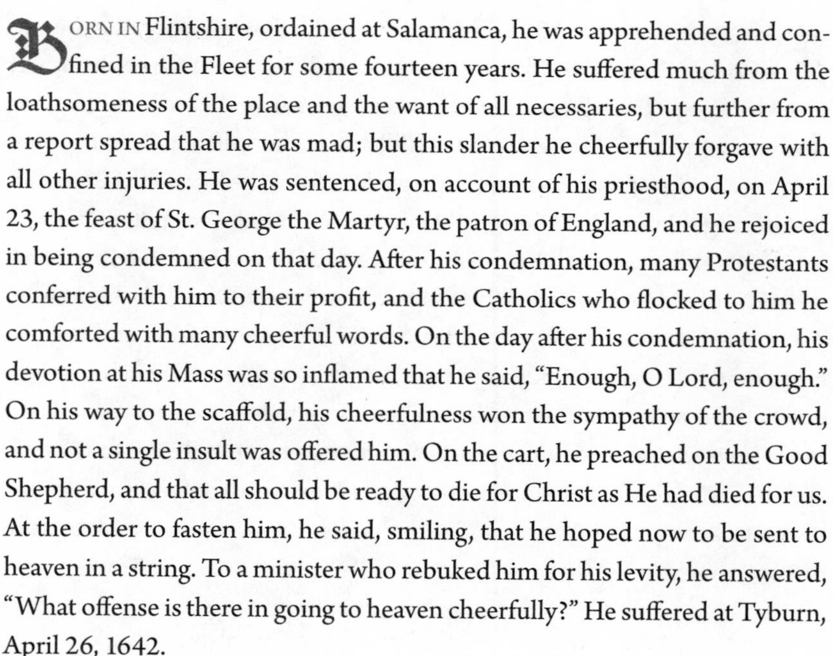

BORN IN Flintshire, ordained at Salamanca, he was apprehended and confined in the Fleet for some fourteen years. He suffered much from the loathsomeness of the place and the want of all necessaries, but further from a report spread that he was mad; but this slander he cheerfully forgave with all other injuries. He was sentenced, on account of his priesthood, on April 23, the feast of St. George the Martyr, the patron of England, and he rejoiced in being condemned on that day. After his condemnation, many Protestants conferred with him to their profit, and the Catholics who flocked to him he comforted with many cheerful words. On the day after his condemnation, his devotion at his Mass was so inflamed that he said, "Enough, O Lord, enough." On his way to the scaffold, his cheerfulness won the sympathy of the crowd, and not a single insult was offered him. On the cart, he preached on the Good Shepherd, and that all should be ready to die for Christ as He had died for us. At the order to fasten him, he said, smiling, that he hoped now to be sent to heaven in a string. To a minister who rebuked him for his levity, he answered, "What offense is there in going to heaven cheerfully?" He suffered at Tyburn, April 26, 1642.

"God loveth a cheerful giver" (2 Cor 9:7).

April 27

LIGHT AND DARKNESS

Ven. Francis Page, S.J., 1602

FR. PAGE learnt from Mr. Floyd, a priest and fellow prisoner, that he was to die on the morrow, for the keeper himself felt unable to be the bearer of such tidings. Fr. Page received the message as from heaven, and, having celebrated the Holy Mysteries, was so filled with joy and supernatural light that it seemed as if nothing could separate him from the love of his Lord. But that he might know that this sensible devotion is God's free gift, and might learn something also of the anguish and agony of His Savior in Gethsemane, he was of a sudden deprived of these extraordinary favors, and, like his Master, became sad, sorrowful, even unto death. In his extremity of fear and anguish he earnestly desired Mr. Floyd's prayers, while his pallor betrayed his inward conflict. The storm continued till the sheriff sent to him to prepare for death as the hour was at hand. The message in a moment restored calm to his soul, and he went to meet death with every sign of joy. The whole way to Tyburn his soul was engaged in prayer, and with the holy name of Jesus on his lips the cart was drawn away. — April 20, 1642

"The Lord gave, and the Lord hath taken away …
blessed be the name of the Lord" (Jb 1:21).

* *Page was beatified by Pope Pius XI on 15 December 1929.*

April 28

LOVE, EARTHLY AND HEAVENLY

Ven. Francis Page, S. J., 1602

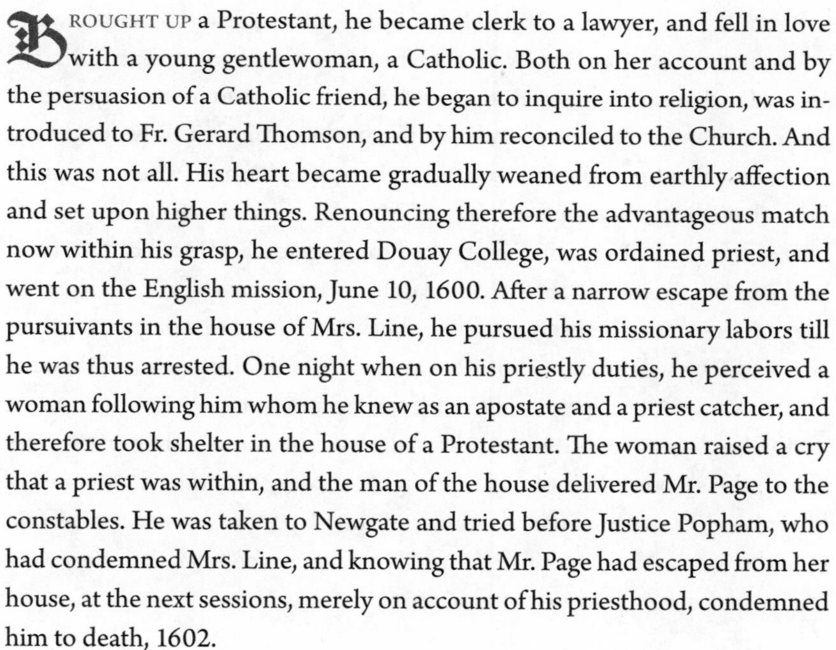

Brought up a Protestant, he became clerk to a lawyer, and fell in love with a young gentlewoman, a Catholic. Both on her account and by the persuasion of a Catholic friend, he began to inquire into religion, was introduced to Fr. Gerard Thomson, and by him reconciled to the Church. And this was not all. His heart became gradually weaned from earthly affection and set upon higher things. Renouncing therefore the advantageous match now within his grasp, he entered Douay College, was ordained priest, and went on the English mission, June 10, 1600. After a narrow escape from the pursuivants in the house of Mrs. Line, he pursued his missionary labors till he was thus arrested. One night when on his priestly duties, he perceived a woman following him whom he knew as an apostate and a priest catcher, and therefore took shelter in the house of a Protestant. The woman raised a cry that a priest was within, and the man of the house delivered Mr. Page to the constables. He was taken to Newgate and tried before Justice Popham, who had condemned Mrs. Line, and knowing that Mr. Page had escaped from her house, at the next sessions, merely on account of his priesthood, condemned him to death, 1602.

"With the robe of justice He hath covered me, as a bridegroom decked with a crown, and a bride adorned with her jewels" (Is 61:10).

April 29

IN THE WAVES

Vens. Robert Anderton and Vens. William Marsden, Prs., 1586

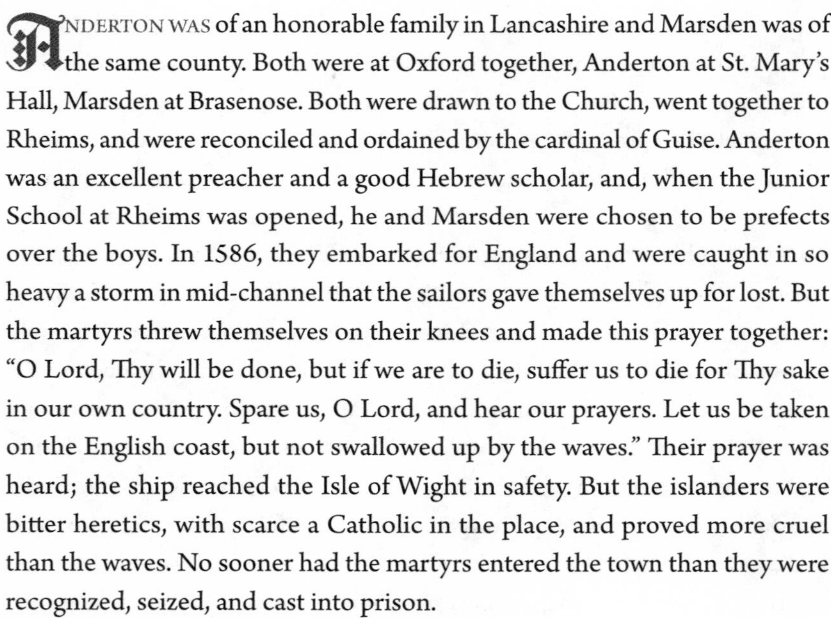

ANDERTON WAS of an honorable family in Lancashire and Marsden was of the same county. Both were at Oxford together, Anderton at St. Mary's Hall, Marsden at Brasenose. Both were drawn to the Church, went together to Rheims, and were reconciled and ordained by the cardinal of Guise. Anderton was an excellent preacher and a good Hebrew scholar, and, when the Junior School at Rheims was opened, he and Marsden were chosen to be prefects over the boys. In 1586, they embarked for England and were caught in so heavy a storm in mid-channel that the sailors gave themselves up for lost. But the martyrs threw themselves on their knees and made this prayer together: "O Lord, Thy will be done, but if we are to die, suffer us to die for Thy sake in our own country. Spare us, O Lord, and hear our prayers. Let us be taken on the English coast, but not swallowed up by the waves." Their prayer was heard; the ship reached the Isle of Wight in safety. But the islanders were bitter heretics, with scarce a Catholic in the place, and proved more cruel than the waves. No sooner had the martyrs entered the town than they were recognized, seized, and cast into prison.

"And they came to Him saying: Lord, save us, we perish" (Mt 8:25).

April 30

THE PHARISEES SILENCED

Ven. Robert Anderton, Pr., 1586

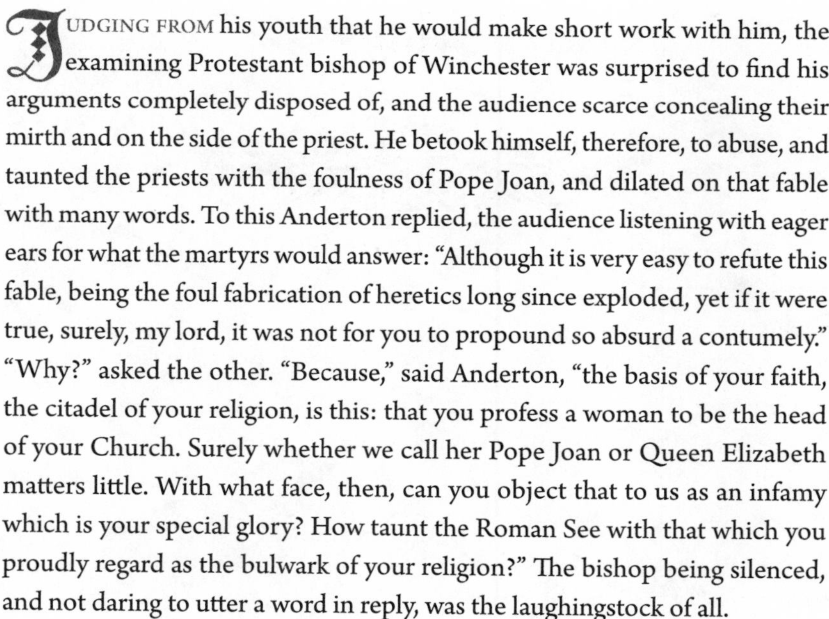

Judging from his youth that he would make short work with him, the examining Protestant bishop of Winchester was surprised to find his arguments completely disposed of, and the audience scarce concealing their mirth and on the side of the priest. He betook himself, therefore, to abuse, and taunted the priests with the foulness of Pope Joan, and dilated on that fable with many words. To this Anderton replied, the audience listening with eager ears for what the martyrs would answer: "Although it is very easy to refute this fable, being the foul fabrication of heretics long since exploded, yet if it were true, surely, my lord, it was not for you to propound so absurd a contumely." "Why?" asked the other. "Because," said Anderton, "the basis of your faith, the citadel of your religion, is this: that you profess a woman to be the head of your Church. Surely whether we call her Pope Joan or Queen Elizabeth matters little. With what face, then, can you object that to us as an infamy which is your special glory? How taunt the Roman See with that which you proudly regard as the bulwark of your religion?" The bishop being silenced, and not daring to utter a word in reply, was the laughingstock of all.

"And they could not answer Him to these things" (Lk 14:6).

May

May 1

THE WITNESS OF TRADITION

Bl. Richard Reynolds, Bridgettine, 1535

Interrogated by the chancellor why he had persisted in an opinion against which so many lords and bishops in Parliament and the whole realm had decreed, he replied: "I had intended to imitate our Lord Jesus Christ when He was questioned by Herod and not to answer. But since you compel me to clear both my own conscience and that of the bystanders, I say that if we propose to maintain opinions by proofs, testimonies, or reasons, mine will be far stronger than yours, because I have all the rest of Christendom in my favor. I dare even say all this kingdom, although the smaller part holds with you, for I am sure the larger part is at heart of our opinion, although outwardly, partly from fear and partly from hope, they profess to be of yours." On this he was commanded by the secretary, under the heaviest penalties of the law, to declare who held with him. He replied: "All good men of the kingdom hold with me." He added: "As to proofs of dead witnesses, I have in my favor all the general councils, all the historians, the holy Doctors of the Church for the last fifteen hundred years, especially St. Ambrose, St. Jerome, St. Augustine, and St. Gregory."

"Remove not the ancient landmarks which thy fathers have set" (Prv 22:28).

* *Reynolds was canonized by Pope Paul VI on 25 October 1970.*

May 2

MASS OF THE HOLY GHOST

Bl. John Houghton, Carthusian, 1535

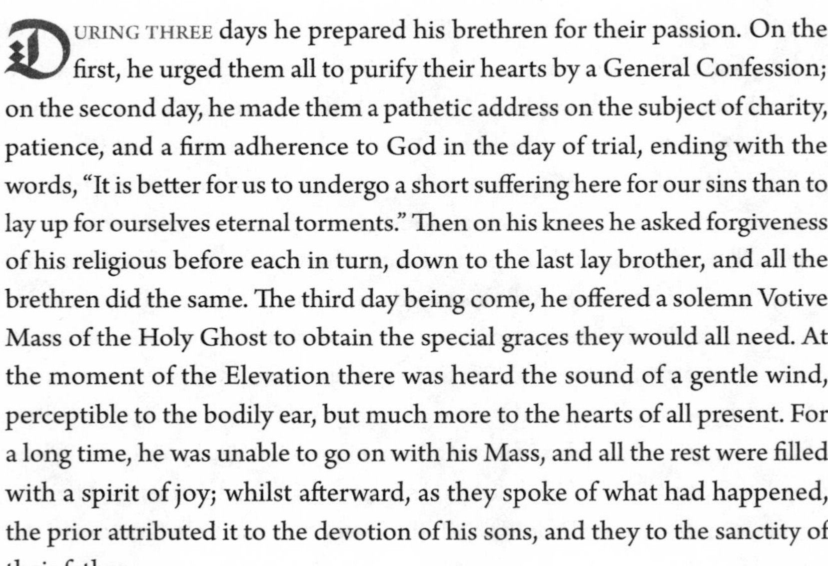

DURING THREE days he prepared his brethren for their passion. On the first, he urged them all to purify their hearts by a General Confession; on the second day, he made them a pathetic address on the subject of charity, patience, and a firm adherence to God in the day of trial, ending with the words, "It is better for us to undergo a short suffering here for our sins than to lay up for ourselves eternal torments." Then on his knees he asked forgiveness of his religious before each in turn, down to the last lay brother, and all the brethren did the same. The third day being come, he offered a solemn Votive Mass of the Holy Ghost to obtain the special graces they would all need. At the moment of the Elevation there was heard the sound of a gentle wind, perceptible to the bodily ear, but much more to the hearts of all present. For a long time, he was unable to go on with his Mass, and all the rest were filled with a spirit of joy; whilst afterward, as they spoke of what had happened, the prior attributed it to the devotion of his sons, and they to the sanctity of their father.

"The Spirit also helpeth our infirmity" (Rom 8:26).

* *Houghton was canonized by Pope Paul VI on 25 October 1970.*

May 3

THE SEAL OF CONFESSION

✠ Fr. Henry Garnet, S. J., 1606

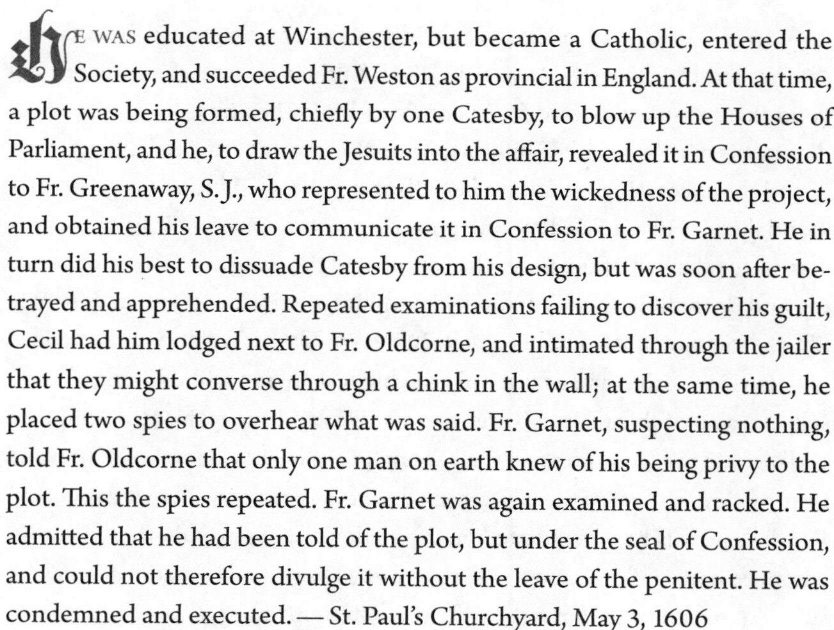

HE WAS educated at Winchester, but became a Catholic, entered the Society, and succeeded Fr. Weston as provincial in England. At that time, a plot was being formed, chiefly by one Catesby, to blow up the Houses of Parliament, and he, to draw the Jesuits into the affair, revealed it in Confession to Fr. Greenaway, S. J., who represented to him the wickedness of the project, and obtained his leave to communicate it in Confession to Fr. Garnet. He in turn did his best to dissuade Catesby from his design, but was soon after betrayed and apprehended. Repeated examinations failing to discover his guilt, Cecil had him lodged next to Fr. Oldcorne, and intimated through the jailer that they might converse through a chink in the wall; at the same time, he placed two spies to overhear what was said. Fr. Garnet, suspecting nothing, told Fr. Oldcorne that only one man on earth knew of his being privy to the plot. This the spies repeated. Fr. Garnet was again examined and racked. He admitted that he had been told of the plot, but under the seal of Confession, and could not therefore divulge it without the leave of the penitent. He was condemned and executed. — St. Paul's Churchyard, May 3, 1606

"Give not that which is holy to dogs" (Mt 7:6).

May 4

HOLY WRATH

✠ Bl. John Haile, Pr., 1535

FELLOW OF King's College, Cambridge, vicar of Chelmsford, he was promoted to Isleworth, August 13, 1521. Little is known of his history beyond that he was respected for his edifying life. When in 1533, Henry repudiating his marriage with Catherine, Anne Boleyn was crowned Queen, June 2, and the succession settled on her offspring, the aged vicar was grievously scandalized. He confided to a neighboring priest, Fern of Teddington, his sorrow for the evil of the times; he reprobated the King's cruelty in oppressing and despoiling the Church, declared him a heretic, denounced his vile life and vicious court, and his unfaithfulness to Catherine, and characterized his marriage with Anne as not only the highest shame and undoing of himself, but also of this realm. "Three parts of England are against the King," he added, "and the Commons see well enough a sufficient cause of rebellion and insurrection, and we of the Church shall never live merrily till that day come." For these words he was indicted on the evidence of Fern and other priests in whom he had confided, and was executed at Tyburn, and is beatified as having suffered for the Faith in resisting the royal supremacy.

"With zeal have I been zealous for the Lord of Hosts, because the children of Israel have forsaken Thy covenant, have destroyed Thy altars and slain Thy prophets" (3 Kgs 19:14).

May 5

THE VOICE OF THE BRIDEGROOM

Bls. Houghton, Lawrence, and Webster, Carthusians, 1535

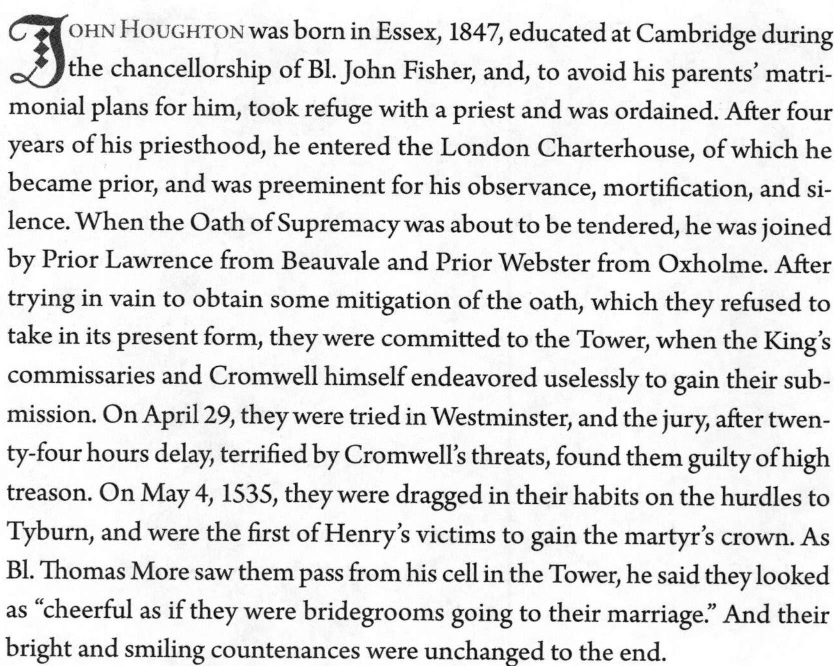

JOHN HOUGHTON was born in Essex, 1847, educated at Cambridge during the chancellorship of Bl. John Fisher, and, to avoid his parents' matrimonial plans for him, took refuge with a priest and was ordained. After four years of his priesthood, he entered the London Charterhouse, of which he became prior, and was preeminent for his observance, mortification, and silence. When the Oath of Supremacy was about to be tendered, he was joined by Prior Lawrence from Beauvale and Prior Webster from Oxholme. After trying in vain to obtain some mitigation of the oath, which they refused to take in its present form, they were committed to the Tower, when the King's commissaries and Cromwell himself endeavored uselessly to gain their submission. On April 29, they were tried in Westminster, and the jury, after twenty-four hours delay, terrified by Cromwell's threats, found them guilty of high treason. On May 4, 1535, they were dragged in their habits on the hurdles to Tyburn, and were the first of Henry's victims to gain the martyr's crown. As Bl. Thomas More saw them pass from his cell in the Tower, he said they looked as "cheerful as if they were bridegrooms going to their marriage." And their bright and smiling countenances were unchanged to the end.

"The friend of the Bridegroom, who standeth and heareth Him, rejoiceth with joy because of the Bridegroom's voice" (Jn 3:29).

May 6

A MODEL OF THE FLOCK

Bl. Richard Reynolds, Bridgettine, 1535

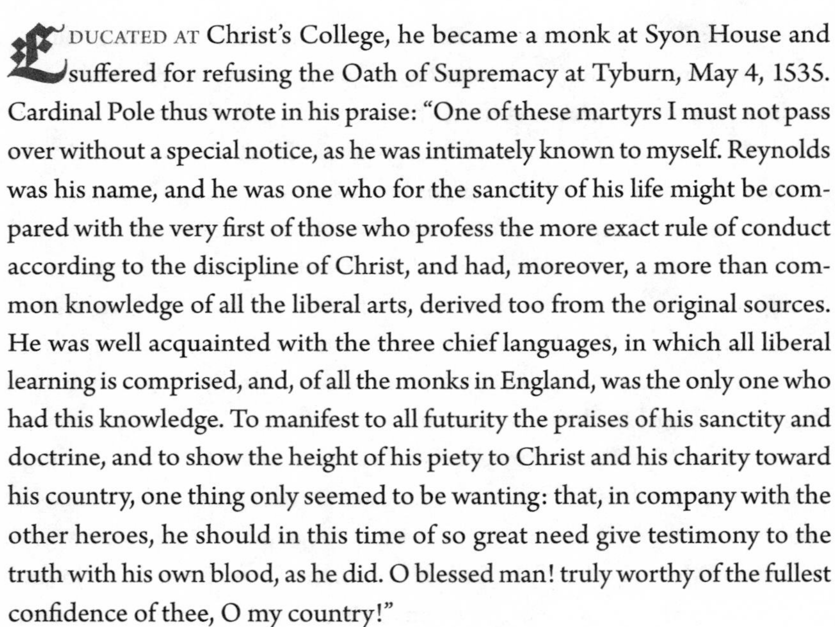

EDUCATED AT Christ's College, he became a monk at Syon House and suffered for refusing the Oath of Supremacy at Tyburn, May 4, 1535. Cardinal Pole thus wrote in his praise: "One of these martyrs I must not pass over without a special notice, as he was intimately known to myself. Reynolds was his name, and he was one who for the sanctity of his life might be compared with the very first of those who profess the more exact rule of conduct according to the discipline of Christ, and had, moreover, a more than common knowledge of all the liberal arts, derived too from the original sources. He was well acquainted with the three chief languages, in which all liberal learning is comprised, and, of all the monks in England, was the only one who had this knowledge. To manifest to all futurity the praises of his sanctity and doctrine, and to show the height of his piety to Christ and his charity toward his country, one thing only seemed to be wanting: that, in company with the other heroes, he should in this time of so great need give testimony to the truth with his own blood, as he did. O blessed man! truly worthy of the fullest confidence of thee, O my country!"

"Being made a pattern of the flock from the heart" (1 Pt 5:3).

May 7

HOLY FEAR

Bl. Thomas Cottam, Pr., 1582

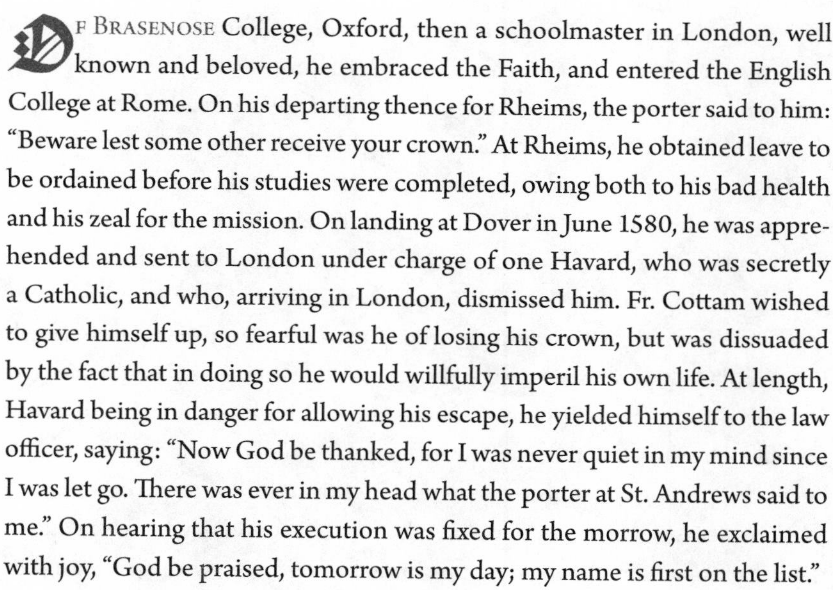

Of Brasenose College, Oxford, then a schoolmaster in London, well known and beloved, he embraced the Faith, and entered the English College at Rome. On his departing thence for Rheims, the porter said to him: "Beware lest some other receive your crown." At Rheims, he obtained leave to be ordained before his studies were completed, owing both to his bad health and his zeal for the mission. On landing at Dover in June 1580, he was apprehended and sent to London under charge of one Havard, who was secretly a Catholic, and who, arriving in London, dismissed him. Fr. Cottam wished to give himself up, so fearful was he of losing his crown, but was dissuaded by the fact that in doing so he would willfully imperil his own life. At length, Havard being in danger for allowing his escape, he yielded himself to the law officer, saying: "Now God be thanked, for I was never quiet in my mind since I was let go. There was ever in my head what the porter at St. Andrews said to me." On hearing that his execution was fixed for the morrow, he exclaimed with joy, "God be praised, tomorrow is my day; my name is first on the list."

"The fear of the Lord is honor and glory and gladness and a crown of joy" (Ecclus 1:11).

May 8

A GARMENT OF CAMEL'S HAIR

Bl. Thomas Cottam, Pr., 1582

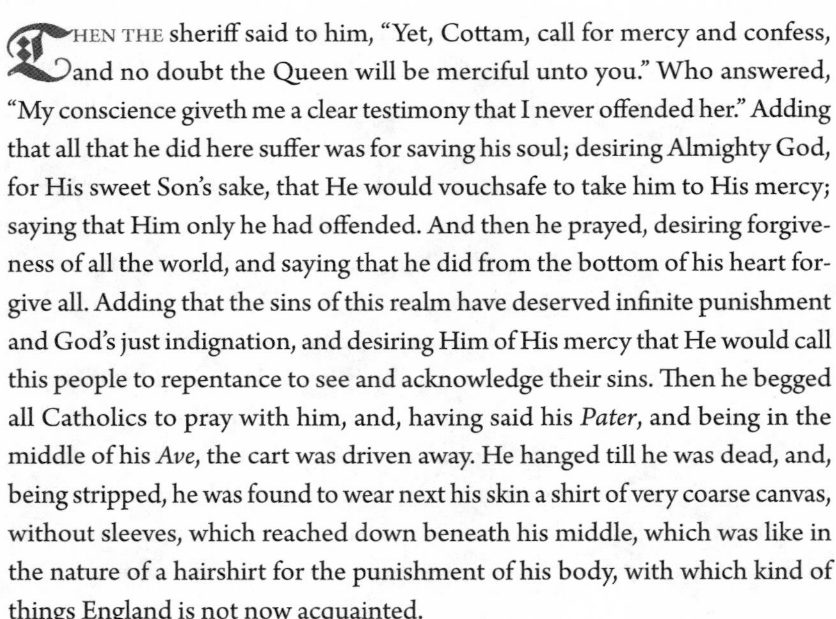

THEN THE sheriff said to him, "Yet, Cottam, call for mercy and confess, and no doubt the Queen will be merciful unto you." Who answered, "My conscience giveth me a clear testimony that I never offended her." Adding that all that he did here suffer was for saving his soul; desiring Almighty God, for His sweet Son's sake, that He would vouchsafe to take him to His mercy; saying that Him only he had offended. And then he prayed, desiring forgiveness of all the world, and saying that he did from the bottom of his heart forgive all. Adding that the sins of this realm have deserved infinite punishment and God's just indignation, and desiring Him of His mercy that He would call this people to repentance to see and acknowledge their sins. Then he begged all Catholics to pray with him, and, having said his *Pater,* and being in the middle of his *Ave,* the cart was driven away. He hanged till he was dead, and, being stripped, he was found to wear next his skin a shirt of very coarse canvas, without sleeves, which reached down beneath his middle, which was like in the nature of a hairshirt for the punishment of his body, with which kind of things England is not now acquainted.

"Those who are Christ's have crucified the flesh with its vices and concupiscences" (Gal 5:24).

May 9

A JOYFUL COUNTENANCE

✠ Bl. Thomas Pickering, O. S. B., 1679

HE WAS a professed lay brother in the Benedictine Monastery at Douay, and was apprehended at the beginning of the Oates Plot. Oates and Bedloe swore that Pickering and Grove were appointed to kill the King, the latter receiving £15,000, the former, being a priest, thirty thousand Masses. Pickering, they swore, had made three attempts on the King's life in St. James's Park; at the first, the flint of the pistol was loose; at the second, there was no powder; at the third, no bullets. Both prisoners absolutely denied the story, and Pickering swore he had never fired a pistol in his life. He was condemned with Ireland and Grove, but reprieved till May 9. At his execution, he expressed great joy at giving his life for God and religion, that being his only fault. Taxed with being a priest, he replied, with a smile, "No, I am only a lay brother." At the moment of his hanging, he was called upon again to confess his fault, at which, pulling up his cap and showing his innocent, smiling countenance, he said, "Is this the face of a dying criminal?" And so he went with a smile to his God, the most harmless of men, the most unlikely, and the most unfit for an attempt to murder. He suffered at Tyburn, May 9, 1679.

"The light of Thy countenance, O Lord, is signed upon us: Thou hast given gladness in my heart" (Ps 4:7).

* *Pickering was beatified by Pope Pius XI on 15 December 1929.*

May 10

THE TRUE PLOTTERS

Bl. Richard Newport, Pr., 1612

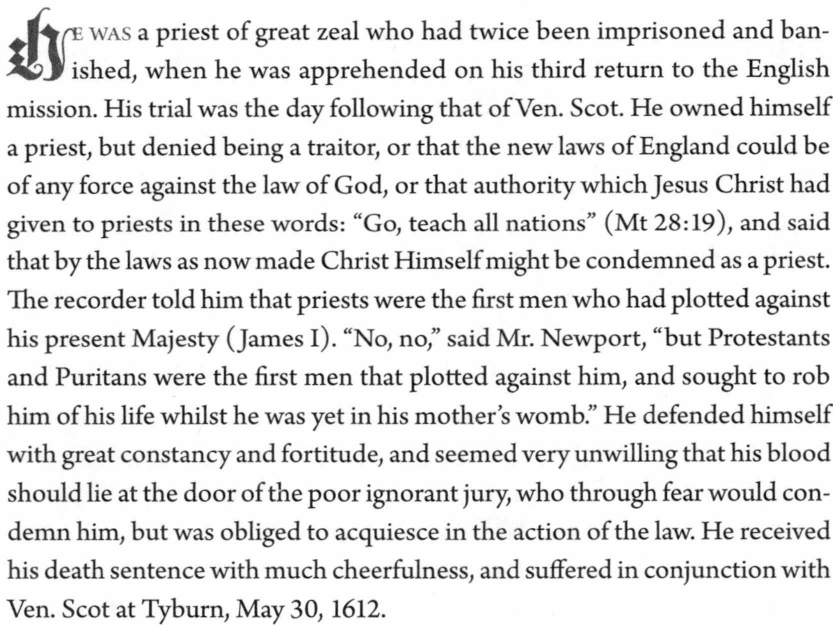

HE WAS a priest of great zeal who had twice been imprisoned and banished, when he was apprehended on his third return to the English mission. His trial was the day following that of Ven. Scot. He owned himself a priest, but denied being a traitor, or that the new laws of England could be of any force against the law of God, or that authority which Jesus Christ had given to priests in these words: "Go, teach all nations" (Mt 28:19), and said that by the laws as now made Christ Himself might be condemned as a priest. The recorder told him that priests were the first men who had plotted against his present Majesty (James I). "No, no," said Mr. Newport, "but Protestants and Puritans were the first men that plotted against him, and sought to rob him of his life whilst he was yet in his mother's womb." He defended himself with great constancy and fortitude, and seemed very unwilling that his blood should lie at the door of the poor ignorant jury, who through fear would condemn him, but was obliged to acquiesce in the action of the law. He received his death sentence with much cheerfulness, and suffered in conjunction with Ven. Scot at Tyburn, May 30, 1612.

"If thou release this man, thou art not Caesar's friend" (Jn 19:12).

May 11

A VIOLATED CLOISTER

✠ Bls. John Rochester and John Walworth, Carthusians, 1537

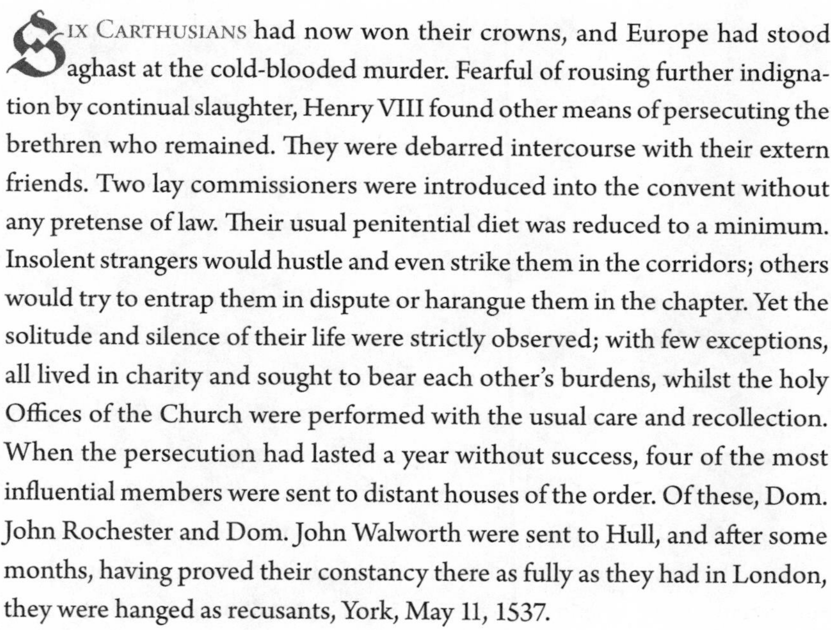

Six Carthusians had now won their crowns, and Europe had stood aghast at the cold-blooded murder. Fearful of rousing further indignation by continual slaughter, Henry VIII found other means of persecuting the brethren who remained. They were debarred intercourse with their extern friends. Two lay commissioners were introduced into the convent without any pretense of law. Their usual penitential diet was reduced to a minimum. Insolent strangers would hustle and even strike them in the corridors; others would try to entrap them in dispute or harangue them in the chapter. Yet the solitude and silence of their life were strictly observed; with few exceptions, all lived in charity and sought to bear each other's burdens, whilst the holy Offices of the Church were performed with the usual care and recollection. When the persecution had lasted a year without success, four of the most influential members were sent to distant houses of the order. Of these, Dom. John Rochester and Dom. John Walworth were sent to Hull, and after some months, having proved their constancy there as fully as they had in London, they were hanged as recusants, York, May 11, 1537.

"The city of the sanctuary has become a desert, Sion is made a desert, Jerusalem is desolate" (Is 64:10).

May 12

CALLED BY NAME

Bl. John Stone, Augustinian, 1538

HE BELONGED to the Convent of the Augustinian Friars, which had been founded in the parish of St. George in Canterbury in 1325 during the reign of Edward III. The house had produced a well-known ecclesiastical writer, the learned John Copgrave, but its honor culminated in being the home of Bl. John. For resisting the King's spiritual supremacy, he was thrown into prison, and Nicholas Harpsfield, archdeacon of Canterbury, his intimate friend, under the name of Alan Cope, records the following event as having occurred during his confinement: "When he was offering fervent prayer to God after an uninterrupted fast of three days, he heard a voice, but seeing no one, calling him by name and exhorting him to be of good courage and suffer with constancy for the opinions he had professed. This heavenly message so much renewed his fervor that no persuasions or terrors could disturb his devotion. No details of his martyrdom finally reached us, but the Corporation of Canterbury account book gives the items of the expenses incurred for the gallows, the carpenter, the hurdle and horse, the halters, and the executioner — the implements of his passion hallowed now by his holy blood."

"Speak, Lord, for Thy servant heareth" (1 Kgs 3:10).

* *Stone was canonized by Pope Paul VI on 25 October 1970.*

May 13

A ROYAL PENITENT

Catherine of Aragon to Bl. John Forest, O. S. F. (1)

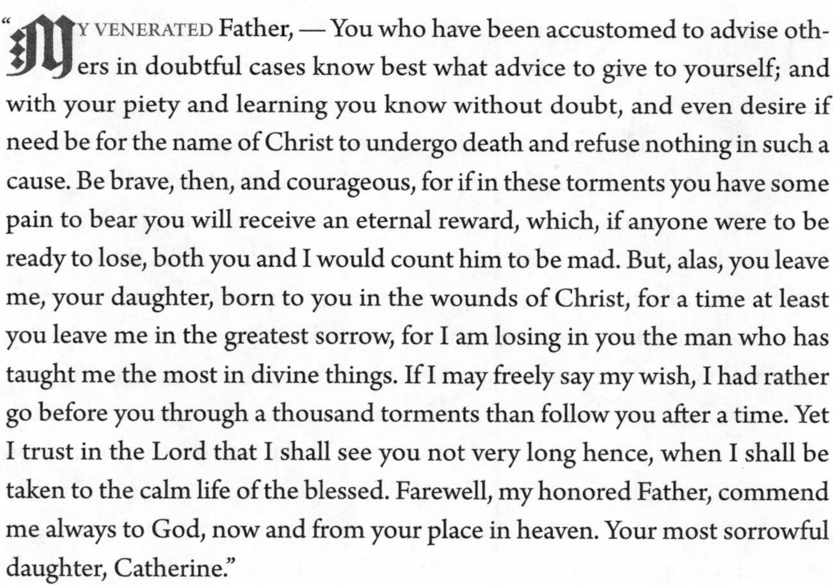

"My venerated Father, — You who have been accustomed to advise others in doubtful cases know best what advice to give to yourself; and with your piety and learning you know without doubt, and even desire if need be for the name of Christ to undergo death and refuse nothing in such a cause. Be brave, then, and courageous, for if in these torments you have some pain to bear you will receive an eternal reward, which, if anyone were to be ready to lose, both you and I would count him to be mad. But, alas, you leave me, your daughter, born to you in the wounds of Christ, for a time at least you leave me in the greatest sorrow, for I am losing in you the man who has taught me the most in divine things. If I may freely say my wish, I had rather go before you through a thousand torments than follow you after a time. Yet I trust in the Lord that I shall see you not very long hence, when I shall be taken to the calm life of the blessed. Farewell, my honored Father, commend me always to God, now and from your place in heaven. Your most sorrowful daughter, Catherine."

"Whither thou goest, I will go; and where thou dwellest, I will dwell; thy people shall be my people, and thy God my God" (Ru 1:16).

May 14

ONE ONLY GOSPEL

Bl. John Forest, O. S. F., to Queen Catherine (2)

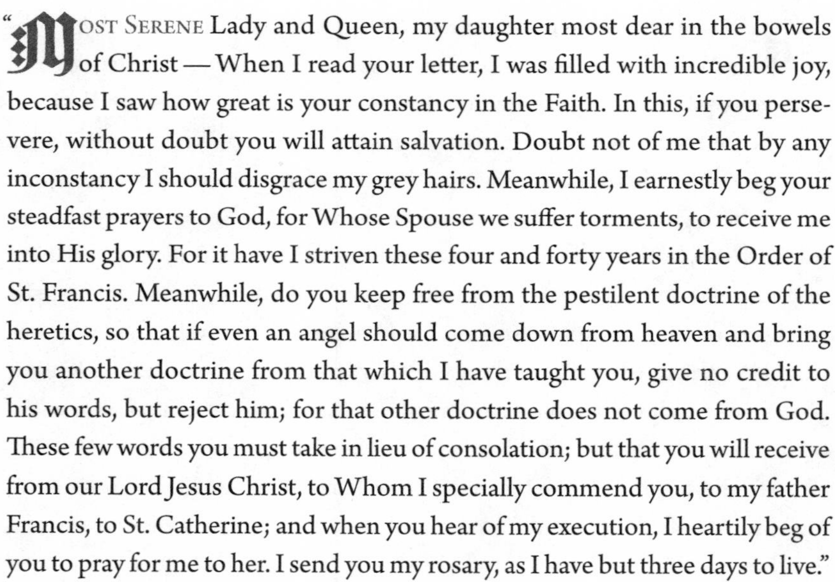

"Most Serene Lady and Queen, my daughter most dear in the bowels of Christ—When I read your letter, I was filled with incredible joy, because I saw how great is your constancy in the Faith. In this, if you persevere, without doubt you will attain salvation. Doubt not of me that by any inconstancy I should disgrace my grey hairs. Meanwhile, I earnestly beg your steadfast prayers to God, for Whose Spouse we suffer torments, to receive me into His glory. For it have I striven these four and forty years in the Order of St. Francis. Meanwhile, do you keep free from the pestilent doctrine of the heretics, so that if even an angel should come down from heaven and bring you another doctrine from that which I have taught you, give no credit to his words, but reject him; for that other doctrine does not come from God. These few words you must take in lieu of consolation; but that you will receive from our Lord Jesus Christ, to Whom I specially commend you, to my father Francis, to St. Catherine; and when you hear of my execution, I heartily beg of you to pray for me to her. I send you my rosary, as I have but three days to live."

"But though we or an angel from heaven preach a gospel to you besides that which we have preached to you, let him be anathema" (Gal 1:8).

RICHARD THIRKELL

"Guarded by the sheriff and his men"

May 15

POINTS IN CONTROVERSY

Bl. Richard Thirkell, Pr., 1583

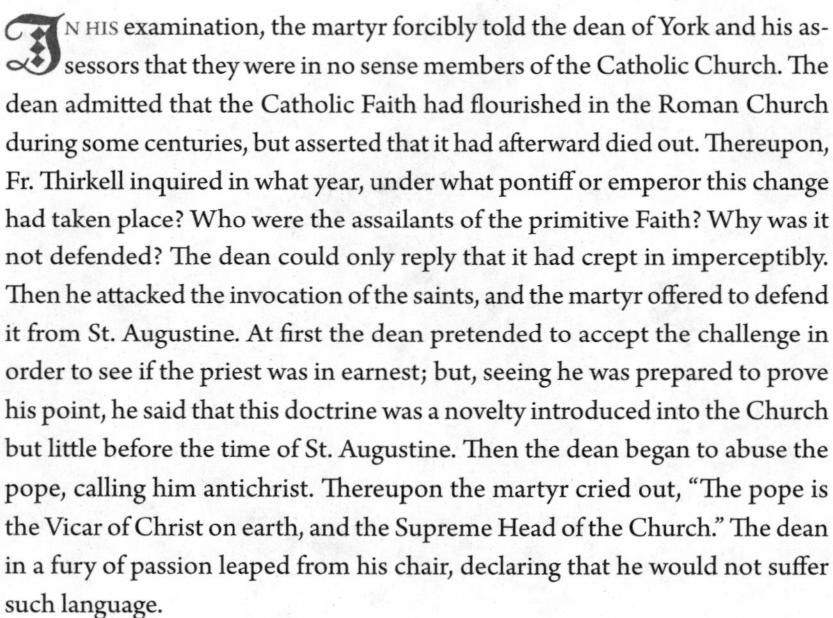

In his examination, the martyr forcibly told the dean of York and his assessors that they were in no sense members of the Catholic Church. The dean admitted that the Catholic Faith had flourished in the Roman Church during some centuries, but asserted that it had afterward died out. Thereupon, Fr. Thirkell inquired in what year, under what pontiff or emperor this change had taken place? Who were the assailants of the primitive Faith? Why was it not defended? The dean could only reply that it had crept in imperceptibly. Then he attacked the invocation of the saints, and the martyr offered to defend it from St. Augustine. At first the dean pretended to accept the challenge in order to see if the priest was in earnest; but, seeing he was prepared to prove his point, he said that this doctrine was a novelty introduced into the Church but little before the time of St. Augustine. Then the dean began to abuse the pope, calling him antichrist. Thereupon the martyr cried out, "The pope is the Vicar of Christ on earth, and the Supreme Head of the Church." The dean in a fury of passion leaped from his chair, declaring that he would not suffer such language.

"Carefully study to present thyself approved unto God,
a workman that needeth not to be ashamed, rightly
handling the word of truth" (2 Tm 2:15).

May 16

THE CONFESSIONS OF AN APOSTATE

Nichols to Bl. Luke Kirby, Pr., 1582

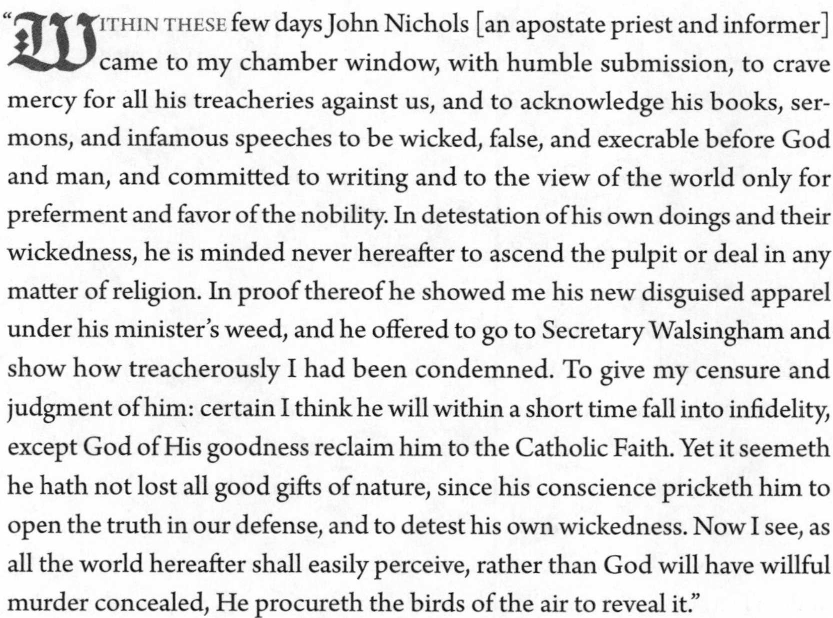

"WITHIN THESE few days John Nichols [an apostate priest and informer] came to my chamber window, with humble submission, to crave mercy for all his treacheries against us, and to acknowledge his books, sermons, and infamous speeches to be wicked, false, and execrable before God and man, and committed to writing and to the view of the world only for preferment and favor of the nobility. In detestation of his own doings and their wickedness, he is minded never hereafter to ascend the pulpit or deal in any matter of religion. In proof thereof he showed me his new disguised apparel under his minister's weed, and he offered to go to Secretary Walsingham and show how treacherously I had been condemned. To give my censure and judgment of him: certain I think he will within a short time fall into infidelity, except God of His goodness reclaim him to the Catholic Faith. Yet it seemeth he hath not lost all good gifts of nature, since his conscience pricketh him to open the truth in our defense, and to detest his own wickedness. Now I see, as all the world hereafter shall easily perceive, rather than God will have willful murder concealed, He procureth the birds of the air to reveal it."

"A man that is an apostate.... with a wicked heart deviseth evil, and at all times soweth discord" (Prv 6:12, 14).

* *Kirby was canonized by Pope Paul VI on 25 October 1970.*

May 17

DEVOTION TO RELICS

Mary Hutton, L., 1583

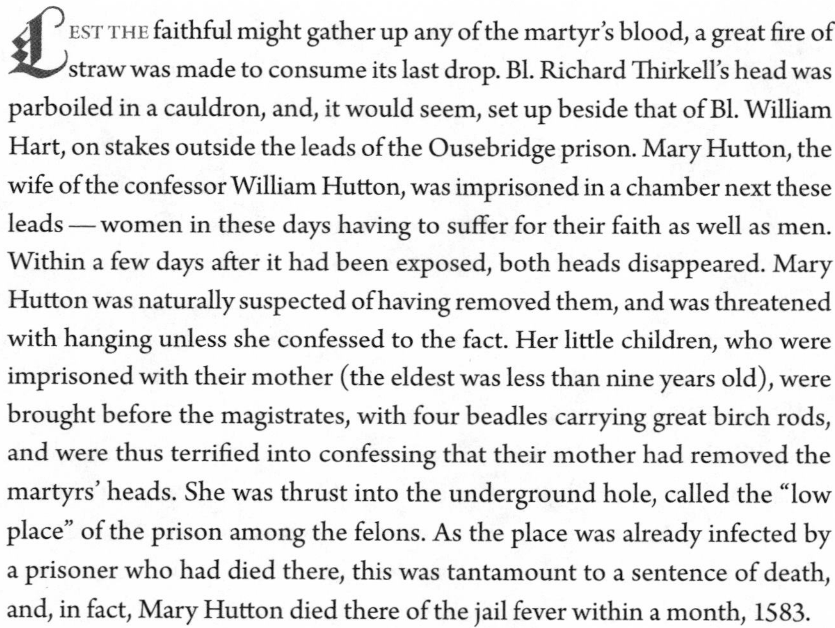

LEST THE faithful might gather up any of the martyr's blood, a great fire of straw was made to consume its last drop. Bl. Richard Thirkell's head was parboiled in a cauldron, and, it would seem, set up beside that of Bl. William Hart, on stakes outside the leads of the Ousebridge prison. Mary Hutton, the wife of the confessor William Hutton, was imprisoned in a chamber next these leads — women in these days having to suffer for their faith as well as men. Within a few days after it had been exposed, both heads disappeared. Mary Hutton was naturally suspected of having removed them, and was threatened with hanging unless she confessed to the fact. Her little children, who were imprisoned with their mother (the eldest was less than nine years old), were brought before the magistrates, with four beadles carrying great birch rods, and were thus terrified into confessing that their mother had removed the martyrs' heads. She was thrust into the underground hole, called the "low place" of the prison among the felons. As the place was already infected by a prisoner who had died there, this was tantamount to a sentence of death, and, in fact, Mary Hutton died there of the jail fever within a month, 1583.

"The Lord keepeth all their bones; not one of them shall be broken" (Ps 33:21).

QUEEN MARY
"Beheaded at Fotheringay"

May 18

THE MOTHER OF THE MACHABEES

Bl. Margaret Pole, W., 1541

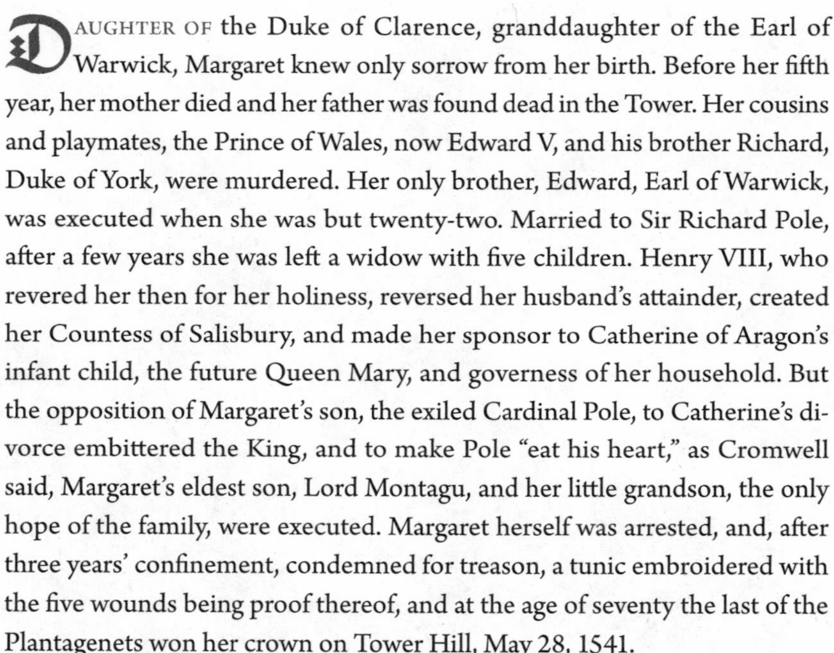

Daughter of the Duke of Clarence, granddaughter of the Earl of Warwick, Margaret knew only sorrow from her birth. Before her fifth year, her mother died and her father was found dead in the Tower. Her cousins and playmates, the Prince of Wales, now Edward V, and his brother Richard, Duke of York, were murdered. Her only brother, Edward, Earl of Warwick, was executed when she was but twenty-two. Married to Sir Richard Pole, after a few years she was left a widow with five children. Henry VIII, who revered her then for her holiness, reversed her husband's attainder, created her Countess of Salisbury, and made her sponsor to Catherine of Aragon's infant child, the future Queen Mary, and governess of her household. But the opposition of Margaret's son, the exiled Cardinal Pole, to Catherine's divorce embittered the King, and to make Pole "eat his heart," as Cromwell said, Margaret's eldest son, Lord Montagu, and her little grandson, the only hope of the family, were executed. Margaret herself was arrested, and, after three years' confinement, condemned for treason, a tunic embroidered with the five wounds being proof thereof, and at the age of seventy the last of the Plantagenets won her crown on Tower Hill, May 28, 1541.

"And last of all, after the sons, the mother also was consumed" (2 Mc 7:41).

May 19

COME QUICKLY

✠ Ven. Peter Wright, S.J., 1651

BORN OF poor but virtuous parents in Northamptonshire, he lost his father in his boyhood, and entered the service of a country lawyer. Living amongst Protestants he conformed, but after a while regained his faith, and, going abroad, was reconciled and became a Jesuit priest. He served first as chaplain to the English soldiers in Flanders, where Colonel Sir Henry Gage became his inseparable companion, and, after his death, in the civil war, he lived with the family of the Marquis of Winchester. There on Candlemas Day, 1651, as he was about to say Mass, the pursuivants entered the house. Fr. Wright escaped to the leads, but was speedily captured. Sentenced to death through the evidence of some apostate, he said joyfully, "God Almighty's holy name be blessed now and forevermore." During the three days before his execution, he confessed and consoled the troops of Catholics who visited him, and for his own part he made a General Confession of his life, celebrated Mass daily, and confided to his brother priest that he had never experienced such joy as at the approach of death. On Whitmonday morning, hearing the knocking at the grate, he took it as a summons from heaven, and said: "I come, sweet Jesus, I come." He suffered at Tyburn, May 19, 1651.

"Surely I come quickly: Amen. Come, Lord Jesus" (Apoc 22:20).

* *Wright was beatified by Pope Pius XI on 15 December 1929.*

ROBERT JOHNSON

"Thou art a traitor most obstinate"

May 20

PRAYERS IN LATIN

Bl. Robert Johnson, Pr., 1582

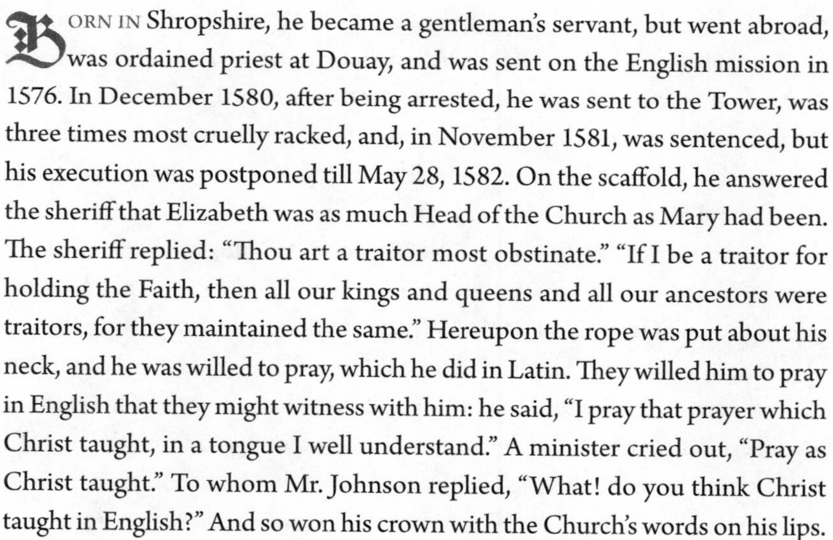

Born in Shropshire, he became a gentleman's servant, but went abroad, was ordained priest at Douay, and was sent on the English mission in 1576. In December 1580, after being arrested, he was sent to the Tower, was three times most cruelly racked, and, in November 1581, was sentenced, but his execution was postponed till May 28, 1582. On the scaffold, he answered the sheriff that Elizabeth was as much Head of the Church as Mary had been. The sheriff replied: "Thou art a traitor most obstinate." "If I be a traitor for holding the Faith, then all our kings and queens and all our ancestors were traitors, for they maintained the same." Hereupon the rope was put about his neck, and he was willed to pray, which he did in Latin. They willed him to pray in English that they might witness with him: he said, "I pray that prayer which Christ taught, in a tongue I well understand." A minister cried out, "Pray as Christ taught." To whom Mr. Johnson replied, "What! do you think Christ taught in English?" And so won his crown with the Church's words on his lips.

"And their children spoke half in the speech of Azotus, and could not speak the Jews' language, and they spoke according to the language of this and that people, and I chide them and laid my curse upon them" (2 Esd 13:24–25).

May 21

HUNG ON PRESUMPTION

Ven. William Scot, O. S. B., 1612

At Trinity Hall, Cambridge, he was converted by reading Catholic books, and became a Benedictine at Valladolid. He was several times in prison. At his first examination before the Protestant archbishop of Canterbury, George Abbot, a noted bigot, he refused the Oath of Allegiance, but neither confessed nor denied his priesthood. The chief proof brought for his being a priest was that, as he came by water from Gravesend to London, for safety's sake, he flung into the Thames a little bag containing his breviary, faculties, and some medals and crosses, which a fisherman, catching in his net, had carried to the said George Abbot. At Newgate, before the recorder, King Bishop of London, and others, he pleaded not guilty, and demanded legal proof that he was a priest, and he told the bishop it did not become one of his cloth to meddle in causes of life and death. The bishop urged against him the fact of a paper giving leave to say Mass above or below ground being found in the bag. "Giving leave," said Fr. Scot; "but to whom? Was my name there expressed? If not, Your Lordship might have kept that argument to yourself, with the rest of the things in the bag." Upon mere presumption he was sentenced and suffered, Tyburn, May 30, 1612.

"Thy princes are faithless companions of thieves; they all love bribes, they run after rewards" (Is 1:23).

* *Scot was beatified by Pope Pius XI on 15 December 1929.*

May 22

A LIVING HOLOCAUST

✠ Bl. John Forest, O. S. F., 1538

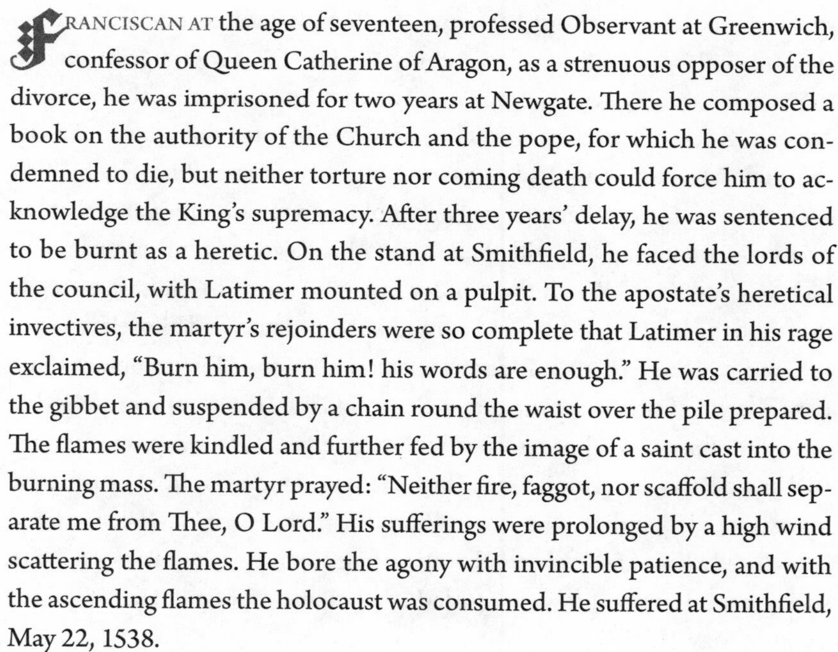

FRANCISCAN AT the age of seventeen, professed Observant at Greenwich, confessor of Queen Catherine of Aragon, as a strenuous opposer of the divorce, he was imprisoned for two years at Newgate. There he composed a book on the authority of the Church and the pope, for which he was condemned to die, but neither torture nor coming death could force him to acknowledge the King's supremacy. After three years' delay, he was sentenced to be burnt as a heretic. On the stand at Smithfield, he faced the lords of the council, with Latimer mounted on a pulpit. To the apostate's heretical invectives, the martyr's rejoinders were so complete that Latimer in his rage exclaimed, "Burn him, burn him! his words are enough." He was carried to the gibbet and suspended by a chain round the waist over the pile prepared. The flames were kindled and further fed by the image of a saint cast into the burning mass. The martyr prayed: "Neither fire, faggot, nor scaffold shall separate me from Thee, O Lord." His sufferings were prolonged by a high wind scattering the flames. He bore the agony with invincible patience, and with the ascending flames the holocaust was consumed. He suffered at Smithfield, May 22, 1538.

"And he went up and offered holocausts and
his own sacrifice" (4 Kgs 16:12).

May 23

PATIENCE UNDER CALUMNY

Bl. Lawrence Richardson, Pr., 1582

✠

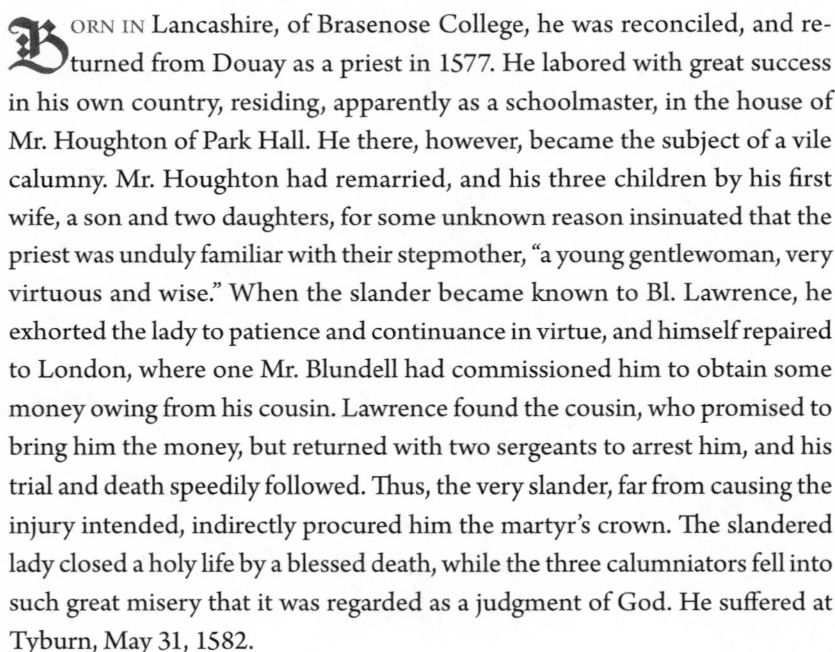

Born in Lancashire, of Brasenose College, he was reconciled, and returned from Douay as a priest in 1577. He labored with great success in his own country, residing, apparently as a schoolmaster, in the house of Mr. Houghton of Park Hall. He there, however, became the subject of a vile calumny. Mr. Houghton had remarried, and his three children by his first wife, a son and two daughters, for some unknown reason insinuated that the priest was unduly familiar with their stepmother, "a young gentlewoman, very virtuous and wise." When the slander became known to Bl. Lawrence, he exhorted the lady to patience and continuance in virtue, and himself repaired to London, where one Mr. Blundell had commissioned him to obtain some money owing from his cousin. Lawrence found the cousin, who promised to bring him the money, but returned with two sergeants to arrest him, and his trial and death speedily followed. Thus, the very slander, far from causing the injury intended, indirectly procured him the martyr's crown. The slandered lady closed a holy life by a blessed death, while the three calumniators fell into such great misery that it was regarded as a judgment of God. He suffered at Tyburn, May 31, 1582.

"I have done judgment and justice: give me not up to them that slander me. Uphold Thy servant unto good" (Ps 118:121–122).

May 24

A CATHOLIC CAVALIER

William Blundell, L., 1695

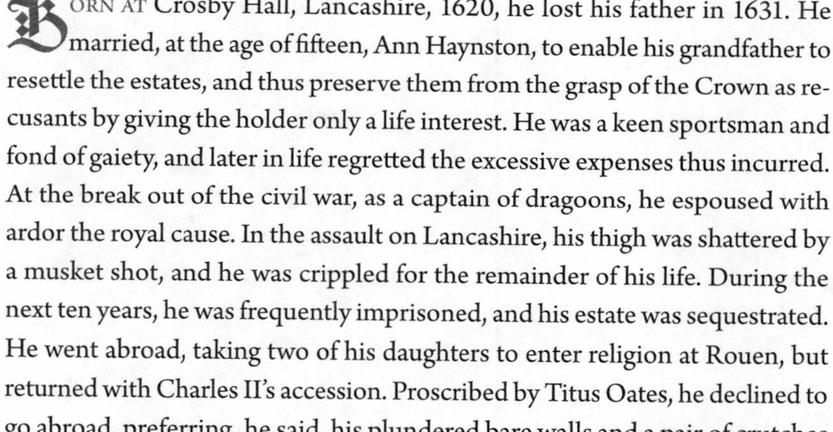

Born at Crosby Hall, Lancashire, 1620, he lost his father in 1631. He married, at the age of fifteen, Ann Haynston, to enable his grandfather to resettle the estates, and thus preserve them from the grasp of the Crown as recusants by giving the holder only a life interest. He was a keen sportsman and fond of gaiety, and later in life regretted the excessive expenses thus incurred. At the break out of the civil war, as a captain of dragoons, he espoused with ardor the royal cause. In the assault on Lancashire, his thigh was shattered by a musket shot, and he was crippled for the remainder of his life. During the next ten years, he was frequently imprisoned, and his estate was sequestrated. He went abroad, taking two of his daughters to enter religion at Rouen, but returned with Charles II's accession. Proscribed by Titus Oates, he declined to go abroad, preferring, he said, his plundered bare walls and a pair of crutches to an outlaw's life. In 1674, he was at the first imprisoned lest he should join James II in Ireland; and in 1695, when he was seventy-five years old, his arrest was attempted, but he was too crippled to be moved. That year he died, having sacrificed limbs, liberty, and goods for his faith and the throne.

"Fear God. Honor the king" (1 Pt 2:17).

May 25

REFUSING A CHALLENGE

William Blundell, L., 1695

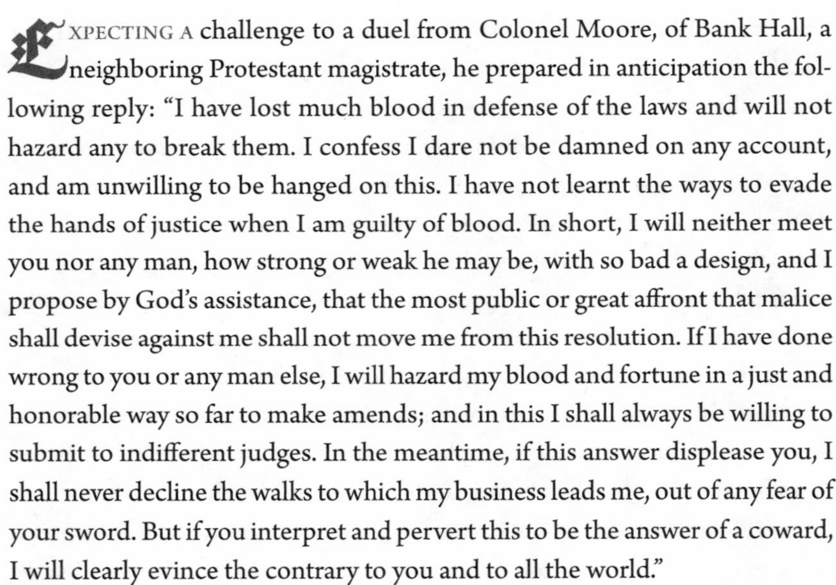

EXPECTING A challenge to a duel from Colonel Moore, of Bank Hall, a neighboring Protestant magistrate, he prepared in anticipation the following reply: "I have lost much blood in defense of the laws and will not hazard any to break them. I confess I dare not be damned on any account, and am unwilling to be hanged on this. I have not learnt the ways to evade the hands of justice when I am guilty of blood. In short, I will neither meet you nor any man, how strong or weak he may be, with so bad a design, and I propose by God's assistance, that the most public or great affront that malice shall devise against me shall not move me from this resolution. If I have done wrong to you or any man else, I will hazard my blood and fortune in a just and honorable way so far to make amends; and in this I shall always be willing to submit to indifferent judges. In the meantime, if this answer displease you, I shall never decline the walks to which my business leads me, out of any fear of your sword. But if you interpret and pervert this to be the answer of a coward, I will clearly evince the contrary to you and to all the world."

"Whosoever shall shed man's blood, his blood shall be shed" (Gn 9:6).

May 26

PRAISE AND THANKSGIVING

Bl. John Shert, Pr., 1582

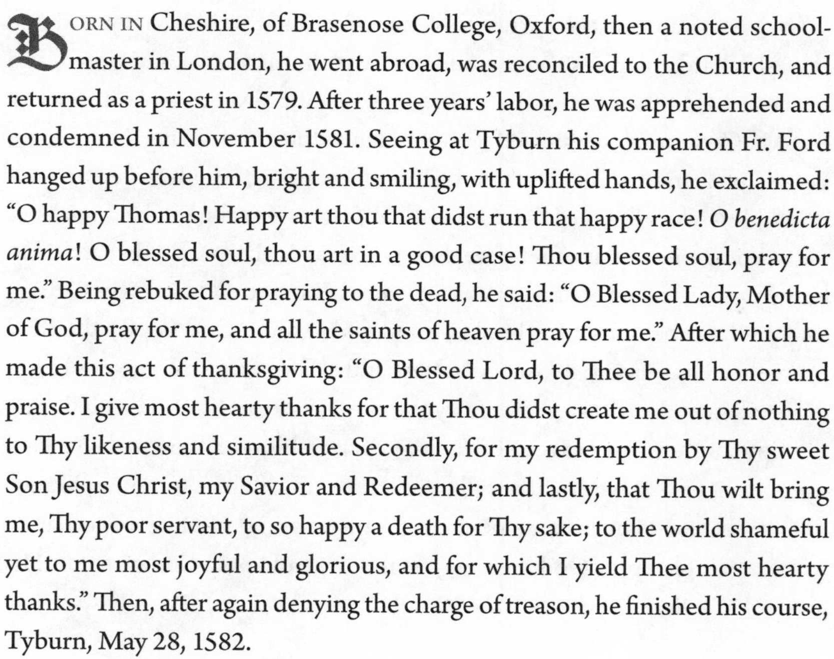

BORN IN Cheshire, of Brasenose College, Oxford, then a noted schoolmaster in London, he went abroad, was reconciled to the Church, and returned as a priest in 1579. After three years' labor, he was apprehended and condemned in November 1581. Seeing at Tyburn his companion Fr. Ford hanged up before him, bright and smiling, with uplifted hands, he exclaimed: "O happy Thomas! Happy art thou that didst run that happy race! *O benedicta anima*! O blessed soul, thou art in a good case! Thou blessed soul, pray for me." Being rebuked for praying to the dead, he said: "O Blessed Lady, Mother of God, pray for me, and all the saints of heaven pray for me." After which he made this act of thanksgiving: "O Blessed Lord, to Thee be all honor and praise. I give most hearty thanks for that Thou didst create me out of nothing to Thy likeness and similitude. Secondly, for my redemption by Thy sweet Son Jesus Christ, my Savior and Redeemer; and lastly, that Thou wilt bring me, Thy poor servant, to so happy a death for Thy sake; to the world shameful yet to me most joyful and glorious, and for which I yield Thee most hearty thanks." Then, after again denying the charge of treason, he finished his course, Tyburn, May 28, 1582.

"Offer to God the sacrifice of praise, and pay thy vows to the Most High" (Ps 49:14).

May 27

FATHER FORGIVE THEM

Bl. Thomas Cottam, 1582

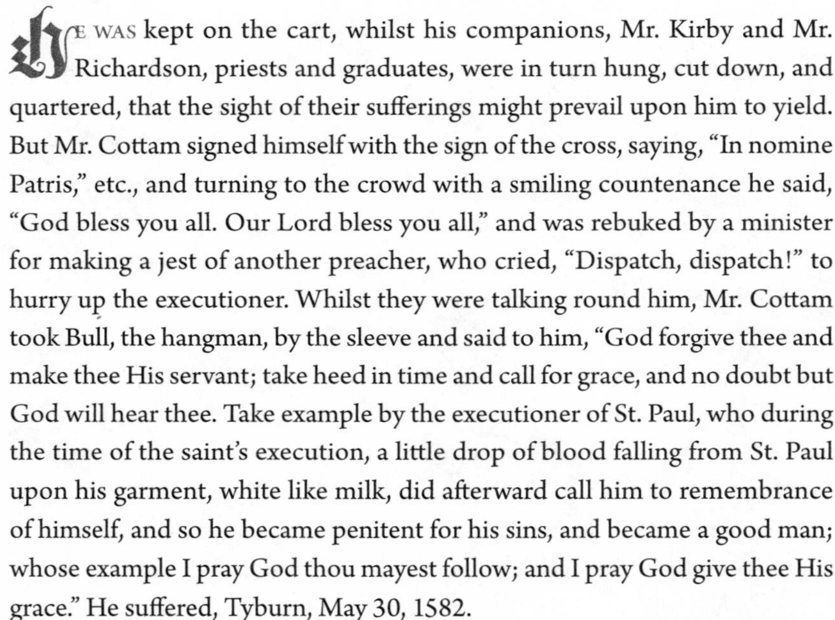

He was kept on the cart, whilst his companions, Mr. Kirby and Mr. Richardson, priests and graduates, were in turn hung, cut down, and quartered, that the sight of their sufferings might prevail upon him to yield. But Mr. Cottam signed himself with the sign of the cross, saying, "In nomine Patris," etc., and turning to the crowd with a smiling countenance he said, "God bless you all. Our Lord bless you all," and was rebuked by a minister for making a jest of another preacher, who cried, "Dispatch, dispatch!" to hurry up the executioner. Whilst they were talking round him, Mr. Cottam took Bull, the hangman, by the sleeve and said to him, "God forgive thee and make thee His servant; take heed in time and call for grace, and no doubt but God will hear thee. Take example by the executioner of St. Paul, who during the time of the saint's execution, a little drop of blood falling from St. Paul upon his garment, white like milk, did afterward call him to remembrance of himself, and so he became penitent for his sins, and became a good man; whose example I pray God thou mayest follow; and I pray God give thee His grace." He suffered, Tyburn, May 30, 1582.

"Father forgive them, for they know not what they do" (Lk 23:34).

May 28

THE SNARES OF THE PHARISEES

Bl. Thomas Ford, Pr., 1582

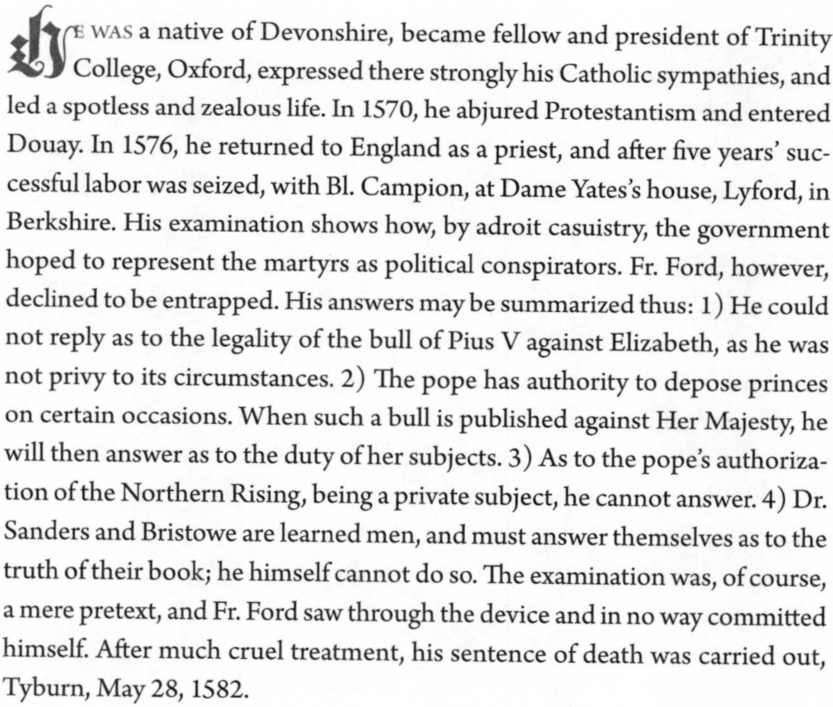

HE WAS a native of Devonshire, became fellow and president of Trinity College, Oxford, expressed there strongly his Catholic sympathies, and led a spotless and zealous life. In 1570, he abjured Protestantism and entered Douay. In 1576, he returned to England as a priest, and after five years' successful labor was seized, with Bl. Campion, at Dame Yates's house, Lyford, in Berkshire. His examination shows how, by adroit casuistry, the government hoped to represent the martyrs as political conspirators. Fr. Ford, however, declined to be entrapped. His answers may be summarized thus: 1) He could not reply as to the legality of the bull of Pius V against Elizabeth, as he was not privy to its circumstances. 2) The pope has authority to depose princes on certain occasions. When such a bull is published against Her Majesty, he will then answer as to the duty of her subjects. 3) As to the pope's authorization of the Northern Rising, being a private subject, he cannot answer. 4) Dr. Sanders and Bristowe are learned men, and must answer themselves as to the truth of their book; he himself cannot do so. The examination was, of course, a mere pretext, and Fr. Ford saw through the device and in no way committed himself. After much cruel treatment, his sentence of death was carried out, Tyburn, May 28, 1582.

"And the Pharisees watched . . . that they might find an accusation against Him" (Lk 6:7).

May 29

HOLY MASS AND MARTYRDOM

✠ Bl. Richard Thirkell, Pr., 1583

Born in Durham; after his ordination, in advanced age, at Douay in 1579, he exclaimed, "God alone knows how great a gift this is that hath been conferred upon me this day!" Holy Mass was his constant thought, and it produced in his soul such daily increase of divine love and heavenly courage that he desired nothing more than, in return for what Christ had done for him, to shed also his blood in Christ and for Christ. For eight whole years his prayers were that he might one day lay down his life for his faith, and this was at length granted him. He was apprehended and tried at York. He appeared at the bar a venerable old man in his priest's cassock, and acknowledged that he was a priest and had performed priestly functions. He was found guilty, and spent the night instructing the criminals and preparing them for death. On entering the court the next morning, he publicly blessed four Catholic prisoners there present, and a brave old woman who knelt to receive it defended his action by saying that as a minister of Christ he had the power to bless in His name. He received the sentence of death with great joy, and so finished his course, York, May 29, 1583.

"They overcame the dragon by the blood of the Lamb and by the word of the testimony, and they loved not their lives unto death" (Apoc 12:11).

May 30

LOVE OF THE CROSS

✠ Bl. William Filbie, Pr., 1582

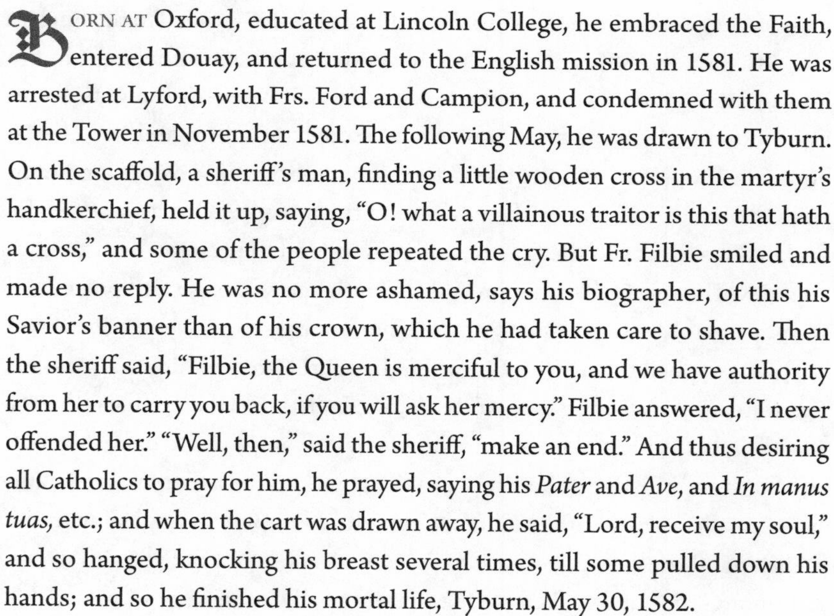

Born at Oxford, educated at Lincoln College, he embraced the Faith, entered Douay, and returned to the English mission in 1581. He was arrested at Lyford, with Frs. Ford and Campion, and condemned with them at the Tower in November 1581. The following May, he was drawn to Tyburn. On the scaffold, a sheriff's man, finding a little wooden cross in the martyr's handkerchief, held it up, saying, "O! what a villainous traitor is this that hath a cross," and some of the people repeated the cry. But Fr. Filbie smiled and made no reply. He was no more ashamed, says his biographer, of this his Savior's banner than of his crown, which he had taken care to shave. Then the sheriff said, "Filbie, the Queen is merciful to you, and we have authority from her to carry you back, if you will ask her mercy." Filbie answered, "I never offended her." "Well, then," said the sheriff, "make an end." And thus desiring all Catholics to pray for him, he prayed, saying his *Pater* and *Ave,* and *In manus tuas,* etc.; and when the cart was drawn away, he said, "Lord, receive my soul," and so hanged, knocking his breast several times, till some pulled down his hands; and so he finished his mortal life, Tyburn, May 30, 1582.

"And then shall appear the sign of the Son of Man in the heavens, and then shall all the tribes of the earth mourn" (Mt 24:30).

May 31

WISDOM IN SPEECH

Bl. Luke Kirby, Pr., 1582

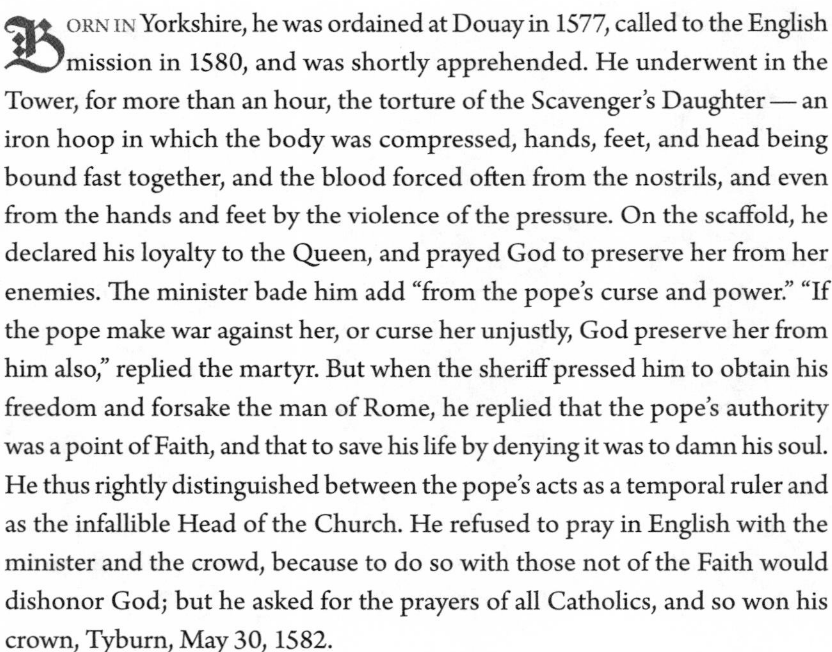

BORN IN Yorkshire, he was ordained at Douay in 1577, called to the English mission in 1580, and was shortly apprehended. He underwent in the Tower, for more than an hour, the torture of the Scavenger's Daughter — an iron hoop in which the body was compressed, hands, feet, and head being bound fast together, and the blood forced often from the nostrils, and even from the hands and feet by the violence of the pressure. On the scaffold, he declared his loyalty to the Queen, and prayed God to preserve her from her enemies. The minister bade him add "from the pope's curse and power." "If the pope make war against her, or curse her unjustly, God preserve her from him also," replied the martyr. But when the sheriff pressed him to obtain his freedom and forsake the man of Rome, he replied that the pope's authority was a point of Faith, and that to save his life by denying it was to damn his soul. He thus rightly distinguished between the pope's acts as a temporal ruler and as the infallible Head of the Church. He refused to pray in English with the minister and the crowd, because to do so with those not of the Faith would dishonor God; but he asked for the prayers of all Catholics, and so won his crown, Tyburn, May 30, 1582.

"O Lord, Thou wilt open my lips, and my mouth shall show forth Thy praise" (Ps 50:17).

June

June 1

REPARATION (1)

Bl. John Storey, L., 1571

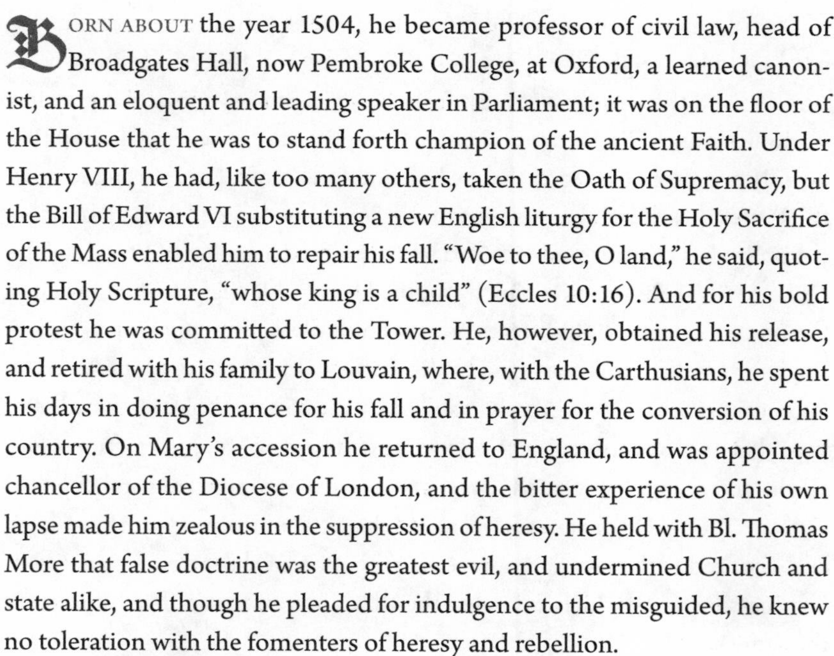

BORN ABOUT the year 1504, he became professor of civil law, head of Broadgates Hall, now Pembroke College, at Oxford, a learned canonist, and an eloquent and leading speaker in Parliament; it was on the floor of the House that he was to stand forth champion of the ancient Faith. Under Henry VIII, he had, like too many others, taken the Oath of Supremacy, but the Bill of Edward VI substituting a new English liturgy for the Holy Sacrifice of the Mass enabled him to repair his fall. "Woe to thee, O land," he said, quoting Holy Scripture, "whose king is a child" (Eccles 10:16). And for his bold protest he was committed to the Tower. He, however, obtained his release, and retired with his family to Louvain, where, with the Carthusians, he spent his days in doing penance for his fall and in prayer for the conversion of his country. On Mary's accession he returned to England, and was appointed chancellor of the Diocese of London, and the bitter experience of his own lapse made him zealous in the suppression of heresy. He held with Bl. Thomas More that false doctrine was the greatest evil, and undermined Church and state alike, and though he pleaded for indulgence to the misguided, he knew no toleration with the fomenters of heresy and rebellion.

"But where sin abounded, grace did more abound" (Rom 5:20).

June 2

REPARATION (2)

Bl. John Storey, L., 1571

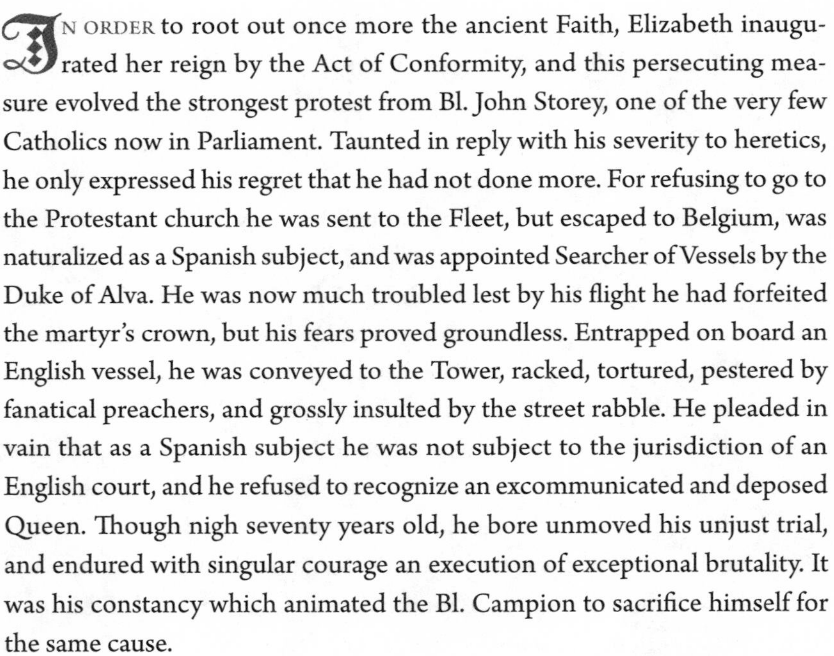

In order to root out once more the ancient Faith, Elizabeth inaugurated her reign by the Act of Conformity, and this persecuting measure evolved the strongest protest from Bl. John Storey, one of the very few Catholics now in Parliament. Taunted in reply with his severity to heretics, he only expressed his regret that he had not done more. For refusing to go to the Protestant church he was sent to the Fleet, but escaped to Belgium, was naturalized as a Spanish subject, and was appointed Searcher of Vessels by the Duke of Alva. He was now much troubled lest by his flight he had forfeited the martyr's crown, but his fears proved groundless. Entrapped on board an English vessel, he was conveyed to the Tower, racked, tortured, pestered by fanatical preachers, and grossly insulted by the street rabble. He pleaded in vain that as a Spanish subject he was not subject to the jurisdiction of an English court, and he refused to recognize an excommunicated and deposed Queen. Though nigh seventy years old, he bore unmoved his unjust trial, and endured with singular courage an execution of exceptional brutality. It was his constancy which animated the Bl. Campion to sacrifice himself for the same cause.

"Thou hast broken my bonds: I will sacrifice to Thee a sacrifice of praise" (Ps 115:16–17).

June 3

THE DIGNITY OF THE PRIESTHOOD

✠ Ven. Francis Ingleby, Pr., 1586

HE WAS the son of Sir John Ingleby, of Ripley, Yorkshire, and studied law in London. After making good way in his profession, he left the world, went to Rheims, was ordained priest, and returned to the English mission in 1584. He worked with great success in his own county, and it was for harboring Fr. Ingleby that Margaret Clitherow underwent her cruel martyrdom. Once when in company with Mr. Lassie, a Catholic gentleman, outside the bishop's palace at York, the latter knelt down to receive his blessing. The action was observed from the windows by two ministers, chaplains of the Protestant bishop, who could not understand paying such a mark of respect to one so poorly dressed. They therefore made inquiries and had him apprehended as a priest. At the council, when reproached as a gentleman of good birth for so far debasing himself as to become a priest, he replied that he made more account of his priesthood than of all other titles whatsoever. During his trial, they endeavored in vain to make him disclose what Catholics he had frequented, and they interrupted his speech on other matters with railings and blasphemies, so that he was never allowed to finish a sentence. He suffered, with great constancy, at York, June 3, 1586.

"And the glory which Thou hast given Me, I have given to them.... I in them, and Thou in Me" (Jn 17:22–23).

* *Ingleby was beatified by Pope John Paul II on 22 November 1987.*

June 4

WISDOM OF THE ANCIENTS

Bp. David Poole of Peterborough, 1568

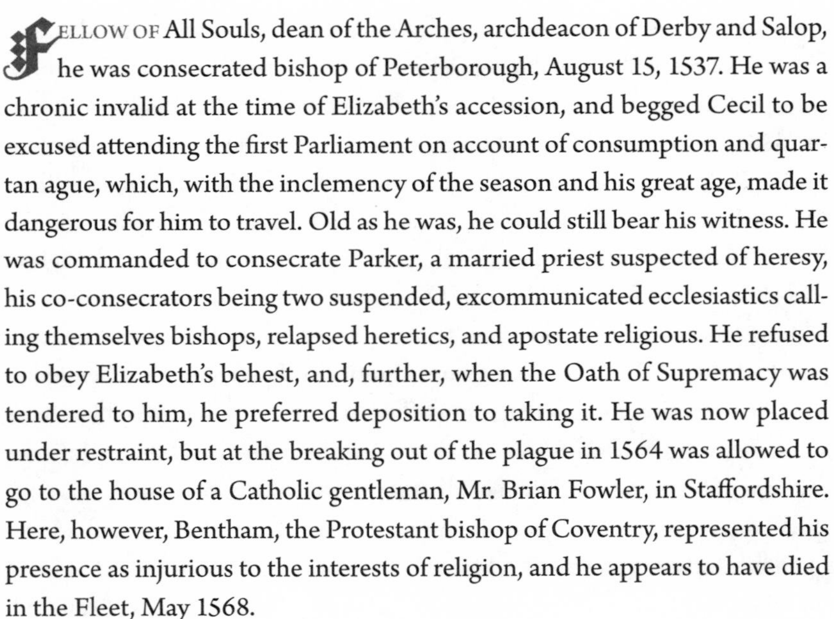

Fellow of All Souls, dean of the Arches, archdeacon of Derby and Salop, he was consecrated bishop of Peterborough, August 15, 1537. He was a chronic invalid at the time of Elizabeth's accession, and begged Cecil to be excused attending the first Parliament on account of consumption and quartan ague, which, with the inclemency of the season and his great age, made it dangerous for him to travel. Old as he was, he could still bear his witness. He was commanded to consecrate Parker, a married priest suspected of heresy, his co-consecrators being two suspended, excommunicated ecclesiastics calling themselves bishops, relapsed heretics, and apostate religious. He refused to obey Elizabeth's behest, and, further, when the Oath of Supremacy was tendered to him, he preferred deposition to taking it. He was now placed under restraint, but at the breaking out of the plague in 1564 was allowed to go to the house of a Catholic gentleman, Mr. Brian Fowler, in Staffordshire. Here, however, Bentham, the Protestant bishop of Coventry, represented his presence as injurious to the interests of religion, and he appears to have died in the Fleet, May 1568.

"Let not the discourse of the ancients escape thee ... for of them thou shalt learn understanding, and shalt give an answer in time of need" (Ecclus 8:11–12).

June 5

THE HOUSE OF MY GOD

✠ Fr. John Gray, O. S. F., 1579

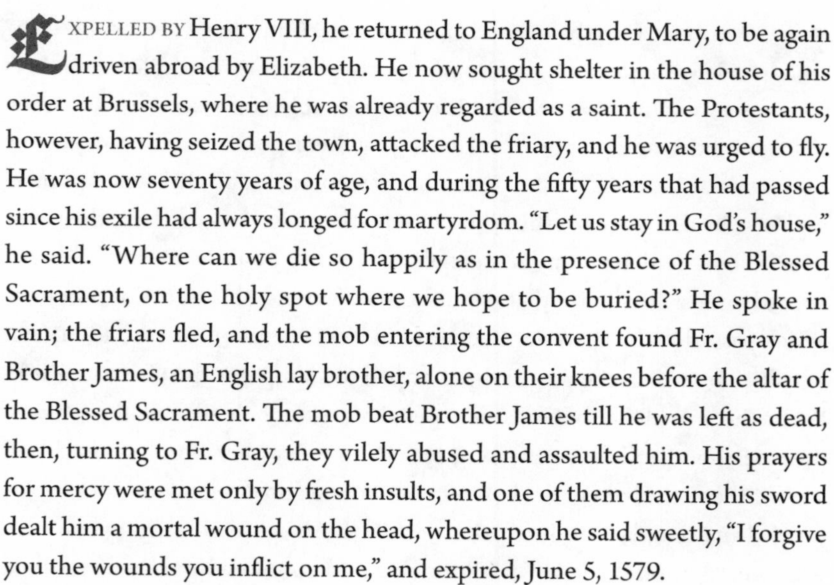

EXPELLED BY Henry VIII, he returned to England under Mary, to be again driven abroad by Elizabeth. He now sought shelter in the house of his order at Brussels, where he was already regarded as a saint. The Protestants, however, having seized the town, attacked the friary, and he was urged to fly. He was now seventy years of age, and during the fifty years that had passed since his exile had always longed for martyrdom. "Let us stay in God's house," he said. "Where can we die so happily as in the presence of the Blessed Sacrament, on the holy spot where we hope to be buried?" He spoke in vain; the friars fled, and the mob entering the convent found Fr. Gray and Brother James, an English lay brother, alone on their knees before the altar of the Blessed Sacrament. The mob beat Brother James till he was left as dead, then, turning to Fr. Gray, they vilely abused and assaulted him. His prayers for mercy were met only by fresh insults, and one of them drawing his sword dealt him a mortal wound on the head, whereupon he said sweetly, "I forgive you the wounds you inflict on me," and expired, June 5, 1579.

"I have chosen to be an abject in the house of my God, rather than to dwell in the tabernacles of sinners" (Ps 83:11).

June 6

A BOON OF THE PENAL LAWS

William Blundell, L., 1698

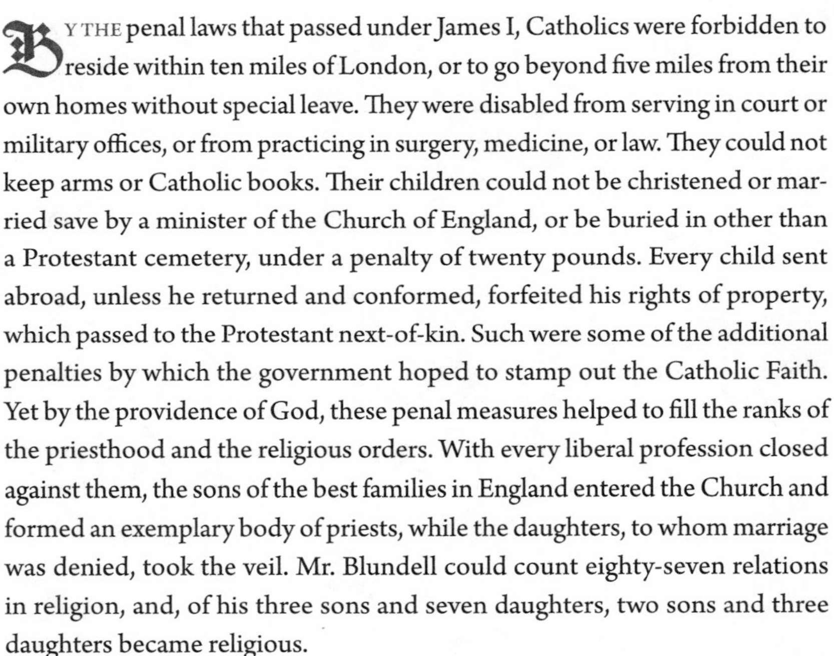

By the penal laws that passed under James I, Catholics were forbidden to reside within ten miles of London, or to go beyond five miles from their own homes without special leave. They were disabled from serving in court or military offices, or from practicing in surgery, medicine, or law. They could not keep arms or Catholic books. Their children could not be christened or married save by a minister of the Church of England, or be buried in other than a Protestant cemetery, under a penalty of twenty pounds. Every child sent abroad, unless he returned and conformed, forfeited his rights of property, which passed to the Protestant next-of-kin. Such were some of the additional penalties by which the government hoped to stamp out the Catholic Faith. Yet by the providence of God, these penal measures helped to fill the ranks of the priesthood and the religious orders. With every liberal profession closed against them, the sons of the best families in England entered the Church and formed an exemplary body of priests, while the daughters, to whom marriage was denied, took the veil. Mr. Blundell could count eighty-seven relations in religion, and, of his three sons and seven daughters, two sons and three daughters became religious.

"I called thee to curse my enemies, and thou on the contrary hast blessed them these three times" (Nm 24:10).

June 7

A PRIEST TO THE RESCUE

Bl. Richard Thirkell, Pr., 1583

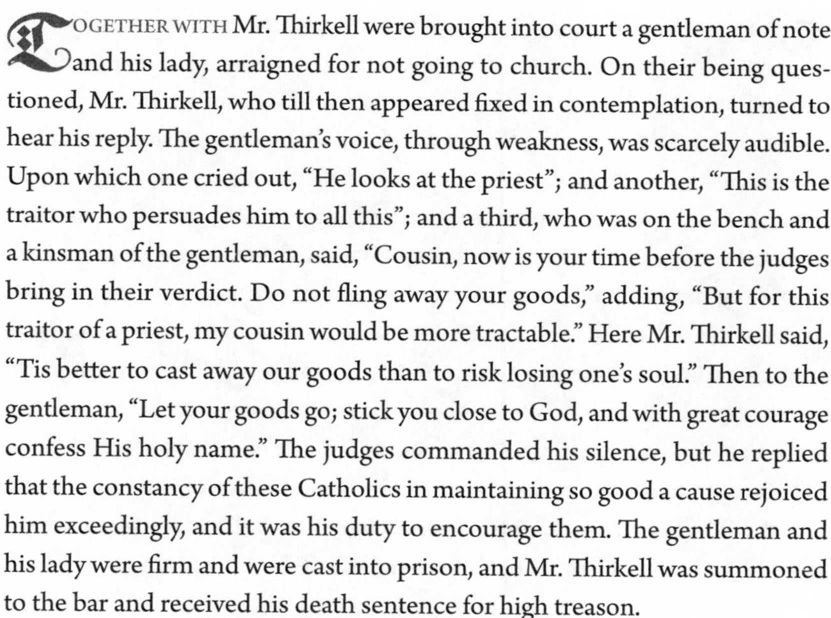

TOGETHER WITH Mr. Thirkell were brought into court a gentleman of note and his lady, arraigned for not going to church. On their being questioned, Mr. Thirkell, who till then appeared fixed in contemplation, turned to hear his reply. The gentleman's voice, through weakness, was scarcely audible. Upon which one cried out, "He looks at the priest"; and another, "This is the traitor who persuades him to all this"; and a third, who was on the bench and a kinsman of the gentleman, said, "Cousin, now is your time before the judges bring in their verdict. Do not fling away your goods," adding, "But for this traitor of a priest, my cousin would be more tractable." Here Mr. Thirkell said, "Tis better to cast away our goods than to risk losing one's soul." Then to the gentleman, "Let your goods go; stick you close to God, and with great courage confess His holy name." The judges commanded his silence, but he replied that the constancy of these Catholics in maintaining so good a cause rejoiced him exceedingly, and it was his duty to encourage them. The gentleman and his lady were firm and were cast into prison, and Mr. Thirkell was summoned to the bar and received his death sentence for high treason.

"I was an eye to the blind, and a foot to the lame" (Jb 29:15).

June 8

OUR LADY OF IPSWICH

Bl. Thomas More, L., 1535

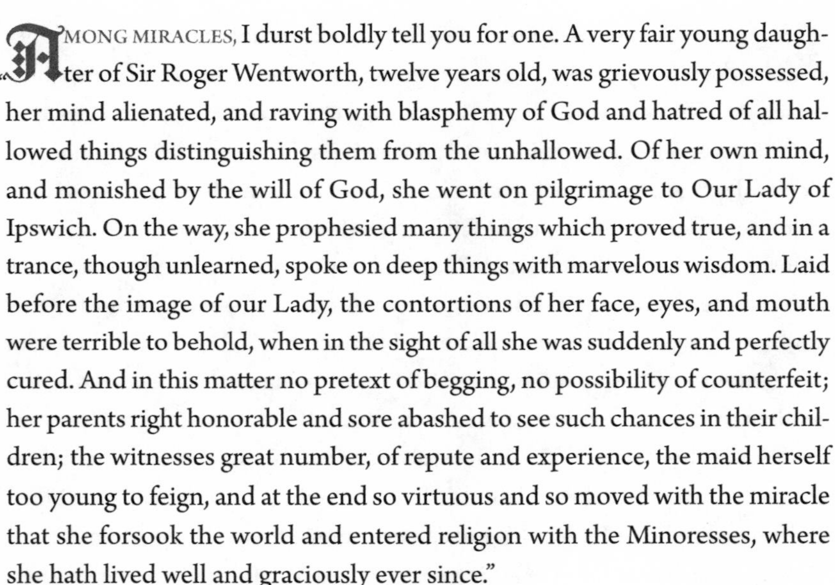

"AMONG MIRACLES, I durst boldly tell you for one. A very fair young daughter of Sir Roger Wentworth, twelve years old, was grievously possessed, her mind alienated, and raving with blasphemy of God and hatred of all hallowed things distinguishing them from the unhallowed. Of her own mind, and monished by the will of God, she went on pilgrimage to Our Lady of Ipswich. On the way, she prophesied many things which proved true, and in a trance, though unlearned, spoke on deep things with marvelous wisdom. Laid before the image of our Lady, the contortions of her face, eyes, and mouth were terrible to behold, when in the sight of all she was suddenly and perfectly cured. And in this matter no pretext of begging, no possibility of counterfeit; her parents right honorable and sore abashed to see such chances in their children; the witnesses great number, of repute and experience, the maid herself too young to feign, and at the end so virtuous and so moved with the miracle that she forsook the world and entered religion with the Minoresses, where she hath lived well and graciously ever since."

"She shall crush thy head, and thou shalt lie in wait for her heel" (Gn 3:15).

June 9

THE END AND THE MEANS

Ven. William Harcourt, S. J., 1679

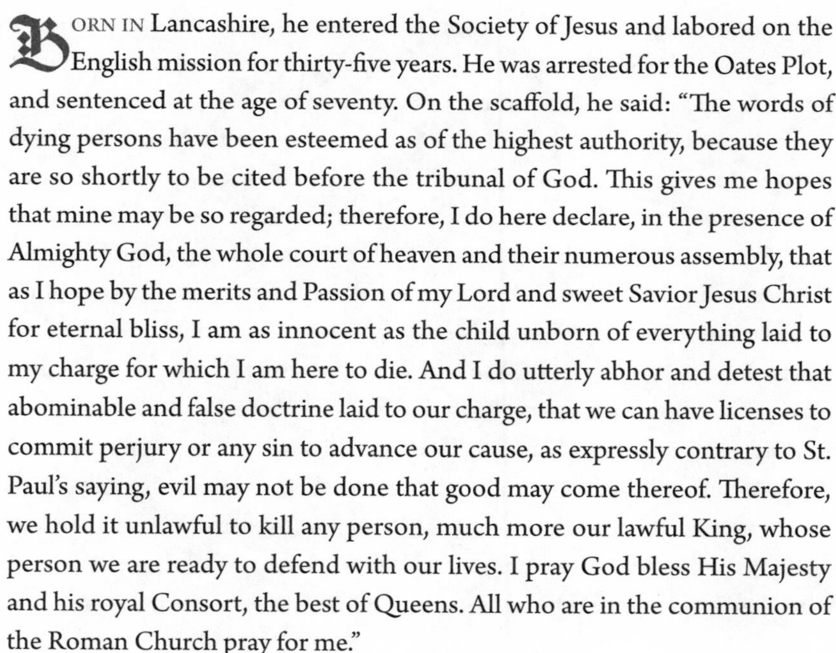

Born in Lancashire, he entered the Society of Jesus and labored on the English mission for thirty-five years. He was arrested for the Oates Plot, and sentenced at the age of seventy. On the scaffold, he said: "The words of dying persons have been esteemed as of the highest authority, because they are so shortly to be cited before the tribunal of God. This gives me hopes that mine may be so regarded; therefore, I do here declare, in the presence of Almighty God, the whole court of heaven and their numerous assembly, that as I hope by the merits and Passion of my Lord and sweet Savior Jesus Christ for eternal bliss, I am as innocent as the child unborn of everything laid to my charge for which I am here to die. And I do utterly abhor and detest that abominable and false doctrine laid to our charge, that we can have licenses to commit perjury or any sin to advance our cause, as expressly contrary to St. Paul's saying, evil may not be done that good may come thereof. Therefore, we hold it unlawful to kill any person, much more our lawful King, whose person we are ready to defend with our lives. I pray God bless His Majesty and his royal Consort, the best of Queens. All who are in the communion of the Roman Church pray for me."

"Not rather as we are slandered, and as some affirm that we say: Let us do evil that good may come of it" (Rom 3:8).

* *Harcourt was beatified by Pope Pius XI on 15 December 1929.*

June 10

"POSSUMUS" (We Can)

Ven. Thomas Whitebread, S.J., 1679

Born of a gentleman's family in Essex, he was educated at St. Omer's, entered the Society of Jesus, and for thirty years labored with great fruit on the English mission. Made provincial, he preached at his visitation at Liege, on St. James's Day, July 25, 1678 (that is, about two months before the Oates persecution began), on the Gospel of the feast. *Potestis libere calicem quern ego bibiturus sum?* " 'Can you drink the chalice which I am to drink?' They say, 'We can.' " He then showed clearly his foresight of the coming storm, and great suffering in store for his brethren and himself. After saying that the times were now quiet, but that God only knew how long they would be so, he then pointedly repeated the text: "Can you drink the chalice? Can you undergo a hard persecution? Are you contented to be falsely betrayed and injured and hurried away to prison? *Possumus* (We can). Blessed be God. *Potestis bibere?* Can you suffer the hardships of a jail, the straw bed, the hard diet, the chains and fetters? Can you endure the rack? *Possumus* (We can). Blessed be God. Can you patiently receive an unjust sentence of a shameful death? We can." And this last clause he uttered as a prayer with his eyes toward heaven.

"Can you drink the chalice which I am to drink?
They say to him: We can" (Mt 20:22).

* *Whitebread was beatified by Pope Pius XI on 15 December 1929.*

June 11

AN UNJUST JUDGE

Ven. Thomas Whitebread, S. J., 1679

OATES AND Bedloe again swore to Whitebread having assisted at the meeting in London to kill the King, save that Bedloe now gave us of his own personal knowledge what he had before spoken of as hearsay, and explained that he had intentionally softened his witness on the previous occasion. Judge Wylde told him that he was a confirmed perjurer and ought never to enter the courts again, but go home and repent. On the other hand, Fr. Whitebread showed the improbability of his conspiring with a man whom he had never seen, and who had been expelled from St. Omer's for his irregular life. He produced fifteen students who swore that Oates was at St. Omer's when he swore he was at the meeting in London. "If this plot existed," urged Fr. Whitebread, "in which so many persons of honor and quality were engaged, why are there no traces of its evidence, no arms bought, no men enlisted, no provision made for its execution? There was no evidence for the jury but hard swearing." Lastly, speaking for himself and his companions, he contrasted the known innocence of their lives and the vicious immorality of their accusers. Nevertheless, Chief Justice Scroggs directed the jury to find them guilty, and himself sentenced them to death.

"O thou art grown old in evil days, now are thy sins come out; . . . the judging unjust judgments, oppressing the innocent, and letting the guilty go free" (Dn 13:52–53).

June 12

LOVE'S SERVILE LOT

Ven. Robert Southwell, S. J., 1595

Love mistress is of many minds,
Yet few know whom they serve;
They reckon least how little love
Their service doth deserve.

The will she robbeth from the wit,
The sense from reason's lore;
She is delightful in the rind,
Corrupted in the core.

She shroudeth vice in virtue's veil,
Pretending good in ill;
She offereth joy, affordeth grief,
A kiss, where she doth kill.

She letteth fall some luring baits
For fools to gather up;
To sweet, to sour, to every taste
She tempereth her cup.

Like tyrant, cruel wounds she gives;
Like surgeon, salves she lends;
But salve and sore have equal force,
For death is both their ends.

Plough not the seas, sow not the sands
Leave off your idle pain;
Seek other mistress for your minds:
Love's service is in vain.

June 13

YEA, YEA, AND NO, NO

✠ Bl. Thomas Woodhouse, S.J., 1573

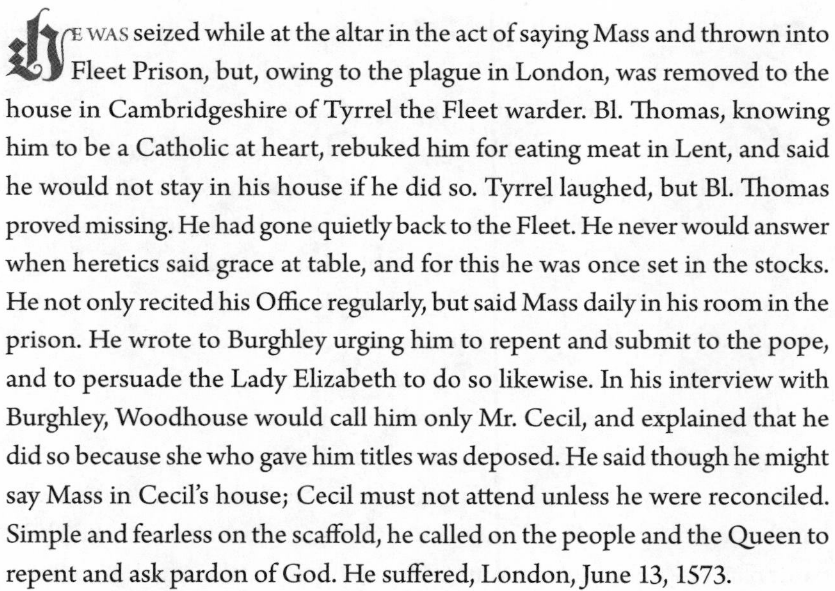

HE WAS seized while at the altar in the act of saying Mass and thrown into Fleet Prison, but, owing to the plague in London, was removed to the house in Cambridgeshire of Tyrrel the Fleet warder. Bl. Thomas, knowing him to be a Catholic at heart, rebuked him for eating meat in Lent, and said he would not stay in his house if he did so. Tyrrel laughed, but Bl. Thomas proved missing. He had gone quietly back to the Fleet. He never would answer when heretics said grace at table, and for this he was once set in the stocks. He not only recited his Office regularly, but said Mass daily in his room in the prison. He wrote to Burghley urging him to repent and submit to the pope, and to persuade the Lady Elizabeth to do so likewise. In his interview with Burghley, Woodhouse would call him only Mr. Cecil, and explained that he did so because she who gave him titles was deposed. He said though he might say Mass in Cecil's house; Cecil must not attend unless he were reconciled. Simple and fearless on the scaffold, he called on the people and the Queen to repent and ask pardon of God. He suffered, London, June 13, 1573.

"And his communication is with the simple" (Prv 3:32).

June 14

THE LEARNING OF THE SIMPLE

Ven. John Rigby, L., 1600

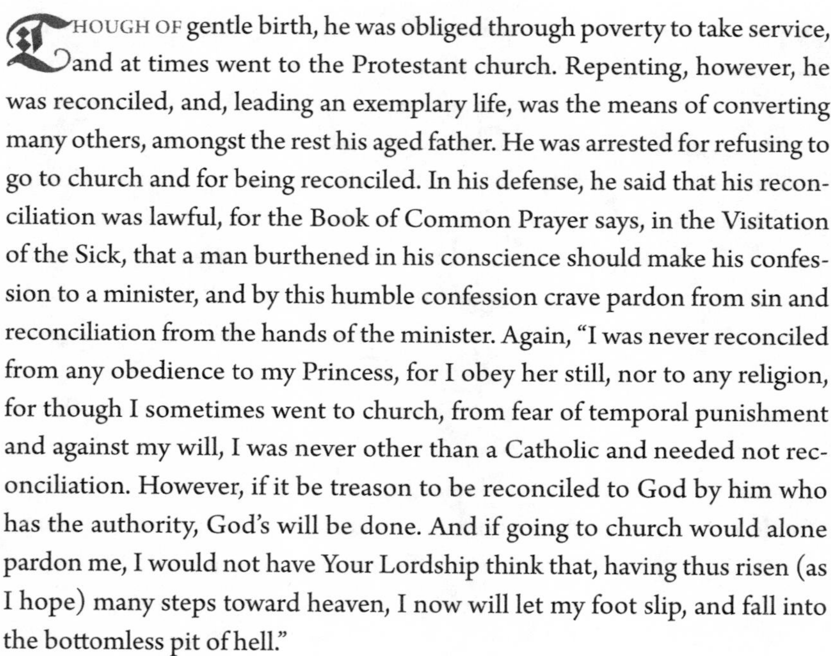

THOUGH OF gentle birth, he was obliged through poverty to take service, and at times went to the Protestant church. Repenting, however, he was reconciled, and, leading an exemplary life, was the means of converting many others, amongst the rest his aged father. He was arrested for refusing to go to church and for being reconciled. In his defense, he said that his reconciliation was lawful, for the Book of Common Prayer says, in the Visitation of the Sick, that a man burthened in his conscience should make his confession to a minister, and by this humble confession crave pardon from sin and reconciliation from the hands of the minister. Again, "I was never reconciled from any obedience to my Princess, for I obey her still, nor to any religion, for though I sometimes went to church, from fear of temporal punishment and against my will, I was never other than a Catholic and needed not reconciliation. However, if it be treason to be reconciled to God by him who has the authority, God's will be done. And if going to church would alone pardon me, I would not have Your Lordship think that, having thus risen (as I hope) many steps toward heaven, I now will let my foot slip, and fall into the bottomless pit of hell."

"Meditate not how you shall answer, for I will give you a mouth and wisdom, which all your adversaries shall not be able to resist and gainsay" (Lk 21:14–15).

* *Rigby was canonized by Pope Paul VI on 25 October 1970.*

June 15

A BRIBE REJECTED

Five Jesuit martyrs, 1679

Fr. Fenwick on the scaffold, addressing the crowd, declared his innocence, and expressed the hope that Christian charity would not let his hearers think that by this last act of his life he would cast away his soul by sealing up his last breath with a damnable lie. Then he joined his companions in their private devotions. At their close, the five stood up — Thomas Whitebread, William Harcourt, John Gavan, John Fenwick, Antony Turner — with the ropes round their necks, when there came a horseman in full speed from Whitehall, crying, "A pardon! a pardon!" With difficulty he made his way through the crowd to the sheriff, who was under the gallows to see the execution carried out. By the terms of the pardon, the King granted them their lives, which by their own treason they had forfeited, from his own inclination to clemency, on condition of their acknowledging the conspiracy and laying open what they knew thereof. They all thanked His Majesty for his inclination of mercy toward them, but they knew of no conspiracy, much less were guilty of any, and could not therefore accept any pardon on these conditions. And so all five together won their crown, Tyburn, June 20, 1679.

"Then Jesus said, Begone, Satan, for it is written: The Lord thy God shalt thou adore, and Him only shalt thou serve" (Mt 4:10).

* *Whitebread, Harcourt, Gavan, Fenwick, and Turner were beatified by Pope Pius XI on 15 December 1929.*

June 16

A PURITAN CONSCIENCE

Ven. John Southworth, Pr., 1654

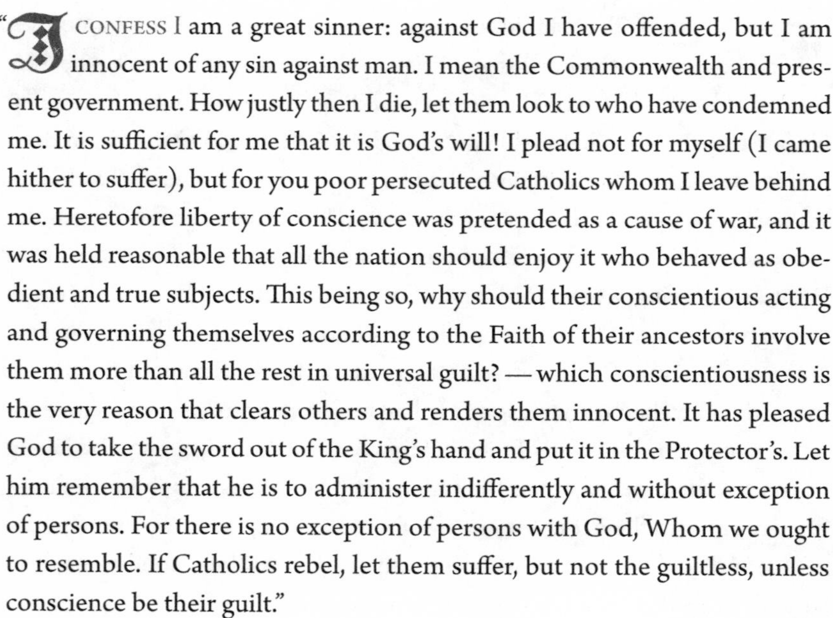

"I confess I am a great sinner: against God I have offended, but I am innocent of any sin against man. I mean the Commonwealth and present government. How justly then I die, let them look to who have condemned me. It is sufficient for me that it is God's will! I plead not for myself (I came hither to suffer), but for you poor persecuted Catholics whom I leave behind me. Heretofore liberty of conscience was pretended as a cause of war, and it was held reasonable that all the nation should enjoy it who behaved as obedient and true subjects. This being so, why should their conscientious acting and governing themselves according to the Faith of their ancestors involve them more than all the rest in universal guilt? — which conscientiousness is the very reason that clears others and renders them innocent. It has pleased God to take the sword out of the King's hand and put it in the Protector's. Let him remember that he is to administer indifferently and without exception of persons. For there is no exception of persons with God, Whom we ought to resemble. If Catholics rebel, let them suffer, but not the guiltless, unless conscience be their guilt."

"I will judge thee according to thy ways, and I will set all thy abominations against thee" (Ez 7:3).

* *Southworth was canonized by Pope Paul VI on 25 October 1970.*

June 17

THE COMMISSION TO PREACH

Ven. John Southworth, Pr., 1654

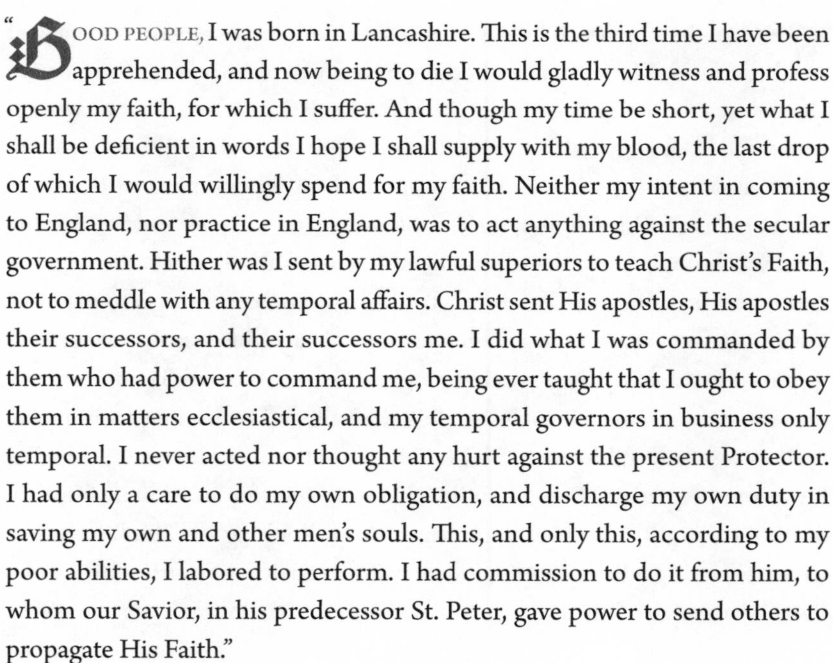

"Good people, I was born in Lancashire. This is the third time I have been apprehended, and now being to die I would gladly witness and profess openly my faith, for which I suffer. And though my time be short, yet what I shall be deficient in words I hope I shall supply with my blood, the last drop of which I would willingly spend for my faith. Neither my intent in coming to England, nor practice in England, was to act anything against the secular government. Hither was I sent by my lawful superiors to teach Christ's Faith, not to meddle with any temporal affairs. Christ sent His apostles, His apostles their successors, and their successors me. I did what I was commanded by them who had power to command me, being ever taught that I ought to obey them in matters ecclesiastical, and my temporal governors in business only temporal. I never acted nor thought any hurt against the present Protector. I had only a care to do my own obligation, and discharge my own duty in saving my own and other men's souls. This, and only this, according to my poor abilities, I labored to perform. I had commission to do it from him, to whom our Savior, in his predecessor St. Peter, gave power to send others to propagate His Faith."

"As the Father hath sent Me, I also send you" (Jn 20:21).

June 18

LOOKING ON JESUS

Ven. John Southworth, Pr., 1654

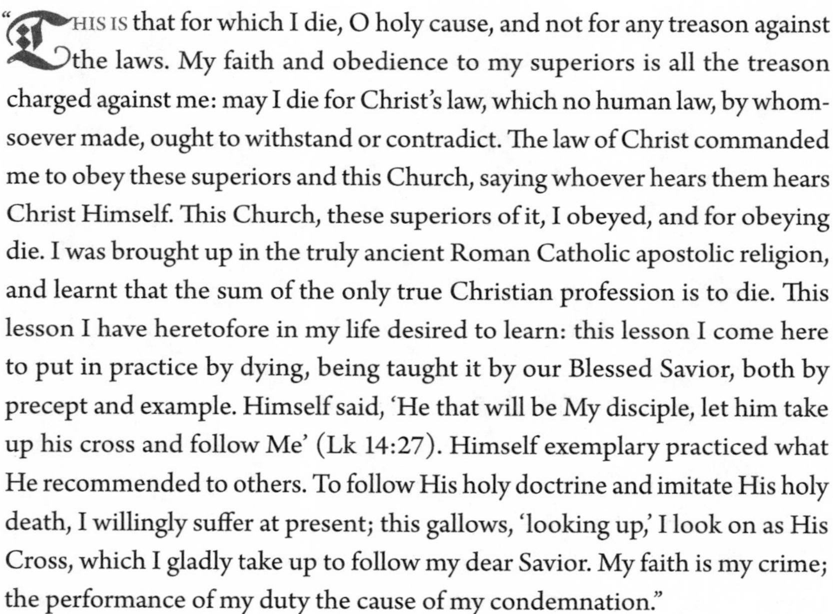

"This is that for which I die, O holy cause, and not for any treason against the laws. My faith and obedience to my superiors is all the treason charged against me: may I die for Christ's law, which no human law, by whomsoever made, ought to withstand or contradict. The law of Christ commanded me to obey these superiors and this Church, saying whoever hears them hears Christ Himself. This Church, these superiors of it, I obeyed, and for obeying die. I was brought up in the truly ancient Roman Catholic apostolic religion, and learnt that the sum of the only true Christian profession is to die. This lesson I have heretofore in my life desired to learn: this lesson I come here to put in practice by dying, being taught it by our Blessed Savior, both by precept and example. Himself said, 'He that will be My disciple, let him take up his cross and follow Me' (Lk 14:27). Himself exemplary practiced what He recommended to others. To follow His holy doctrine and imitate His holy death, I willingly suffer at present; this gallows, 'looking up,' I look on as His Cross, which I gladly take up to follow my dear Savior. My faith is my crime; the performance of my duty the cause of my condemnation."

"Looking on Jesus, the author and finisher of our faith, Who, having joy set before Him, endured the Cross" (Heb 12:2).

June 19

THE WHIMS OF A KING

✠ Bl. Sebastian Newdigate, Carthusian, 1535

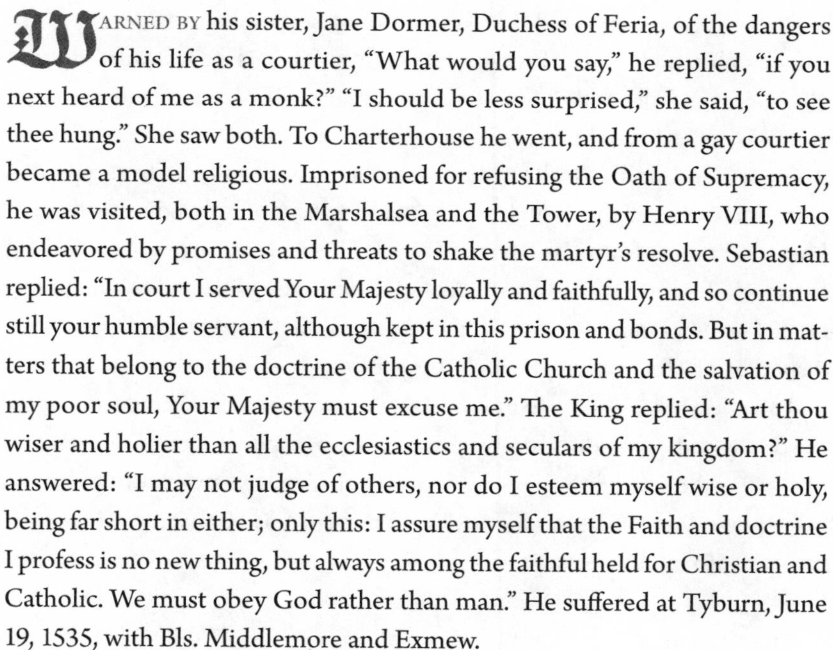

Warned by his sister, Jane Dormer, Duchess of Feria, of the dangers of his life as a courtier, "What would you say," he replied, "if you next heard of me as a monk?" "I should be less surprised," she said, "to see thee hung." She saw both. To Charterhouse he went, and from a gay courtier became a model religious. Imprisoned for refusing the Oath of Supremacy, he was visited, both in the Marshalsea and the Tower, by Henry VIII, who endeavored by promises and threats to shake the martyr's resolve. Sebastian replied: "In court I served Your Majesty loyally and faithfully, and so continue still your humble servant, although kept in this prison and bonds. But in matters that belong to the doctrine of the Catholic Church and the salvation of my poor soul, Your Majesty must excuse me." The King replied: "Art thou wiser and holier than all the ecclesiastics and seculars of my kingdom?" He answered: "I may not judge of others, nor do I esteem myself wise or holy, being far short in either; only this: I assure myself that the Faith and doctrine I profess is no new thing, but always among the faithful held for Christian and Catholic. We must obey God rather than man." He suffered at Tyburn, June 19, 1535, with Bls. Middlemore and Exmew.

"Put not your trust in princes: in the children of men,
in whom there is no salvation" (Ps 145:2–3).

June 20

LEAVE TO LIE

✠ Ven. Thomas Whitebread, S.J., 1679, on the scaffold

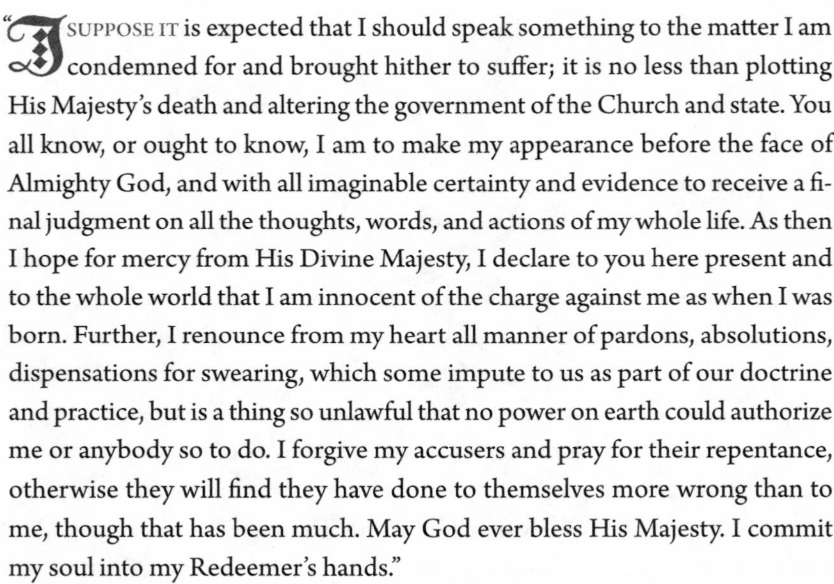

"I suppose it is expected that I should speak something to the matter I am condemned for and brought hither to suffer; it is no less than plotting His Majesty's death and altering the government of the Church and state. You all know, or ought to know, I am to make my appearance before the face of Almighty God, and with all imaginable certainty and evidence to receive a final judgment on all the thoughts, words, and actions of my whole life. As then I hope for mercy from His Divine Majesty, I declare to you here present and to the whole world that I am innocent of the charge against me as when I was born. Further, I renounce from my heart all manner of pardons, absolutions, dispensations for swearing, which some impute to us as part of our doctrine and practice, but is a thing so unlawful that no power on earth could authorize me or anybody so to do. I forgive my accusers and pray for their repentance, otherwise they will find they have done to themselves more wrong than to me, though that has been much. May God ever bless His Majesty. I commit my soul into my Redeemer's hands."

"Wherefore putting away lying, speak ye the truth every man with his neighbor; for we are members one of another" (Eph 4:25).

June 21

FETTERS UNLOOSED

✠ Ven. John Rigby, L., 1600

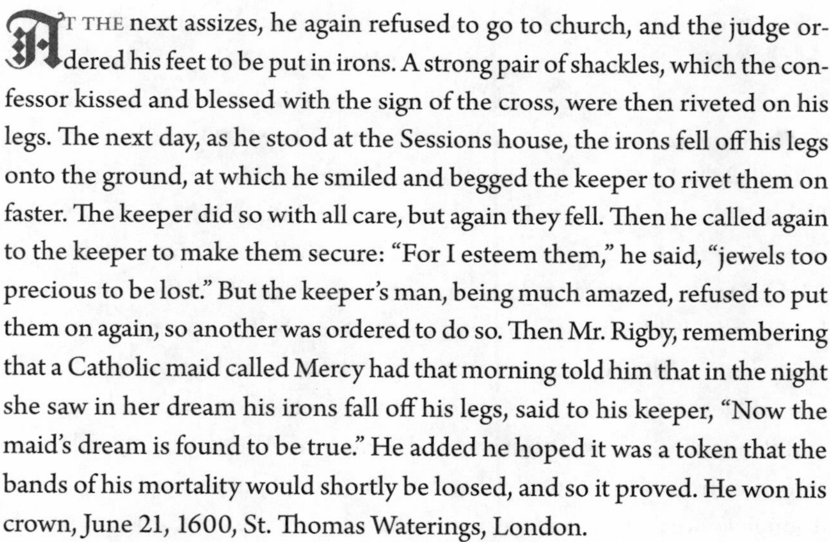

AT THE next assizes, he again refused to go to church, and the judge ordered his feet to be put in irons. A strong pair of shackles, which the confessor kissed and blessed with the sign of the cross, were then riveted on his legs. The next day, as he stood at the Sessions house, the irons fell off his legs onto the ground, at which he smiled and begged the keeper to rivet them on faster. The keeper did so with all care, but again they fell. Then he called again to the keeper to make them secure: "For I esteem them," he said, "jewels too precious to be lost." But the keeper's man, being much amazed, refused to put them on again, so another was ordered to do so. Then Mr. Rigby, remembering that a Catholic maid called Mercy had that morning told him that in the night she saw in her dream his irons fall off his legs, said to his keeper, "Now the maid's dream is found to be true." He added he hoped it was a token that the bands of his mortality would shortly be loosed, and so it proved. He won his crown, June 21, 1600, St. Thomas Waterings, London.

"Thou hast broken my bonds: I will sacrifice to Thee a sacrifice of praise" (Ps 115:16–17).

June 22

ASCENDING THE STEPS

Bl. John Fisher, Card. Bp., 1535

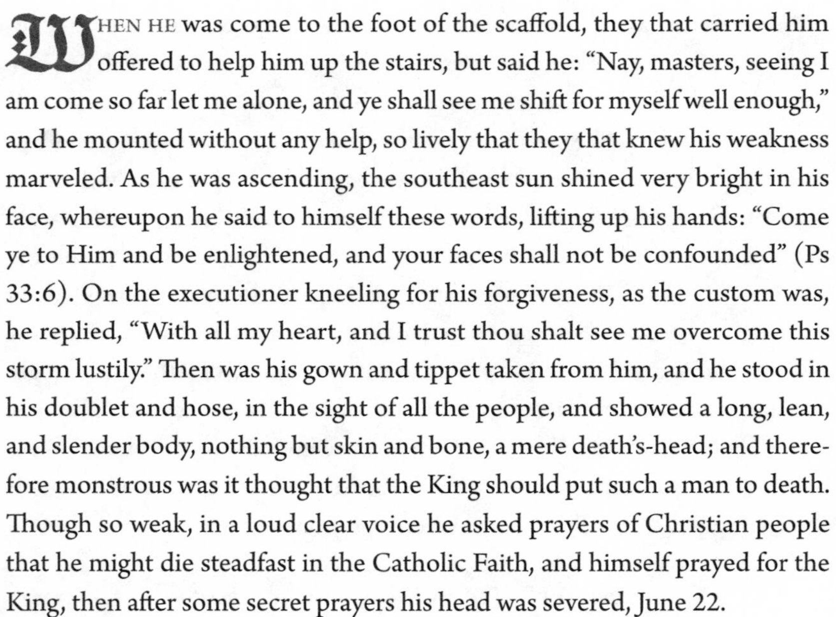

When he was come to the foot of the scaffold, they that carried him offered to help him up the stairs, but said he: "Nay, masters, seeing I am come so far let me alone, and ye shall see me shift for myself well enough," and he mounted without any help, so lively that they that knew his weakness marveled. As he was ascending, the southeast sun shined very bright in his face, whereupon he said to himself these words, lifting up his hands: "Come ye to Him and be enlightened, and your faces shall not be confounded" (Ps 33:6). On the executioner kneeling for his forgiveness, as the custom was, he replied, "With all my heart, and I trust thou shalt see me overcome this storm lustily." Then was his gown and tippet taken from him, and he stood in his doublet and hose, in the sight of all the people, and showed a long, lean, and slender body, nothing but skin and bone, a mere death's-head; and therefore monstrous was it thought that the King should put such a man to death. Though so weak, in a loud clear voice he asked prayers of Christian people that he might die steadfast in the Catholic Faith, and himself prayed for the King, then after some secret prayers his head was severed, June 22.

"In his heart he hath disposed to ascend by steps in the vale of tears" (Ps 83:6–7).

June 23

LEARNING FOR LIFE

Bl. John Fisher, Card. Bp., 1535

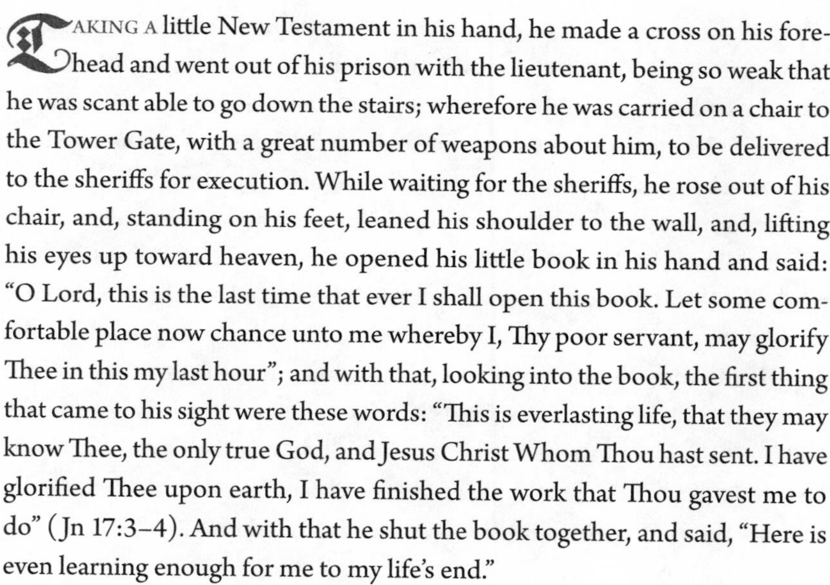

TAKING A little New Testament in his hand, he made a cross on his forehead and went out of his prison with the lieutenant, being so weak that he was scant able to go down the stairs; wherefore he was carried on a chair to the Tower Gate, with a great number of weapons about him, to be delivered to the sheriffs for execution. While waiting for the sheriffs, he rose out of his chair, and, standing on his feet, leaned his shoulder to the wall, and, lifting his eyes up toward heaven, he opened his little book in his hand and said: "O Lord, this is the last time that ever I shall open this book. Let some comfortable place now chance unto me whereby I, Thy poor servant, may glorify Thee in this my last hour"; and with that, looking into the book, the first thing that came to his sight were these words: "This is everlasting life, that they may know Thee, the only true God, and Jesus Christ Whom Thou hast sent. I have glorified Thee upon earth, I have finished the work that Thou gavest me to do" (Jn 17:3–4). And with that he shut the book together, and said, "Here is even learning enough for me to my life's end."

"Thy knowledge is become wonderful to me" (Ps 138:6).

June 24

THE WEDDING GARMENT

Bl. John Fisher, Card. Bp., 1535

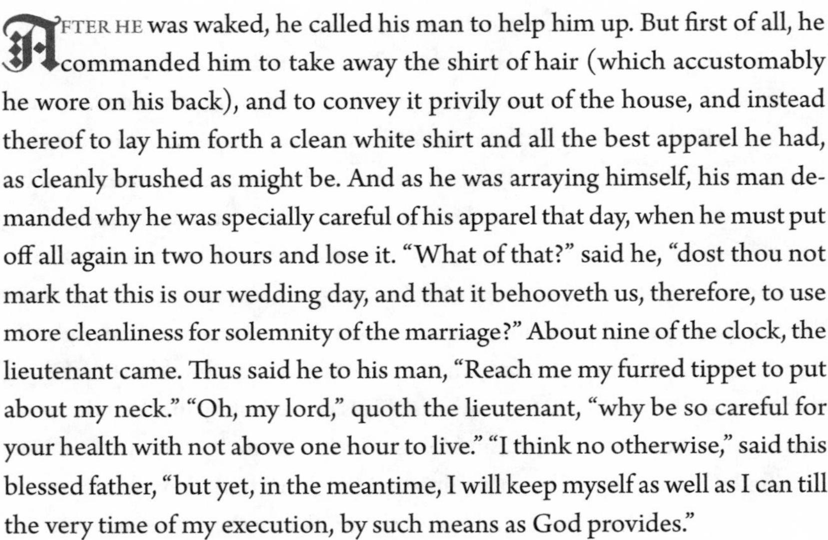

AFTER HE was waked, he called his man to help him up. But first of all, he commanded him to take away the shirt of hair (which accustomably he wore on his back), and to convey it privily out of the house, and instead thereof to lay him forth a clean white shirt and all the best apparel he had, as cleanly brushed as might be. And as he was arraying himself, his man demanded why he was specially careful of his apparel that day, when he must put off all again in two hours and lose it. "What of that?" said he, "dost thou not mark that this is our wedding day, and that it behooveth us, therefore, to use more cleanliness for solemnity of the marriage?" About nine of the clock, the lieutenant came. Thus said he to his man, "Reach me my furred tippet to put about my neck." "Oh, my lord," quoth the lieutenant, "why be so careful for your health with not above one hour to live." "I think no otherwise," said this blessed father, "but yet, in the meantime, I will keep myself as well as I can till the very time of my execution, by such means as God provides."

"But thou hast a few names in Sardis which have not denied their garments; and they shall walk with Me in white, because they are worthy" (Apoc 3:4).

June 25

A MARTYR'S SLEEP

Bl. John Fisher, Card. Bp., 1535

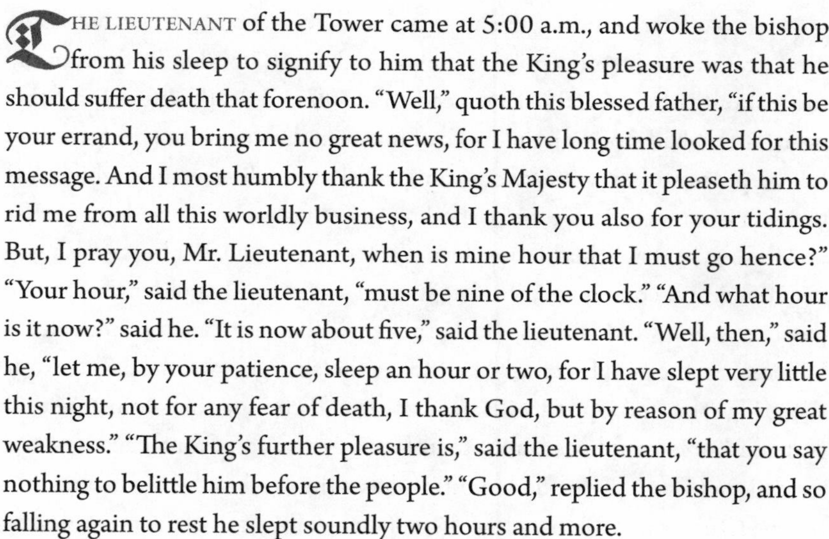

THE LIEUTENANT of the Tower came at 5:00 a.m., and woke the bishop from his sleep to signify to him that the King's pleasure was that he should suffer death that forenoon. "Well," quoth this blessed father, "if this be your errand, you bring me no great news, for I have long time looked for this message. And I most humbly thank the King's Majesty that it pleaseth him to rid me from all this worldly business, and I thank you also for your tidings. But, I pray you, Mr. Lieutenant, when is mine hour that I must go hence?" "Your hour," said the lieutenant, "must be nine of the clock." "And what hour is it now?" said he. "It is now about five," said the lieutenant. "Well, then," said he, "let me, by your patience, sleep an hour or two, for I have slept very little this night, not for any fear of death, I thank God, but by reason of my great weakness." "The King's further pleasure is," said the lieutenant, "that you say nothing to belittle him before the people." "Good," replied the bishop, and so falling again to rest he slept soundly two hours and more.

"Thou shalt rest, and thy sleep shall be sweet" (Prv 3:24).

June 26

THE BONES OF ELIAS

Bl. John Fisher, Card. Bp., 1535

THE DAY after his burial, the head, being somewhat parboiled in hot water, was pricked upon a pole and set on high upon London Bridge, among the rest of the holy Carthusians' heads that suffered death before him. This head, after it had stood up the space of fourteen days upon the bridge, could not be perceived to waste or consume, neither for the weather, which was then very hot, neither for the parboiling in hot water, but grew daily fresher and fresher, so that in his lifetime he never looked so well. For his cheek being beautified by a comely red, the face looked as if it had beholden the people passing by, and would have spoke to them, which many took for a miracle.... Whereupon the people coming daily to see this strange sight, the passage over the bridge was so stopped with their going and coming that almost neither cart nor horse could pass; and, therefore, at the end of fourteen days, the executioner was commanded to throw down the head in the night-time into the river Thames, and in the place thereof was set the head of the most blessed and constant martyr, Sir Thomas More, who suffered his passion on the 6th day of July next following.

"No word could overcome him, and after death his body prophesied" (Ecclus 48:14).

June 27

FEEDING THE HUNGRY

Margaret Clement, L., 1537

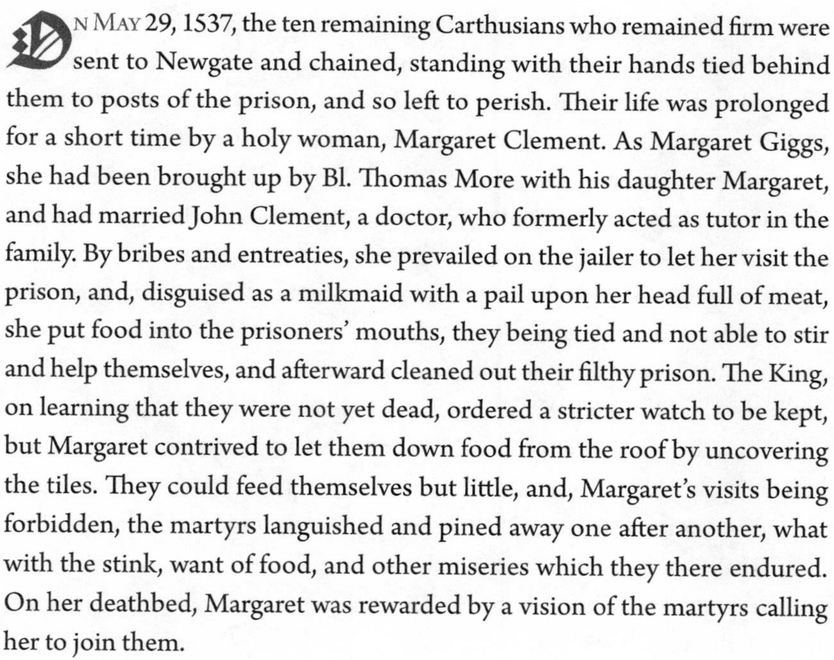

On May 29, 1537, the ten remaining Carthusians who remained firm were sent to Newgate and chained, standing with their hands tied behind them to posts of the prison, and so left to perish. Their life was prolonged for a short time by a holy woman, Margaret Clement. As Margaret Giggs, she had been brought up by Bl. Thomas More with his daughter Margaret, and had married John Clement, a doctor, who formerly acted as tutor in the family. By bribes and entreaties, she prevailed on the jailer to let her visit the prison, and, disguised as a milkmaid with a pail upon her head full of meat, she put food into the prisoners' mouths, they being tied and not able to stir and help themselves, and afterward cleaned out their filthy prison. The King, on learning that they were not yet dead, ordered a stricter watch to be kept, but Margaret contrived to let them down food from the roof by uncovering the tiles. They could feed themselves but little, and, Margaret's visits being forbidden, the martyrs languished and pined away one after another, what with the stink, want of food, and other miseries which they there endured. On her deathbed, Margaret was rewarded by a vision of the martyrs calling her to join them.

"I was hungry, and you gave me to eat" (*Mt 25:35*).

June 28

A DANGEROUS SEDUCER

✠ Ven. John Southworth, Pr., 1654

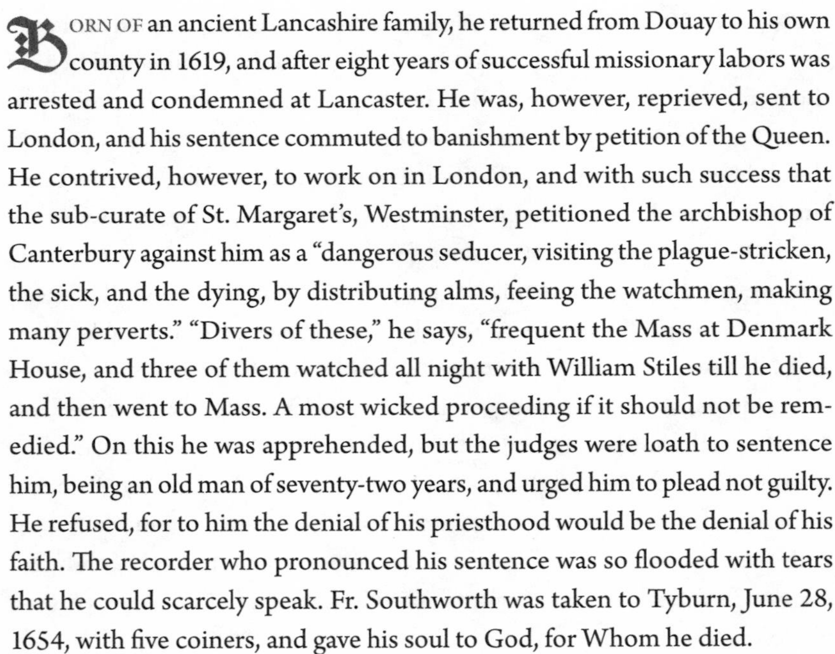

Born of an ancient Lancashire family, he returned from Douay to his own county in 1619, and after eight years of successful missionary labors was arrested and condemned at Lancaster. He was, however, reprieved, sent to London, and his sentence commuted to banishment by petition of the Queen. He contrived, however, to work on in London, and with such success that the sub-curate of St. Margaret's, Westminster, petitioned the archbishop of Canterbury against him as a "dangerous seducer, visiting the plague-stricken, the sick, and the dying, by distributing alms, feeing the watchmen, making many perverts." "Divers of these," he says, "frequent the Mass at Denmark House, and three of them watched all night with William Stiles till he died, and then went to Mass. A most wicked proceeding if it should not be remedied." On this he was apprehended, but the judges were loath to sentence him, being an old man of seventy-two years, and urged him to plead not guilty. He refused, for to him the denial of his priesthood would be the denial of his faith. The recorder who pronounced his sentence was so flooded with tears that he could scarcely speak. Fr. Southworth was taken to Tyburn, June 28, 1654, with five coiners, and gave his soul to God, for Whom he died.

"He stirreth up the people, teaching through all Judea" (Lk 23:5).

June 29

ST. PETER'S REMORSE

Ven. Robert Southwell, S.J., 1595

It is a small relief
To say I was Thy child,
If, as an ill-deserving foe,
From grace I am exiled.

I was, I had, I could —
All words importing want;
They are but dust of dead supplies,
Where needful helps are scant.

Once to have been in bliss
That hardly can return,
Doth but bewray from whence I fell,
And wherefore now I mourn.

All thoughts of passed hopes
Increase my present cross;
Like ruins of decayed joys,
They still upbraid my loss.

O mild and mighty Lord!
Amend that is amiss;
My sin, my sore, Thy love my salve,
Thy cure my comfort is.

Confirm Thy former deed,
Reform that is defiled;
I was, I am, I will remain
Thy charge, Thy choice, Thy child.

June 30

A GOOD DAY

✠ Ven. Philip Powell, O. S. B., 1646

TO THE judge's question on which day he would die, he answered pleasantly, "It is not an easy question or soon compassed to be provided to die well. We have all much to answer for, and myself not the least share; therefore, my lord, consider what time Your Lordship would allot to yourself, and appoint that to me." The proffer being twice repeated, he answered he could by no means be an allotter of his own death, so the judge promised he should have sufficient notice. In the prison, his courtesy and cheerfulness so won the hearts of his fellow prisoners that twenty-nine gentlemen, all Protestants, save six whom he converted, drew up a certificate of his innocent and virtuous behavior. His cheerfulness increased day by day as he drew nearer heaven. When the officer brought the date fixed for his death, he joyfully said, "Welcome whatever comes, God's Name be praised." On the scaffold he said, "You are come to see a sad spectacle, but to me it is not. It is the happiest day and greatest joy that ever befell me, for I am condemned to die as a Catholic priest and a Benedictine monk, a dignity and honor for which I give God thanks." He suffered June 30, 1646.

"Who is the man that desireth life: who loveth to see good days?" (Ps 33:13).

* *Powell was beatified by Pope Pius XI on 15 December 1929.*

July

July 1

THE FRUITS OF THE SPIRIT

✠ Ven. Oliver Plunket, Abp., 1681

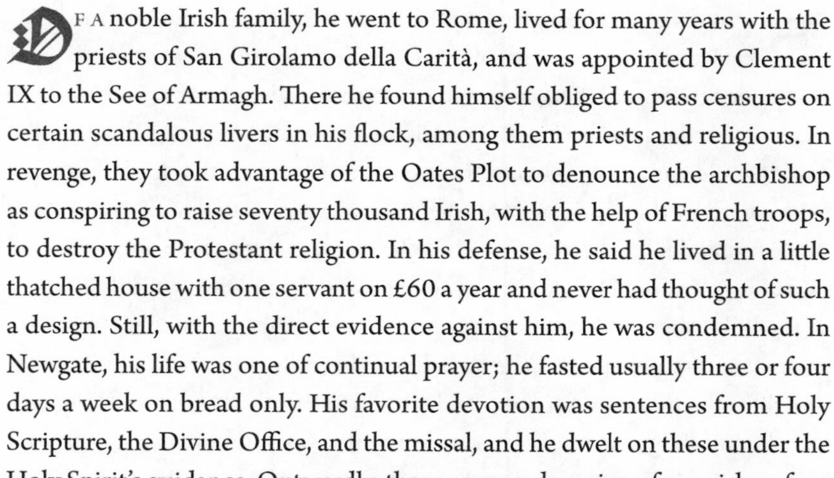

Of a noble Irish family, he went to Rome, lived for many years with the priests of San Girolamo della Carità, and was appointed by Clement IX to the See of Armagh. There he found himself obliged to pass censures on certain scandalous livers in his flock, among them priests and religious. In revenge, they took advantage of the Oates Plot to denounce the archbishop as conspiring to raise seventy thousand Irish, with the help of French troops, to destroy the Protestant religion. In his defense, he said he lived in a little thatched house with one servant on £60 a year and never had thought of such a design. Still, with the direct evidence against him, he was condemned. In Newgate, his life was one of continual prayer; he fasted usually three or four days a week on bread only. His favorite devotion was sentences from Holy Scripture, the Divine Office, and the missal, and he dwelt on these under the Holy Spirit's guidance. Outwardly, there appeared no sign of anguish or fear, but a sweet and holy recollection, a gentle courtesy, an unfailing cheerfulness, devoting his fitness for the sacrifice and ripeness for heaven. His very presence kindled in men's hearts a desire to suffer for Christ.

"The fruits of the Spirit are charity, joy, peace" (Gal 5:22).

* *Plunket was canonized by Pope Paul VI on 12 October 1975.*

July 2

PRAYER WITHOUT CEASING

✠ Ven. Monford Scott, Pr., 1591

Born in Norfolk, he arrived on the English mission from Douay in 1577. "He was a man," we are told, "of wonderful meekness and of so great abstinence that his diet on common days was bread and water, and but little more on Sundays and holidays. So addicted also was he to prayer that he often spent whole days and nights in this exercise, insomuch that his knees were grown hard by the assiduity of his devotions, as it is related of St. James. One of the bystanders perceiving this when the martyr's body was being quartered said aloud, 'I should be glad to see any one of our ministers with their knees as much hardened by constant prayer as we see this man's knees are.' And so great and so general was the veneration this holy priest had acquired that Topcliffe, the noted persecutor, loudly boasted that the Queen and kingdom were highly obliged to him for having brought to the gallows a priest so devout and mortified." Fr. Scott was prosecuted and condemned solely on account of his priestly character. He suffered with wonderful constancy, and no less modesty and spiritual joy, to the great edification of the spectators, and the admiration even of the greatest enemies of his faith and profession, Tyburn, July 2, 1591.

"By all prayer and supplication praying at all times in the Spirit" (Eph 6:18).

* *Scott was beatified by Pope John Paul II on 22 November 1987.*

July 3

TYBURN IN GALA

Ven. Thomas Maxfield, Pr., 1616

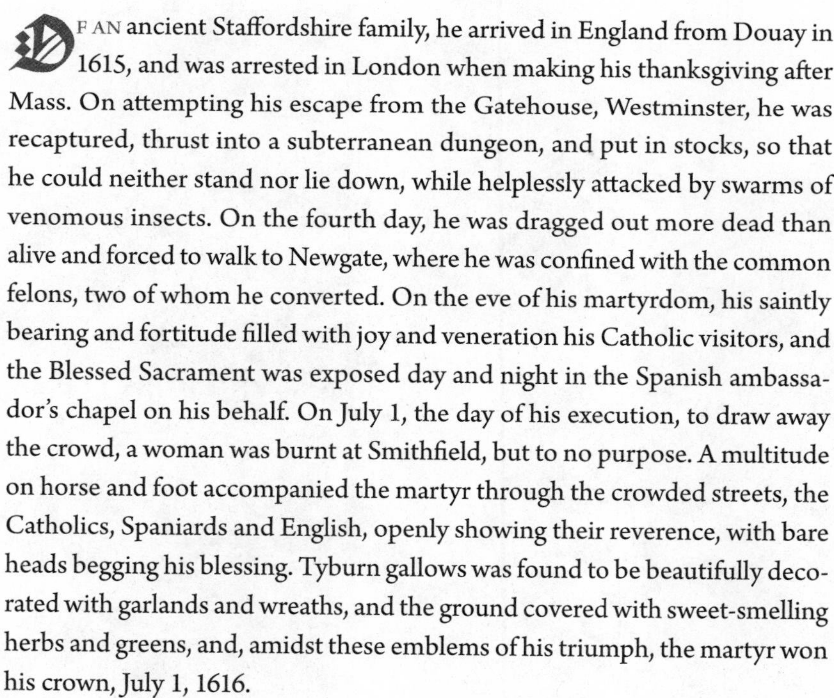

Of an ancient Staffordshire family, he arrived in England from Douay in 1615, and was arrested in London when making his thanksgiving after Mass. On attempting his escape from the Gatehouse, Westminster, he was recaptured, thrust into a subterranean dungeon, and put in stocks, so that he could neither stand nor lie down, while helplessly attacked by swarms of venomous insects. On the fourth day, he was dragged out more dead than alive and forced to walk to Newgate, where he was confined with the common felons, two of whom he converted. On the eve of his martyrdom, his saintly bearing and fortitude filled with joy and veneration his Catholic visitors, and the Blessed Sacrament was exposed day and night in the Spanish ambassador's chapel on his behalf. On July 1, the day of his execution, to draw away the crowd, a woman was burnt at Smithfield, but to no purpose. A multitude on horse and foot accompanied the martyr through the crowded streets, the Catholics, Spaniards and English, openly showing their reverence, with bare heads begging his blessing. Tyburn gallows was found to be beautifully decorated with garlands and wreaths, and the ground covered with sweet-smelling herbs and greens, and, amidst these emblems of his triumph, the martyr won his crown, July 1, 1616.

"As a tree planted by the running water bringing forth its fruit in due season" (Ps 1:3).

THOMAS MAXFIELD

"A lady of quality found means to make him a charitable visit"

July 4

A MAN OF GOD

✠ Ven. John Cornelius, S.J., 1594

He said Mass every day at five o'clock in the morning, and never without tears. At the reading of the Passion in Holy Week, again he wept exceedingly. He was sometimes in an ecstasy when praying, and was found once on his knees, his hands crossed on his breast, and his eyes raised to heaven, so absorbed in God that it was doubtful whether he was alive or dead. He always wore a rough hairshirt, used frequent disciplines, and for many years fasted four days a week. He gave to the poor all that came to his hands, committing the care of himself to God's providence. He preached twice a week, gave catechetical instructions for almost an hour, and read some pious lessons for about half an hour in the evening to those aspiring to perfection. The mortification of his senses and his recollection in God were so great that for three whole years that he lodged in a room, the windows of which looked upon the parish church, he had never observed it, nor did he know whether the house in which he lived was leaded or tiled. Upon several occasions, his face was illuminated with a heavenly light. He suffered at Dorchester, July 4, 1594.

"But thou, O man of God ... pursue justice, godliness, faith, charity, patience, mildness" (1 Tm 6:11).

* *Cornelius was beatified by Pope Pius XI on 15 December 1929.*

July 5

THE LAST FIRST

✠ Ven. George Nicols, Pr., 1589

Born at Oxford, he was ordained at Rheims, and sent on the mission, 1583. Oxford was the chief scene of his labors, and they bore fruit in abundance. Amongst the souls he won to God was that of a noted highwayman under sentence of death in Oxford Castle. Through the conversation of his Catholic fellow prisoners, he became thoroughly contrite, and longed to be able to make his Confession. On the very morning of his execution, Fr. Nicols came to the jail with a crowd of other persons, and, passing for a kinsman and acquaintance of the prisoner, after mutual salutations took him aside, heard his Confession, for which he had carefully prepared the night before, and gave him absolution. The prisoner, now wonderfully comforted, declared himself a Catholic, was deaf to all the persuasions of the minister to return to Protestantism, and suffered joyfully professing the Faith. Fr. Nicols and Fr. Yaxley, his companion, were sent up to London with legs tied under the horses' bellies, being insulted all along the route. An Oxford undergraduate, who from compassion attended them on their journey, was confined for some time in Bedlam as insane. The priests were sent back to Oxford, and executed July 1, 1589.

"So the last shall be first and the first last, for many are called but few chosen" (Mt 20:16).

* *Nicols was beatified by Pope John Paul II on 22 November 1987.*

July 6

THE PRIVILEGES OF MARTYRDOM

✠ Bl. Thomas More, L., 1535

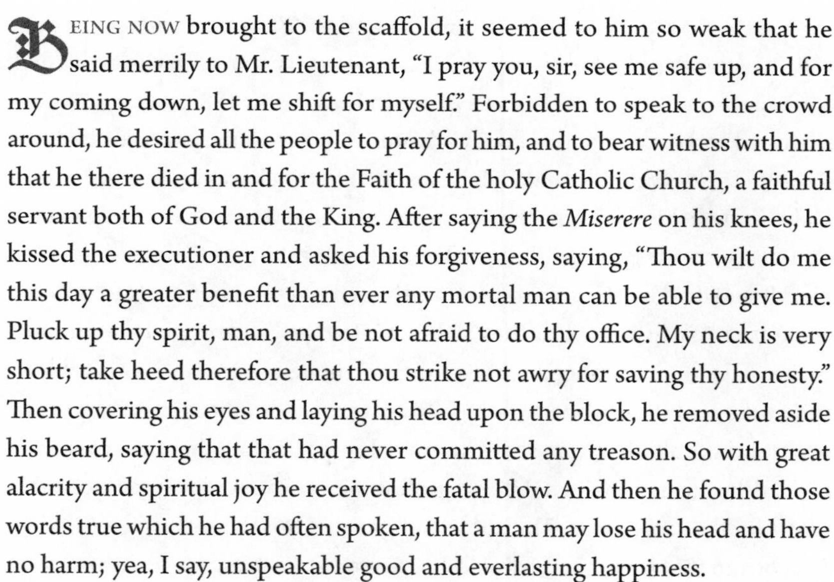

Being now brought to the scaffold, it seemed to him so weak that he said merrily to Mr. Lieutenant, "I pray you, sir, see me safe up, and for my coming down, let me shift for myself." Forbidden to speak to the crowd around, he desired all the people to pray for him, and to bear witness with him that he there died in and for the Faith of the holy Catholic Church, a faithful servant both of God and the King. After saying the *Miserere* on his knees, he kissed the executioner and asked his forgiveness, saying, "Thou wilt do me this day a greater benefit than ever any mortal man can be able to give me. Pluck up thy spirit, man, and be not afraid to do thy office. My neck is very short; take heed therefore that thou strike not awry for saving thy honesty." Then covering his eyes and laying his head upon the block, he removed aside his beard, saying that that had never committed any treason. So with great alacrity and spiritual joy he received the fatal blow. And then he found those words true which he had often spoken, that a man may lose his head and have no harm; yea, I say, unspeakable good and everlasting happiness.

"He that shall lose his life for Me shall find it" (Mt 10:39).

July 7

THE SPOUSE OF THE CANTICLES

✠ Ven. Roger Dicconson, Pr., and companions, 1591

FR. DICCONSON was born in Lincoln, and though apparently as a youth he attended the Protestant church, he must have been early reconciled, for he returned from Rheims as a priest to England in 1583. After being imprisoned and exiled, he was finally arrested at Winchester, and executed July 7, 1591. The devotion with which he inspired his flock was seen in the case of Ralph Milner, his fellow martyr, and in that of the seven maiden gentlewomen who were condemned with him. The judge, thinking they would be sufficiently terrified by the sentence of death, gave them a reprieve and ordered them back to prison. At this they all burst into tears, and begged that the sentence of death pronounced against them might be carried out, and that they might die with their ghostly father. They were accomplices in his supposed guilt, and should therefore share his punishment, adding that they trusted to God, Who, having enabled them to profess their faith, would strengthen them to die for the same cause. The judge, indignant at this demonstration, told Fr. Dicconson that their blood should be exacted at his hands. "Yes, my lord, so Pilate turned his fault on the Jews. May our blood not be exacted from you." The maidens remained martyrs in will.

"Thy Name is as oil poured out: therefore young maidens have loved thee" (Cant 1:2).

* *Dicconson was beatified by Pope Pius XI on 15 December 1929.*

July 8

THE SHIELD OF TRUTH

✠ Bl. Adrian Fortescue, L., 1539

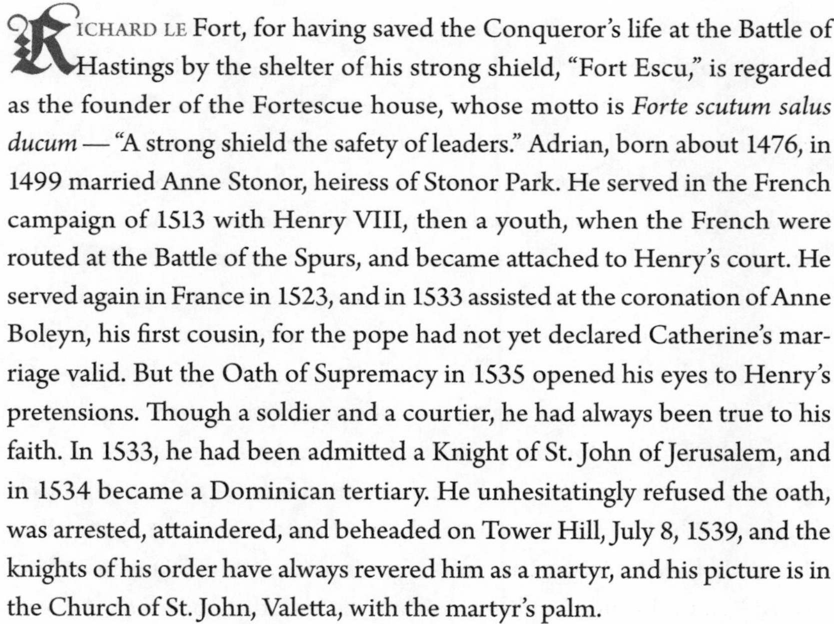

Richard le Fort, for having saved the Conqueror's life at the Battle of Hastings by the shelter of his strong shield, "Fort Escu," is regarded as the founder of the Fortescue house, whose motto is *Forte scutum salus ducum* — "A strong shield the safety of leaders." Adrian, born about 1476, in 1499 married Anne Stonor, heiress of Stonor Park. He served in the French campaign of 1513 with Henry VIII, then a youth, when the French were routed at the Battle of the Spurs, and became attached to Henry's court. He served again in France in 1523, and in 1533 assisted at the coronation of Anne Boleyn, his first cousin, for the pope had not yet declared Catherine's marriage valid. But the Oath of Supremacy in 1535 opened his eyes to Henry's pretensions. Though a soldier and a courtier, he had always been true to his faith. In 1533, he had been admitted a Knight of St. John of Jerusalem, and in 1534 became a Dominican tertiary. He unhesitatingly refused the oath, was arrested, attaindered, and beheaded on Tower Hill, July 8, 1539, and the knights of his order have always revered him as a martyr, and his picture is in the Church of St. John, Valetta, with the martyr's palm.

"His truth shall compass thee as a shield: thou shalt not fear the terror of the night" (Ps 90:5).

July 9

INTRODUCER TO CHRIST

Ven. Ralph Milner, L., 1591

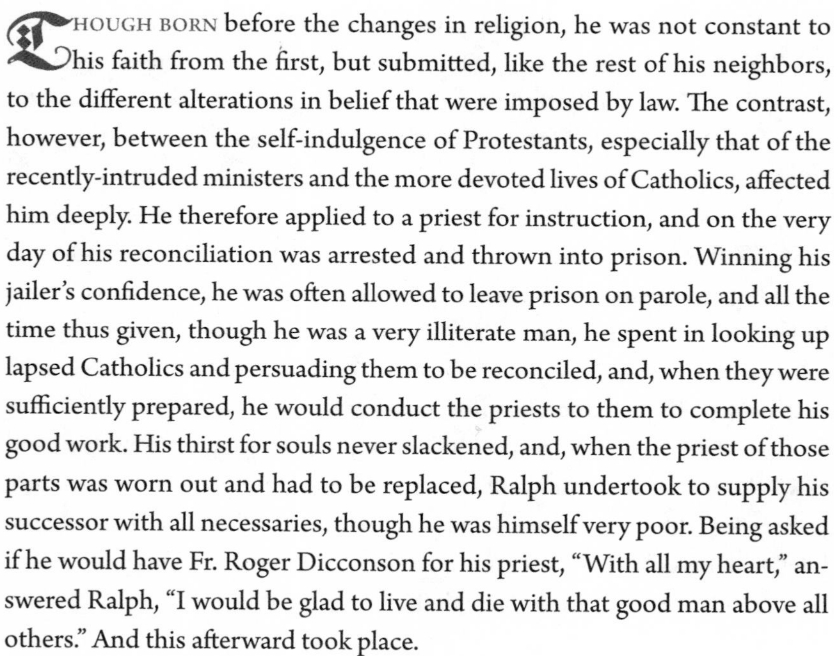

Though born before the changes in religion, he was not constant to his faith from the first, but submitted, like the rest of his neighbors, to the different alterations in belief that were imposed by law. The contrast, however, between the self-indulgence of Protestants, especially that of the recently-intruded ministers and the more devoted lives of Catholics, affected him deeply. He therefore applied to a priest for instruction, and on the very day of his reconciliation was arrested and thrown into prison. Winning his jailer's confidence, he was often allowed to leave prison on parole, and all the time thus given, though he was a very illiterate man, he spent in looking up lapsed Catholics and persuading them to be reconciled, and, when they were sufficiently prepared, he would conduct the priests to them to complete his good work. His thirst for souls never slackened, and, when the priest of those parts was worn out and had to be replaced, Ralph undertook to supply his successor with all necessaries, though he was himself very poor. Being asked if he would have Fr. Roger Dicconson for his priest, "With all my heart," answered Ralph, "I would be glad to live and die with that good man above all others." And this afterward took place.

"Andrew findeth his brother Simon.... and he brought him to Jesus" (Jn 1:41–42).

* *Milner was beatified by Pope Pius XI on 15 December 1929.*

July 10

THE WINDING-SHEET

Bl. Thomas More, L., 1535

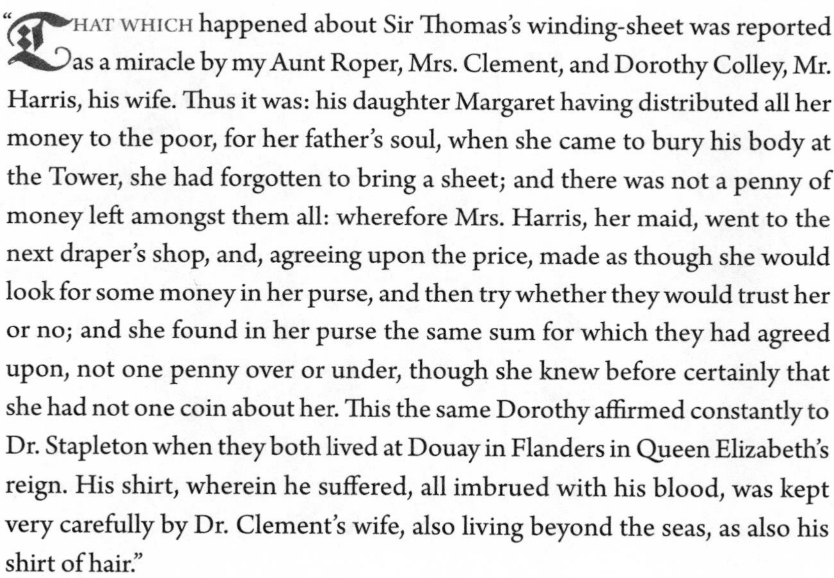

"THAT WHICH happened about Sir Thomas's winding-sheet was reported as a miracle by my Aunt Roper, Mrs. Clement, and Dorothy Colley, Mr. Harris, his wife. Thus it was: his daughter Margaret having distributed all her money to the poor, for her father's soul, when she came to bury his body at the Tower, she had forgotten to bring a sheet; and there was not a penny of money left amongst them all: wherefore Mrs. Harris, her maid, went to the next draper's shop, and, agreeing upon the price, made as though she would look for some money in her purse, and then try whether they would trust her or no; and she found in her purse the same sum for which they had agreed upon, not one penny over or under, though she knew before certainly that she had not one coin about her. This the same Dorothy affirmed constantly to Dr. Stapleton when they both lived at Douay in Flanders in Queen Elizabeth's reign. His shirt, wherein he suffered, all imbrued with his blood, was kept very carefully by Dr. Clement's wife, also living beyond the seas, as also his shirt of hair."

"And Joseph, buying fine linen, and taking Him, wrapped Him in the fine linen, and laid Him in a sepulchre" (Mk 15:46).

July 11

"FOR MY SAKE AND THE GOSPEL"

Ven. Ralph Milner, L., 1591

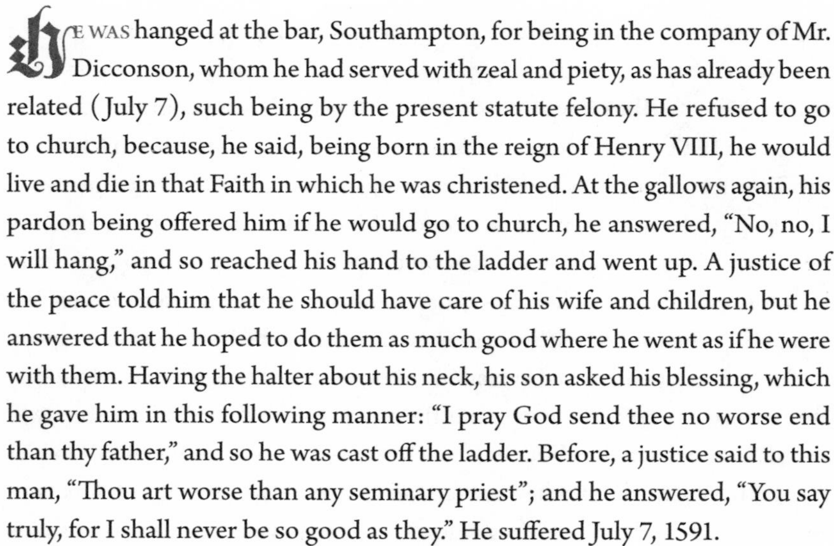

HE WAS hanged at the bar, Southampton, for being in the company of Mr. Dicconson, whom he had served with zeal and piety, as has already been related (July 7), such being by the present statute felony. He refused to go to church, because, he said, being born in the reign of Henry VIII, he would live and die in that Faith in which he was christened. At the gallows again, his pardon being offered him if he would go to church, he answered, "No, no, I will hang," and so reached his hand to the ladder and went up. A justice of the peace told him that he should have care of his wife and children, but he answered that he hoped to do them as much good where he went as if he were with them. Having the halter about his neck, his son asked his blessing, which he gave him in this following manner: "I pray God send thee no worse end than thy father," and so he was cast off the ladder. Before, a justice said to this man, "Thou art worse than any seminary priest"; and he answered, "You say truly, for I shall never be so good as they." He suffered July 7, 1591.

"He that loveth father or mother more than
Me is not worthy of Me" (Mt 10:37).

July 12

APOSTOLIC CHARITY

✠ Ven. John Buckley, O. S. F., 1598

THE PRISON of the Marshalsea was the first field of his priestly labors. In confinement there were many so-called Protestants, who, if not apostates, were at least the children of Catholics, and in their affections more easily reconciled. There were also Catholics of all ranks and classes, separated from their families, some perhaps racked and tortured, all suffering scarcely less from the filth and foul air of the dungeons. The rich were drained by exorbitant charges, the poor subjected to unauthorized barbarities by mercenary jailers. Among these, Fr. Buckley found ample work, consoling the dejected, upholding the weak, raising the fallen. From the Marshalsea he was transferred to Wisbeach, and after three years' confinement there, whether banished or by making his escape, he went to Rome. There he was enrolled as a Franciscan; but in 1593, after three years' apostolic work in England, he was again put in prison, where, as before, he did incalculable good, and was made provincial of his order. In 1598, he was arraigned and condemned for having, as a priest, returned to England against the statute. He suffered at St. Thomas Waterings, Southwark, July 12, 1598.

"For I long to see you … to strengthen you; that is to say, that I may be comforted together in you by that which is common to us both, your faith and mine" (Rom 1:11–12).

* *Buckley was canonized by Pope Paul VI on 25 October 1970.*

July 13

PILATE'S WIFE

✠ Ven. Thomas Tunstall, Pr., 1616

Of an old Lancashire family, he returned from Douay to the English mission in 1610, and soon falling into the hands of the persecutors, spent four or five years in different prisons, the last of which was Wisbeach. From this prison he made his escape by letting himself down by a rope, and took shelter in a friend's house near Lynn, Norfolk. His hands being much galled and wounded by the friction of the rope, and having no proper remedies, he applied to a charitable lady, Lady l'Estrange, who was skilled in surgery and did much service to the poor. She received him kindly, dressed his wounds, and promised him her best assistance. She could not, however, forbear describing to her husband (a justice of the peace), Sir Hammond l'Estrange, her new strange patient. The justice immediately cried out that he was the priest escaped from Wisbeach, and must be seized. The lady on her knees begged her husband to forget what she had said, adding that she would be unhappy all her life if the priest suffered through her. He, however, was apprehended, and, in spite of her repeated entreaties, was condemned and executed at Norwich, thanking Sir Hammond for being chiefly instrumental in bringing him to his end.

"And as he was sitting in the place of judgment, his wife sent to him, saying: Have thou nothing to do with that just man" (Mt 27:19).

* *Tunstall was beatified by Pope Pius XI on 15 December 1929.*

July 14

THE LAW ETERNAL

✠ Ven. Richard Langhorne, L., 1679

In spite of the penal statute forbidding Catholics to follow the law, he had risen to eminence in that profession, while at the same time he was known as a zealous Catholic. For this reason, he was impeached by Oates as a ringleader in his pretended plot. He defended himself with great ability, proved an alibi against Oates's statement as to where he lodged for the plot, but all in vain; he was condemned, and drawn to Tyburn, July 14, 1679. In his printed speech, he declares his allegiance to the King, his innocency of the plot, and the sinfulness of treason. He then continued: "I take it to be clear that my religion alone is the cause for which I am accused and condemned. I have had not only a pardon, but also great advantages as to preferments and estates offered me in case I would forsake my religion, own myself guilty, and charge others with the same crime. By God's grace, I have chosen rather this death than charge others against the truth." Great as an exponent of human law, he was greater still in sealing with his blood his adhesion to the eternal law of God. With the words, "Into Thy hands I commend my spirit," he went to his reward.

"Thy justice is justice forever, and Thy law is the truth" (Ps 118:142).

* *Langhorne was beatified by Pope Pius XI on 15 December 1929.*

July 15

NO COMPROMISE

Bl. Thomas More, L., 1535

His keenest trial arose from the endeavor of his beloved daughter to persuade him to take the oath, as she had done herself. She urged that he was more to the King than any man in England, and therefore ought to obey him in what was not evidently repugnant to God's law. That in favor of the oath were all the learned men of England, and nearly all the bishops and doctors, save Fisher. More answered that he condemned no one for taking the oath, "for some may do it upon temporal hopes, or fear of great losses, for which I will never think any have taken it; for I imagine that nobody is so frail and fearful as myself. Some may hope that God will not impute it unto them for a sin, because they do it by constraint. Some may hope to do penance presently after, and others are of opinion that God is not offended with our mouth, so our heart be pure; but as for my part, I dare not jeopardy myself upon these vain hopes." As to the numbers against him, he had on his side many more in other parts of Christendom, and all the doctors of the Church.

"He that is not with Me, is against Me: and he that gathereth not with Me, scattereth" (Mt 12:30).

July 16

THE CONTINUITY THEORY

✠ Ven. John Sugar, Pr., 1604

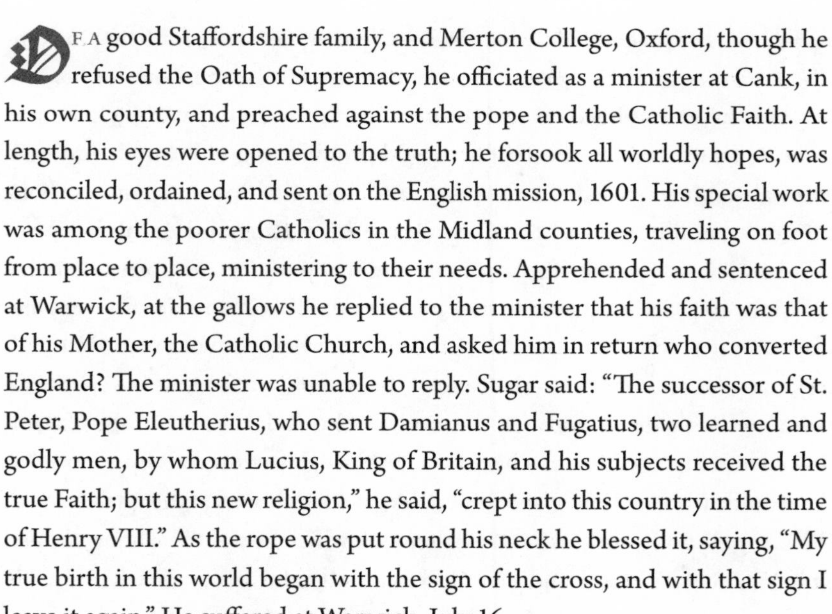

Of a good Staffordshire family, and Merton College, Oxford, though he refused the Oath of Supremacy, he officiated as a minister at Cank, in his own county, and preached against the pope and the Catholic Faith. At length, his eyes were opened to the truth; he forsook all worldly hopes, was reconciled, ordained, and sent on the English mission, 1601. His special work was among the poorer Catholics in the Midland counties, traveling on foot from place to place, ministering to their needs. Apprehended and sentenced at Warwick, at the gallows he replied to the minister that his faith was that of his Mother, the Catholic Church, and asked him in return who converted England? The minister was unable to reply. Sugar said: "The successor of St. Peter, Pope Eleutherius, who sent Damianus and Fugatius, two learned and godly men, by whom Lucius, King of Britain, and his subjects received the true Faith; but this new religion," he said, "crept into this country in the time of Henry VIII." As the rope was put round his neck he blessed it, saying, "My true birth in this world began with the sign of the cross, and with that sign I leave it again." He suffered at Warwick, July 16.

"You are fellow citizens with the saints ... built upon the foundation of the apostles and prophets, Jesus Christ Himself being the chief cornerstone" (Eph 2:19–20).

* *Sugar was beatified by Pope John Paul II on 22 November 1987.*

July 17

ZEAL FOR MARTYRDOM

Ven. Robert Grissold, L., 1604

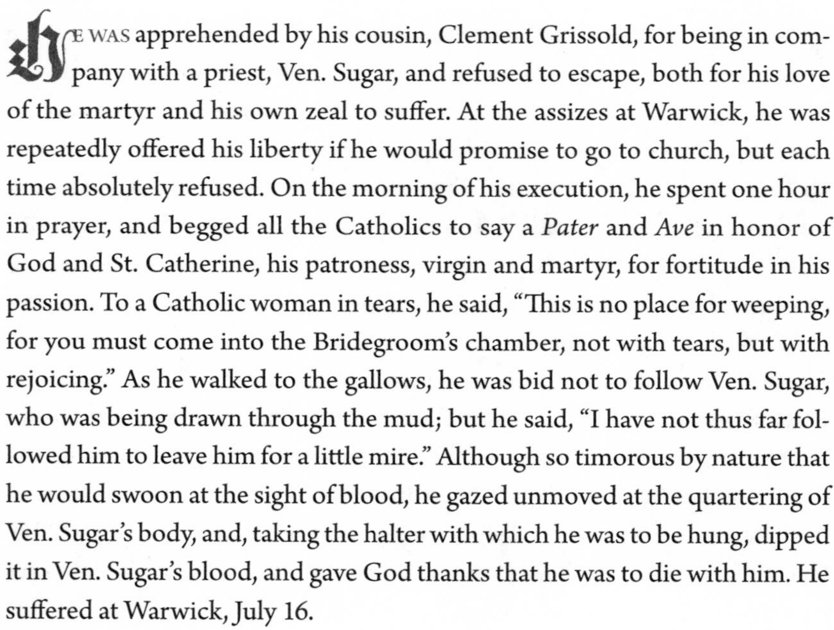

He was apprehended by his cousin, Clement Grissold, for being in company with a priest, Ven. Sugar, and refused to escape, both for his love of the martyr and his own zeal to suffer. At the assizes at Warwick, he was repeatedly offered his liberty if he would promise to go to church, but each time absolutely refused. On the morning of his execution, he spent one hour in prayer, and begged all the Catholics to say a *Pater* and *Ave* in honor of God and St. Catherine, his patroness, virgin and martyr, for fortitude in his passion. To a Catholic woman in tears, he said, "This is no place for weeping, for you must come into the Bridegroom's chamber, not with tears, but with rejoicing." As he walked to the gallows, he was bid not to follow Ven. Sugar, who was being drawn through the mud; but he said, "I have not thus far followed him to leave him for a little mire." Although so timorous by nature that he would swoon at the sight of blood, he gazed unmoved at the quartering of Ven. Sugar's body, and, taking the halter with which he was to be hung, dipped it in Ven. Sugar's blood, and gave God thanks that he was to die with him. He suffered at Warwick, July 16.

"For I am ready not only to be bound, but to die also in Jerusalem, for the name of the Lord Jesus" (Acts 21:13).

* *Grissold was beatified by Pope John Paul II on 22 November 1987.*

July 18

HIS FATHER'S SON

Ven. William Davies, Pr., 1593

BORN OF an old family in Carnarvonshire, he studied at Rheims, was ordained, and sent on the English mission in 1585. He labored in his own county, and brought many lost sheep back to the fold. On March 20, 1592, while endeavoring to procure a passage for four young men to Ireland, who were going to Valladolid to study for the priesthood, he and his companions were arrested and hurried off to Beaumaris. Having confessed himself a priest, he was separated from his companions and cast into a fetid dungeon, but after a month he was allowed more liberty, and was constantly consulted by the Catholics for miles round. At the assizes, he was condemned to death, and his companions found guilty of felony. After being removed to various prisons, he was brought to Beaumaris, and the day of his execution fixed. He was, however, so beloved that no one could be found to act as hangman or to supply the materials required; at length, by the hands of strangers, he suffered, July 27, 1593. The youngest of his four companions was entrusted to a schoolmaster to be whipped into conformity with the established religion. The boy, however, was whipped in vain, and at length escaped to Ireland, when, with a schoolfellow he had converted, he found his way to Valladolid.

"He walked in the steps of his father" (2 Par 34:2).

* *Davies was beatified by Pope John Paul II on 22 November 1987.*

July 19

"BONES THOU HAST HUMBLED"

✠ Ven. Anthony Brookby, O. S. F., 1537

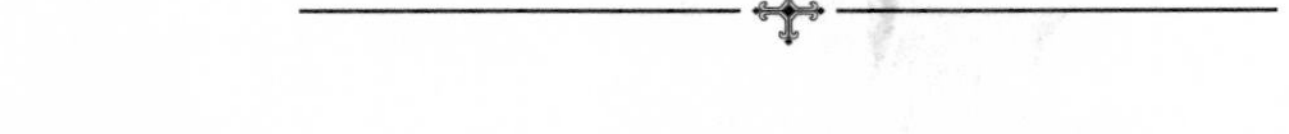

AMONG THE two hundred Observants cast into prison by Henry VIII was Fr. Brookby, professor of divinity in Magdalen College, Oxford. He was very learned in Greek and Hebrew, and was distinguished as an eloquent preacher. One day as he was preaching in the Church of St. Laurence in London, he inveighed strongly against the King's late proceedings. He was consequently taken up by His Majesty's express commands, and was thrown into a loathsome dungeon. Here he was placed on the rack in order to induce him to retract his words. But he bore all the tortures with wonderful courage and constancy, and, far from yielding a single point, he only expressed an ardent desire to suffer yet more cruel torments for the love of God. So unusually barbarous was his racking that every joint in his body was dislocated, and he could not move or even raise his hand to his mouth. For twenty-five days a devout old woman charitably waited on him and fed him. At the end of that time, an executioner came to him, by the King's command, and as he lay in bed strangled him with the rope which he wore as a girdle. He suffered, July 19, 1537.

"And the bones that have been humbled shall rejoice" (Ps 50:10).

July 20

NO PRIEST, NO RELIGION

Ven. William Plessington, Pr., 1679

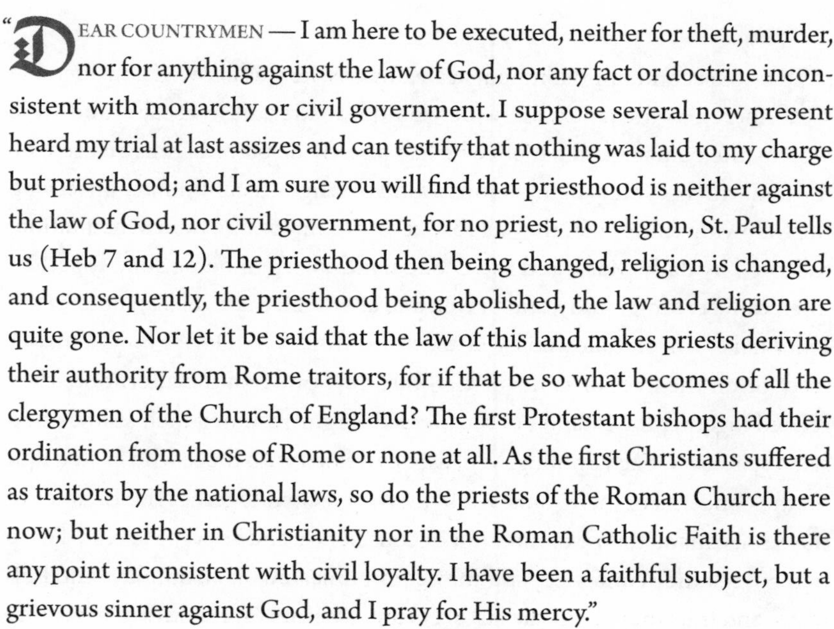

“DEAR COUNTRYMEN — I am here to be executed, neither for theft, murder, nor for anything against the law of God, nor any fact or doctrine inconsistent with monarchy or civil government. I suppose several now present heard my trial at last assizes and can testify that nothing was laid to my charge but priesthood; and I am sure you will find that priesthood is neither against the law of God, nor civil government, for no priest, no religion, St. Paul tells us (Heb 7 and 12). The priesthood then being changed, religion is changed, and consequently, the priesthood being abolished, the law and religion are quite gone. Nor let it be said that the law of this land makes priests deriving their authority from Rome traitors, for if that be so what becomes of all the clergymen of the Church of England? The first Protestant bishops had their ordination from those of Rome or none at all. As the first Christians suffered as traitors by the national laws, so do the priests of the Roman Church here now; but neither in Christianity nor in the Roman Catholic Faith is there any point inconsistent with civil loyalty. I have been a faithful subject, but a grievous sinner against God, and I pray for His mercy.”

“And the others were made many priests, because by reason of death they were not suffered to continue: but this, for that He continueth forever, hath an everlasting priesthood” (Heb 7:23–24).

* *Plessington was canonized by Pope Paul VI on 25 October 1970.*

July 21

THE THREE CHILDREN IN THE FURNACE

Ven. William Davies, Pr., and companions, 1592

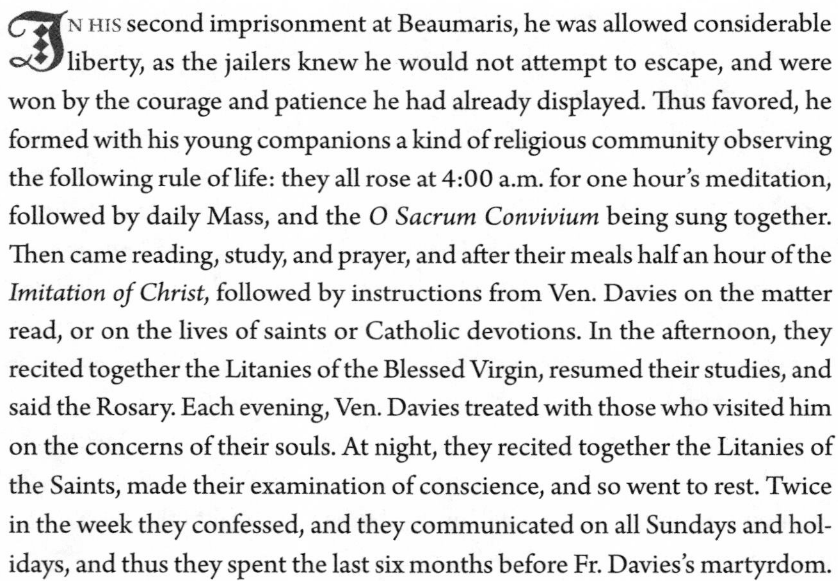

In his second imprisonment at Beaumaris, he was allowed considerable liberty, as the jailers knew he would not attempt to escape, and were won by the courage and patience he had already displayed. Thus favored, he formed with his young companions a kind of religious community observing the following rule of life: they all rose at 4:00 a.m. for one hour's meditation, followed by daily Mass, and the *O Sacrum Convivium* being sung together. Then came reading, study, and prayer, and after their meals half an hour of the *Imitation of Christ,* followed by instructions from Ven. Davies on the matter read, or on the lives of saints or Catholic devotions. In the afternoon, they recited together the Litanies of the Blessed Virgin, resumed their studies, and said the Rosary. Each evening, Ven. Davies treated with those who visited him on the concerns of their souls. At night, they recited together the Litanies of the Saints, made their examination of conscience, and so went to rest. Twice in the week they confessed, and they communicated on all Sundays and holidays, and thus they spent the last six months before Fr. Davies's martyrdom.

"And they walked in the midst of the flame, praising God and blessing the Lord" (Dn 3:24).

July 22

ALWAYS READY

Ven. Philip Evans, S.J., 1679

Born in Monmouthshire, educated at St. Omer's, he entered the Society, and labored for four years with great fruit on the English mission. On the breaking out of the Oates Plot persecution, he was urged to fly, but chose rather to risk his life amidst his flock. Apprehended, he was condemned at Cardiff with Mr. John Lloyd, a secular priest, who was his companion to the end. The execution was so long deferred that it was thought they would not suffer, and they were allowed considerable liberty. One day when Fr. Evans was out of doors engaged in some recreation, the jailer brought him the news that he was to be executed on the morrow, and must return to prison. "Why so much haste?" said Fr. Evans, "let me finish my game first." And so he did, and then returned to prison, and felt he could scarce contain himself for joy, and taking his harp, for he was a musician, he made it tell his soul's happiness. His irons were so firmly riveted that their removal lasted an hour and caused great pain, but his patience was never disturbed. On the scaffold he declared his innocence, and with a bright and cheerful countenance went to his reward. He was but thirty-four years of age, and had spent fourteen in the Society.

"My heart is ready, O God, my heart is ready: I will sing and will give praise" (Ps 107:2).

* *Evans was canonized by Pope Paul VI on 25 October 1970.*

July 23

A FALL AND A RISING

Ven. Richard Sympson, Pr., 1588

FROM THE Protestant ministry he became a priest. After being several times imprisoned, he was finally condemned at York, 1588. Having a reprieve, he appears to have given some semblance of conformity, but was reclaimed by his fellow prisoners, Vens. Garlick and Ludlam, and on July 24 martyred with them, as an eyewitness and poet thus describes:

When Garlick did the ladder kiss,
And Sympson after hie,
Methought that there St. Andrew was
Desirous for to die.

When Ludlam looked smilingly
And joyful did remain,
It seemed St. Stephen was standing by
For to be stoned again.

And what if Sympson seemed to yield
For doubt and dread to die,
He rose again and won the field,
And died more constantly.

His watching, fast, and shirt of hair,
His speech and death and all,
Do record give, do witness bear,
He wailed his former fall.

"To him that shall overcome, I will give to sit with Me on My throne" (Apoc 3:21).

* *Sympson was beatified by Pope John Paul II on 22 November 1987.*

July 24

ANOTHER JUDAS

✠ Ven. John Bost, Pr., 1594

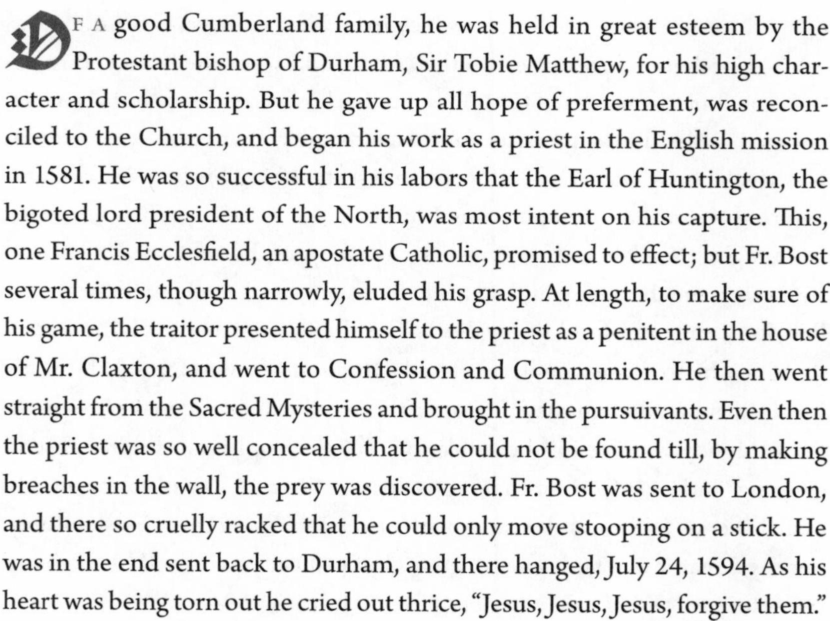

Of a good Cumberland family, he was held in great esteem by the Protestant bishop of Durham, Sir Tobie Matthew, for his high character and scholarship. But he gave up all hope of preferment, was reconciled to the Church, and began his work as a priest in the English mission in 1581. He was so successful in his labors that the Earl of Huntington, the bigoted lord president of the North, was most intent on his capture. This, one Francis Ecclesfield, an apostate Catholic, promised to effect; but Fr. Bost several times, though narrowly, eluded his grasp. At length, to make sure of his game, the traitor presented himself to the priest as a penitent in the house of Mr. Claxton, and went to Confession and Communion. He then went straight from the Sacred Mysteries and brought in the pursuivants. Even then the priest was so well concealed that he could not be found till, by making breaches in the wall, the prey was discovered. Fr. Bost was sent to London, and there so cruelly racked that he could only move stooping on a stick. He was in the end sent back to Durham, and there hanged, July 24, 1594. As his heart was being torn out he cried out thrice, "Jesus, Jesus, Jesus, forgive them."

"And after the morsel, Satan entered into him" (Jn 13:27).

* *Bost was canonized by Pope Paul VI on 25 October 1970.*

July 25

THE SEED OF THE CHURCH

Ven. John Ingram, Pr., 1594

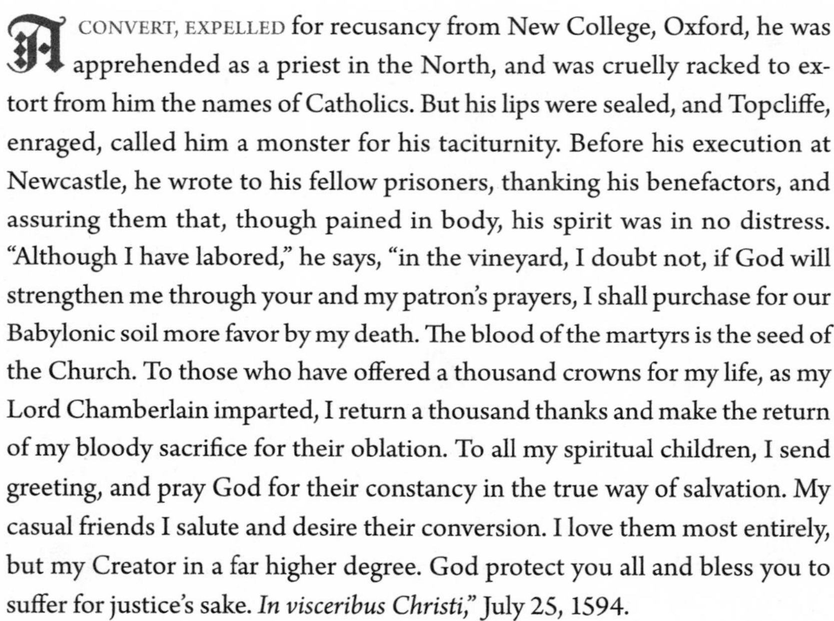

A CONVERT, EXPELLED for recusancy from New College, Oxford, he was apprehended as a priest in the North, and was cruelly racked to extort from him the names of Catholics. But his lips were sealed, and Topcliffe, enraged, called him a monster for his taciturnity. Before his execution at Newcastle, he wrote to his fellow prisoners, thanking his benefactors, and assuring them that, though pained in body, his spirit was in no distress. "Although I have labored," he says, "in the vineyard, I doubt not, if God will strengthen me through your and my patron's prayers, I shall purchase for our Babylonic soil more favor by my death. The blood of the martyrs is the seed of the Church. To those who have offered a thousand crowns for my life, as my Lord Chamberlain imparted, I return a thousand thanks and make the return of my bloody sacrifice for their oblation. To all my spiritual children, I send greeting, and pray God for their constancy in the true way of salvation. My casual friends I salute and desire their conversion. I love them most entirely, but my Creator in a far higher degree. God protect you all and bless you to suffer for justice's sake. *In visceribus Christi*," July 25, 1594.

"As dying, and behold we live" (2 Cor 6:9).

* *Ingram was beatified by Pope Pius XI on 15 December 1929.*

GEORGE SWALLOWELL
"Behold the head of a traitor"

July 26

A BROTHER IN NEED

Ven. George Swallowell, L., 1594

A Protestant reader in the Bishopric of Durham, he paid a visit to a Catholic gentleman imprisoned for recusancy, who pressed him on the question of his authority to preach. Convinced of the absurdity of making a woman the Head of the Church, against the words of St. Paul, he publicly professed from the pulpit his conviction that he was no true minister, and would no longer officiate in that Church. Upon this he was arrested, and, after a year's imprisonment in Durham jail, was brought to the bar with Frs. Bost and Ingram. At first, through fear of death, he promised the judges to conform, on which Fr. Bost, looking at him, said, "George Swallowell, what hast thou done?" and he, horrified, begged in return to have his word back. Cautioned that death would be the consequence, he boldly said that he "professed the same Faith as the two priests, and would die their death." With that Fr. Bost looked at him again and said, "Hold thee there, Swallowell, and my soul for thine," and with these words laid his hand on his head. Then the lord president said, "Away with Bost, for he is reconciling him." Swallowell won his crown with great constancy, Darlington, July 26.

"A brother that is helped by a brother is
like a strong city" (Prv 18:19).

* *Swallowell was beatified by Pope Pius XI on 15 December 1929.*

July 27

VOICES FROM HEAVEN

✠ Ven. Robert Sutton, Pr., 1587

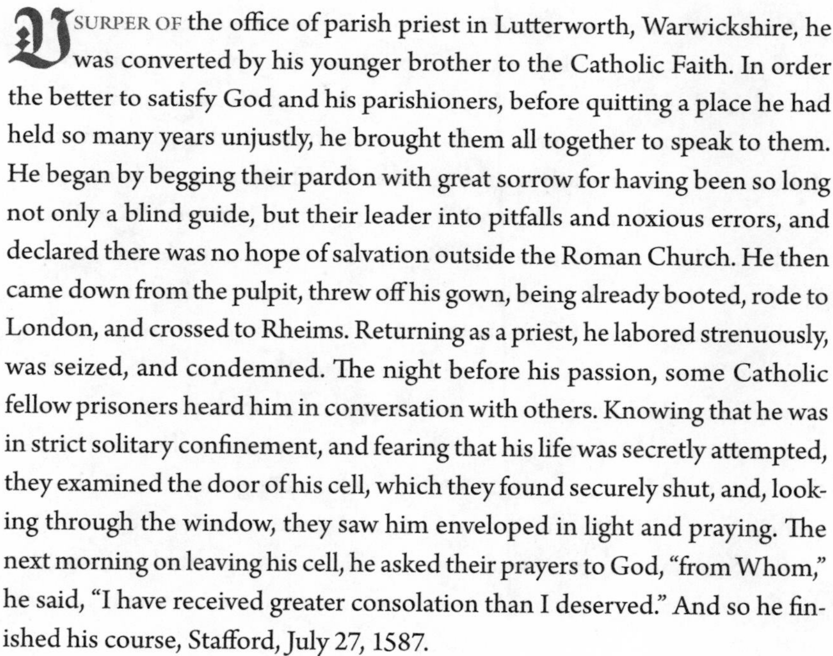

Usurper of the office of parish priest in Lutterworth, Warwickshire, he was converted by his younger brother to the Catholic Faith. In order the better to satisfy God and his parishioners, before quitting a place he had held so many years unjustly, he brought them all together to speak to them. He began by begging their pardon with great sorrow for having been so long not only a blind guide, but their leader into pitfalls and noxious errors, and declared there was no hope of salvation outside the Roman Church. He then came down from the pulpit, threw off his gown, being already booted, rode to London, and crossed to Rheims. Returning as a priest, he labored strenuously, was seized, and condemned. The night before his passion, some Catholic fellow prisoners heard him in conversation with others. Knowing that he was in strict solitary confinement, and fearing that his life was secretly attempted, they examined the door of his cell, which they found securely shut, and, looking through the window, they saw him enveloped in light and praying. The next morning on leaving his cell, he asked their prayers to God, "from Whom," he said, "I have received greater consolation than I deserved." And so he finished his course, Stafford, July 27, 1587.

"I heard a voice from heaven saying to me: Write: Blessed are the dead who die in the Lord" (Apoc 14:13).

* *Sutton was beatified by Pope John Paul II on 22 November 1987.*

July 28

A CLIENT OF ST. ANNE

✠ Ven. William Ward, O. S. F., 1641

HE WAS the first martyr under the persecution, renewed in spite of his promises, by Charles I. Born a Protestant, of a good Westmorland family, educated at Brasenose College, Oxford, he became a Catholic traveling abroad. On his return, he practiced his religion so openly that he was in prison at different times for nearly ten years. He entered Douay, was ordained priest 1608, and embarked for England. A contrary wind, however, drove him to Scotland, where, as a suspected priest, he was kept in an underground dungeon, in total darkness, for three years. Set free, he returned to England, and for thirty years, twenty of which were spent in prison, in spite of continuous suffering from a corrosive fistula and chronic toothache, he toiled for souls. He never preached, but holy conversation and the Sacrament of Penance were the weapons of his apostolate, and the harvest reaped was abundant. When over eighty years of age, he was sentenced for saying Mass. He had a true Franciscan devotion to our Blessed Lady, and had always kept the feast of her mother St. Anne with great solemnity, and he was now granted to die on that day. In the morning, he said Mass, and, going forth with joy, won his crown.

"Give her of the fruit of her hands, and let her works praise her in the gates" (Prv 31:31).

* *Ward was beatified by Pope Pius XI on 15 December 1929.*

July 29

A BURNING HEART

✠ Ven. William Ward, O. S. F., 1641

"BEHOLD THE heart of a traitor!" cried the hangman, with the martyr's heart still palpitating in his hand, and threw it into the fire. Eager to obtain a relic, Count Egmont, a pious Catholic then in England, sent his servant with his handkerchief to dip it in the martyr's blood. Others, however, had been before him and not a drop remained. Searching in the ashes, the servant found a heap of flesh singed with the fiery coals, and hastily wrapped the whole mass in his handkerchief. An attempt being now made to seize him, he fled across Hyde Park; but as his pursuers gained, he pretended to stumble, and hid his treasure in a bush as he fell. Taken before the magistrates, he was released through the count's interest. The next day, he returned and found his treasure, which proved to be the martyr's heart. As with St. Laurence, the divine fire within was stronger than the outward earthly flame. The hot coals adhering to the flesh had not burned the handkerchief, and the heart itself remained fifteen days incorrupt, when the count had it embalmed, and took it to Paris with the relics of fourteen other martyrs whose executions he had witnessed, and on July 26, 1650, he signed and sealed the formal deed of authentication now in the archives of Lille.

"And there came in my heart as a burning fire shut up in my bones" (Jer 20:9).

July 30

AT LAST

✠ Bl. Thomas Abel, Pr., 1540

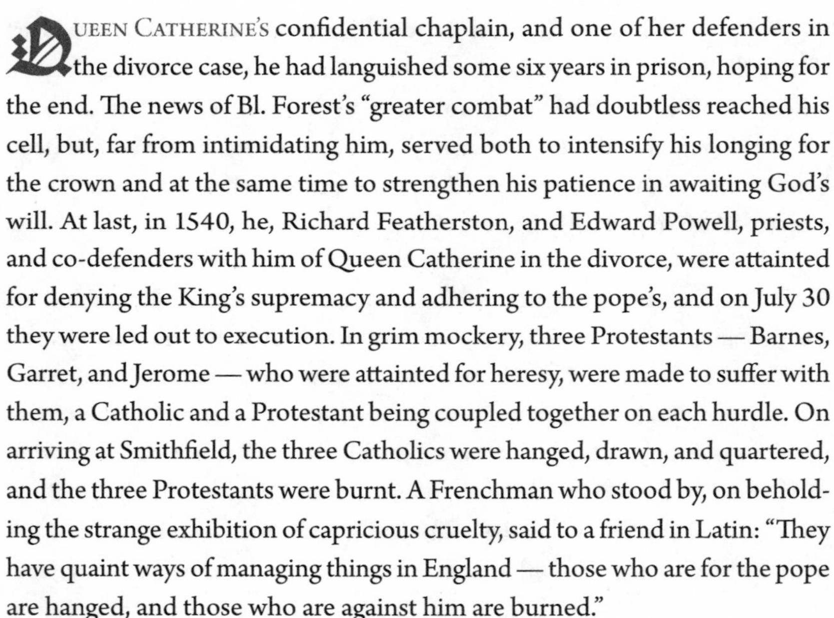

Queen Catherine's confidential chaplain, and one of her defenders in the divorce case, he had languished some six years in prison, hoping for the end. The news of Bl. Forest's "greater combat" had doubtless reached his cell, but, far from intimidating him, served both to intensify his longing for the crown and at the same time to strengthen his patience in awaiting God's will. At last, in 1540, he, Richard Featherston, and Edward Powell, priests, and co-defenders with him of Queen Catherine in the divorce, were attainted for denying the King's supremacy and adhering to the pope's, and on July 30 they were led out to execution. In grim mockery, three Protestants — Barnes, Garret, and Jerome — who were attainted for heresy, were made to suffer with them, a Catholic and a Protestant being coupled together on each hurdle. On arriving at Smithfield, the three Catholics were hanged, drawn, and quartered, and the three Protestants were burnt. A Frenchman who stood by, on beholding the strange exhibition of capricious cruelty, said to a friend in Latin: "They have quaint ways of managing things in England — those who are for the pope are hanged, and those who are against him are burned."

"Wait on God with patience; join thyself to God and endure, that thy life may be increased in the latter end" (Ecclus 2:3).

July 31

SHOD FOR THE GOSPEL

✠ Bl. Everard Hanse, Pr., 1581

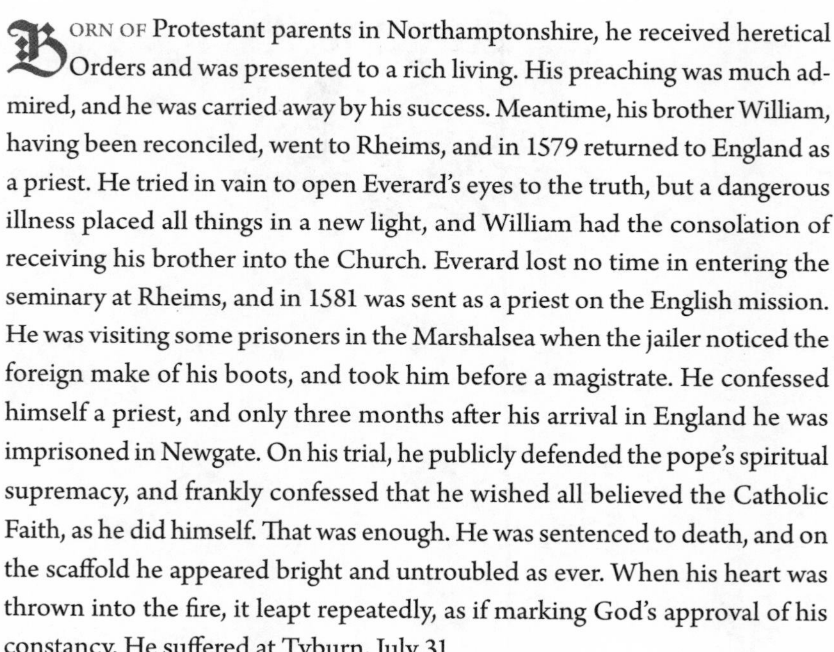

Born of Protestant parents in Northamptonshire, he received heretical Orders and was presented to a rich living. His preaching was much admired, and he was carried away by his success. Meantime, his brother William, having been reconciled, went to Rheims, and in 1579 returned to England as a priest. He tried in vain to open Everard's eyes to the truth, but a dangerous illness placed all things in a new light, and William had the consolation of receiving his brother into the Church. Everard lost no time in entering the seminary at Rheims, and in 1581 was sent as a priest on the English mission. He was visiting some prisoners in the Marshalsea when the jailer noticed the foreign make of his boots, and took him before a magistrate. He confessed himself a priest, and only three months after his arrival in England he was imprisoned in Newgate. On his trial, he publicly defended the pope's spiritual supremacy, and frankly confessed that he wished all believed the Catholic Faith, as he did himself. That was enough. He was sentenced to death, and on the scaffold he appeared bright and untroubled as ever. When his heart was thrown into the fire, it leapt repeatedly, as if marking God's approval of his constancy. He suffered at Tyburn, July 31.

"How beautiful are the feet of those that preach the gospel of peace, that bring glad tidings of good things" (Rom 10:15).

August

August 1

PETER REPENTANT

John Thomas, L., 1593

He was condemned, together with Bird, but, horrified at the sentence of death, promised the judge he would go to church. The judge could not recall the sentence given, so countermanded his execution till the Queen's pardon should arrive. On his return to prison, helped probably by Bird's exhortations, he conquered the fear of death by the fear of hell, and sent word at once to the judge that he repented of his cowardice, and would do nothing contrary to his duty as a Catholic. The judge said, "Is he in such a hurry for the gallows? Let him not be afraid; if he persists, we can hang him at the next assizes." Yet he appeared at the gallows with the other criminals, carrying his winding-sheet, and said to the sheriff he had been condemned and had come to die. But the sheriff said that, though he would meet his wishes with the greatest pleasure were it in his power, he could not do so, as his name was not on the list. So Thomas retired, lamenting his sin and his past life, for he had been a Calvinist minister; but God did not fail him, and, purged by a long penance, with a large increase of merits, in the August following he obtained what he desired, at Bardich, Winchester.

"And the Lord turning looked on Peter. . . . And Peter going out, wept bitterly" (Lk 22:61–62).

August 2

CASTING OUT FEAR

Ven. Thomas Whitaker, Pr., 1646

His father was master of a noted free school in Burnley, Lancashire, and Thomas, showing promise, was sent to the English College, Valladolid, at the charge of a neighboring Catholic family, Townley of Townley. He entered on the English mission in 1638, and gained many souls, facing bravely all dangers, notwithstanding his naturally timorous disposition. Being urged, on the road to Lancaster, to effect his escape from the room in which he was confined, he stripped himself, and, forgetting to throw out his clothes before him, the passage gained he found himself free, but naked. After wandering some miles in this strange condition, he providentially met with a Catholic, who gave him shelter and clothing. Again arrested, he was cruelly beaten and cast into Lancaster jail. There for three years his life was spent in continual prayer to God to strengthen him for the combat, and in ministering to the two priests, Fr. Bramber and Fr. Woodcock, O. S. B., his seniors, who were his fellow prisoners. His trial and sentence were quickly dispatched as he had confessed himself a priest. At the place of execution, his anguish of soul was evident, but grace triumphed over nature. He absolutely refused a proffered pardon, and with Fr. Bramber and Fr. Woodcock, O. S. B., he won his crown, Lancaster, August 7.

"Perfect charity casteth out fear" (1 Jn 4:18).

* *Whitaker was beatified by Pope John Paul II on 22 November 1987.*

August 3

THE BAPTIST AND HEROD

✠ Ven. Thomas Belchiam, O. S. F., 1538

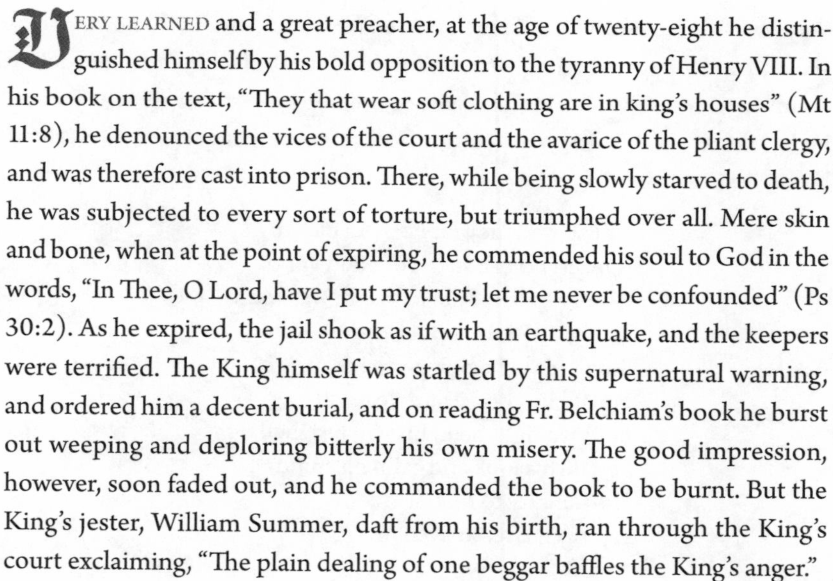

VERY LEARNED and a great preacher, at the age of twenty-eight he distinguished himself by his bold opposition to the tyranny of Henry VIII. In his book on the text, "They that wear soft clothing are in king's houses" (Mt 11:8), he denounced the vices of the court and the avarice of the pliant clergy, and was therefore cast into prison. There, while being slowly starved to death, he was subjected to every sort of torture, but triumphed over all. Mere skin and bone, when at the point of expiring, he commended his soul to God in the words, "In Thee, O Lord, have I put my trust; let me never be confounded" (Ps 30:2). As he expired, the jail shook as if with an earthquake, and the keepers were terrified. The King himself was startled by this supernatural warning, and ordered him a decent burial, and on reading Fr. Belchiam's book he burst out weeping and deploring bitterly his own misery. The good impression, however, soon faded out, and he commanded the book to be burnt. But the King's jester, William Summer, daft from his birth, ran through the King's court exclaiming, "The plain dealing of one beggar baffles the King's anger."

"And the king was struck sad; yet because of his oath and for them that sat with him at table . . . he sent and beheaded John in prison" (Mt 14:9–10).

August 4

Hermit and Martyr

Ven. Nicholas Postgate, Pr., 1679

Born in Yorkshire of parents great sufferers for the Faith, he returned from Douay to the English mission, June 1630. He labored in his native county and converted hundreds from sin and heresy. With all his active work, he led the life of a solitary in a hut on Blackamoor, which is thus described by a contemporary:

Nor spared they Fr. Posket's blood,
A reverend priest, devout and good,
Whose spotless life in length was spun
To eighty years and three times one.
Sweet his behavior, grave his speech,
He did by good example teach.
His love right bent, his will resigned,
Serene his look and calm his mind;
His sanctity to that degree
As angels live, so lived he.

A thatched cottage was the cell
Where this contemplative did dwell,
Two miles from Mulgrave Castle 't stood,
Sheltered by snowdrifts, not by wood.
Tho' there he lived to that great age
It was a dismal hermitage,
But God placed there the Saint's abode
For Blackamoor's greater good.

"You are dead: and your life is hid with Christ in God" (Col 3:3).

* *Postgate was beatified by Pope John Paul II on 22 November 1987.*

August 5

THE WINGS OF A DOVE

Ven. Nicholas Postgate, Pr., 1679

HUNTED ABOUT during the Oates persecution, he was at last arrested and condemned, not as a plotter, but for high treason as a priest. On the eve of his martyrdom at York, came, with other visitors, Mrs. Charles Fairfax and Mrs. Meynel of Kilvington in great grief at taking leave of him. But the confessor, bright and cheerful, laid his right hand on one and his left on the other and said, "Be of good heart, you shall both be delivered of sons, and they will be both saved." The two ladies gave birth to sons, who were baptized and died in infancy. In his weary hunted life, he prayed as follows:

And thus, dear Lord, I fly about
In weak and weary case;
And, like a dove in Noe's Ark,
I find no resting place.

My wearied limbs, sweet Jesus, mark;
And when Thou thinkest best,
Stretch forth Thy hand out of the ark
And take me to Thy breast.

The new mission of Pickering is a memorial of the martyr's ministry.

"Who will give me wings like a dove, and I will fly and be at rest?" (Ps 54:7).

August 6

TWICE HANGED

Ven. John Woodcock, O. S. F., 1646

On hearing his sentence, he was filled with inexpressible joy and exclaimed, "Praise be to God; God be thanked." Frs. Bamber and Reding, two secular priests, were condemned at the same time. The following night Fr. Woodcock spent in prayer and joyful contemplation. At the dawn of day, August 7th, he and his two companions were led out in the usual way to execution. An immense and noisy crowd followed them with abuse and insult. The Catholics who were present were greatly edified and consoled, and not a few Protestants were astonished at their constancy. Fr. Woodcock was the first to mount the ladder. After he had said a few words on the Catholic and Roman Faith he was cast off, but by some accident, or through the carelessness of the executioner, the rope broke and he fell to the ground. He was stunned for a moment, but quickly recovered himself and rose to his feet unhurt. At the sheriff's order he mounted the ladder again, and, after being thus hanged a second time, he was cut down and butchered alive. As the executioner's hand was within his body, "Jesus" broke from his lips.

"Thy dead men shall live, my slain shall rise again: awake and give praise, ye that dwell in the dust: for thy dew is the dew of the light: and the land of the giants thou shalt pull down into ruin" (Is 26:19).

* *Woodcock was beatified by Pope John Paul II on 22 November 1987.*

August 7

A PUBLIC CONFESSION

✠ Ven. Edward Bamber, Pr., 1646

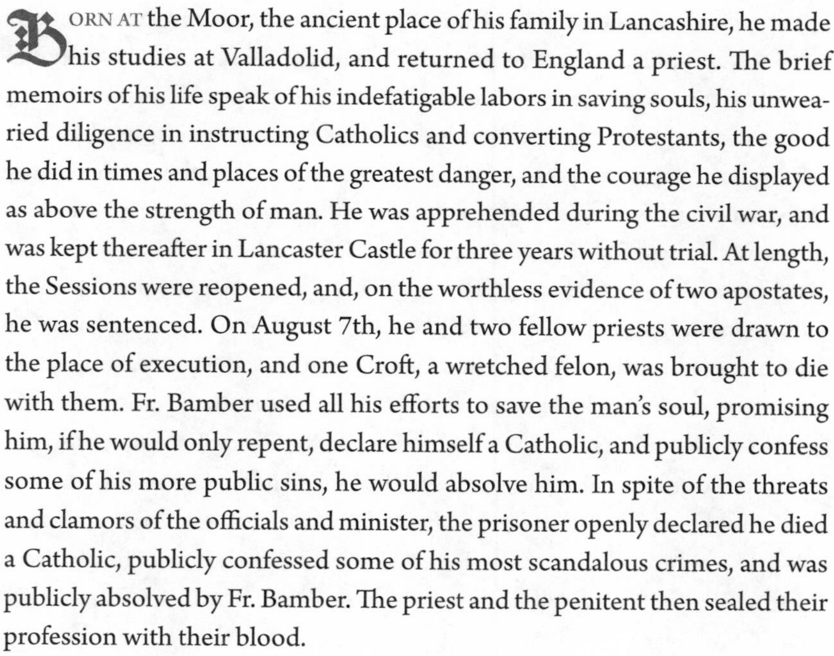

BORN AT the Moor, the ancient place of his family in Lancashire, he made his studies at Valladolid, and returned to England a priest. The brief memoirs of his life speak of his indefatigable labors in saving souls, his unwearied diligence in instructing Catholics and converting Protestants, the good he did in times and places of the greatest danger, and the courage he displayed as above the strength of man. He was apprehended during the civil war, and was kept thereafter in Lancaster Castle for three years without trial. At length, the Sessions were reopened, and, on the worthless evidence of two apostates, he was sentenced. On August 7th, he and two fellow priests were drawn to the place of execution, and one Croft, a wretched felon, was brought to die with them. Fr. Bamber used all his efforts to save the man's soul, promising him, if he would only repent, declare himself a Catholic, and publicly confess some of his more public sins, he would absolve him. In spite of the threats and clamors of the officials and minister, the prisoner openly declared he died a Catholic, publicly confessed some of his most scandalous crimes, and was publicly absolved by Fr. Bamber. The priest and the penitent then sealed their profession with their blood.

"Confess your sins one to another" (Jas 5:16).

* *Bamber was beatified by Pope John Paul II on 22 November 1987.*

August 8

A CHAMPION OF THE POPE

✠ Bl. John Felton, L., 1570

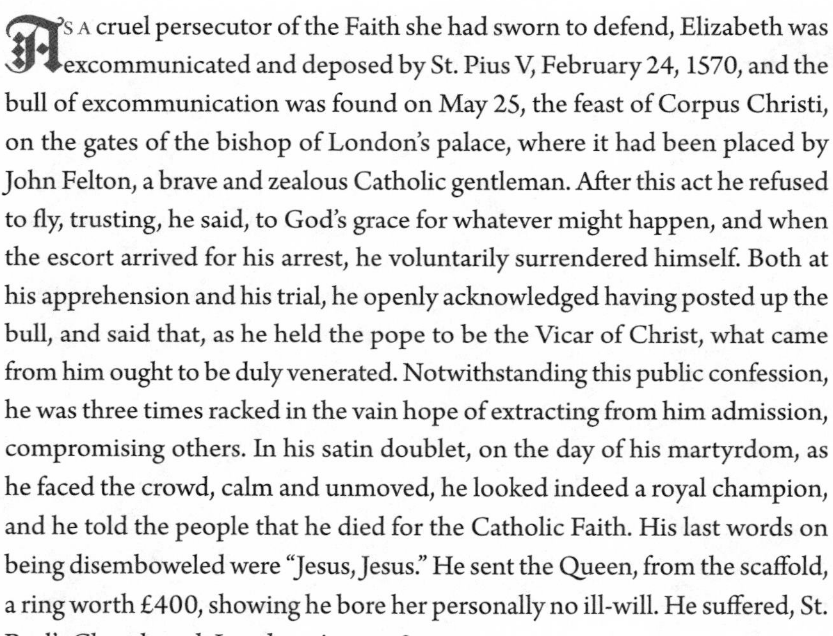

As a cruel persecutor of the Faith she had sworn to defend, Elizabeth was excommunicated and deposed by St. Pius V, February 24, 1570, and the bull of excommunication was found on May 25, the feast of Corpus Christi, on the gates of the bishop of London's palace, where it had been placed by John Felton, a brave and zealous Catholic gentleman. After this act he refused to fly, trusting, he said, to God's grace for whatever might happen, and when the escort arrived for his arrest, he voluntarily surrendered himself. Both at his apprehension and his trial, he openly acknowledged having posted up the bull, and said that, as he held the pope to be the Vicar of Christ, what came from him ought to be duly venerated. Notwithstanding this public confession, he was three times racked in the vain hope of extracting from him admission, compromising others. In his satin doublet, on the day of his martyrdom, as he faced the crowd, calm and unmoved, he looked indeed a royal champion, and he told the people that he died for the Catholic Faith. His last words on being disemboweled were "Jesus, Jesus." He sent the Queen, from the scaffold, a ring worth £400, showing he bore her personally no ill-will. He suffered, St. Paul's Churchyard, London, August 8.

"Thou art Peter, and upon this rock I will build My Church" (Mt 16:18).

August 9

POISON DETECTED

✠ Ven. Thomas Palasor, Pr., 1600

A Yorkshire man by birth, he was apprehended as a priest in the house of Mr. John Norton in that county, with his host and Mr. John Talbot, and all three were confined in Durham jail. There at dinner, some broth was set before Mr. Palasor, and, on his preparing to taste it, the bone of mutton in the dish ran blood in the form of crosses and of *O*'s in the broth. He therefore abstained from taking it. The maid, noticing this, carried the broth back to her mistress, who spiced it over and sent it by the same maid to Mr. Talbot and Mr. Norton, when the same phenomenon was repeated. The maid, by name Mary Day, seeing this, came to Palasor, confessed that the broth had been poisoned by the malice of her mistress, the jailer's wife, and on her knees begged his forgiveness, and asked him to make her one of his Faith. She was instructed and reconciled, and became servant to a Catholic gentlewoman, Eleanor Forcer, who bore testimony to the above occurrence. Palasor was condemned to death for returning to England as a priest, contrary to the statute, and Mr. Norton and Mr. Talbot received the same sentence for harboring and assisting him, and all three together were executed at Durham.

"They shall take up serpents, and, if they shall drink any deadly thing, it shall not hurt them" (Mk 16:18).

* *Palasor was beatified by Pope John Paul II on 22 November 1987.*

August 10

FORWARD TO THE MARK

Ven. John Woodcock, O. S. F., 1646

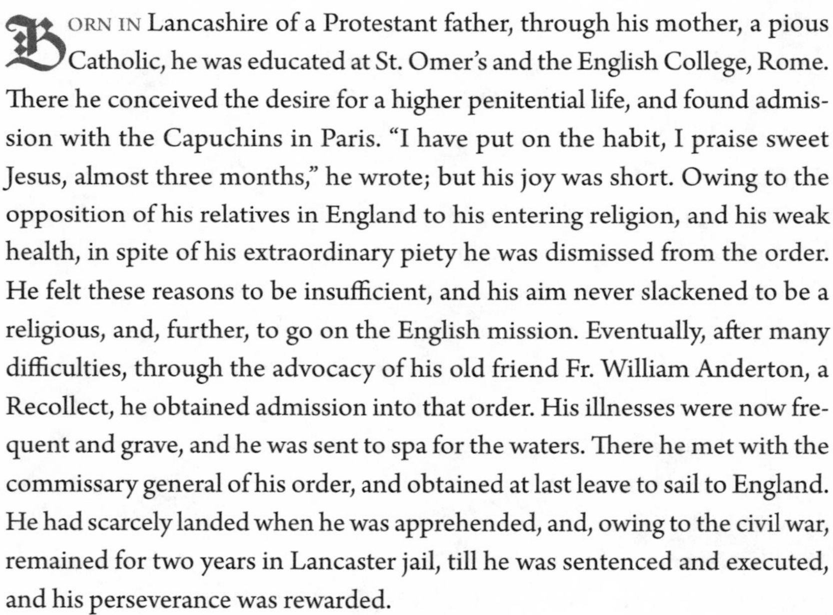

Born in Lancashire of a Protestant father, through his mother, a pious Catholic, he was educated at St. Omer's and the English College, Rome. There he conceived the desire for a higher penitential life, and found admission with the Capuchins in Paris. "I have put on the habit, I praise sweet Jesus, almost three months," he wrote; but his joy was short. Owing to the opposition of his relatives in England to his entering religion, and his weak health, in spite of his extraordinary piety he was dismissed from the order. He felt these reasons to be insufficient, and his aim never slackened to be a religious, and, further, to go on the English mission. Eventually, after many difficulties, through the advocacy of his old friend Fr. William Anderton, a Recollect, he obtained admission into that order. His illnesses were now frequent and grave, and he was sent to spa for the waters. There he met with the commissary general of his order, and obtained at last leave to sail to England. He had scarcely landed when he was apprehended, and, owing to the civil war, remained for two years in Lancaster jail, till he was sentenced and executed, and his perseverance was rewarded.

"One thing I do: forgetting the things that are behind…
I press forward to the mark, to the prize of the supernal
vocation of God in Christ Jesus" (Phil 3:13–14).

August 11

THE NORTHERN RISING

Letter of St. Pius V

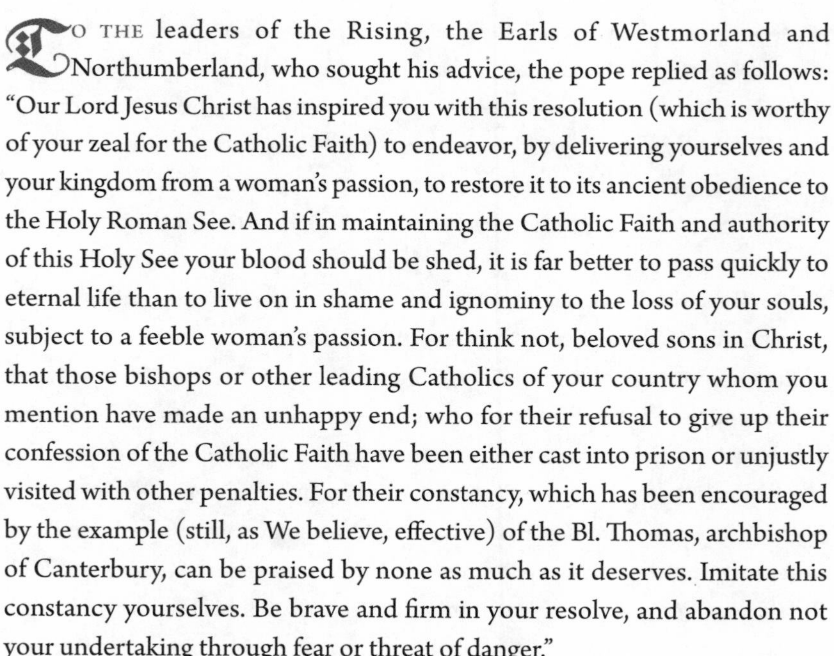

TO THE leaders of the Rising, the Earls of Westmorland and Northumberland, who sought his advice, the pope replied as follows: "Our Lord Jesus Christ has inspired you with this resolution (which is worthy of your zeal for the Catholic Faith) to endeavor, by delivering yourselves and your kingdom from a woman's passion, to restore it to its ancient obedience to the Holy Roman See. And if in maintaining the Catholic Faith and authority of this Holy See your blood should be shed, it is far better to pass quickly to eternal life than to live on in shame and ignominy to the loss of your souls, subject to a feeble woman's passion. For think not, beloved sons in Christ, that those bishops or other leading Catholics of your country whom you mention have made an unhappy end; who for their refusal to give up their confession of the Catholic Faith have been either cast into prison or unjustly visited with other penalties. For their constancy, which has been encouraged by the example (still, as We believe, effective) of the Bl. Thomas, archbishop of Canterbury, can be praised by none as much as it deserves. Imitate this constancy yourselves. Be brave and firm in your resolve, and abandon not your undertaking through fear or threat of danger."

"Behold, He shall neither slumber nor sleep,
that keepeth Israel" (Ps 120:4).

August 12

THE ABOMINATION OF DESOLATION

Bl. Thomas Percy, L., 1572

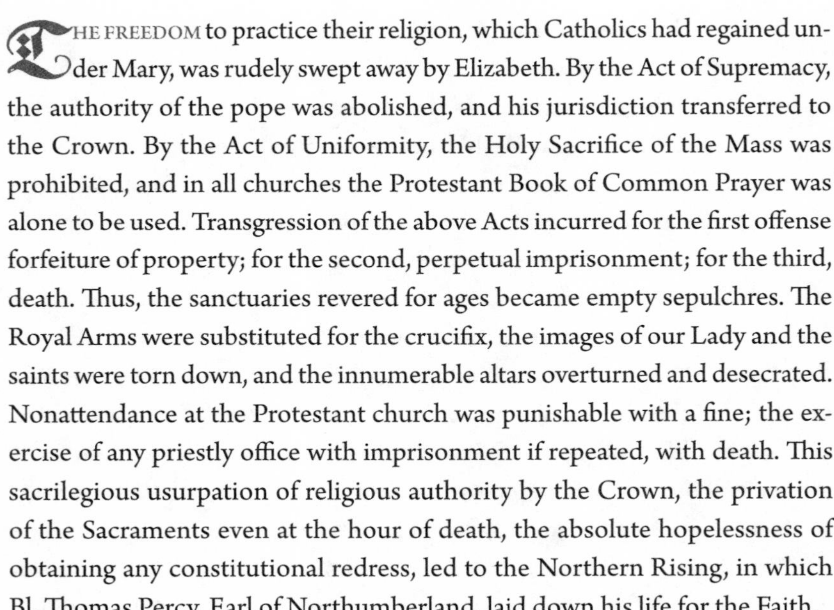

THE FREEDOM to practice their religion, which Catholics had regained under Mary, was rudely swept away by Elizabeth. By the Act of Supremacy, the authority of the pope was abolished, and his jurisdiction transferred to the Crown. By the Act of Uniformity, the Holy Sacrifice of the Mass was prohibited, and in all churches the Protestant Book of Common Prayer was alone to be used. Transgression of the above Acts incurred for the first offense forfeiture of property; for the second, perpetual imprisonment; for the third, death. Thus, the sanctuaries revered for ages became empty sepulchres. The Royal Arms were substituted for the crucifix, the images of our Lady and the saints were torn down, and the innumerable altars overturned and desecrated. Nonattendance at the Protestant church was punishable with a fine; the exercise of any priestly office with imprisonment if repeated, with death. This sacrilegious usurpation of religious authority by the Crown, the privation of the Sacraments even at the hour of death, the absolute hopelessness of obtaining any constitutional redress, led to the Northern Rising, in which Bl. Thomas Percy, Earl of Northumberland, laid down his life for the Faith.

"And behold our sanctuary and our beauty and our glory is laid waste, and the Gentiles have defiled them. To what end, then, should we live any longer?" (1 Mc 2:12–13).

August 13

CLEANSING THE TEMPLE

Bl. Thomas Percy, L., 1572

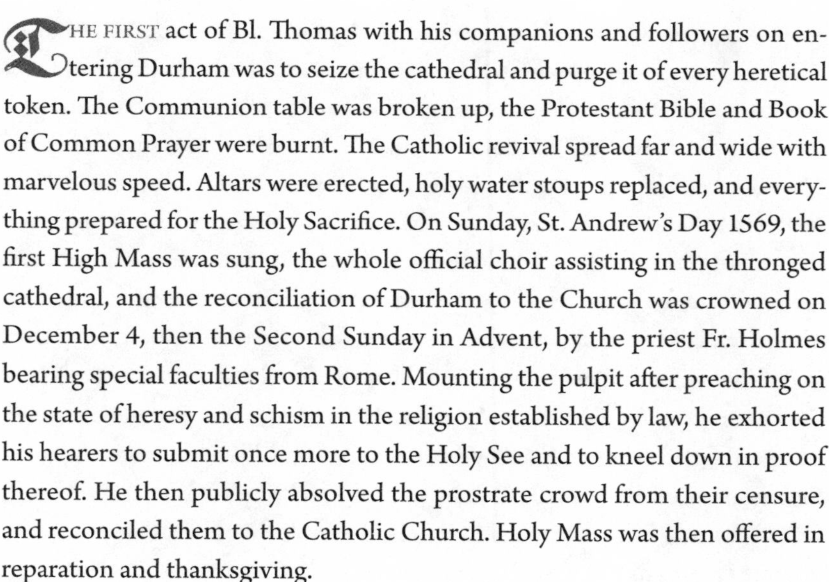

THE FIRST act of Bl. Thomas with his companions and followers on entering Durham was to seize the cathedral and purge it of every heretical token. The Communion table was broken up, the Protestant Bible and Book of Common Prayer were burnt. The Catholic revival spread far and wide with marvelous speed. Altars were erected, holy water stoups replaced, and everything prepared for the Holy Sacrifice. On Sunday, St. Andrew's Day 1569, the first High Mass was sung, the whole official choir assisting in the thronged cathedral, and the reconciliation of Durham to the Church was crowned on December 4, then the Second Sunday in Advent, by the priest Fr. Holmes bearing special faculties from Rome. Mounting the pulpit after preaching on the state of heresy and schism in the religion established by law, he exhorted his hearers to submit once more to the Holy See and to kneel down in proof thereof. He then publicly absolved the prostrate crowd from their censure, and reconciled them to the Catholic Church. Holy Mass was then offered in reparation and thanksgiving.

"In the same day wherein the heathen had defiled it was it dedicated anew with canticles, and harps, and lutes, and cymbals. And all the people fell upon their faces, and adored and blessed up to heaven Him that had prospered them" (1 Mc 4:54–55).

August 14

ABSOLVED FROM AFAR

Ven. Hugh Green, Pr., 1642

Born in London, and a convert from Cambridge, he was arrested in attempting to leave England, in consequence of Charles I's banishment of priests, and sentenced after five months' imprisonment. Dame Willoughby, an eyewitness, says that "his devotion on his way to death was most edifying. He was taken from the hurdle and kept on the hill at some distance from the scaffold until three poor women were hanged. Two of them had sent him word the night before that they would die in his Faith. This comforted him much, for he had done his utmost to speak with them, but failed. They therefore sent again to desire him that when they had made a confession of their sinful lives at the foot of the gallows, on their making the sign he should absolve them. This with great joy in his heart, and much benefit (as it is hoped) on theirs, was performed. They then turned their faces toward us, and throwing forth their arms cried out to him, 'God be with you, sir,' and so died. But the third woman turned from us toward the press of people, her face or speech never tending toward us."

"The Spirit breatheth where He will" (Jn 3:8).

* *Green was beatified by Pope Pius XI on 15 December 1929.*

August 15

THE FOUR LAST THINGS

Ven. Hugh Green, Pr., 1642, on the scaffold

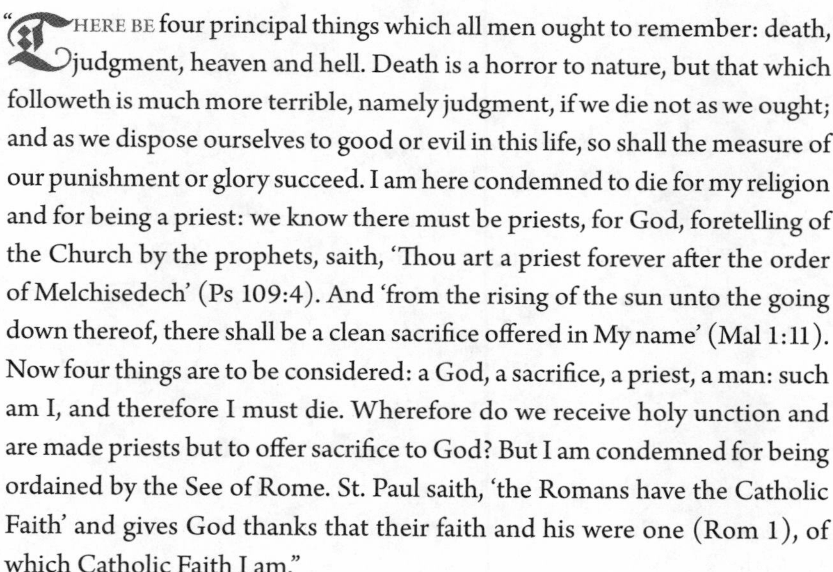

"THERE BE four principal things which all men ought to remember: death, judgment, heaven and hell. Death is a horror to nature, but that which followeth is much more terrible, namely judgment, if we die not as we ought; and as we dispose ourselves to good or evil in this life, so shall the measure of our punishment or glory succeed. I am here condemned to die for my religion and for being a priest: we know there must be priests, for God, foretelling of the Church by the prophets, saith, 'Thou art a priest forever after the order of Melchisedech' (Ps 109:4). And 'from the rising of the sun unto the going down thereof, there shall be a clean sacrifice offered in My name' (Mal 1:11). Now four things are to be considered: a God, a sacrifice, a priest, a man: such am I, and therefore I must die. Wherefore do we receive holy unction and are made priests but to offer sacrifice to God? But I am condemned for being ordained by the See of Rome. St. Paul saith, 'the Romans have the Catholic Faith' and gives God thanks that their faith and his were one (Rom 1), of which Catholic Faith I am."

"In all thy works remember thy last end, and thou shalt never sin" (Ecclus 7:40).

August 16

FOUR THINGS MORE

Ven. Hugh Green, Pr., 1642, on the scaffold

"There be four things more: one God, one Faith, one Baptism, one Church. That there is one God we all acknowledge, in Whom, from Whom, and by Whom all things remain and have their being. That there is one Faith appears by Christ's praying that St. Peter's faith (He said not 'faiths') should never fail (Lk 22:32); and He promised to be with it to the end of the world. That there is one Baptism: we are all cleansed 'by the laver of water in the Word' (Eph 5:26). That there is one Church, holy and sanctified: Doth not St. Paul say that it is a glorious Church 'without spot or wrinkle or any such thing' (Eph 5:27)? Now the marks of this Church are sanctity, unity, antiquity, universality, which all of us in all points of faith believe. But some will say we are fallen off from this Church of Rome, but in what pope's time, in what prince's reign, or what are the errors, none can discover. No, this holy Church of Christ did never err. By the law I am now to die for being a priest. Judge you, can these new laws overthrow the authority of God's Church? Nevertheless, I forgive you, and pray God for all."

"That they may be one, as We also are one" (Jn 17:22).

August 17

A HUNTED LIFE

Ven. Thomas Holford, Pr., 1588

THE SON of a Protestant minister in Cheshire, he was reconciled by Fr. Davis, and ordained, and his life as a priest seems to have been a fulfillment of the Gospel precept of flight under persecution. "He was first searched for," says Fr. Davis, "in the house where I lay, on All Souls' Day, but escaped. Again, after being nearly taken in the search for Babington, he repaired again to a house where I was staying, but we escaped to a hay barn, through a secret place at the foot of the stairs. He then labored for souls in his own county, Cheshire, was apprehended, sent to London, and lodged in an inn at Holborn. Then, rising early, he managed to pass the pursuivants, who had drunk hard and were asleep. On Holborn Viaduct he met a Catholic gentleman, who, seeing him half-dressed, thought him a madman. Pulling off his yellow stocking and white boothose, he walked barefoot by unfrequented paths till he arrived, late at night, at a house where I lay, about eight miles from London. He had eaten nothing, and his feet were bleeding and torn with briars and thorns. My hosts and their daughters tended him and put him to bed. The next year, he was apprehended and executed, August 28, at Clerkenwell."

"They wandered about in sheepskins and goatskins, being in want, distressed, afflicted: of whom the world was not worthy" (Heb 11:37–38).

* *Holford was beatified by Pope Pius XI on 15 December 1929.*

August 18

THE ETERNAL PRIESTHOOD

Ven. Roger Cadwallador, Pr., 1610

A native of Herefordshire, very learned and a noted Greek scholar, he began his priestly labors in England about 1594, and during sixteen years won many souls to the Church. Apprehended on Easter Day, in the house of Mrs. Winefride Scroope, near Hereford, he acknowledged to the Protestant bishop that he was a priest, and added that he supposed that this would not be against him with the bishop, whose special concern it was to maintain the sacerdotal dignity. "For, my lord, either you must admit yourself to be a priest, or I can prove you to be no bishop." The bishop insisted that Christ was the only sacrificing priest of the New Testament, in that sense of the word, which is not common to all Christians, and hoped thus to free himself from being a priest. On which the martyr replied, "Make that good, I pray you, my lord, for so you will prove that I am no more a priest than other men, and consequently no traitor or offender against your law"; on which one, Holkins, to cover the bishop's disgrace, said that the King himself had said that these kind of men were so numerous that he should never have done if he put them all to death.

"But this [Jesus], for that He continueth forever, hath an everlasting priesthood" (Heb 7:24).

* *Cadwallador was beatified by Pope John Paul II on 22 November 1987.*

August 19

A LAMENTATION FULFILLED

✠ Ven. Hugh Green, Pr., 1642

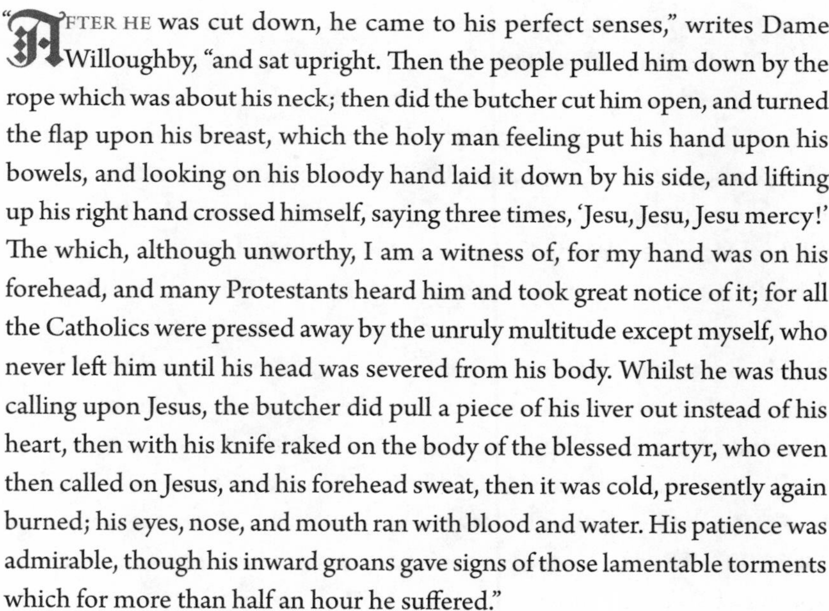

“After he was cut down, he came to his perfect senses,” writes Dame Willoughby, “and sat upright. Then the people pulled him down by the rope which was about his neck; then did the butcher cut him open, and turned the flap upon his breast, which the holy man feeling put his hand upon his bowels, and looking on his bloody hand laid it down by his side, and lifting up his right hand crossed himself, saying three times, ‘Jesu, Jesu, Jesu mercy!’ The which, although unworthy, I am a witness of, for my hand was on his forehead, and many Protestants heard him and took great notice of it; for all the Catholics were pressed away by the unruly multitude except myself, who never left him until his head was severed from his body. Whilst he was thus calling upon Jesus, the butcher did pull a piece of his liver out instead of his heart, then with his knife raked on the body of the blessed martyr, who even then called on Jesus, and his forehead sweat, then it was cold, presently again burned; his eyes, nose, and mouth ran with blood and water. His patience was admirable, though his inward groans gave signs of those lamentable torments which for more than half an hour he suffered.”

“My eyes have failed with weeping, my bowels are troubled,
my liver is poured out upon the earth” (Lam 2:11).

August 20

THIRTY PIECES OF SILVER

Bl. Thomas Percy, L., 1572

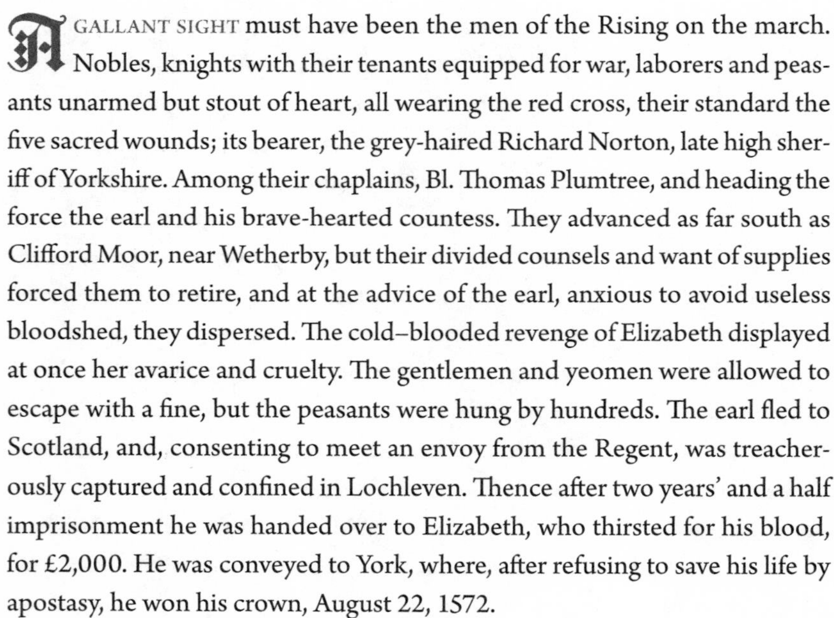

A GALLANT SIGHT must have been the men of the Rising on the march. Nobles, knights with their tenants equipped for war, laborers and peasants unarmed but stout of heart, all wearing the red cross, their standard the five sacred wounds; its bearer, the grey-haired Richard Norton, late high sheriff of Yorkshire. Among their chaplains, Bl. Thomas Plumtree, and heading the force the earl and his brave-hearted countess. They advanced as far south as Clifford Moor, near Wetherby, but their divided counsels and want of supplies forced them to retire, and at the advice of the earl, anxious to avoid useless bloodshed, they dispersed. The cold–blooded revenge of Elizabeth displayed at once her avarice and cruelty. The gentlemen and yeomen were allowed to escape with a fine, but the peasants were hung by hundreds. The earl fled to Scotland, and, consenting to meet an envoy from the Regent, was treacherously captured and confined in Lochleven. Thence after two years' and a half imprisonment he was handed over to Elizabeth, who thirsted for his blood, for £2,000. He was conveyed to York, where, after refusing to save his life by apostasy, he won his crown, August 22, 1572.

"But they appointed him thirty pieces of silver, and from thenceforth he sought opportunity to betray Him" (Mt 26:15–16).

August 21

THE FRIDAY ABSTINENCE

Bl. Thomas Percy, L., 1572

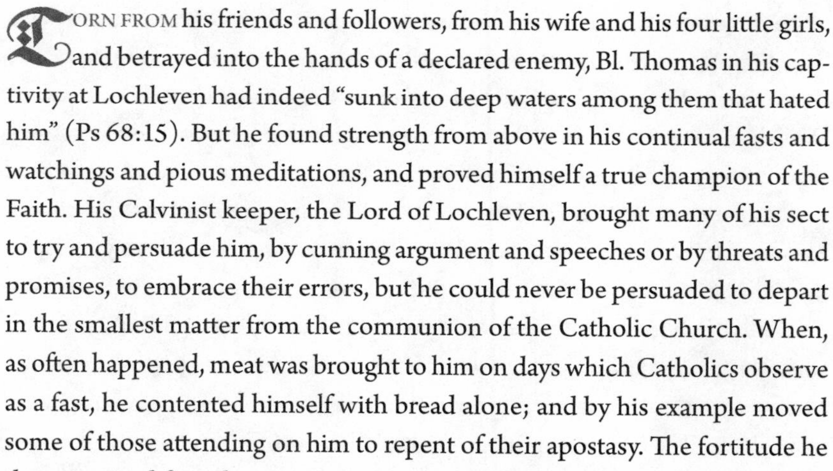

TORN FROM his friends and followers, from his wife and his four little girls, and betrayed into the hands of a declared enemy, Bl. Thomas in his captivity at Lochleven had indeed "sunk into deep waters among them that hated him" (Ps 68:15). But he found strength from above in his continual fasts and watchings and pious meditations, and proved himself a true champion of the Faith. His Calvinist keeper, the Lord of Lochleven, brought many of his sect to try and persuade him, by cunning argument and speeches or by threats and promises, to embrace their errors, but he could never be persuaded to depart in the smallest matter from the communion of the Catholic Church. When, as often happened, meat was brought to him on days which Catholics observe as a fast, he contented himself with bread alone; and by his example moved some of those attending on him to repent of their apostasy. The fortitude he thus acquired found a witness in Lord Hunsdon, who reported "that he is readier to talk of hawks and hounds than anything else, though very sorrowful and fearing for his life."

"Eleazer, one of the chief of the scribes . . . was pressed to eat swine's flesh. But he, choosing rather a most glorious death than a hateful life, went forward voluntarily to the torment" (2 Mc 6:18–19).

August 22

THE HOLY HOUSE OF LORETO

✠ Bl. William Lacy, Pr., 1582

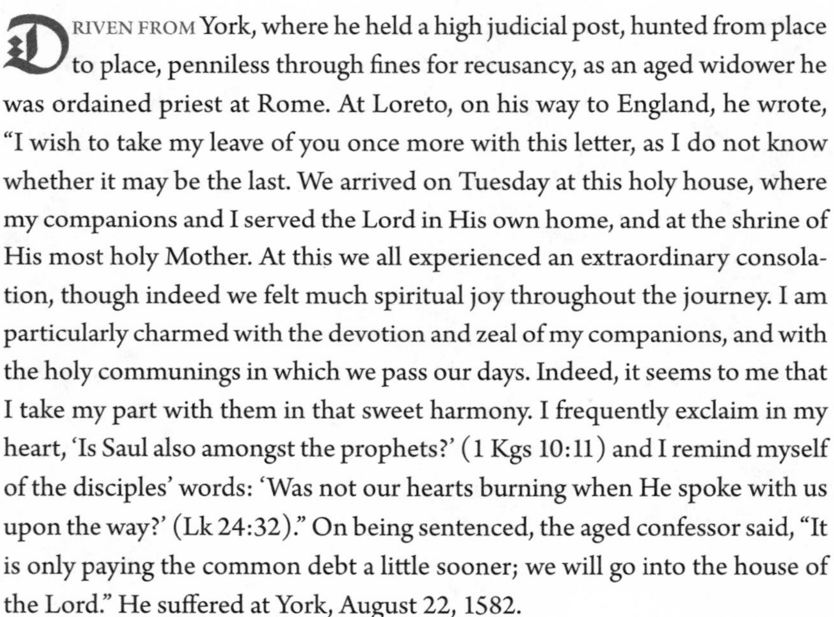

Driven from York, where he held a high judicial post, hunted from place to place, penniless through fines for recusancy, as an aged widower he was ordained priest at Rome. At Loreto, on his way to England, he wrote, "I wish to take my leave of you once more with this letter, as I do not know whether it may be the last. We arrived on Tuesday at this holy house, where my companions and I served the Lord in His own home, and at the shrine of His most holy Mother. At this we all experienced an extraordinary consolation, though indeed we felt much spiritual joy throughout the journey. I am particularly charmed with the devotion and zeal of my companions, and with the holy communings in which we pass our days. Indeed, it seems to me that I take my part with them in that sweet harmony. I frequently exclaim in my heart, 'Is Saul also amongst the prophets?' (1 Kgs 10:11) and I remind myself of the disciples' words: 'Was not our hearts burning when He spoke with us upon the way?' (Lk 24:32)." On being sentenced, the aged confessor said, "It is only paying the common debt a little sooner; we will go into the house of the Lord." He suffered at York, August 22, 1582.

"This is no other but the house of God, and the gate of heaven" (Gn 28:17).

August 23

THE CROWN OF DIGNITY

Ven. John Kemble, Pr., 1679

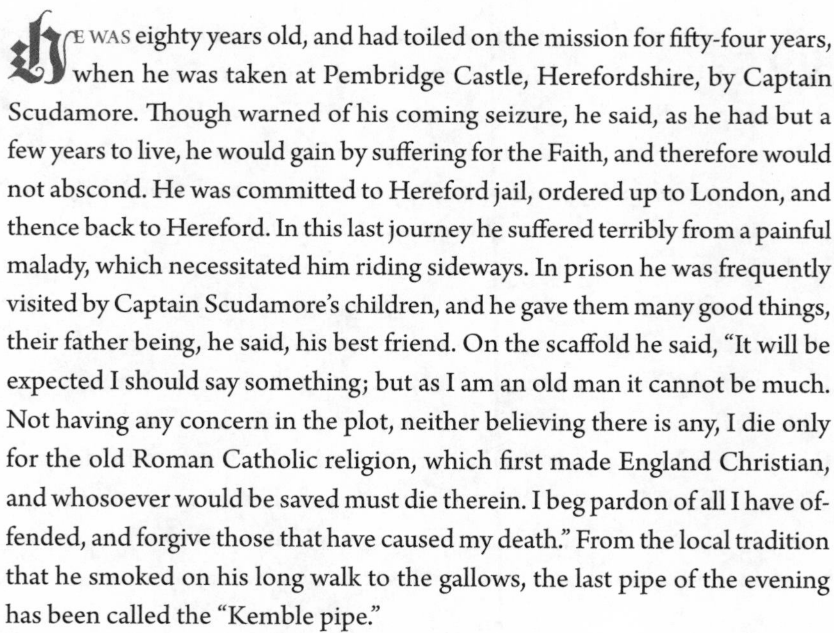

HE WAS eighty years old, and had toiled on the mission for fifty-four years, when he was taken at Pembridge Castle, Herefordshire, by Captain Scudamore. Though warned of his coming seizure, he said, as he had but a few years to live, he would gain by suffering for the Faith, and therefore would not abscond. He was committed to Hereford jail, ordered up to London, and thence back to Hereford. In this last journey he suffered terribly from a painful malady, which necessitated him riding sideways. In prison he was frequently visited by Captain Scudamore's children, and he gave them many good things, their father being, he said, his best friend. On the scaffold he said, "It will be expected I should say something; but as I am an old man it cannot be much. Not having any concern in the plot, neither believing there is any, I die only for the old Roman Catholic religion, which first made England Christian, and whosoever would be saved must die therein. I beg pardon of all I have offended, and forgive those that have caused my death." From the local tradition that he smoked on his long walk to the gallows, the last pipe of the evening has been called the "Kemble pipe."

"Old age is a crown of dignity, when it is found in the ways of justice" (Prv 16:31).

* *Kemble was canonized by Pope Paul VI on 25 October 1970.*

August 24

A VOLUNTARY OFFERING

Ven. John Wall, O. S. F., 1679

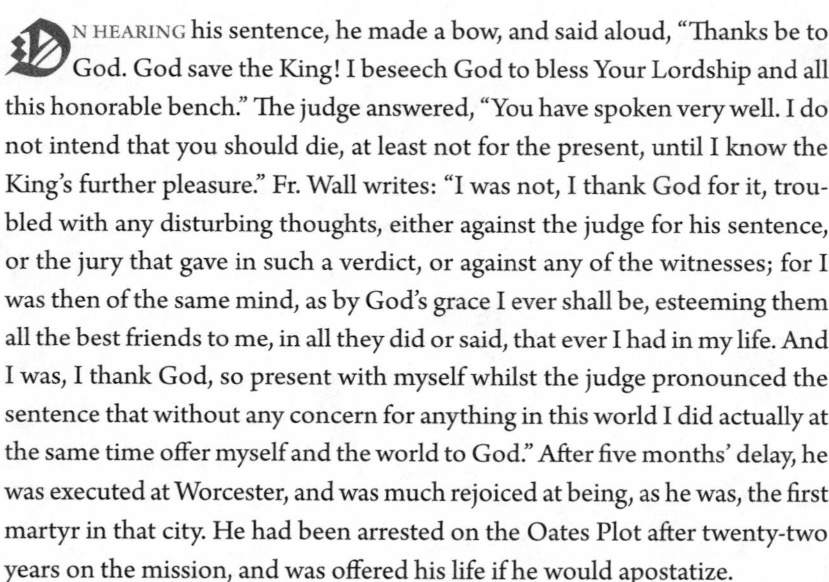

On hearing his sentence, he made a bow, and said aloud, "Thanks be to God. God save the King! I beseech God to bless Your Lordship and all this honorable bench." The judge answered, "You have spoken very well. I do not intend that you should die, at least not for the present, until I know the King's further pleasure." Fr. Wall writes: "I was not, I thank God for it, troubled with any disturbing thoughts, either against the judge for his sentence, or the jury that gave in such a verdict, or against any of the witnesses; for I was then of the same mind, as by God's grace I ever shall be, esteeming them all the best friends to me, in all they did or said, that ever I had in my life. And I was, I thank God, so present with myself whilst the judge pronounced the sentence that without any concern for anything in this world I did actually at the same time offer myself and the world to God." After five months' delay, he was executed at Worcester, and was much rejoiced at being, as he was, the first martyr in that city. He had been arrested on the Oates Plot after twenty-two years on the mission, and was offered his life if he would apostatize.

"He was offered, because it was His own will" (Is 53:7).

* *Wall was canonized by Pope Paul VI on 25 October 1970.*

August 25

REPROACHED FOR CHRIST

Ven. Charles Baker, S.J., 1679

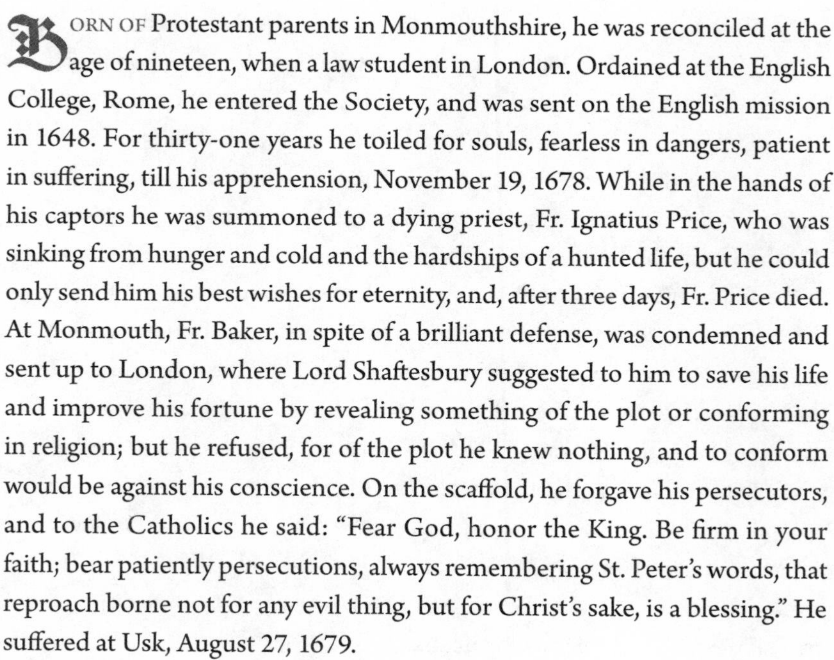

BORN OF Protestant parents in Monmouthshire, he was reconciled at the age of nineteen, when a law student in London. Ordained at the English College, Rome, he entered the Society, and was sent on the English mission in 1648. For thirty-one years he toiled for souls, fearless in dangers, patient in suffering, till his apprehension, November 19, 1678. While in the hands of his captors he was summoned to a dying priest, Fr. Ignatius Price, who was sinking from hunger and cold and the hardships of a hunted life, but he could only send him his best wishes for eternity, and, after three days, Fr. Price died. At Monmouth, Fr. Baker, in spite of a brilliant defense, was condemned and sent up to London, where Lord Shaftesbury suggested to him to save his life and improve his fortune by revealing something of the plot or conforming in religion; but he refused, for of the plot he knew nothing, and to conform would be against his conscience. On the scaffold, he forgave his persecutors, and to the Catholics he said: "Fear God, honor the King. Be firm in your faith; bear patiently persecutions, always remembering St. Peter's words, that reproach borne not for any evil thing, but for Christ's sake, is a blessing." He suffered at Usk, August 27, 1679.

> *"If you be reproached for the name of Christ, you shall be blessed: for that which is the honor of God . . . resteth on you" (1 Pt 4:14).*

* *Baker was canonized by Pope Paul VI on 25 October 1970.*

August 26

CHEERFUL IN ADVERSITY

✠ Bp. Thomas Thirlby of Ely, 1570

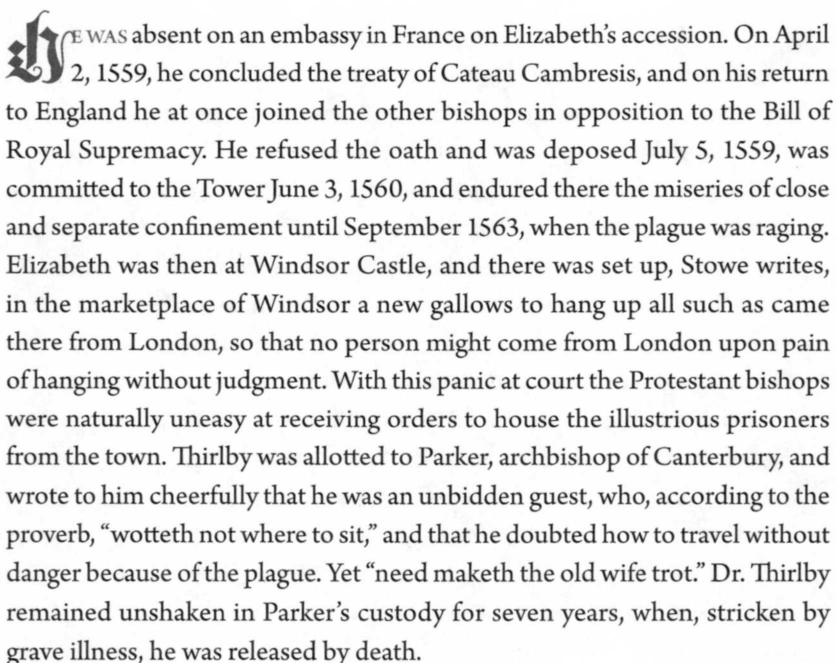

HE WAS absent on an embassy in France on Elizabeth's accession. On April 2, 1559, he concluded the treaty of Cateau Cambresis, and on his return to England he at once joined the other bishops in opposition to the Bill of Royal Supremacy. He refused the oath and was deposed July 5, 1559, was committed to the Tower June 3, 1560, and endured there the miseries of close and separate confinement until September 1563, when the plague was raging. Elizabeth was then at Windsor Castle, and there was set up, Stowe writes, in the marketplace of Windsor a new gallows to hang up all such as came there from London, so that no person might come from London upon pain of hanging without judgment. With this panic at court the Protestant bishops were naturally uneasy at receiving orders to house the illustrious prisoners from the town. Thirlby was allotted to Parker, archbishop of Canterbury, and wrote to him cheerfully that he was an unbidden guest, who, according to the proverb, "wotteth not where to sit," and that he doubted how to travel without danger because of the plague. Yet "need maketh the old wife trot." Dr. Thirlby remained unshaken in Parker's custody for seven years, when, stricken by grave illness, he was released by death.

"According to the multitude of the sorrows of my heart,
Thy comforts have given joy to my soul" (Ps 93:19).

August 27

GLORIFYING GOD

✠ Ven. Roger Cadwallador, Pr., 1610

WHEN HE was near his crown he wrote, "Comfort yourselves, my friends, in this that I die in an assurance of salvation; which, if you truly love me as you ought to do, should please you better than to have me alive a little while among you for your content, and then to die with great uncertainty either to be saved or damned. If this manner of death be shameful, yet not more than my Savior's was: if it be painful, yet not more than was His. Only have you care to persevere in God's true Faith and charity, and then we shall meet again to our greater comfort that shall never end." On the morning of his execution, having spent some five hours in prayer, he took some broth and claret to make himself strong, he said, like Bishop Fisher, to suffer for God, and dressed himself in a new suit of clothes as his wedding garment. On the scaffold, asked to give his opinion as to the oath, he replied that his opinion mattered little; they should regard rather the sentiments of the Church, for his swearing would neither diminish the pope's authority nor increase the King's. His constancy under the terrible butchery which attended his end confirmed the faith of the Herefordshire Catholics.

"But let none of you suffer as a murderer or a thief. . . .
But, if as a Christian, let him not be ashamed, but let
him glorify God in His name" (1 Pt 4:15–16).

August 28

STRIKING THEIR BREASTS

✠ Ven. Edmund Arrowsmith, S.J., 1628

HE WAS sentenced at Lancaster for being a priest, a Jesuit, and a persuader of religion, and the judge ordered that he was to be hung at noon, when most men would be at dinner; but as it fell out, the whole place of execution was covered with great multitudes of people of all sorts, ages, sexes, and religions, expecting the end of the tragedy. As he was carried through the castle yard, Fr. Southworth, his fellow prisoner under reprieve, appeared at the prison window and received his absolution. He was then bound on the hurdle, with his head toward the horse's tail, "for greater ignominy." Most of his friends were prevented to approach him, and the executioner went before the horse and hurdle with a club in his hand in a kind of barbarous triumph. On the scaffold, he refused to save his life by taking the oath, professed that he died for the Catholic Faith, and prayed for the conversion of England. His last words, as he was cast off the ladder, were *"Bone Jesu."* Divers Protestants, beholders of this bloody spectacle, wished their souls with his. Others wished they had never come there. Others said it was a barbarous act to use men so for their religion.

"And all the multitude of them that were come together to that sight, and saw the things that were done, returned striking their breasts" (Lk 23:48).

* *Arrowsmith was canonized by Pope Paul VI on 25 October 1970.*

August 29

MURDER FOR EXAMPLE

✠ Ven. Richard Herst, L., 1628

A CONVICTED RECUSANT, he was ploughing his field when one Dewhurst came to serve him with a warrant. Herst fled, and Dewhurst, following in pursuit, received a blow from Herst's maid, and afterward, in the heat of the pursuit, fell and broke his leg. From that wound in the leg he died, yet Herst, who had never been within thirty yards of him, was charged with his death. Herst's pardon was offered him if he would take the oath, but he refused, and he declined also to go to church, so he was trailed there by his legs and much hurt. In the church he stopped his ears, not to hear false doctrine, and, on returning, said, "They have tortured my body, but, thank God, they have not hurt my soul." At his trial at Lancaster, though his innocence of Dewhurst's death was evident, the judge told the jury that he was a recusant, had resisted the bishop's authority, and that they must find it murder for an example, which was done. At the gallows, he said to the hangman, who was bungling with the rope, "Tom, I think I must come and help you." Then, after repeating the holy names of Jesus and Mary, he passed to immortality, Lancaster, August 29.

"Cursed shalt thou be upon the earth, which hath opened her mouth and received the blood of thy brother at thy hand" (Gn 4:11).

* *Herst was beatified by Pope Pius XI on 15 December 1929.*

August 30

VISITING THE PRISONER

✠ Ven. Margaret Ward, L., 1588

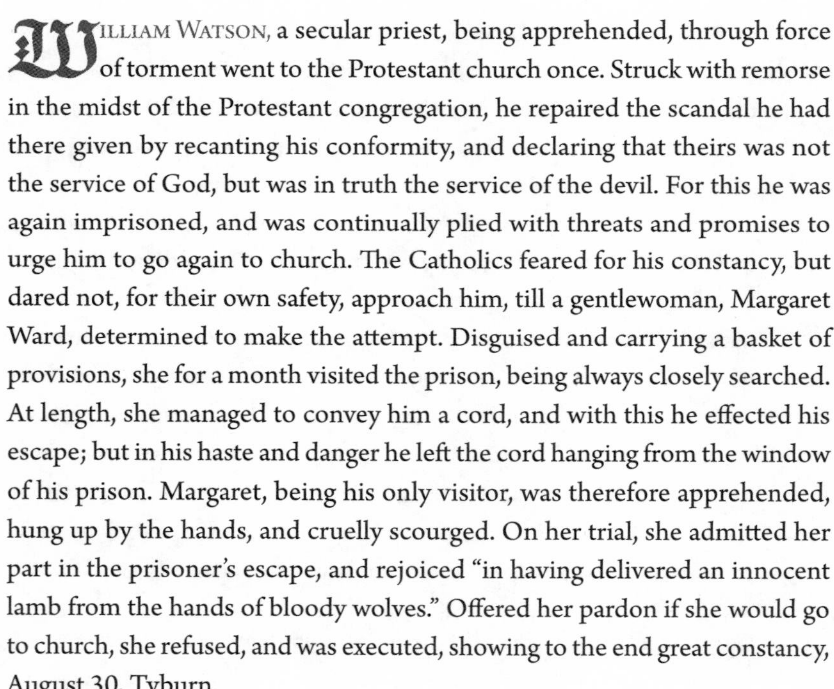

William Watson, a secular priest, being apprehended, through force of torment went to the Protestant church once. Struck with remorse in the midst of the Protestant congregation, he repaired the scandal he had there given by recanting his conformity, and declaring that theirs was not the service of God, but was in truth the service of the devil. For this he was again imprisoned, and was continually plied with threats and promises to urge him to go again to church. The Catholics feared for his constancy, but dared not, for their own safety, approach him, till a gentlewoman, Margaret Ward, determined to make the attempt. Disguised and carrying a basket of provisions, she for a month visited the prison, being always closely searched. At length, she managed to convey him a cord, and with this he effected his escape; but in his haste and danger he left the cord hanging from the window of his prison. Margaret, being his only visitor, was therefore apprehended, hung up by the hands, and cruelly scourged. On her trial, she admitted her part in the prisoner's escape, and rejoiced "in having delivered an innocent lamb from the hands of bloody wolves." Offered her pardon if she would go to church, she refused, and was executed, showing to the end great constancy, August 30, Tyburn.

"I was in prison, and you visited me" (Mt 25:36).

* *Ward was canonized by Pope Paul VI on 25 October 1970.*

August 31

THE TABERNACLE OF KORE

✠ Ven. Thomas Felton, O. F M., 1588

A MARTYR HIMSELF and the son of a martyr, his father having suffered for putting up St. Pius V's bull of excommunication, he was apprehended as a suspected papist for the third time, though but a layman, when only twenty years of age. Tortured in the "Little Ease," starved, hanged up by the hands till the blood sprang from his finger ends, he remained steadfast. Upon a Sunday, he was violently taken by certain officers and carried betwixt two, fast bound in a chair, into the chapel at Bridewell to their service. He, having his hands at first at liberty, stopped his ears with his fingers that he might not hear what the minister said. Then they bound down his hands also to the chair; but being set down to the ground, bound in the manner aforesaid, he stamped with his feet, and made such noise with his mouth, shouting and hallowing, and crying oftentimes, "Jesus, Jesus," that the minister's voice could not be heard. Asked by the judge if he acknowledged the Queen's supremacy, he made answer that he "had read divers chronicles, but never read that God ordained a woman should be Supreme Head of the Church." For this speech he was condemned, and hung the next day near Hounslow, Middlesex.

"Depart from the tents of these wicked men, and touch nothing of theirs, lest you be involved in their sins" (Nm 16:26).

* *Felton was beatified by Pope Pius XI on 15 December 1929.*

September

September 1

A LIFE-OFFERING FOR THE PEOPLE

Ven. John Goodman, Pr., 1645

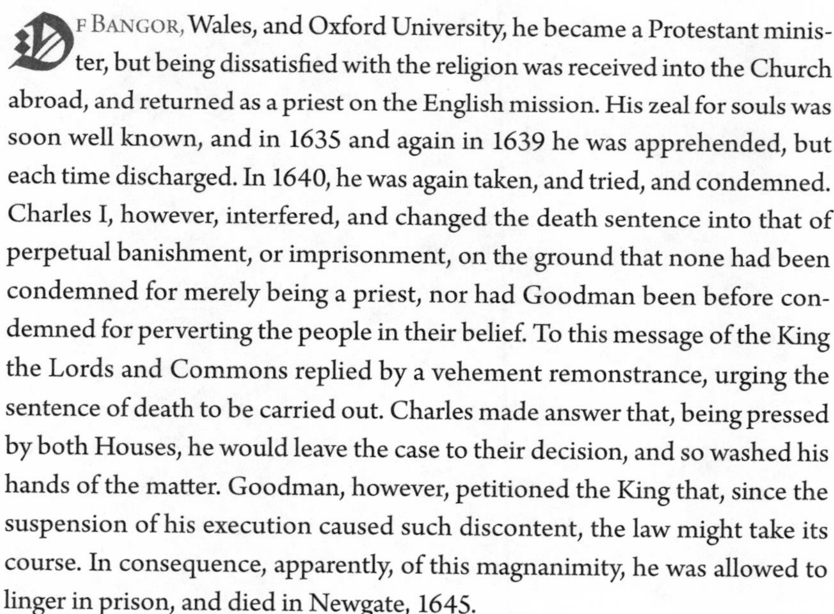

Of Bangor, Wales, and Oxford University, he became a Protestant minister, but being dissatisfied with the religion was received into the Church abroad, and returned as a priest on the English mission. His zeal for souls was soon well known, and in 1635 and again in 1639 he was apprehended, but each time discharged. In 1640, he was again taken, and tried, and condemned. Charles I, however, interfered, and changed the death sentence into that of perpetual banishment, or imprisonment, on the ground that none had been condemned for merely being a priest, nor had Goodman been before condemned for perverting the people in their belief. To this message of the King the Lords and Commons replied by a vehement remonstrance, urging the sentence of death to be carried out. Charles made answer that, being pressed by both Houses, he would leave the case to their decision, and so washed his hands of the matter. Goodman, however, petitioned the King that, since the suspension of his execution caused such discontent, the law might take its course. In consequence, apparently, of this magnanimity, he was allowed to linger in prison, and died in Newgate, 1645.

"And he said, Take me up and cast me into the sea, and the sea shall be calm to you; for I know that for my sake this great tempest is upon you" (Jon 1:12).

September 2

TIME AND ETERNITY

Bl. Thomas More, L., 1535

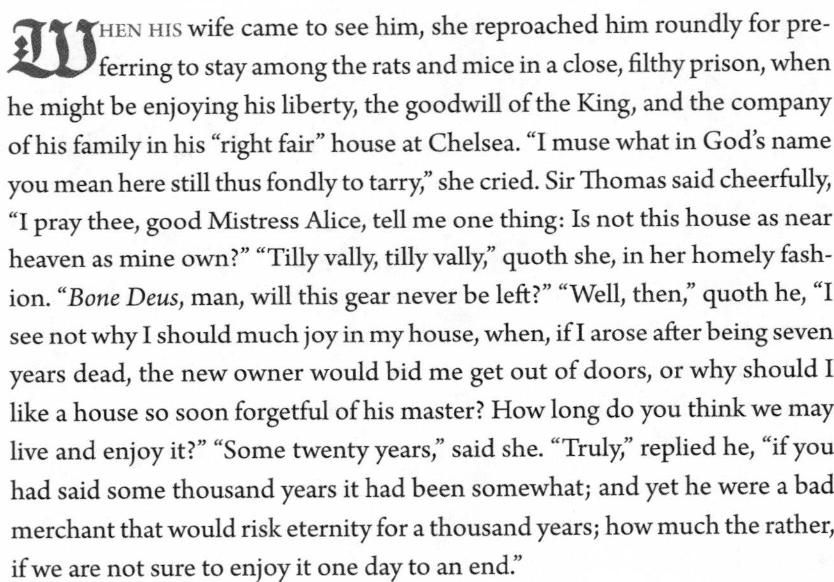

When his wife came to see him, she reproached him roundly for preferring to stay among the rats and mice in a close, filthy prison, when he might be enjoying his liberty, the goodwill of the King, and the company of his family in his "right fair" house at Chelsea. "I muse what in God's name you mean here still thus fondly to tarry," she cried. Sir Thomas said cheerfully, "I pray thee, good Mistress Alice, tell me one thing: Is not this house as near heaven as mine own?" "Tilly vally, tilly vally," quoth she, in her homely fashion. "*Bone Deus*, man, will this gear never be left?" "Well, then," quoth he, "I see not why I should much joy in my house, when, if I arose after being seven years dead, the new owner would bid me get out of doors, or why should I like a house so soon forgetful of his master? How long do you think we may live and enjoy it?" "Some twenty years," said she. "Truly," replied he, "if you had said some thousand years it had been somewhat; and yet he were a bad merchant that would risk eternity for a thousand years; how much the rather, if we are not sure to enjoy it one day to an end."

"One day with the Lord is as a thousand years, and a thousand years as one day" (2 Pt 3:8).

September 3

HOW LONG, O LORD?

Bl. Thomas Abel, Pr., to Bl. John Forest, O. S. F.

"ALTHOUGH HUMAN nature is terrified by the intensity of tortures, yet our faith demands and requires us to bear them. I said, 'My foot is moved because Thou hast turned away Thy face from me. Thou turnest away Thy face from me, and I became troubled'; troubled, I say, because the pain of the tortures which I desire is prolonged, and at the same time I am humbled; humbled, and not raised up, because not drawn to my Savior; not drawn, because I am burdened with the weight of my sins, burdened and not refreshed by Him. What, then, profits my condemnation, if there be longer to wait? Wherefore, I ask? Because you have not availingly implored the mercy of God. For I know how much the prayer of the just man weighs before God. Because with the Lord there is mercy, and with Him plentiful redemption. In Thee have our fathers hoped; they have hoped, and Thou hast delivered them for the sake of David, Thy servant. Why, then, is there not an end put to these tortures? I have now suffered seven and thirty days, and I find no rest. But my hope is that we shall die together by the same punishment."

"How long, O Lord, wilt Thou forget me unto the end?" (Ps 12:1).

September 4

PERSEVERANCE

Bl. John Forest to Bl. Thomas Abel

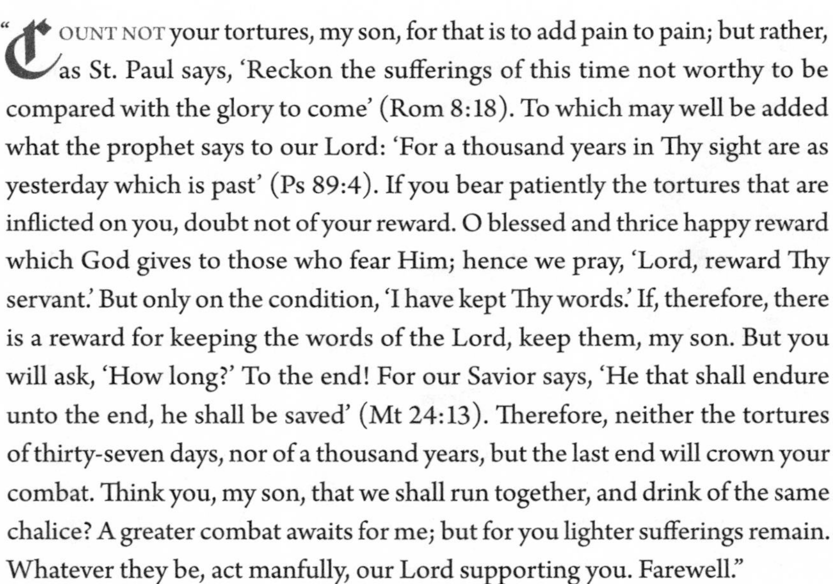

"COUNT NOT your tortures, my son, for that is to add pain to pain; but rather, as St. Paul says, 'Reckon the sufferings of this time not worthy to be compared with the glory to come' (Rom 8:18). To which may well be added what the prophet says to our Lord: 'For a thousand years in Thy sight are as yesterday which is past' (Ps 89:4). If you bear patiently the tortures that are inflicted on you, doubt not of your reward. O blessed and thrice happy reward which God gives to those who fear Him; hence we pray, 'Lord, reward Thy servant.' But only on the condition, 'I have kept Thy words.' If, therefore, there is a reward for keeping the words of the Lord, keep them, my son. But you will ask, 'How long?' To the end! For our Savior says, 'He that shall endure unto the end, he shall be saved' (Mt 24:13). Therefore, neither the tortures of thirty-seven days, nor of a thousand years, but the last end will crown your combat. Think you, my son, that we shall run together, and drink of the same chalice? A greater combat awaits for me; but for you lighter sufferings remain. Whatever they be, act manfully, our Lord supporting you. Farewell."

"He that shall endure to the end, he shall be saved" (Mk 13:13).

September 5

FAITHFUL IN THE END

Bp. Edmund Bonner of London, 1569

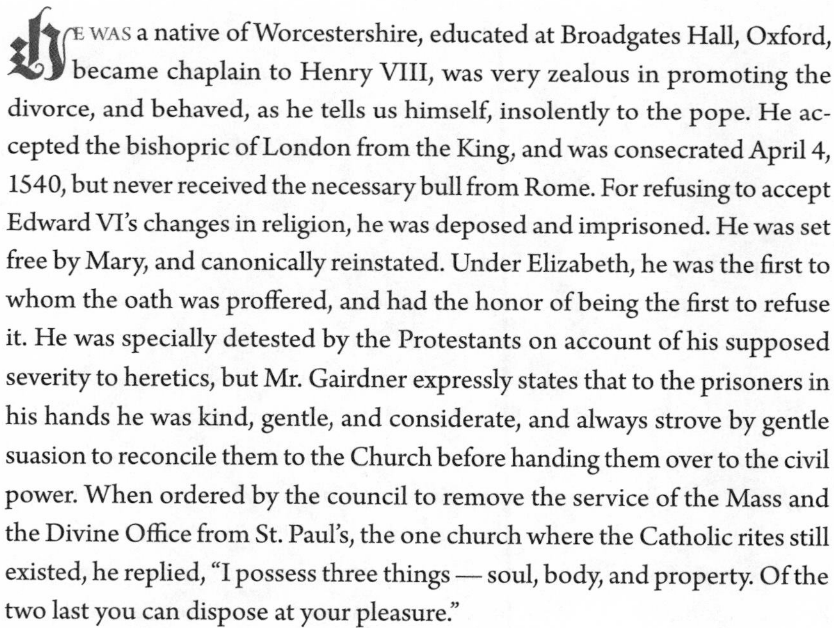

He was a native of Worcestershire, educated at Broadgates Hall, Oxford, became chaplain to Henry VIII, was very zealous in promoting the divorce, and behaved, as he tells us himself, insolently to the pope. He accepted the bishopric of London from the King, and was consecrated April 4, 1540, but never received the necessary bull from Rome. For refusing to accept Edward VI's changes in religion, he was deposed and imprisoned. He was set free by Mary, and canonically reinstated. Under Elizabeth, he was the first to whom the oath was proffered, and had the honor of being the first to refuse it. He was specially detested by the Protestants on account of his supposed severity to heretics, but Mr. Gairdner expressly states that to the prisoners in his hands he was kind, gentle, and considerate, and always strove by gentle suasion to reconcile them to the Church before handing them over to the civil power. When ordered by the council to remove the service of the Mass and the Divine Office from St. Paul's, the one church where the Catholic rites still existed, he replied, "I possess three things — soul, body, and property. Of the two last you can dispose at your pleasure."

"Restore unto me the joy of Thy salvation, and strengthen me with a perfect spirit" (Ps 50:14).

September 6

AN EASTER OFFERING

Ven. Edward Barlow, O. S. B., 1641

He was beginning to recover from his illness, but was still very weak, when he was apprehended on Easter Day, 1641. A neighboring minister proposed to his congregation that, instead of their service, they should show their zeal by capturing the noted popish priest, whom they would surely now find in the midst of his flock, but would lose when church time was over. Some four hundred went therefore with clubs and swords, the parson marching at their head in his surplice. Fr. Barlow had finished Mass, and was making a discourse to his people on the subject of patience, when the house was found to be surrounded by armed men. He refused to hide himself in any of the secret places provided in the house for that purpose, or leave his sheep, as he said, to the mercy of the wolves. He exhorted them to constancy, and reminded them that these light and momentary tribulations worked an eternal weight of glory, and, telling them that he was ready to offer all things for Christ, he bid them open the door. The mob rushed in, shouting, "Where is Barlow? He is the man we want," and, laying hands on him, they secured him and let the rest go, upon giving caution for their appearance. He suffered at Lancaster, September 10, 1641.

"For Christ our pasch is sacrificed" (1 Cor 5:7).

* *Barlow was canonized by Pope Paul VI on 25 October 1970.*

September 7

THE CONTEMPLATIVE WAY

✠ Ven. John Duckett, Pr., 1644

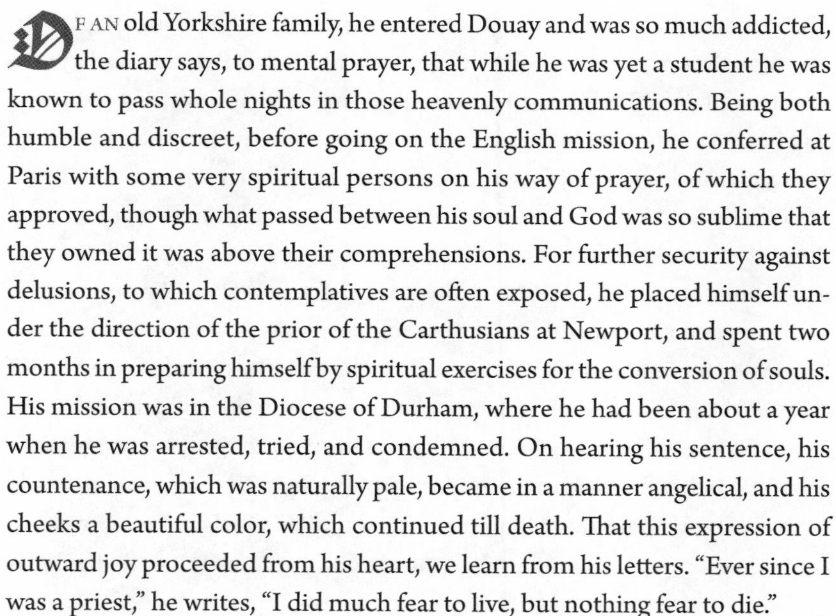

OF AN old Yorkshire family, he entered Douay and was so much addicted, the diary says, to mental prayer, that while he was yet a student he was known to pass whole nights in those heavenly communications. Being both humble and discreet, before going on the English mission, he conferred at Paris with some very spiritual persons on his way of prayer, of which they approved, though what passed between his soul and God was so sublime that they owned it was above their comprehensions. For further security against delusions, to which contemplatives are often exposed, he placed himself under the direction of the prior of the Carthusians at Newport, and spent two months in preparing himself by spiritual exercises for the conversion of souls. His mission was in the Diocese of Durham, where he had been about a year when he was arrested, tried, and condemned. On hearing his sentence, his countenance, which was naturally pale, became in a manner angelical, and his cheeks a beautiful color, which continued till death. That this expression of outward joy proceeded from his heart, we learn from his letters. "Ever since I was a priest," he writes, "I did much fear to live, but nothing fear to die."

"This is my rest forever and ever: here will I dwell, for I have chosen it" (Ps 131:14).

* *Duckett was beatified by Pope Pius XI on 15 December 1929.*

September 8

HOLY RIVALRY

Vens. Ralph Corby, S. J., and John Duckett, Pr., 1644

RALPH CORBY, alias Darlington, was born near Dublin of English parents, natives of Durham, who had gone over to Ireland for the free exercise of their religion. The piety of the family is sufficiently attested by the fact that both parents and children entered into religion: the father and his three sons into the Society of Jesus, the mother and her daughters into the Order of St. Benedict. After twelve years' hard work, notwithstanding continuous ill-health, among the poorer Catholics in Durham, he was arrested and sent up to London with Fr. Duckett. They were escorted from Westminster to Newgate by a company of Parliament soldiers, with a captain at their head, beating drums and firing off their muskets through the crowded streets, as if they had been the enemy's generals taken in war as in the old Roman battles. In prison, the life of one of them could have been saved by an exchange made for a prisoner in the hand of the emperor of Germany. The offer was first made to Fr. Corby, who declined it on the ground that Fr. Duckett, being younger, could do more work than himself; but he in his turn refused it with thanks, as Fr. Corby's life, on account of his experience, was of greater value.

"Behold what manner of charity the Father hath bestowed upon us" (1 Jn 3:1).

* *Corby was beatified by Pope Pius XI on 15 December 1929.*

September 9

THE KISS OF PEACE

Vens. Ralph Corby, S. J., and John Duckett, Pr., 1644

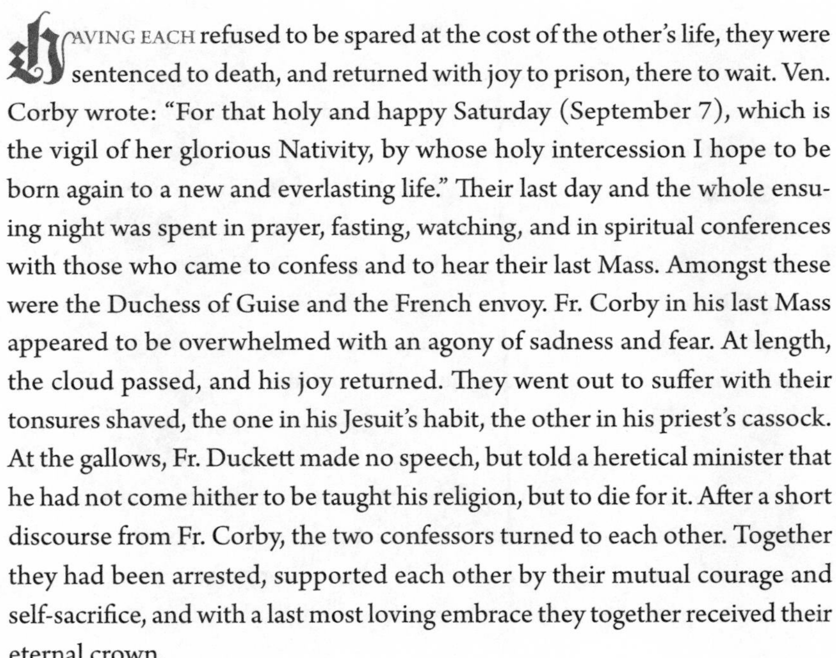

HAVING EACH refused to be spared at the cost of the other's life, they were sentenced to death, and returned with joy to prison, there to wait. Ven. Corby wrote: "For that holy and happy Saturday (September 7), which is the vigil of her glorious Nativity, by whose holy intercession I hope to be born again to a new and everlasting life." Their last day and the whole ensuing night was spent in prayer, fasting, watching, and in spiritual conferences with those who came to confess and to hear their last Mass. Amongst these were the Duchess of Guise and the French envoy. Fr. Corby in his last Mass appeared to be overwhelmed with an agony of sadness and fear. At length, the cloud passed, and his joy returned. They went out to suffer with their tonsures shaved, the one in his Jesuit's habit, the other in his priest's cassock. At the gallows, Fr. Duckett made no speech, but told a heretical minister that he had not come hither to be taught his religion, but to die for it. After a short discourse from Fr. Corby, the two confessors turned to each other. Together they had been arrested, supported each other by their mutual courage and self-sacrifice, and with a last most loving embrace they together received their eternal crown.

"Salute one another with a holy kiss. All the saints salute you" (2 Cor 13:12).

September 10

PRESSED OUT OF MEASURE

Bp. Gilbert Bourne of Bath and Wells, 1569

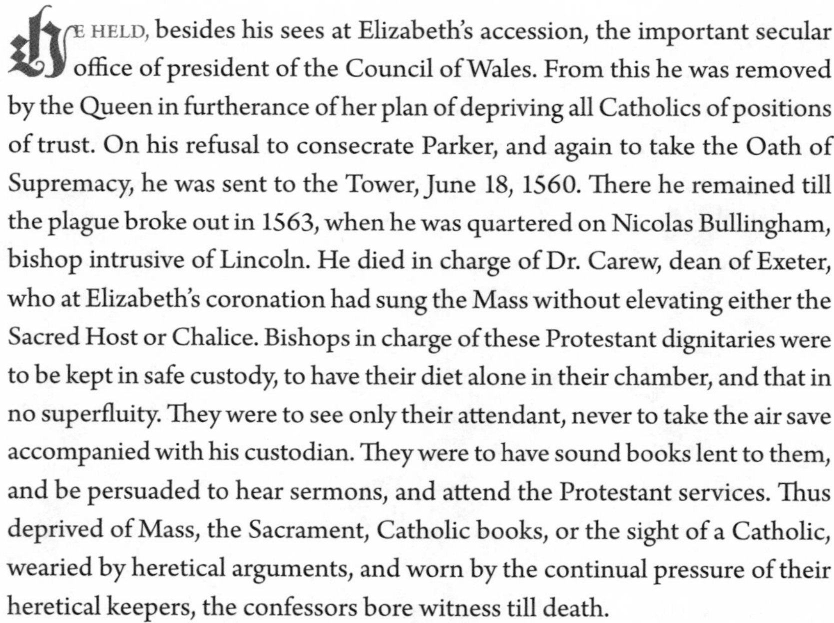

He held, besides his sees at Elizabeth's accession, the important secular office of president of the Council of Wales. From this he was removed by the Queen in furtherance of her plan of depriving all Catholics of positions of trust. On his refusal to consecrate Parker, and again to take the Oath of Supremacy, he was sent to the Tower, June 18, 1560. There he remained till the plague broke out in 1563, when he was quartered on Nicolas Bullingham, bishop intrusive of Lincoln. He died in charge of Dr. Carew, dean of Exeter, who at Elizabeth's coronation had sung the Mass without elevating either the Sacred Host or Chalice. Bishops in charge of these Protestant dignitaries were to be kept in safe custody, to have their diet alone in their chamber, and that in no superfluity. They were to see only their attendant, never to take the air save accompanied with his custodian. They were to have sound books lent to them, and be persuaded to hear sermons, and attend the Protestant services. Thus deprived of Mass, the Sacrament, Catholic books, or the sight of a Catholic, wearied by heretical arguments, and worn by the continual pressure of their heretical keepers, the confessors bore witness till death.

"We would not have you ignorant, brethren, of our tribulation . . . we were pressed out of measure, so that we were weary even of life" (2 Cor 1:8).

September 11

HEREDITARY CHAMPION OF ENGLAND

Robert Dymoke, L., 1580

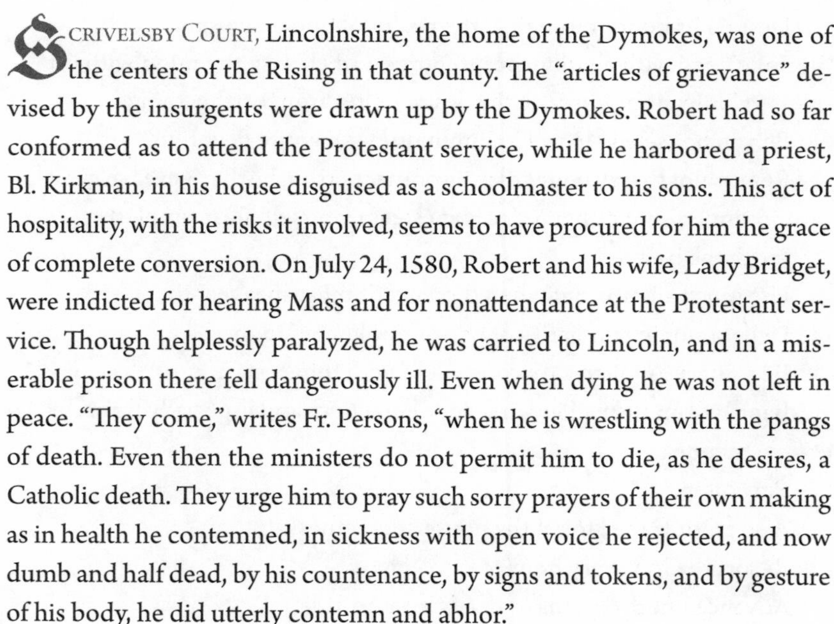

Scrivelsby Court, Lincolnshire, the home of the Dymokes, was one of the centers of the Rising in that county. The "articles of grievance" devised by the insurgents were drawn up by the Dymokes. Robert had so far conformed as to attend the Protestant service, while he harbored a priest, Bl. Kirkman, in his house disguised as a schoolmaster to his sons. This act of hospitality, with the risks it involved, seems to have procured for him the grace of complete conversion. On July 24, 1580, Robert and his wife, Lady Bridget, were indicted for hearing Mass and for nonattendance at the Protestant service. Though helplessly paralyzed, he was carried to Lincoln, and in a miserable prison there fell dangerously ill. Even when dying he was not left in peace. "They come," writes Fr. Persons, "when he is wrestling with the pangs of death. Even then the ministers do not permit him to die, as he desires, a Catholic death. They urge him to pray such sorry prayers of their own making as in health he contemned, in sickness with open voice he rejected, and now dumb and half dead, by his countenance, by signs and tokens, and by gesture of his body, he did utterly contemn and abhor."

"Who by faith conquered kingdoms, wrought justice, obtained promises, stopped the mouths of lions" (Heb 11:33).

September 12

A MARTYR'S MAXIMS (1)

Bl. Adrian Fortescue, L., 1539

Above all things love God with all thy heart.

Desire His honor more than the health of thine own soul.

Take heed with all diligence to purge and cleanse thy mind with oft Confession, and raise thy desire or lust from earthly things.

Be you houseled [Holy Communion] with entire devotion.

Repute not thyself better than any other person, be they never so great sinners, but rather judge and esteem yourself most simplest.

Judge the best.

Use much silence, but when thou needs must speak.

Delight not in familiarity of persons unknown to thee.

Be solitary as much as is convenient with thine estate.

Banish from thee all judging and detraction, and especially from thy tongue.

Pray often.

Also enforce thee to set thy house at quietness.

Resort to God every hour.

Advance not thy words or deeds by any pride.

Be not too much familiar, but show a serious and prudent countenance with gentleness.

Show before all people a good example of virtues.

"The wisdom from above is first chaste" (Jas 3:17).

September 13

A MARTYR'S MAXIMS (2)

Bl. Adrian Fortescue, L., 1539

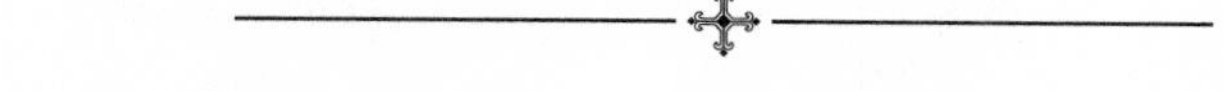

Be not partial for favor, lucre, or malice, but according to truth, equity, justice, and reason.

Be pitiful to poor folk and help them to thy power, for then thou shalt greatly please God.

Give fair language to all persons, and especially to the poor and needy.

Also be diligent in giving of alms.

In prosperity, be meek of heart, and in adversity, patient.

And pray continually to God that you may do what is His pleasure.

Also apply diligently the cooperations of the Holy Ghost whatever thou hast therein to do.

Pray for perseverance.

Continue in dread, and ever have God before thine eyes.

Renew every day thy good purpose.

What thou hast to do, do it diligently.

'Stablish thyself always in well-doing.

If by chance you fall into sin, despair not, and if you keep these precepts, the Holy Ghost will strengthen thee in all other things necessary, and, thus doing, you shall be with Christ in heaven, to Whom be glory, laud, honor, and praise everlasting.

"She conducted the just ... through the right ways, and showed him the kingdom of God, and gave him the knowledge of holy things" (Ws 10:10).

September 14

SEPARATED UNTO THE GOSPEL

Ven. Edward Barlow, O. S. B., 1641

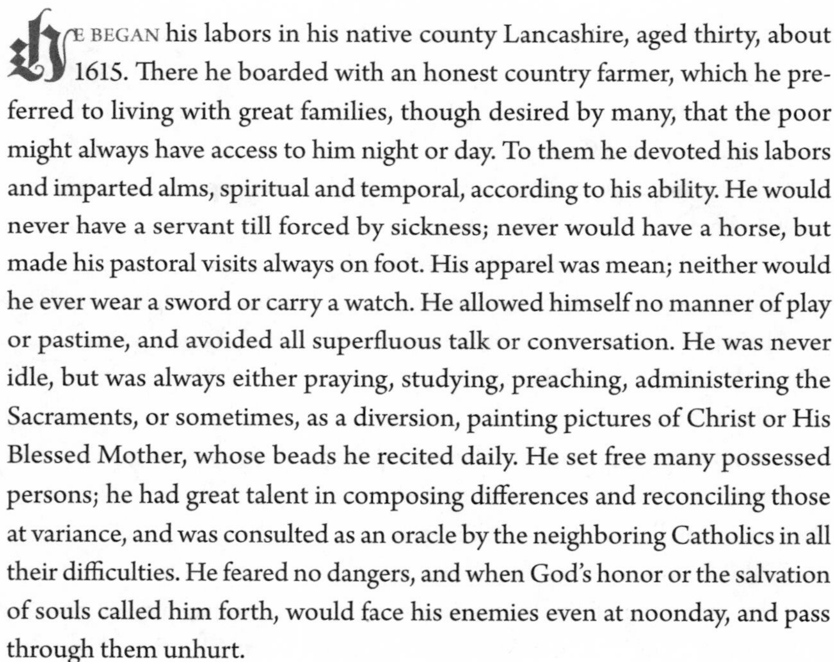

HE BEGAN his labors in his native county Lancashire, aged thirty, about 1615. There he boarded with an honest country farmer, which he preferred to living with great families, though desired by many, that the poor might always have access to him night or day. To them he devoted his labors and imparted alms, spiritual and temporal, according to his ability. He would never have a servant till forced by sickness; never would have a horse, but made his pastoral visits always on foot. His apparel was mean; neither would he ever wear a sword or carry a watch. He allowed himself no manner of play or pastime, and avoided all superfluous talk or conversation. He was never idle, but was always either praying, studying, preaching, administering the Sacraments, or sometimes, as a diversion, painting pictures of Christ or His Blessed Mother, whose beads he recited daily. He set free many possessed persons; he had great talent in composing differences and reconciling those at variance, and was consulted as an oracle by the neighboring Catholics in all their difficulties. He feared no dangers, and when God's honor or the salvation of souls called him forth, would face his enemies even at noonday, and pass through them unhurt.

"Paul, a servant of Jesus Christ, called to be an apostle, separated unto the Gospel of God" (Rom 1:1).

September 15

THE PRIMITIVE CHURCH

Ven. Edward Barlow, O. S. B., 1641

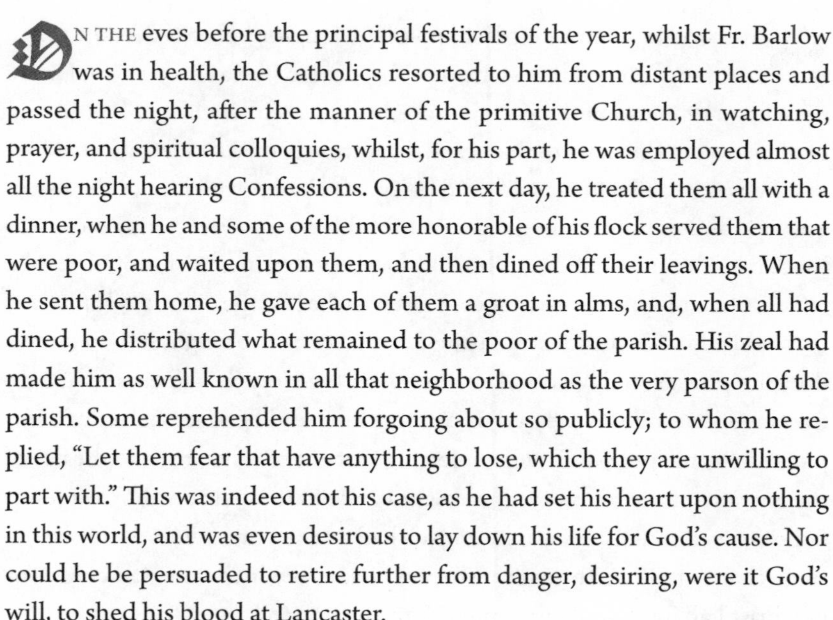

On the eves before the principal festivals of the year, whilst Fr. Barlow was in health, the Catholics resorted to him from distant places and passed the night, after the manner of the primitive Church, in watching, prayer, and spiritual colloquies, whilst, for his part, he was employed almost all the night hearing Confessions. On the next day, he treated them all with a dinner, when he and some of the more honorable of his flock served them that were poor, and waited upon them, and then dined off their leavings. When he sent them home, he gave each of them a groat in alms, and, when all had dined, he distributed what remained to the poor of the parish. His zeal had made him as well known in all that neighborhood as the very parson of the parish. Some reprehended him forgoing about so publicly; to whom he replied, "Let them fear that have anything to lose, which they are unwilling to part with." This was indeed not his case, as he had set his heart upon nothing in this world, and was even desirous to lay down his life for God's cause. Nor could he be persuaded to retire further from danger, desiring, were it God's will, to shed his blood at Lancaster.

"And the multitude of believers had but one heart and one soul.... All things were common unto them" (Acts 4:32).

September 16

HORROR OF SCANDAL

Ven. Edward Barlow, O. S. B., 1641

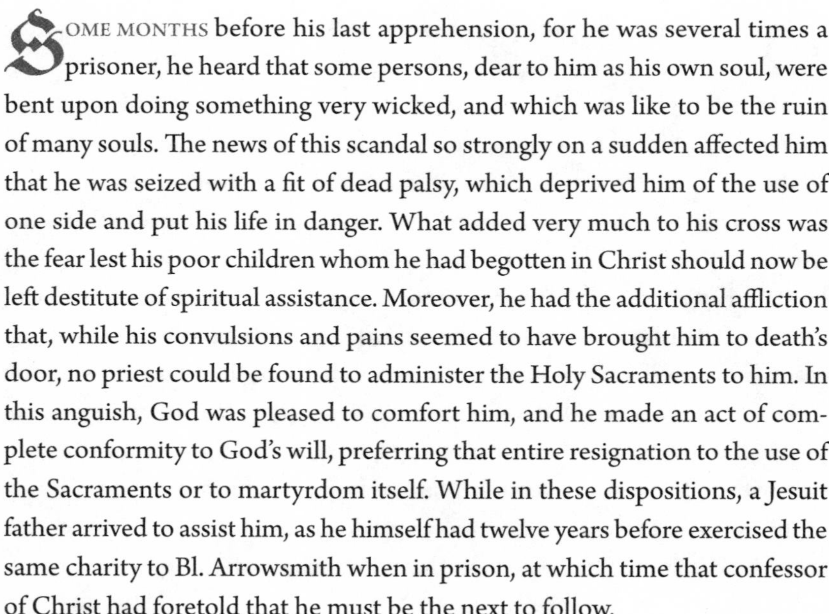

SOME MONTHS before his last apprehension, for he was several times a prisoner, he heard that some persons, dear to him as his own soul, were bent upon doing something very wicked, and which was like to be the ruin of many souls. The news of this scandal so strongly on a sudden affected him that he was seized with a fit of dead palsy, which deprived him of the use of one side and put his life in danger. What added very much to his cross was the fear lest his poor children whom he had begotten in Christ should now be left destitute of spiritual assistance. Moreover, he had the additional affliction that, while his convulsions and pains seemed to have brought him to death's door, no priest could be found to administer the Holy Sacraments to him. In this anguish, God was pleased to comfort him, and he made an act of complete conformity to God's will, preferring that entire resignation to the use of the Sacraments or to martyrdom itself. While in these dispositions, a Jesuit father arrived to assist him, as he himself had twelve years before exercised the same charity to Bl. Arrowsmith when in prison, at which time that confessor of Christ had foretold that he must be the next to follow.

"Who is weak, and I am not weak? Who is scandalized, and I am not on fire?" (2 Cor 11:29).

September 17

ROMANS THE ONLY PRIESTS

Ven. Edward Barlow, O. S. B., 1641

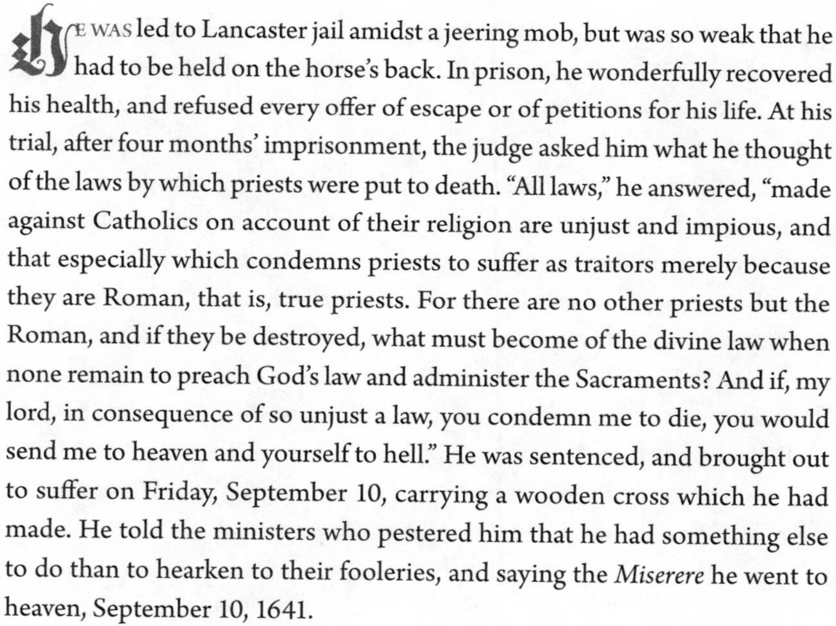

HE WAS led to Lancaster jail amidst a jeering mob, but was so weak that he had to be held on the horse's back. In prison, he wonderfully recovered his health, and refused every offer of escape or of petitions for his life. At his trial, after four months' imprisonment, the judge asked him what he thought of the laws by which priests were put to death. "All laws," he answered, "made against Catholics on account of their religion are unjust and impious, and that especially which condemns priests to suffer as traitors merely because they are Roman, that is, true priests. For there are no other priests but the Roman, and if they be destroyed, what must become of the divine law when none remain to preach God's law and administer the Sacraments? And if, my lord, in consequence of so unjust a law, you condemn me to die, you would send me to heaven and yourself to hell." He was sentenced, and brought out to suffer on Friday, September 10, carrying a wooden cross which he had made. He told the ministers who pestered him that he had something else to do than to hearken to their fooleries, and saying the *Miserere* he went to heaven, September 10, 1641.

"But I chose Jerusalem, that My name might be there: and I chose David to set him over My people" (2 Par 6:6).

September 18

STRONGER THAN DEATH

Ven. Richard Herst, L., 1628

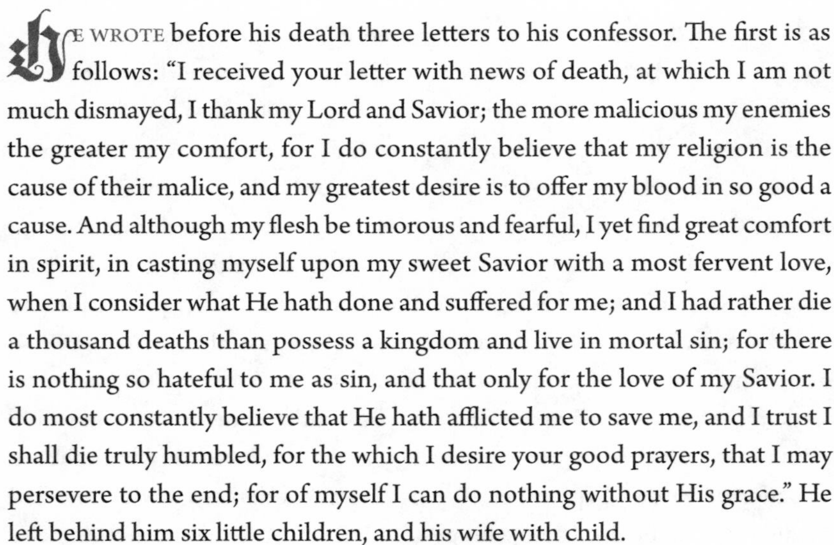

He wrote before his death three letters to his confessor. The first is as follows: "I received your letter with news of death, at which I am not much dismayed, I thank my Lord and Savior; the more malicious my enemies the greater my comfort, for I do constantly believe that my religion is the cause of their malice, and my greatest desire is to offer my blood in so good a cause. And although my flesh be timorous and fearful, I yet find great comfort in spirit, in casting myself upon my sweet Savior with a most fervent love, when I consider what He hath done and suffered for me; and I had rather die a thousand deaths than possess a kingdom and live in mortal sin; for there is nothing so hateful to me as sin, and that only for the love of my Savior. I do most constantly believe that He hath afflicted me to save me, and I trust I shall die truly humbled, for the which I desire your good prayers, that I may persevere to the end; for of myself I can do nothing without His grace." He left behind him six little children, and his wife with child.

"Lord, Thou knowest all things: Thou knowest that I love Thee" (Jn 21:17).

September 19

PRAYERS FOR THE DEAD

Ven. Richard Herst, L., 1628

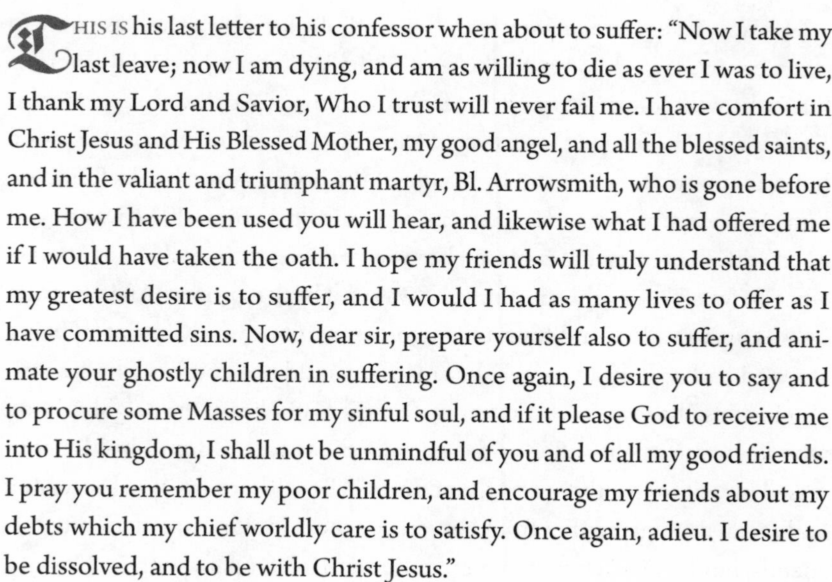

THIS IS his last letter to his confessor when about to suffer: "Now I take my last leave; now I am dying, and am as willing to die as ever I was to live, I thank my Lord and Savior, Who I trust will never fail me. I have comfort in Christ Jesus and His Blessed Mother, my good angel, and all the blessed saints, and in the valiant and triumphant martyr, Bl. Arrowsmith, who is gone before me. How I have been used you will hear, and likewise what I had offered me if I would have taken the oath. I hope my friends will truly understand that my greatest desire is to suffer, and I would I had as many lives to offer as I have committed sins. Now, dear sir, prepare yourself also to suffer, and animate your ghostly children in suffering. Once again, I desire you to say and to procure some Masses for my sinful soul, and if it please God to receive me into His kingdom, I shall not be unmindful of you and of all my good friends. I pray you remember my poor children, and encourage my friends about my debts which my chief worldly care is to satisfy. Once again, adieu. I desire to be dissolved, and to be with Christ Jesus."

> *"He sent twelve thousand drachms of silver for sacrifice to be offered for the sins of the dead, thinking well and religiously concerning the resurrection"* (2 Mc 12:43).

September 20

TO SAVE OTHERS

Ven. John Duckett, Pr., 1644

He was taken, in company with two Catholic laymen, as he was going to baptize two children on the feast of the Visitation, July 2. His captors, the Parliament soldiers, carried him before a committee of the sequestrators at Sunderland. He declined to answer as to his priesthood and demanded proof, but was committed to prison by reason of the holy oils and books found on him. Again examined, and again refusing to inculpate himself, he was threatened with lighted matches placed between his fingers to make him confess what he was. This availing nothing, he was sent back to prison. After an hour, he was again called, and found his two companions on the point of being shipped and sent away, merely because he would not confess who he was. "Seeing this," he says, "and also fearing that the Catholics of the neighborhood who knew me might suffer, and especially those with whom I lived, I confessed myself to free them and the country." His self-sacrifice was successful, and seemed an inspiration from heaven. No more inquiry was made after his friends, but Fr. Duckett was sent up to London in company with Fr. Corby, a Jesuit, who was taken in these parts as he was going up to the altar to say Mass.

"If therefore ye seek Me, let these go their way" (Jn 18:8).

September 21

A HOLY YOUTH

Ven. Edmund Arrowsmith, S.J., 1628

HIS FAMILY were great sufferers for the Faith. His maternal grandfather, Mr. Nicholas Gerard, being unable to move with the gout, was carried to the Protestant church and placed close to the minister, but he sang psalms in Latin so loud that the minister was inaudible, and he had to be removed. His parents and their household were driven, tied two and two, to Lancaster jail, the four youngest children, of which Edmund was one, being left homeless and unclad until some charitable neighbors took compassion on them. After some years, to ease his now widowed mother of her burden, a venerable priest took charge of Edmund. As the boy went to school, about a mile distant, his daily practice was to recite with his companions the little hours of Our Lady's Office, and, on his way back, the Vespers and Compline. After his return home, he would withdraw to his oratory and there perform his customary devotions of the Jesus Psalter, the Seven Psalms, and so on, and so engaging were his temper and manners that he won the affection of even the Protestant schoolmaster. His priestly studies, though often interrupted by his bad health, were completed at Douay, whence he went on the English mission, 1613.

"When he was yet a boy, he began to seek the God of his father David" (2 Par 34:3).

September 22

LOWLY, BUT BOLD

Ven. Edmund Arrowsmith, S.J., 1628

He is described as being, like St. Paul, of mean presence, but of great innocency of life, and so zealous, witty, and fervent that his eagerness to dispute with heretics, had he not been restrained, would have brought him too soon into danger of death. A Protestant gentleman, thinking from his appearance he might be easily befooled, tried to jest upon him, but his retorts were so sharp that the gentleman swore that where he thought he had met a mere simpleton he had found a foolish scholar or a learned fool. He had such great power in freeing possessed persons, during his fifteen years of priestly labor, first as a secular then as a Jesuit, that at his last trial the judge pleaded for his death as too dangerous a seducer to be set at liberty. Dr. Bridgman, bishop of Chester, before whom he was once brought at suppertime in Lent, excused himself for eating flesh, as being dispensed on account of weakness. "But who dispenses your lusty ministers there, who have no such need, and all eat flesh?" As divers ministers together attacked him, he said to the bishop, "Turn all your dogs at once against me, and let us have a loose bait."

"Now I, Paul, beseech you by the mildness and modesty of Christ, who in presence indeed am lowly among you, but being absent am bold toward you" (2 Cor 10:1).

September 23

THE NARROW WAY

Ven. John Wall, O. S. F., 1679

Born of a Lancashire gentleman's family, he received the habit of St. Francis at Douay in 1651, being then thirty-two years of age. He entered on the English mission, 1656, and labored successfully for twelve years. At the breaking out of the Oates Plot, he was apprehended, and, refusing to take the Oath of Allegiance, was imprisoned in Worcester jail. Of his sentiments then he writes: "Imprisonment in these times, when none can send to their friends or their friends come to them, is the best means to teach us how to put our confidence in God alone in all things, and then He will make His promise good that 'all things shall be added unto us' (Lk 12:31), which chapter, if everyone would read and made good use of, a prison would be better than a palace, and a confinement for religion and a good conscience's sake more pleasant than all the liberties the world could afford. As for my own part, God give me His grace and all faithful Christians their prayers; I am happy enough. We all ought to follow the narrow way, though there be many difficulties in it. It is an easy thing to run the blind way of liberty, but God deliver us from all broad, sweet ways."

"How narrow is the gate and straight the way that leadeth to life, and few there are that find it" (Mt 7:14).

September 24

A MARTYR'S LEGACIES

Bl. Everard Hanse, Pr., 1581

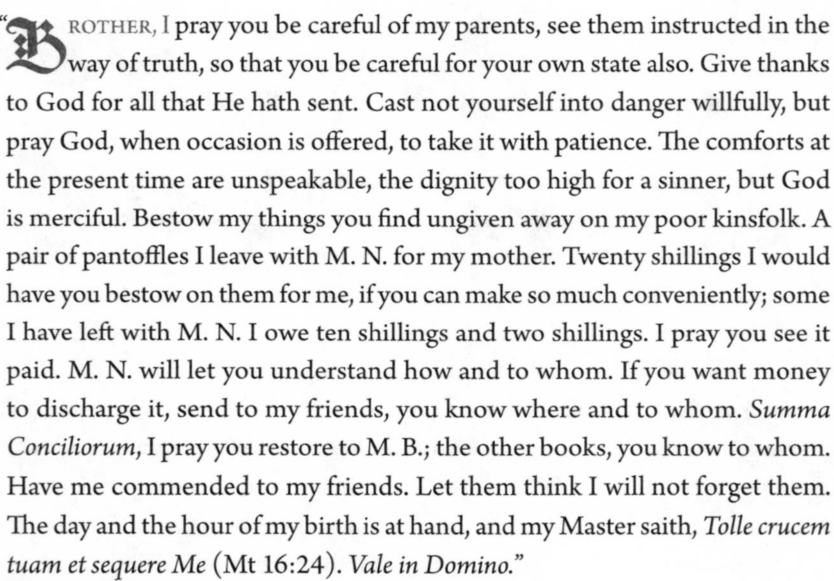

"BROTHER, I pray you be careful of my parents, see them instructed in the way of truth, so that you be careful for your own state also. Give thanks to God for all that He hath sent. Cast not yourself into danger willfully, but pray God, when occasion is offered, to take it with patience. The comforts at the present time are unspeakable, the dignity too high for a sinner, but God is merciful. Bestow my things you find ungiven away on my poor kinsfolk. A pair of pantoffles I leave with M. N. for my mother. Twenty shillings I would have you bestow on them for me, if you can make so much conveniently; some I have left with M. N. I owe ten shillings and two shillings. I pray you see it paid. M. N. will let you understand how and to whom. If you want money to discharge it, send to my friends, you know where and to whom. *Summa Conciliorum*, I pray you restore to M. B.; the other books, you know to whom. Have me commended to my friends. Let them think I will not forget them. The day and the hour of my birth is at hand, and my Master saith, *Tolle crucem tuam et sequere Me* (Mt 16:24). *Vale in Domino.*"

"Well done, thou good and faithful servant: because thou hast been faithful over a few things, I will place thee over many things. Enter thou into the joy of thy Lord" (Mt 25:23).

September 25

A REPROVER OF SIN

Ven. Oliver Plunket, Abp., on the scaffold, 1681

"I WAS BROUGHT to the bar here after six months imprisonment for a crime for which before I was arraigned in Ireland; a fact almost without precedent in five hundred years. Five weeks were allowed me to bring over my records and witnesses, which, owing to many difficulties, was insufficient. I asked for five days more. This was refused, and I was exposed, with my hands tied, as it were, to these merciless perjurers. You see what position I am in, and you have heard the protestations of my innocency, and I hope you will believe the words of a dying man. In support of my credit, I assure you that I was offered my life if I would accuse other conspirators, but as I know of none I could not. I admit that I endeavored to establish a proper discipline among the clergy according to my duty, and you see how I am rewarded. By false oaths they have brought me to this untimely death. But this wicked act, being a defect of person, ought not to reflect on the Order of St. Francis or on the Roman Catholic clergy. There was a Judas among the apostles, and a Nicholas among the seven deacons, and as St. Stephen, the holy deacon, prayed for his enemies, so do I." And so he went to his reward.

"Them that sin reprove before all that the rest may have fear" (1 Tm 5:20).

September 26

A FAIR TRIAL

Ven. Oliver Plunket, Abp., 1681

AFTER HIS condemnation, he wrote to Fr. Corker, his fellow prisoner, as follows: "I am obliged to you for the favor and charity of the 20th, and for all your former benevolences; and whereas I cannot in this country remunerate you, with God's grace I hope to be grateful in that kingdom which is properly our country. And truly God gave me, though unworthy of it, that grace to have *fortem animum mortis terrore carentem*, 'a courage fearless of death.' I have many sins to answer for before the Supreme Judge of the high bench, where no false witnesses can have audience. But as for the bench yesterday, I am not guilty of any crime there objected to me. I would I could be so clear at the bench of the All-Powerful. *Ut ut sit*, there is one comfort that He cannot be deceived, because He is omniscious, and knows all secrets, even of hearts, and cannot deceive because all goodness, so that I may be sure of a fair trial, and will get time sufficient to call witnesses; nay, the Judge will bring them in a moment if there be need of any. You and your comrade's prayers will be powerful advocates at that trial. Here none are admitted for your affectionate friend, Oliver Plunket."

"But there is no other God but Thou, Who hast care of all, that Thou shouldst show that Thou dost not give judgment unjustly" (Ws 12:13).

September 27

A PEACEMAKER

✠ Bp. Thomas Watson of Lincoln, 1584

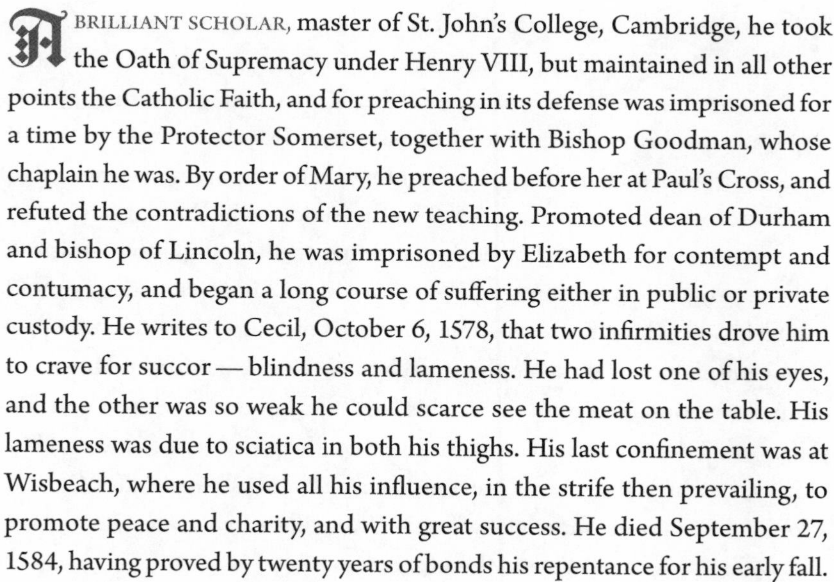

A BRILLIANT SCHOLAR, master of St. John's College, Cambridge, he took the Oath of Supremacy under Henry VIII, but maintained in all other points the Catholic Faith, and for preaching in its defense was imprisoned for a time by the Protector Somerset, together with Bishop Goodman, whose chaplain he was. By order of Mary, he preached before her at Paul's Cross, and refuted the contradictions of the new teaching. Promoted dean of Durham and bishop of Lincoln, he was imprisoned by Elizabeth for contempt and contumacy, and began a long course of suffering either in public or private custody. He writes to Cecil, October 6, 1578, that two infirmities drove him to crave for succor — blindness and lameness. He had lost one of his eyes, and the other was so weak he could scarce see the meat on the table. His lameness was due to sciatica in both his thighs. His last confinement was at Wisbeach, where he used all his influence, in the strife then prevailing, to promote peace and charity, and with great success. He died September 27, 1584, having proved by twenty years of bonds his repentance for his early fall.

"I beseech you, brethren, by the name of our Lord Jesus Christ, that you all speak the same thing, and that there be no schisms among you" (1 Cor 1:10).

September 28

PETITION FOR READMISSION

Ven. John Woodcock, O. S. F., 1646

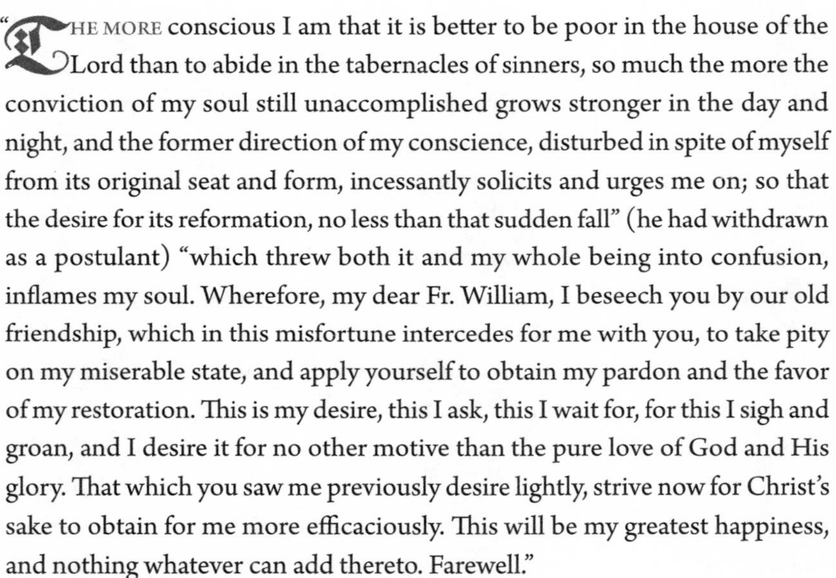

"THE MORE conscious I am that it is better to be poor in the house of the Lord than to abide in the tabernacles of sinners, so much the more the conviction of my soul still unaccomplished grows stronger in the day and night, and the former direction of my conscience, disturbed in spite of myself from its original seat and form, incessantly solicits and urges me on; so that the desire for its reformation, no less than that sudden fall" (he had withdrawn as a postulant) "which threw both it and my whole being into confusion, inflames my soul. Wherefore, my dear Fr. William, I beseech you by our old friendship, which in this misfortune intercedes for me with you, to take pity on my miserable state, and apply yourself to obtain my pardon and the favor of my restoration. This is my desire, this I ask, this I wait for, for this I sigh and groan, and I desire it for no other motive than the pure love of God and His glory. That which you saw me previously desire lightly, strive now for Christ's sake to obtain for me more efficaciously. This will be my greatest happiness, and nothing whatever can add thereto. Farewell."

"The prayer of him that humbleth himself shall pierce the clouds" (Ecclus 35:21).

September 29

LOVE OF PARENTS

✠ Ven. William Spenser, Pr., 1589

Born in the Craven district of York, he was educated by his maternal uncle, Horn, a Marian priest, at his benefice near Chipping Norton. He then entered Trinity College, Oxford, and became fellow and master of arts in 1580. There, though outwardly conforming, he showed such zeal for the Faith as to embitter the heretics and to win many youths by his instructions in Catholic doctrine. After two years thus living with a troubled conscience, he sought peace by leaving Oxford for Rheims, and in 1584 returned as a priest to England. His first care was the conversion of his parents, whom he contrived after much difficulty to meet in a field disguised as a laborer, with the result that they were both reconciled. His uncle also by his influence resigned his benefice, which he had only held by tampering with heresy, and found a home in a Catholic household. He now devoted himself to the Catholic prisoners at York, and managed to secure a hiding place with them in the castle. After laboring with much fruit, he was arrested when on a journey and suffered with great constancy at York, September 27, 1589, thus washing out with his blood the heretical stains of his youth.

"Honor thy father, and forget not the groanings of thy mother, . . . and make a return to them as they have done for thee" (Ecclus 7:29–30).

* *Spenser was beatified by Pope John Paul II on 22 November 1987.*

September 30

LITTLE BELLS OF GOLD

Bl. Roger Cadwallador, Pr., 1610

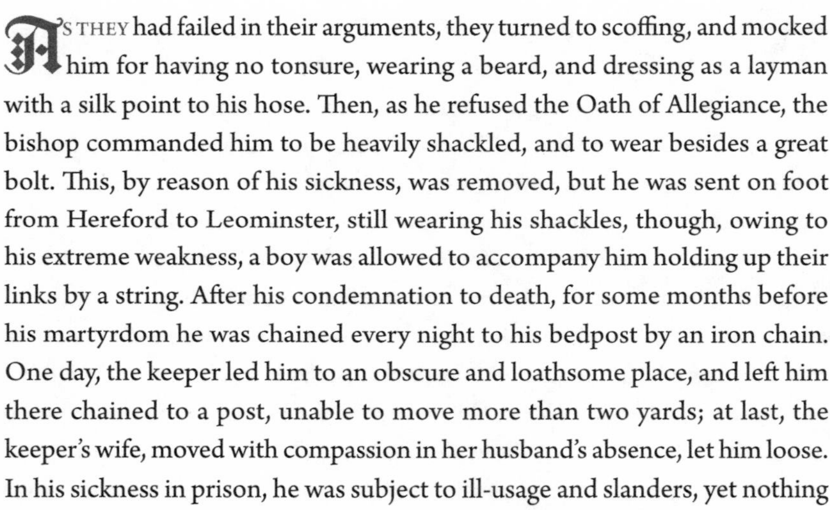

AS THEY had failed in their arguments, they turned to scoffing, and mocked him for having no tonsure, wearing a beard, and dressing as a layman with a silk point to his hose. Then, as he refused the Oath of Allegiance, the bishop commanded him to be heavily shackled, and to wear besides a great bolt. This, by reason of his sickness, was removed, but he was sent on foot from Hereford to Leominster, still wearing his shackles, though, owing to his extreme weakness, a boy was allowed to accompany him holding up their links by a string. After his condemnation to death, for some months before his martyrdom he was chained every night to his bedpost by an iron chain. One day, the keeper led him to an obscure and loathsome place, and left him there chained to a post, unable to move more than two yards; at last, the keeper's wife, moved with compassion in her husband's absence, let him loose. In his sickness in prison, he was subject to ill-usage and slanders, yet nothing daunted his courage or cheerfulness, and to a friend he said, shaking his shackles as he lay prostrate, "Hear, O Lord! these are my little bells."

"He clothed him with a robe of glory.... and encompassed him with many little bells of gold ... that a noise might be heard in the temple, for a memorial to the children of his people" (Ecclus 45:9–11).

October

October 1

A TRUE ISRAELITE

✠ Ven. John Robinson, Pr., 1588

Born at Fernsby, Yorkshire, he lived for some time in the world in the married state, but on becoming a widower he went over to Rheims, was ordained, and sent on the mission. He was a man of great simplicity and sincerity, and he used to say that if he could not dispute for the Faith as well as some of the others, he could die for it as well as the best. He was apprehended in the very port where he landed, and cast into the Clink prison. His fellow prisoners, in respect to his age and probity, called him "Father," and he in return styled them his "bairns," and when they were sent off to be executed in different parts of the kingdom, the good old man lamented for days exceedingly, until at last the warrant for his own execution arrived. To the bearer of the warrant, he gave all his money, and on his knees gave God thanks. He was sent to suffer at Ipswich, a long journey taken on foot, but he refused to put on boots, as he said, "These feet of mine have never worn them, and they can well travel now without them, for they will be well repaid." He was executed October 1, 1588.

"Behold a true Israelite, in whom there is no guile" (Jn 1:47).

* *Robinson was beatified by Pope Pius XI on 15 December 1929.*

October 2

THE UNITY OF CHRISTENDOM

Bl. Thomas More, L., 1535

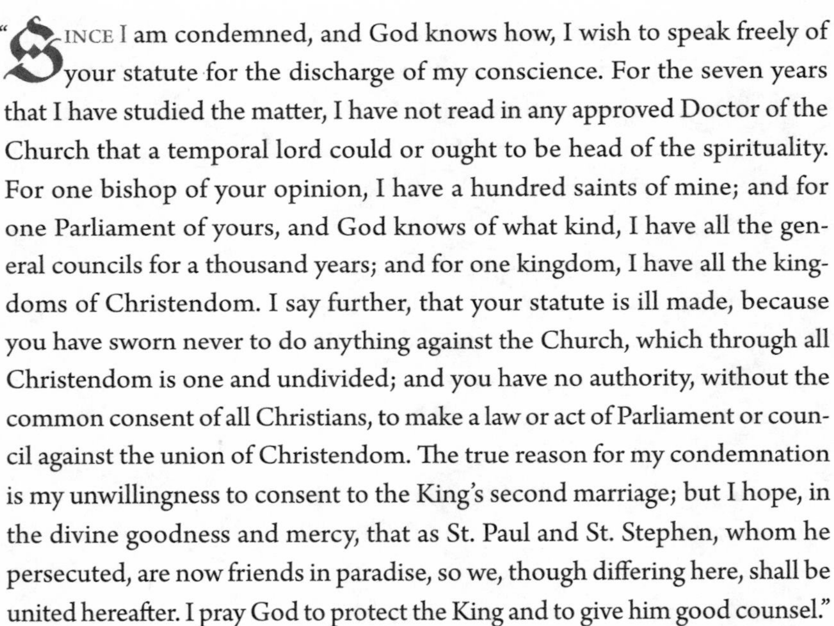

"Since I am condemned, and God knows how, I wish to speak freely of your statute for the discharge of my conscience. For the seven years that I have studied the matter, I have not read in any approved Doctor of the Church that a temporal lord could or ought to be head of the spirituality. For one bishop of your opinion, I have a hundred saints of mine; and for one Parliament of yours, and God knows of what kind, I have all the general councils for a thousand years; and for one kingdom, I have all the kingdoms of Christendom. I say further, that your statute is ill made, because you have sworn never to do anything against the Church, which through all Christendom is one and undivided; and you have no authority, without the common consent of all Christians, to make a law or act of Parliament or council against the union of Christendom. The true reason for my condemnation is my unwillingness to consent to the King's second marriage; but I hope, in the divine goodness and mercy, that as St. Paul and St. Stephen, whom he persecuted, are now friends in paradise, so we, though differing here, shall be united hereafter. I pray God to protect the King and to give him good counsel."

"Every kingdom divided against itself shall be made desolate, and every city or house divided against itself shall not stand" (Mt 12:25).

October 3

AN ADVOCATE OF CHRIST

Ven. Philip Powell, O. S. B., 1646

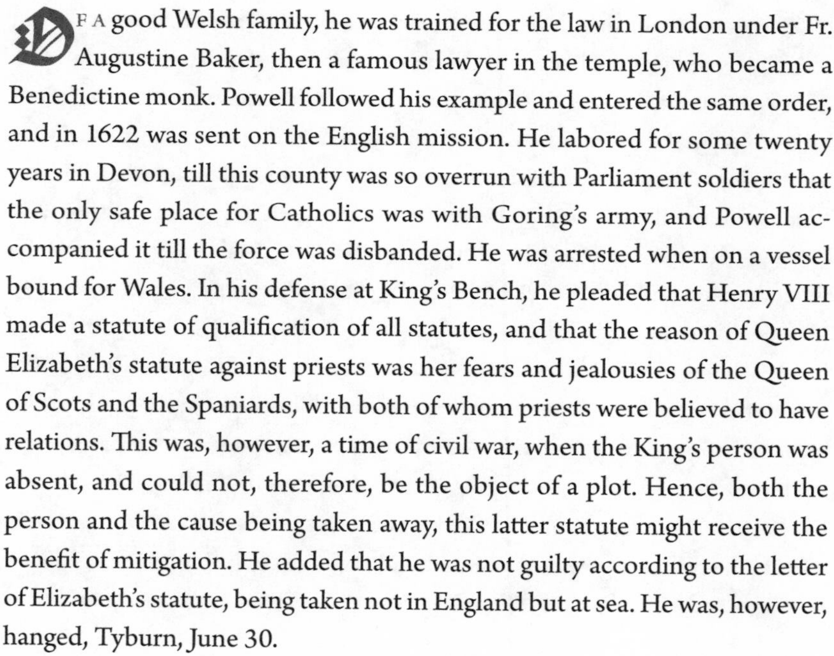

OF A good Welsh family, he was trained for the law in London under Fr. Augustine Baker, then a famous lawyer in the temple, who became a Benedictine monk. Powell followed his example and entered the same order, and in 1622 was sent on the English mission. He labored for some twenty years in Devon, till this county was so overrun with Parliament soldiers that the only safe place for Catholics was with Goring's army, and Powell accompanied it till the force was disbanded. He was arrested when on a vessel bound for Wales. In his defense at King's Bench, he pleaded that Henry VIII made a statute of qualification of all statutes, and that the reason of Queen Elizabeth's statute against priests was her fears and jealousies of the Queen of Scots and the Spaniards, with both of whom priests were believed to have relations. This was, however, a time of civil war, when the King's person was absent, and could not, therefore, be the object of a plot. Hence, both the person and the cause being taken away, this latter statute might receive the benefit of mitigation. He added that he was not guilty according to the letter of Elizabeth's statute, being taken not in England but at sea. He was, however, hanged, Tyburn, June 30.

"And all that heard Him were astonished at His wisdom and His answers" (Lk 2:47).

October 4

THE FINAL JUDGMENT

Bl. Edmund Campion, S. J., 1581

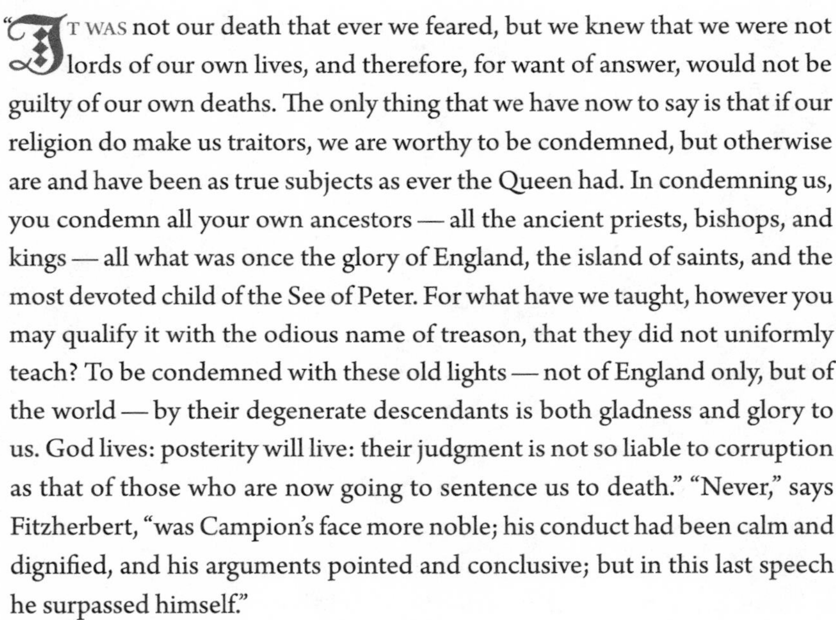

"It was not our death that ever we feared, but we knew that we were not lords of our own lives, and therefore, for want of answer, would not be guilty of our own deaths. The only thing that we have now to say is that if our religion do make us traitors, we are worthy to be condemned, but otherwise are and have been as true subjects as ever the Queen had. In condemning us, you condemn all your own ancestors — all the ancient priests, bishops, and kings — all what was once the glory of England, the island of saints, and the most devoted child of the See of Peter. For what have we taught, however you may qualify it with the odious name of treason, that they did not uniformly teach? To be condemned with these old lights — not of England only, but of the world — by their degenerate descendants is both gladness and glory to us. God lives: posterity will live: their judgment is not so liable to corruption as that of those who are now going to sentence us to death." "Never," says Fitzherbert, "was Campion's face more noble; his conduct had been calm and dignified, and his arguments pointed and conclusive; but in this last speech he surpassed himself."

"And after this the judgment" (Heb 9:27).

October 5

A MOTHER'S SACRIFICE

Ven. William Hartley, Pr., 1588

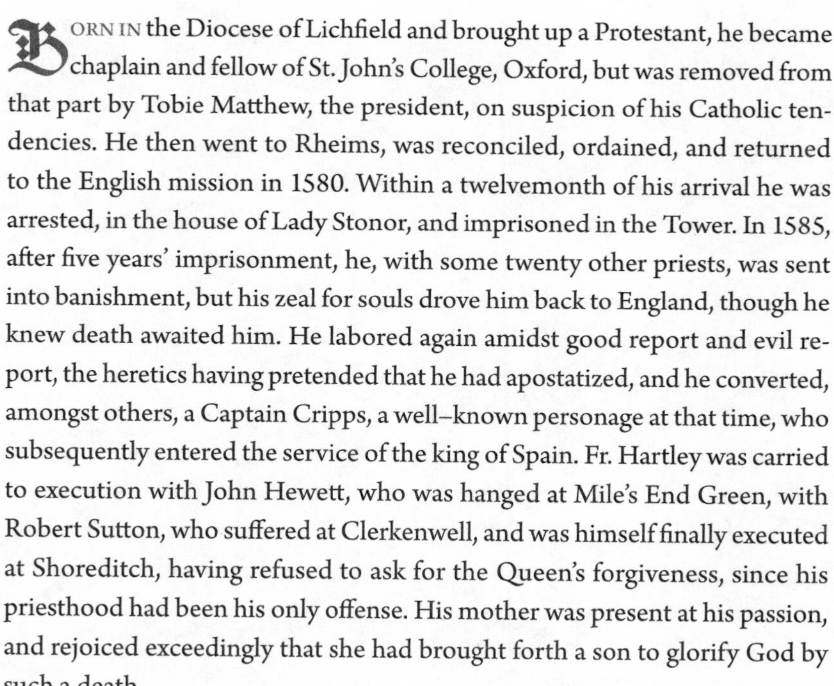

Born in the Diocese of Lichfield and brought up a Protestant, he became chaplain and fellow of St. John's College, Oxford, but was removed from that part by Tobie Matthew, the president, on suspicion of his Catholic tendencies. He then went to Rheims, was reconciled, ordained, and returned to the English mission in 1580. Within a twelvemonth of his arrival he was arrested, in the house of Lady Stonor, and imprisoned in the Tower. In 1585, after five years' imprisonment, he, with some twenty other priests, was sent into banishment, but his zeal for souls drove him back to England, though he knew death awaited him. He labored again amidst good report and evil report, the heretics having pretended that he had apostatized, and he converted, amongst others, a Captain Cripps, a well-known personage at that time, who subsequently entered the service of the king of Spain. Fr. Hartley was carried to execution with John Hewett, who was hanged at Mile's End Green, with Robert Sutton, who suffered at Clerkenwell, and was himself finally executed at Shoreditch, having refused to ask for the Queen's forgiveness, since his priesthood had been his only offense. His mother was present at his passion, and rejoiced exceedingly that she had brought forth a son to glorify God by such a death.

"There stood by the Cross of Jesus His Mother" (Jn 19:25).

* *Hartley was beatified by Pope Pius XI on 15 December 1929.*

October 6

THE CATHOLIC ASSOCIATION

George Gilbert, S.J., 1583

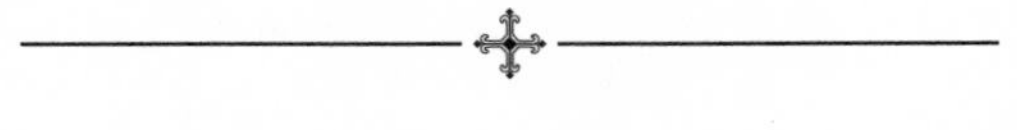

Of an old Suffolk family, possessed of a large fortune, a Puritan by profession, he followed in his youth the life of a gay cavalier. Going abroad, however, his eyes were opened to the Faith, and he was reconciled by Fr. Parsons at Rome. Returning to England, he devoted himself to the services of the missionary priests, and formed for this purpose, with Lord Henry Howard, Lord Oxford, Mr. Southwell, Lord Paget, and other young men, a "Catholic Association," which was solemnly blessed by Gregory XIII, April 14, 1580. The members promised to imitate the lives of the apostles, and to devote themselves wholly to the salvation of souls and the conversion of heretics. They were to be content with the necessaries of their state, and to bestow all the rest for the good of the Catholic cause. They supplied the priests with altar requisites, with horses, and various changes of apparel, and disguised themselves as grooms or servants and escorted the priests through the country from house to house. To Gilbert is due the first idea of the frescoes of the English martyrs in the English College, Rome. He was admitted to the Society of Jesus on his deathbed.

"And the multitude of believers had but one heart and one soul. Neither did anyone say that aught of the things he possessed was his own: but all things were common unto them" (Acts 4:32).

October 7

POVERTY PREFERRED

Bp. Edmund Bonner of London, 1569

SUMMONED BY the council and requested to resign, with the assurance of a good pension if he would do so, he replied that he preferred death. "How then," they asked, "will you live?" "Nothing indeed remains to me; but I hope in God, Who will not fail me, and in my friends, the more that I may be able to gain my livelihood by teaching children, which profession I did not disdain to exercise although I was a bishop. And should no one be found willing to accept my teaching, I am a doctor of law and will resume the study of what I have forgotten, and will thus gain my bread. And should this not succeed, I know how to labor with my hands in gardens and orchards, as planting, grafting, sowing, and so on, as well as any gardener in the kingdom. And should this also be insufficient, I desire no other grace, favor, or privilege from Her Majesty than what she grants to the mendicants who go through London from door-to-door begging, that I may do the like if necessary." When the council heard this, his final denunciation, they said, "We have nothing more to do with you at present. Her Majesty then will provide herself with another bishop."

"Hath not God chosen the poor in this world, rich in faith and heirs of the kingdom which God hath promised to them that love Him?" (Jas 2:5).

October 8

CASTING OUT DEVILS

✠ Ven. Richard Dibdale, Pr., 1586

Born in Worcestershire, ordained at Rheims, he began his labors in the English mission in 1584. He was specially renowned as an exorcist. At Sir George Peckham's, Denham, near Uxbridge, and other places, by the virtue and power which Christ has bequeathed to the ministers of His Church, the martyr showed his mastery over evil spirits. They were forced to leave the bodies of the possessed, and to bring from their mouths pieces of metal and other things which could never have entered a human body. In obedience to the prayers and exorcisms of the Church, they declared, to their own confusion, the virtue of the sign of the cross, holy water, and relics, both of the ancient saints and of those suffering in England in those days for the Catholic Faith. These manifestations were slighted indeed by some incredulous and hard-hearted heretics; yet others who were not so biased by passion, but more reasonable, were convinced by what they saw, and thereupon renounced their errors. Fr. Dibdale was condemned to die for his priestly character and functions, and accordingly was, together with Bls. Lowe and Adams, driven to Tyburn, and there hanged, drawn, and quartered, October 8, 1586.

"He gave them power over unclean spirits,
to cast them out" (Mt 10:1).

* *Dibdale was beatified by Pope John Paul II on 22 November 1987.*

October 9

OUR CAPTAIN CHRIST (1)

Bl. Thirkell to the Catholic prisoners (1)

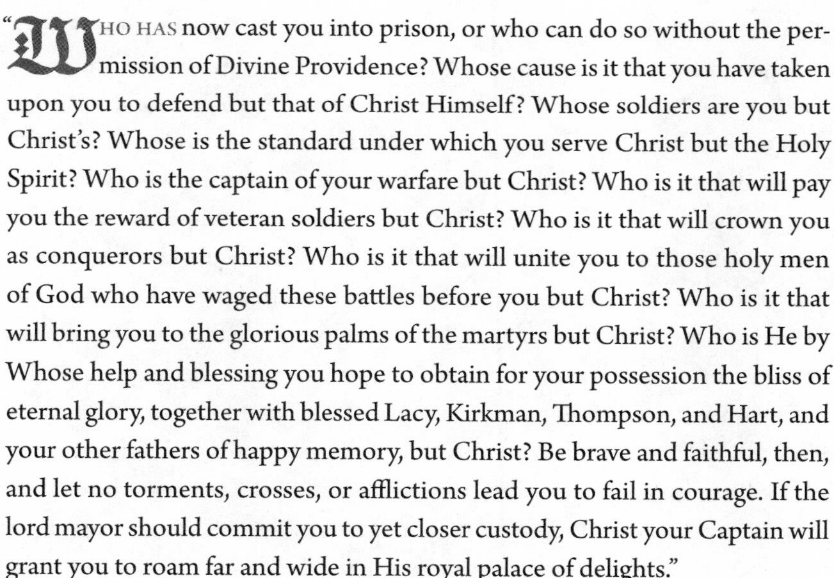

"WHO HAS now cast you into prison, or who can do so without the permission of Divine Providence? Whose cause is it that you have taken upon you to defend but that of Christ Himself? Whose soldiers are you but Christ's? Whose is the standard under which you serve Christ but the Holy Spirit? Who is the captain of your warfare but Christ? Who is it that will pay you the reward of veteran soldiers but Christ? Who is it that will crown you as conquerors but Christ? Who is it that will unite you to those holy men of God who have waged these battles before you but Christ? Who is it that will bring you to the glorious palms of the martyrs but Christ? Who is He by Whose help and blessing you hope to obtain for your possession the bliss of eternal glory, together with blessed Lacy, Kirkman, Thompson, and Hart, and your other fathers of happy memory, but Christ? Be brave and faithful, then, and let no torments, crosses, or afflictions lead you to fail in courage. If the lord mayor should commit you to yet closer custody, Christ your Captain will grant you to roam far and wide in His royal palace of delights."

"But we see Jesus, Who was made a little lower than the angels, for the suffering of death, crowned with glory and honor" (Heb 2:9).

October 10

OUR CAPTAIN CHRIST (2)

Bl. Thirkell to the Catholic prisoners (2)

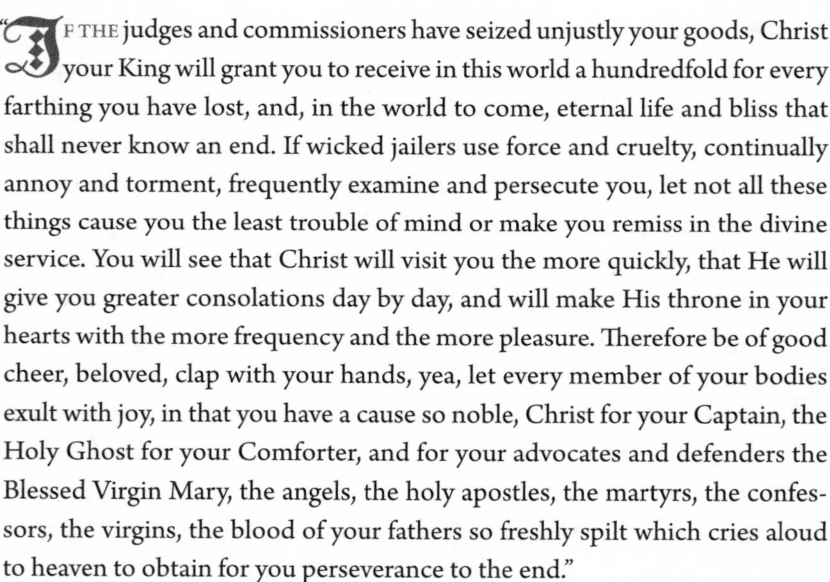

"If the judges and commissioners have seized unjustly your goods, Christ your King will grant you to receive in this world a hundredfold for every farthing you have lost, and, in the world to come, eternal life and bliss that shall never know an end. If wicked jailers use force and cruelty, continually annoy and torment, frequently examine and persecute you, let not all these things cause you the least trouble of mind or make you remiss in the divine service. You will see that Christ will visit you the more quickly, that He will give you greater consolations day by day, and will make His throne in your hearts with the more frequency and the more pleasure. Therefore be of good cheer, beloved, clap with your hands, yea, let every member of your bodies exult with joy, in that you have a cause so noble, Christ for your Captain, the Holy Ghost for your Comforter, and for your advocates and defenders the Blessed Virgin Mary, the angels, the holy apostles, the martyrs, the confessors, the virgins, the blood of your fathers so freshly spilt which cries aloud to heaven to obtain for you perseverance to the end."

"For it became Him ... Who had brought many children into glory, to perfect the author of their salvation, by His passion" (Heb 2:10).

October 11

THE IMAGE OF CHRIST

Ven. Thomas Bullaker, O. S. F., 1642

"IF YOU go on as you have begun, before many years," he said to the sheriff, "the law will make it treason to believe in Jesus Christ. You must hate Him greatly since you cannot bear to behold the statue and image which is a memorial of His Passion and our Redemption, and which the most praiseworthy piety of your forefathers erected at great cost." Hereupon those who stood around cried out, "Where in the Scripture did Christ order an image of Himself to be made?" Bullaker replied: "The precise words do not occur, yet the natural law, to which the divine law is never opposed, approves of the practice. Reason teaches and experience proves that an injury done to a statue is done to him whose person it represents. To make the thing clearer, if anyone insulted, trampled underfoot, or broke to pieces the statue of the King, would you not say that he was guilty of treason? And if it be so, ask yourselves, I entreat you, how much greater a crime it must be to injure and abuse the statue of Jesus Christ our Savior, the King of Kings, as you have lately done."

"Whom He foreknew, He also predestinated to be made conformable to the image of His Son" (Rom 8:29).

* *Bullaker was beatified by Pope John Paul II on 22 November 1987.*

October 12

FIRE FROM HEAVEN

✠ Ven. Thomas Bullaker, O. S. F., 1642

SON OF a well-known Catholic physician at Chichester, he was sent to St. Omer's, and thence entered the Franciscan Order in Spain. He first offered himself for the mission in the West Indies, but England being pointed out as a richer field for his labors, thither he went. On landing at Plymouth, he was arrested and imprisoned, and his sufferings then endured affected his health for the remainder of his life. As nothing could be proved against him, he was discharged, and for eleven years labored in the country. The heroic sufferings of Fr. Ward enkindled in him, however, a holy envy, and he obtained leave to remove to London. He chose that part of the city where he was most in peril, but his hope for martyrdom was constantly deferred. Pursuivants came to his house, but would not take him, though he declared himself a priest. The next day they returned, and, though his breviary was on the table, they left without arresting him. Deeming himself unworthy of the crown, he redoubled his prayers and tears, and was arrested on Sunday, September 11, 1642, at the beginning of his Mass, and to his great joy was executed at Tyburn, October 12, 1642.

"I am come to cast fire on the earth, and what will I but that it be enkindled?" (Lk 12:49).

October 13

THE LAST GLORIA

Ven. Thomas Bullaker, O. S. F., 1642

"IN THE year 1642," he writes, "on September 11, which fell on a Sunday, it pleased the Most High and Mighty God to put an end to my sufferings, and give me, His most unworthy servant, the consolation and hope that what I have so long desired and prayed for would shortly come to pass. Blessed be His holy name for all eternity. After having finished the Divine Office on the morning of this day, in order that I might better offer the unbloody Sacrifice of the Body and Blood of our Lord Jesus Christ to God, I recollected myself as was fitting and as best I could, and I prayed His Divine Majesty of His infinite goodness to grant me for love of Him to exchange life, and, knowing my own unworthiness, of His overflowing and infinite goodness to make up for my poverty. After having prayed thus with the greatest fervor that God granted me, I rose, and having washed my hands and said the Litany of the Blessed Virgin as usual, I began the Mass. But lo, as I was intoning the *Gloria in Excelsis*, the apostate pursuivant Wadsworth came into the room, laid hands on me at the altar, and took me to the sheriff."

"Father, glorify Thy name. A voice came from heaven: I have glorified it and will glorify it again" (Jn 12:28).

October 14

THE DWELLERS OF CAPHARNAUM

Ven. Thomas Bullaker, O. S. F., 1642

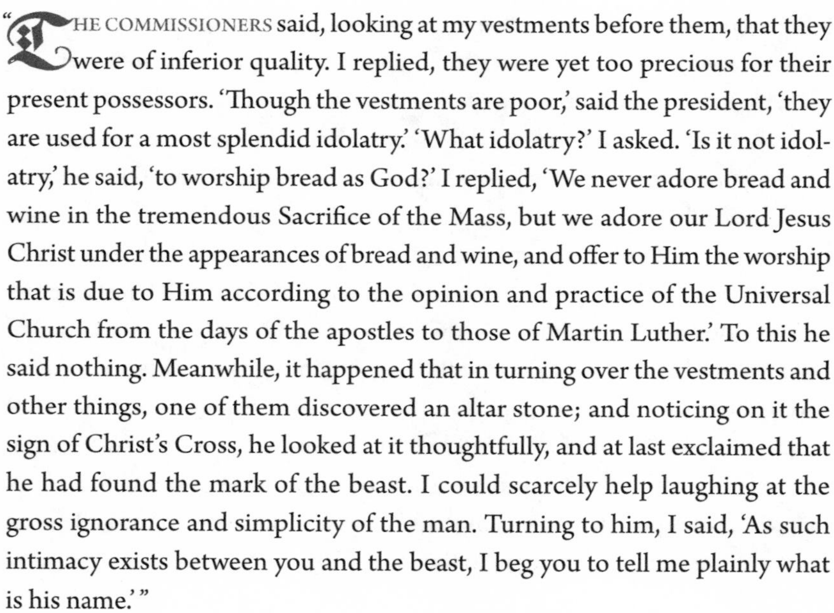

"THE COMMISSIONERS said, looking at my vestments before them, that they were of inferior quality. I replied, they were yet too precious for their present possessors. 'Though the vestments are poor,' said the president, 'they are used for a most splendid idolatry.' 'What idolatry?' I asked. 'Is it not idolatry,' he said, 'to worship bread as God?' I replied, 'We never adore bread and wine in the tremendous Sacrifice of the Mass, but we adore our Lord Jesus Christ under the appearances of bread and wine, and offer to Him the worship that is due to Him according to the opinion and practice of the Universal Church from the days of the apostles to those of Martin Luther.' To this he said nothing. Meanwhile, it happened that in turning over the vestments and other things, one of them discovered an altar stone; and noticing on it the sign of Christ's Cross, he looked at it thoughtfully, and at last exclaimed that he had found the mark of the beast. I could scarcely help laughing at the gross ignorance and simplicity of the man. Turning to him, I said, 'As such intimacy exists between you and the beast, I beg you to tell me plainly what is his name.' "

"How can this man give us His flesh to eat?" (Jn 6:53).

October 15

A PROPHECY FULFILLED

Ven. Thomas Bullaker, O. S. F., 1642

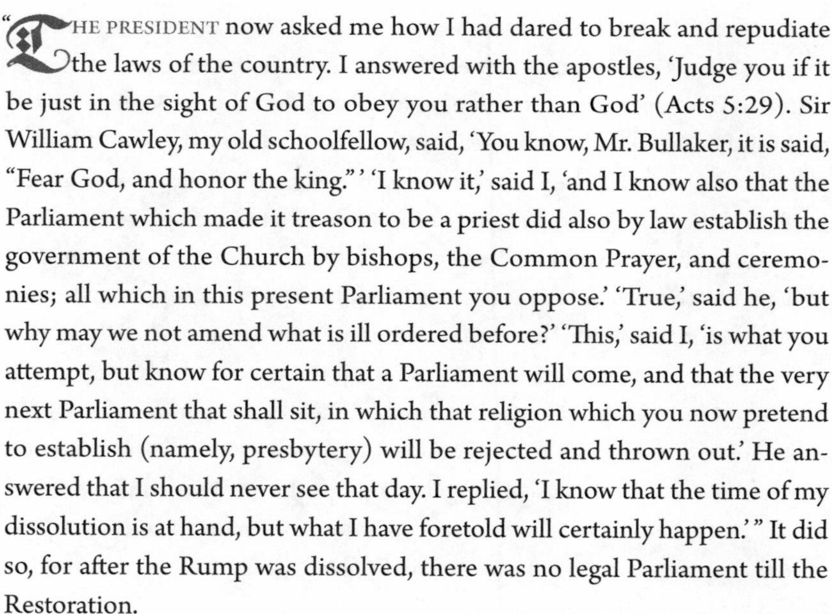

"The president now asked me how I had dared to break and repudiate the laws of the country. I answered with the apostles, 'Judge you if it be just in the sight of God to obey you rather than God' (Acts 5:29). Sir William Cawley, my old schoolfellow, said, 'You know, Mr. Bullaker, it is said, "Fear God, and honor the king." ' 'I know it,' said I, 'and I know also that the Parliament which made it treason to be a priest did also by law establish the government of the Church by bishops, the Common Prayer, and ceremonies; all which in this present Parliament you oppose.' 'True,' said he, 'but why may we not amend what is ill ordered before?' 'This,' said I, 'is what you attempt, but know for certain that a Parliament will come, and that the very next Parliament that shall sit, in which that religion which you now pretend to establish (namely, presbytery) will be rejected and thrown out.' He answered that I should never see that day. I replied, 'I know that the time of my dissolution is at hand, but what I have foretold will certainly happen.' " It did so, for after the Rump was dissolved, there was no legal Parliament till the Restoration.

"The lame walk, the lepers are cleansed.... And blessed is he that shall not be scandalized in Me" (Mt 11:5–6).

October 16

FATHER OF MANY SONS

✠ William Allen, Card., 1594

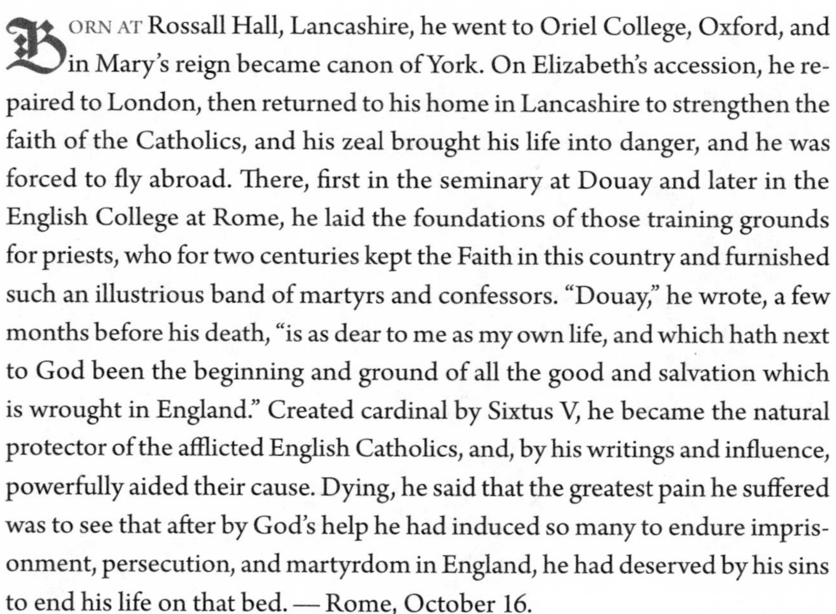

Born at Rossall Hall, Lancashire, he went to Oriel College, Oxford, and in Mary's reign became canon of York. On Elizabeth's accession, he repaired to London, then returned to his home in Lancashire to strengthen the faith of the Catholics, and his zeal brought his life into danger, and he was forced to fly abroad. There, first in the seminary at Douay and later in the English College at Rome, he laid the foundations of those training grounds for priests, who for two centuries kept the Faith in this country and furnished such an illustrious band of martyrs and confessors. "Douay," he wrote, a few months before his death, "is as dear to me as my own life, and which hath next to God been the beginning and ground of all the good and salvation which is wrought in England." Created cardinal by Sixtus V, he became the natural protector of the afflicted English Catholics, and, by his writings and influence, powerfully aided their cause. Dying, he said that the greatest pain he suffered was to see that after by God's help he had induced so many to endure imprisonment, persecution, and martyrdom in England, he had deserved by his sins to end his life on that bed. — Rome, October 16.

"For if you have ten thousand instructors in Christ, yet not many fathers. For in Christ Jesus, by the gospel, I have begotten you" (1 Cor 4:15).

October 17

ON ATTENDANCE AT PROTESTANT SERVICES

William Allen, Card., 1594

"NEVER TEACH nor defend the lawfulness of communicating with the Protestants in their prayers, or services, or conventicles where they meet to minister their untrue Sacraments; for this is contrary to the practice of the Church and the holy Fathers of all ages, who never communicated nor allowed in any Catholic person to pray together with Arians, Donatists, or what other soever. Neither is it a positive law of the Church, and therefore dispensable on occasions, but it is forbidden by God's eternal law, as by many evident arguments I could convince, and it hath been largely proved in sundry treatises in our own tongue, and we have practiced it from the beginning of our miseries. And lest any of my brethren should distrust my judgment, or be not satisfied by the proofs adduced, or myself be beguiled therein in my own conceit, I have not only taken the opinion of learned divines here, but, to make sure, I have asked the judgment of His Holiness [Clement VIII] thereon. And he expressly said that participation in prayers with Protestants, or going to their services was neither lawful nor dispensable."

"And their speech spreadeth like a canker.... Let everyone depart from iniquity who nameth the name of the Lord" (2 Tm 2:17, 19).

October 18

AN APOSTATE LAND

William Allen, Card., 1594

IN HIS defense of the seminary priests, he wrote thus: "First and foremost for the clergy, it is wholly distrained and destroyed, as the world knoweth. The chief prelates, bishops, and others, all spoiled of their dignities and livelihoods, thrust into prisons, forced into banishment, till by manifold and long miseries they be almost all wasted and worn away. These, then, so many, so notable, and so worthy, for whom God, nature, and their place of birth do challenge a part of that so much prized prosperity, feel none of it; but for mere conscience and confession of the truth, which their holy predecessors laid and left with them in deposition, have lost their terrene lot, and either are dead or have passed so many years in misery, as those other good fellows, their intruders, have lived in joy and felicity; who, indeed, are *filii hominum qui nubunt et nubuntur* (Lk 20:34), that is, certain fleshly companions, unordered apostates, and contemptible ministers, who, entering into the right and room of others, provided not for them, do think all fair weather in England, and have good cause to like the luck of these late years, which maketh true men mourners, while these thieves be merry."

"They have changed my delightful portion into a desolate wilderness. They have laid it waste, and it hath mourned for me" (Jer 12:10–11).

October 19

FROM PRISON TO PARADISE

✠ Ven. Philip Howard, L., 1595

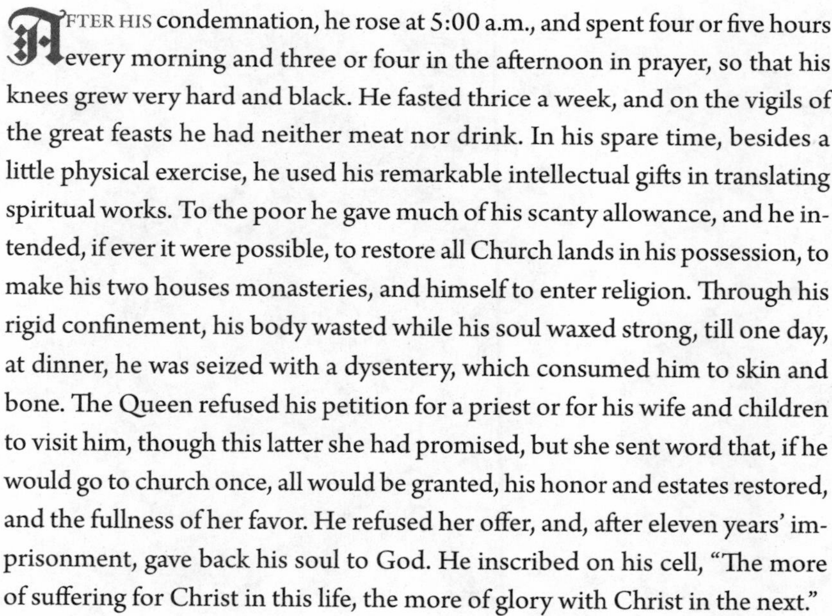

After his condemnation, he rose at 5:00 a.m., and spent four or five hours every morning and three or four in the afternoon in prayer, so that his knees grew very hard and black. He fasted thrice a week, and on the vigils of the great feasts he had neither meat nor drink. In his spare time, besides a little physical exercise, he used his remarkable intellectual gifts in translating spiritual works. To the poor he gave much of his scanty allowance, and he intended, if ever it were possible, to restore all Church lands in his possession, to make his two houses monasteries, and himself to enter religion. Through his rigid confinement, his body wasted while his soul waxed strong, till one day, at dinner, he was seized with a dysentery, which consumed him to skin and bone. The Queen refused his petition for a priest or for his wife and children to visit him, though this latter she had promised, but she sent word that, if he would go to church once, all would be granted, his honor and estates restored, and the fullness of her favor. He refused her offer, and, after eleven years' imprisonment, gave back his soul to God. He inscribed on his cell, "The more of suffering for Christ in this life, the more of glory with Christ in the next."

"The sufferings of this life are not worthy to be compared with the glory to come" (Rom 8:18).

* *Howard was canonized by Pope Paul VI on 25 October 1970.*

PHILIP EARL OF ARUNDEL

"In the Tower under sentence of death"

October 20

THE HATRED OF HERODIAS (1)

Ven. Philip Howard, L., 1595

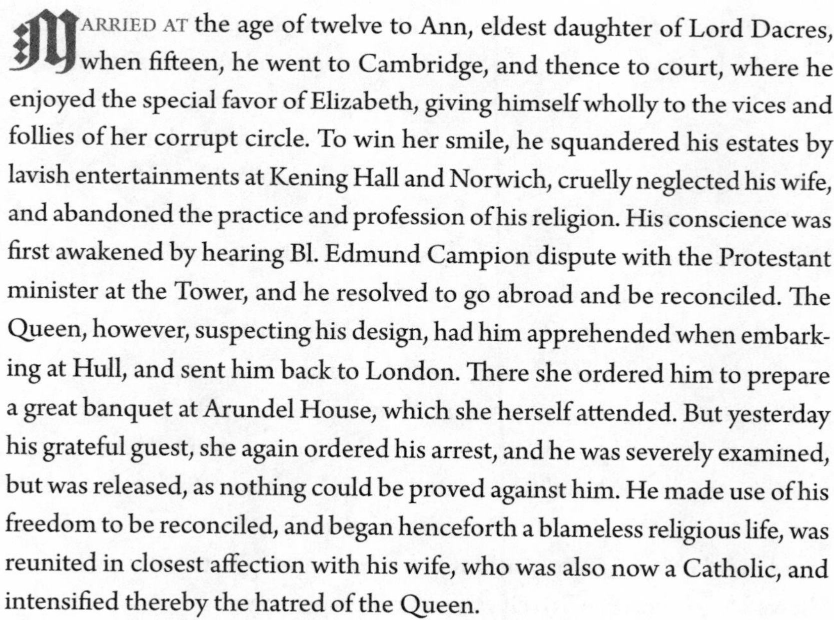

Married at the age of twelve to Ann, eldest daughter of Lord Dacres, when fifteen, he went to Cambridge, and thence to court, where he enjoyed the special favor of Elizabeth, giving himself wholly to the vices and follies of her corrupt circle. To win her smile, he squandered his estates by lavish entertainments at Kening Hall and Norwich, cruelly neglected his wife, and abandoned the practice and profession of his religion. His conscience was first awakened by hearing Bl. Edmund Campion dispute with the Protestant minister at the Tower, and he resolved to go abroad and be reconciled. The Queen, however, suspecting his design, had him apprehended when embarking at Hull, and sent him back to London. There she ordered him to prepare a great banquet at Arundel House, which she herself attended. But yesterday his grateful guest, she again ordered his arrest, and he was severely examined, but was released, as nothing could be proved against him. He made use of his freedom to be reconciled, and began henceforth a blameless religious life, was reunited in closest affection with his wife, who was also now a Catholic, and intensified thereby the hatred of the Queen.

"But she being instructed before by her mother, said: Give me now in a dish the head of John the Baptist" (Mt 14:8).

October 21

THE HATRED OF HERODIAS (2)

Ven. Philip Howard, L., 1595

PHILIP'S LIFE as a recusant, which he now was, made his residence in England even more perilous, and he determined to seek safety abroad. He had, however, scarcely embarked when his vessel was stopped by order of the council, and he was taken prisoner. For leaving the kingdom without the Queen's leave and for being reconciled to the Church, he was fined £1,000, and sentenced to prison during the Queen's pleasure. At first, in the Tower, he had considerable liberty, and with his fellow Catholics contrived to have Mass; but on the falsified charge of having prayed for the success of the Armada, he was tried for high treason and condemned to death. The sentence was not carried out, but he was subjected instead to a series of hardships and sufferings, the joint product of feminine malice and despotic power. For several years, a keeper, specially appointed by the Queen, never left his presence, heard his every word, and constantly, by false reports, further increased the Queen's wrath. His room was dark and exhaled a pestilential stench. He was slandered to his wife as unfaithful to her and intemperate, nor was he ever allowed to see her. She herself was reduced to poverty.

"Let them bear false witness that he hath blasphemed God and the king, and then carry him out and stone him, and so let him die" (3 Kgs 21:10).

October 22

A FILIAL APPEAL

Ven. Robert Southwell, S. J., to his Protestant father (1)

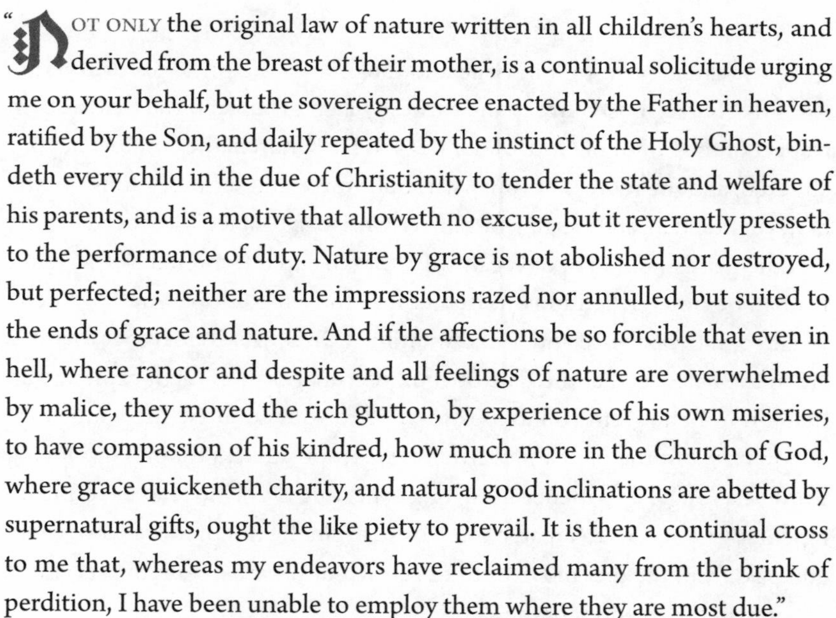

"Not only the original law of nature written in all children's hearts, and derived from the breast of their mother, is a continual solicitude urging me on your behalf, but the sovereign decree enacted by the Father in heaven, ratified by the Son, and daily repeated by the instinct of the Holy Ghost, bindeth every child in the due of Christianity to tender the state and welfare of his parents, and is a motive that alloweth no excuse, but it reverently presseth to the performance of duty. Nature by grace is not abolished nor destroyed, but perfected; neither are the impressions razed nor annulled, but suited to the ends of grace and nature. And if the affections be so forcible that even in hell, where rancor and despite and all feelings of nature are overwhelmed by malice, they moved the rich glutton, by experience of his own miseries, to have compassion of his kindred, how much more in the Church of God, where grace quickeneth charity, and natural good inclinations are abetted by supernatural gifts, ought the like piety to prevail. It is then a continual cross to me that, whereas my endeavors have reclaimed many from the brink of perdition, I have been unable to employ them where they are most due."

"He that feareth the Lord honoreth his parents and will serve them as his masters" (Ecclus 3:8).

October 23

THE STRICTNESS OF THE RECKONING

Ven. Robert Southwell, S. J., to his Protestant father (2)

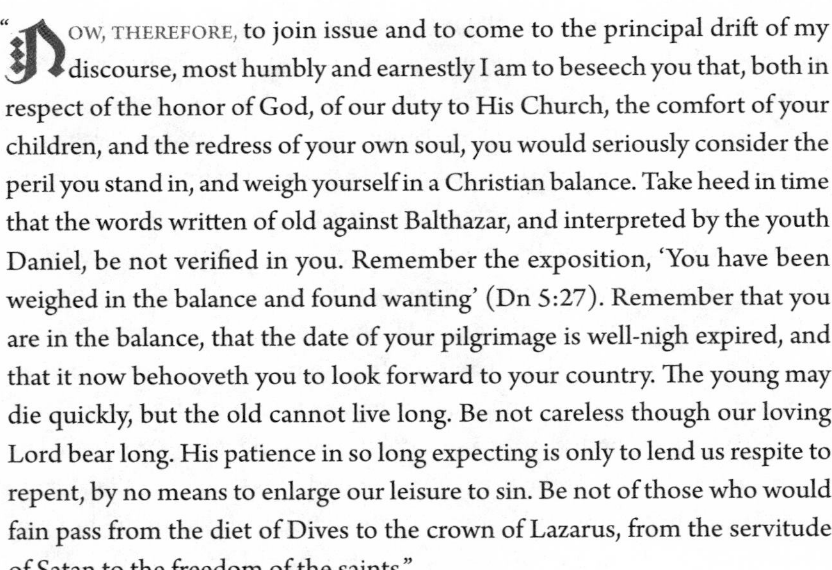

"NOW, THEREFORE, to join issue and to come to the principal drift of my discourse, most humbly and earnestly I am to beseech you that, both in respect of the honor of God, of our duty to His Church, the comfort of your children, and the redress of your own soul, you would seriously consider the peril you stand in, and weigh yourself in a Christian balance. Take heed in time that the words written of old against Balthazar, and interpreted by the youth Daniel, be not verified in you. Remember the exposition, 'You have been weighed in the balance and found wanting' (Dn 5:27). Remember that you are in the balance, that the date of your pilgrimage is well-nigh expired, and that it now behooveth you to look forward to your country. The young may die quickly, but the old cannot live long. Be not careless though our loving Lord bear long. His patience in so long expecting is only to lend us respite to repent, by no means to enlarge our leisure to sin. Be not of those who would fain pass from the diet of Dives to the crown of Lazarus, from the servitude of Satan to the freedom of the saints."

"Take heed to thyself" (1 Tm 4:16).

October 24

AND THEN THE JUDGMENT

Ven. Robert Southwell, S. J., to his Protestant father (3)

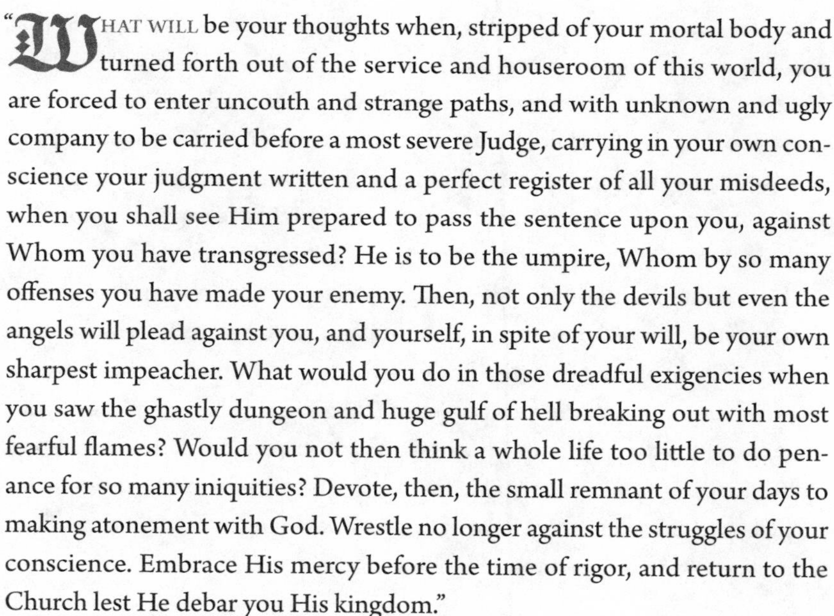

“What will be your thoughts when, stripped of your mortal body and turned forth out of the service and houseroom of this world, you are forced to enter uncouth and strange paths, and with unknown and ugly company to be carried before a most severe Judge, carrying in your own conscience your judgment written and a perfect register of all your misdeeds, when you shall see Him prepared to pass the sentence upon you, against Whom you have transgressed? He is to be the umpire, Whom by so many offenses you have made your enemy. Then, not only the devils but even the angels will plead against you, and yourself, in spite of your will, be your own sharpest impeacher. What would you do in those dreadful exigencies when you saw the ghastly dungeon and huge gulf of hell breaking out with most fearful flames? Would you not then think a whole life too little to do penance for so many iniquities? Devote, then, the small remnant of your days to making atonement with God. Wrestle no longer against the struggles of your conscience. Embrace His mercy before the time of rigor, and return to the Church lest He debar you His kingdom.”

“Thou hast sealed my offenses, as it were in a bag” (Jb 14:17).

October 25

OUR HOME IN HEAVEN

Ven. Robert Southwell, S. J., to his Protestant father (4)

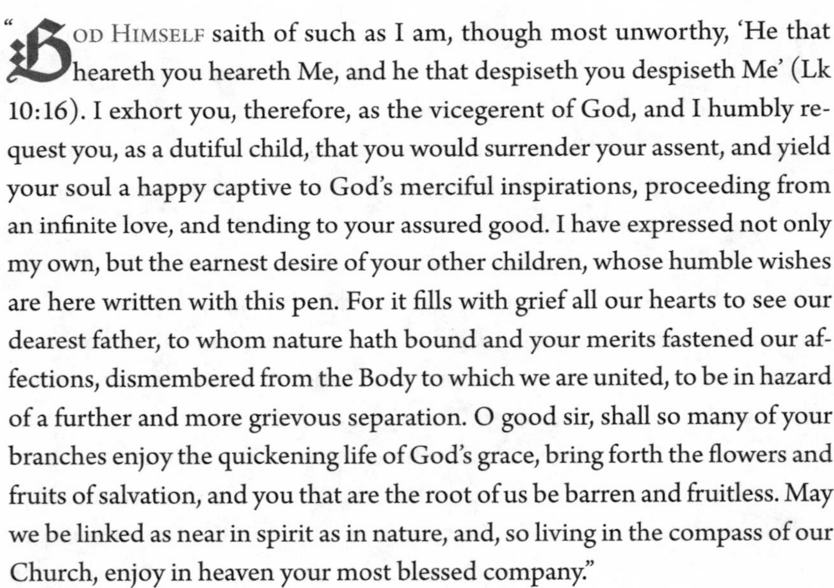

"God Himself saith of such as I am, though most unworthy, 'He that heareth you heareth Me, and he that despiseth you despiseth Me' (Lk 10:16). I exhort you, therefore, as the vicegerent of God, and I humbly request you, as a dutiful child, that you would surrender your assent, and yield your soul a happy captive to God's merciful inspirations, proceeding from an infinite love, and tending to your assured good. I have expressed not only my own, but the earnest desire of your other children, whose humble wishes are here written with this pen. For it fills with grief all our hearts to see our dearest father, to whom nature hath bound and your merits fastened our affections, dismembered from the Body to which we are united, to be in hazard of a further and more grievous separation. O good sir, shall so many of your branches enjoy the quickening life of God's grace, bring forth the flowers and fruits of salvation, and you that are the root of us be barren and fruitless. May we be linked as near in spirit as in nature, and, so living in the compass of our Church, enjoy in heaven your most blessed company."

"Until we all meet into the unity of faith, and the knowledge of the Son of God, unto a perfect man" (Eph 4:13).

October 26

WISDOM LEARNT IN CHAINS

Bl. Richard Thirkell, Pr., 1583

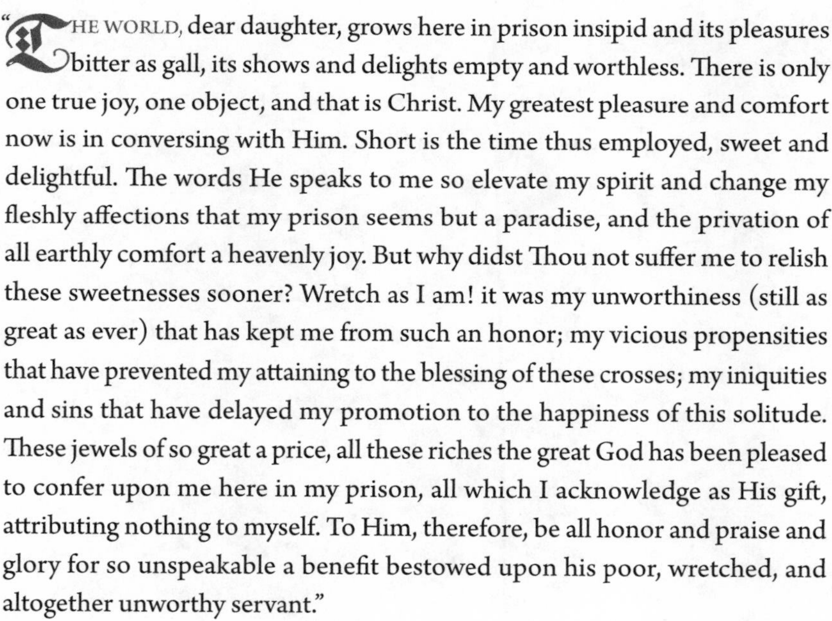

"The world, dear daughter, grows here in prison insipid and its pleasures bitter as gall, its shows and delights empty and worthless. There is only one true joy, one object, and that is Christ. My greatest pleasure and comfort now is in conversing with Him. Short is the time thus employed, sweet and delightful. The words He speaks to me so elevate my spirit and change my fleshly affections that my prison seems but a paradise, and the privation of all earthly comfort a heavenly joy. But why didst Thou not suffer me to relish these sweetnesses sooner? Wretch as I am! it was my unworthiness (still as great as ever) that has kept me from such an honor; my vicious propensities that have prevented my attaining to the blessing of these crosses; my iniquities and sins that have delayed my promotion to the happiness of this solitude. These jewels of so great a price, all these riches the great God has been pleased to confer upon me here in my prison, all which I acknowledge as His gift, attributing nothing to myself. To Him, therefore, be all honor and praise and glory for so unspeakable a benefit bestowed upon his poor, wretched, and altogether unworthy servant."

"According to the multitude of the sorrows of my heart,
Thy comforts have given joy to my soul" (Ps 93:19).

October 27

A WORM AND NO MAN

Bl. Alexander Briant, S. J., 1581

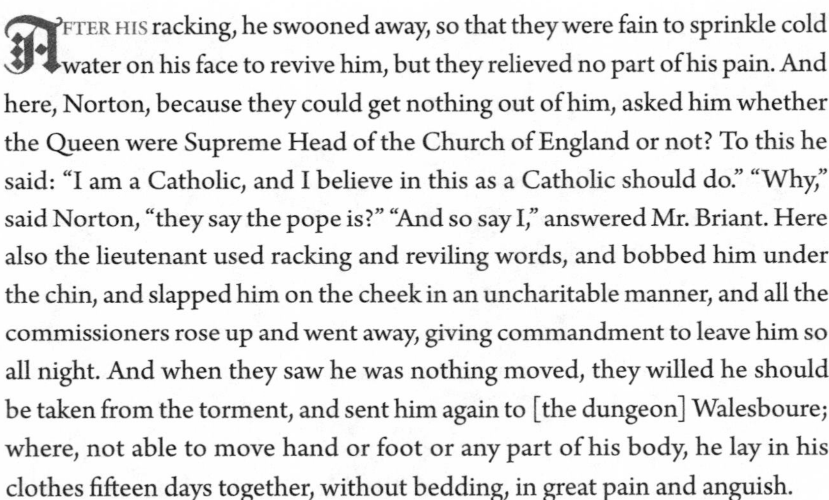

AFTER HIS racking, he swooned away, so that they were fain to sprinkle cold water on his face to revive him, but they relieved no part of his pain. And here, Norton, because they could get nothing out of him, asked him whether the Queen were Supreme Head of the Church of England or not? To this he said: "I am a Catholic, and I believe in this as a Catholic should do." "Why," said Norton, "they say the pope is?" "And so say I," answered Mr. Briant. Here also the lieutenant used racking and reviling words, and bobbed him under the chin, and slapped him on the cheek in an uncharitable manner, and all the commissioners rose up and went away, giving commandment to leave him so all night. And when they saw he was nothing moved, they willed he should be taken from the torment, and sent him again to [the dungeon] Walesboure; where, not able to move hand or foot or any part of his body, he lay in his clothes fifteen days together, without bedding, in great pain and anguish.

"My strength is dried up like a potsherd, and my tongue
hath cleaved to my jaws: and Thou hast brought
me down into the dust of death" (Ps 21:16).

* *Briant was canonized by Pope Paul VI on 25 October 1970.*

October 28

THE MORE EXCELLENT WAY

Bl. Alexander Briant, S.J., 1581

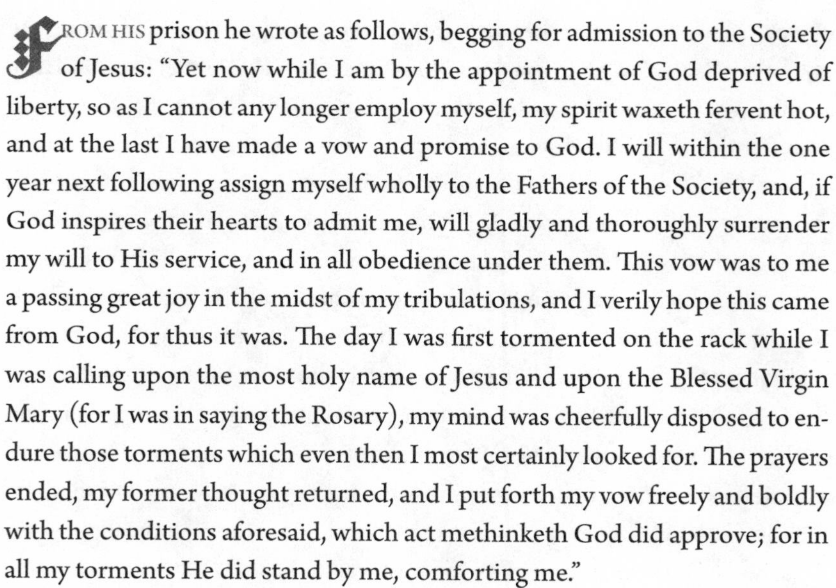

FROM HIS prison he wrote as follows, begging for admission to the Society of Jesus: "Yet now while I am by the appointment of God deprived of liberty, so as I cannot any longer employ myself, my spirit waxeth fervent hot, and at the last I have made a vow and promise to God. I will within the one year next following assign myself wholly to the Fathers of the Society, and, if God inspires their hearts to admit me, will gladly and thoroughly surrender my will to His service, and in all obedience under them. This vow was to me a passing great joy in the midst of my tribulations, and I verily hope this came from God, for thus it was. The day I was first tormented on the rack while I was calling upon the most holy name of Jesus and upon the Blessed Virgin Mary (for I was in saying the Rosary), my mind was cheerfully disposed to endure those torments which even then I most certainly looked for. The prayers ended, my former thought returned, and I put forth my vow freely and boldly with the conditions aforesaid, which act methinketh God did approve; for in all my torments He did stand by me, comforting me."

"But be zealous for the better gifts. And I show unto you a yet more excellent way" (1 Cor 12:31).

October 29

WITH ARMS OUTSTRETCHED

Ven. Henry Heath, O. S. F., 1643

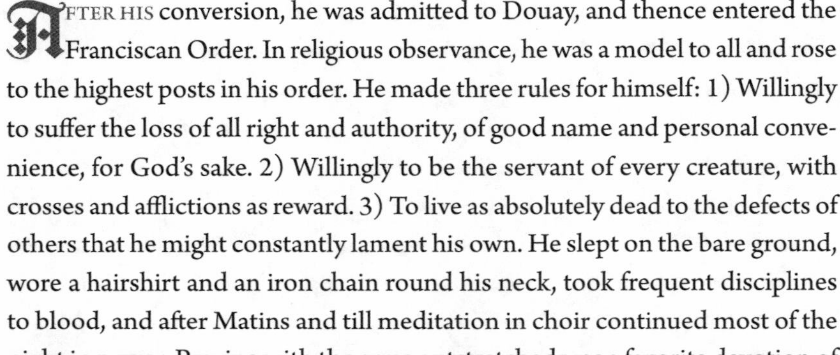

AFTER HIS conversion, he was admitted to Douay, and thence entered the Franciscan Order. In religious observance, he was a model to all and rose to the highest posts in his order. He made three rules for himself: 1) Willingly to suffer the loss of all right and authority, of good name and personal convenience, for God's sake. 2) Willingly to be the servant of every creature, with crosses and afflictions as reward. 3) To live as absolutely dead to the defects of others that he might constantly lament his own. He slept on the bare ground, wore a hairshirt and an iron chain round his neck, took frequent disciplines to blood, and after Matins and till meditation in choir continued most of the night in prayer. Praying with the arms outstretched was a favorite devotion of the Friars Minor, and this was one of the means by which he prepared himself to shed his blood for the Crucified. By it, he obtained many favors. Once when attacked by a contagious disorder, of which many of the friars had died, he remained on his knees with his arms outstretched till they fell through weakness, but at the same moment he was restored to health.

"And when Moses lifted up his hands, Israel overcame" (Ex 17:11).

October 30

THE VOICE OF THE PEOPLE

✠ Ven. John Slade, L., 1583

On Wednesday, 30th October, John Slade, a schoolmaster, was drawn from the prison at Winchester to the marketplace for his execution. Being taken off the hurdle, he knelt down by the gallows and made the sign of the cross on the posts. Questioned on the Queen's spiritual supremacy, he replied, "The supremacy hath and doth belong to the pope by right from Peter, and the pope hath received it as by divine providence. Therefore, we must not give those things belonging to God to any other than Him alone. And because I will not do otherwise, I may say with the three children in the fiery oven, and the first of the widow's seven sons in the Machabees: *Parati sumus mori magis quam patrias Dei leges praevaricari* (2 Mc 7:2)." Again pressed by the Protestant chaplain on the same subject, Slade said, "Sir, you are very busy in words: if the pope hath excommunicated the Queen, I think he hath done no more than he may or than he ought to do. I will acknowledge no other Head of the Church, but only the pope, and Her Majesty hath only that authority in temporal causes that he allows her." On this the people cried, "Away with the traitor! Hang him! hang him!"

"But they cried again, saying: Crucify Him, crucify Him" (Lk 23:21).

* *Slade was beatified by Pope Pius XI on 15 December 1929.*

October 31

THIRST FOR MARTYRDOM

Ven. Henry Heath, O. S. F., 1643

After nineteen years at Douay, the news of his brothers martyred in England urged him to petition to be sent there also. "When I remember," he wrote to his superior, "their unconquerable fortitude, their constancy in the Faith, their recklessness of flesh and blood, I am overwhelmed with shame that, while they fight, I remain at home in idleness and peace. Alas, my dearest sir, I await only a command from you; nothing else detains me. This my petition is not new or unheard of, or aught else than what stones and plants and other inanimate things by a natural inclination covet and pursue, for, verily, all things of their own accord tend toward the center and end for which they were created. I confess, indeed, that I am both wholly unfit and unworthy to exercise the apostolic office, or to receive reproaches and insults for the name of Jesus. But strength is made perfect in weakness, and God chooses the foolish to confound the wise. Moreover, I am convinced that I am no less bound than others to serve Jesus Christ and to suffer for Him. May our most gracious Lord inspire you to hasten your consent, and I shall remain to all eternity your poor son, P. M."

"Lo, here am I, send me" (Is 6:8).

November

November 1

UPON THE IMAGE OF DEATH

Ven. Robert Southwell, S.J., 1595

Before my face the picture hangs
That daily should me put in mind
Of those cold names and bitter pangs
That shortly I am like to find:
But yet, alas! full little I
Do think hereon that I must die.

I often look upon a face,
Most ugly, grisly, bare, and thin;
I often view the hollow place
Where eyes and nose had sometime been;
I see the bones across that lie,
Yet little think that I must die.

My ancestors are turned to clay,
And many of my mates are gone;
My youngers daily drop away,
And can I think to 'scape alone?
No, no, I know that I must die,
And yet my life amend not I.

If none can 'scape Death's dreadful dart,
If rich and poor his beck obey;
If strong, if wise, if all do smart,
Then I to 'scape shall have no way.
Oh! grant me grace, O God, that I
My life may mend, sith I must die.

November 2

THE WATERS OF MARA

✠ Ven. John Bodey, L., 1583

On Saturday, November 2nd, he was drawn to the gallows, and being laid on the hurdle, he said thus, "O sweet bed, the happiest bed that ever man laid on! Thou art welcome to me." When the hangman put the halter about his neck, he kissed it and said, "O blessed chain, the sweetest chain and richest that ever came about any man's neck!" And so kissing it, he suffered the hangman to put it about his neck. Being told that he was dying for high treason, he replied, "I have been sufficiently condemned, for I have been convicted twice. You make the hearing of a blessed Mass, or the saying of an *Ave Maria,* treason, but I have committed none, though I am punished for treason." In reply to the sheriff he said, "I must needs ask Her Majesty's forgiveness, for I have offended her many ways, as in using unlawful games, excess in apparel, and in other offenses to her laws; but in this matter you shall pardon me. And for the people, as they and I am different in religion, I will not have them pray for me, but I pray God to preserve Her Majesty." At length, saying "Jesu, Jesu, esto mihi Jesu," he was put beside the ladder.

"And they could not drink the waters of Mara because they were bitter.... But he cried to the Lord, and He showed him a tree, which when he had cast into the waters, they were turned into sweetness" (Ex 15:23, 25).

* *Bodey was beatified by Pope Pius XI on 15 December 1929.*

November 3

A VISION IN THE NIGHT

Ven. John Bodey, L., 1583

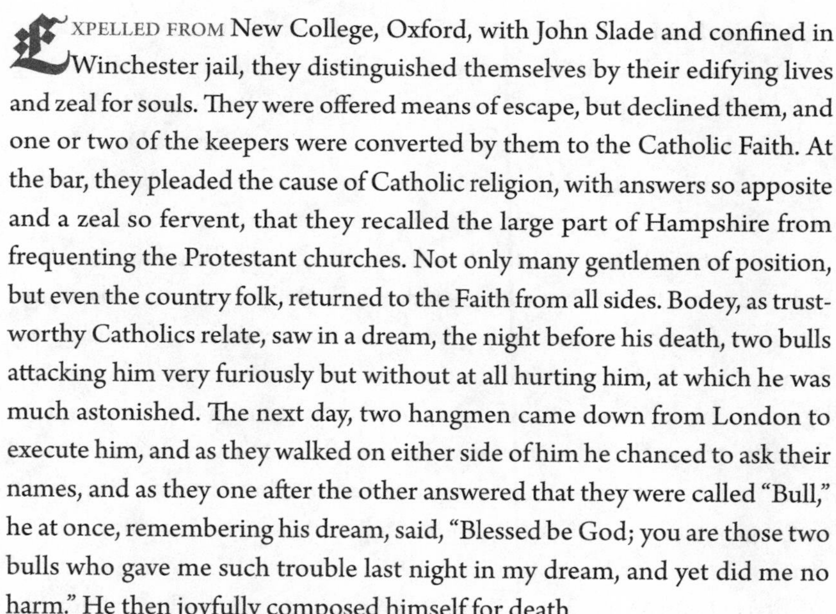

Expelled from New College, Oxford, with John Slade and confined in Winchester jail, they distinguished themselves by their edifying lives and zeal for souls. They were offered means of escape, but declined them, and one or two of the keepers were converted by them to the Catholic Faith. At the bar, they pleaded the cause of Catholic religion, with answers so apposite and a zeal so fervent, that they recalled the large part of Hampshire from frequenting the Protestant churches. Not only many gentlemen of position, but even the country folk, returned to the Faith from all sides. Bodey, as trustworthy Catholics relate, saw in a dream, the night before his death, two bulls attacking him very furiously but without at all hurting him, at which he was much astonished. The next day, two hangmen came down from London to execute him, and as they walked on either side of him he chanced to ask their names, and as they one after the other answered that they were called "Bull," he at once, remembering his dream, said, "Blessed be God; you are those two bulls who gave me such trouble last night in my dream, and yet did me no harm." He then joyfully composed himself for death.

"And the Lord said to Paul in the night by vision: Do not fear" (Acts 18:9).

November 4

MASSES FOR THE DEAD

Ven. John Cornelius, S. J., 1594

He was born of Irish parents at Bodmin in Cornwall, and on account of his rare abilities he was sent to Oxford by Sir John Arundel. Preferring the old religion, he left the university, was ordained in Rome, and was chosen to make a Latin oration in the pope's chapel on St. Stephen's Day. He was noted for his sanctity, zeal for souls, power as a preacher, and his dominion as an exorcist over evil spirits, and for a singular vision granted him. John Lord Stourton, though a Catholic at heart, had outwardly conformed, and had died unreconciled, but with great desire for the Sacraments and extraordinary marks of repentance. When Cornelius was saying Mass for the repose of his soul, at the Memento for the dead, he excited the wonder of all present by remaining apparently transfixed by some apparition on the Gospel side of the altar. At the conclusion of the Mass, he explained that the soul of the said Lord Stourton, then in purgatory, had appeared to him desiring his prayers, and begging him to request his mother to have Masses said for his soul. The vision was also seen by Brother Patrick Salmon, S. J. Fr. Cornelius was apprehended in Lady Arundel's house, and was executed with Brother Salmon and others at Dorchester, July 4, 1594.

"It is therefore a holy and wholesome thought to pray for the dead, that they may be loosed from their sins" (2 Mc 12:46).

November 5

THE BLACKFRIARS COLLAPSE

Robert Drury, S.J., 1653

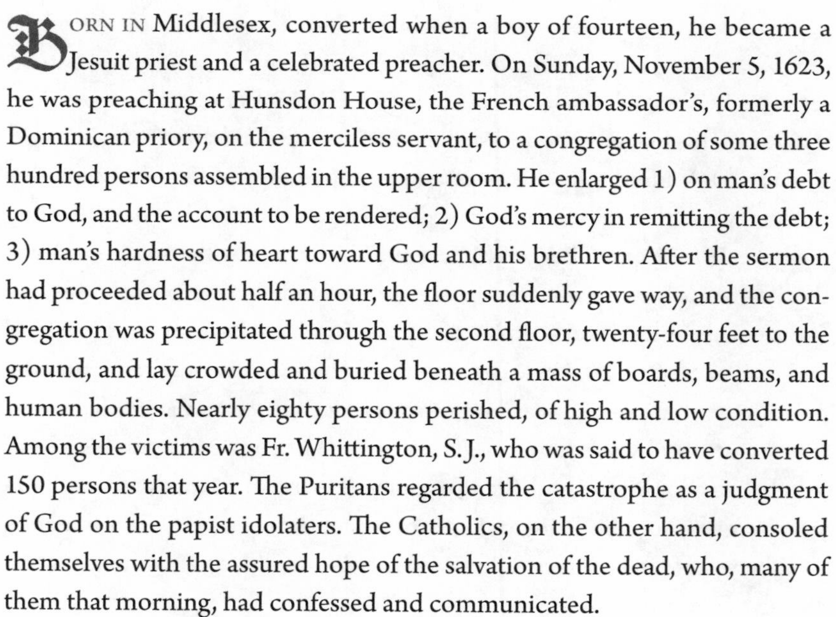

Born in Middlesex, converted when a boy of fourteen, he became a Jesuit priest and a celebrated preacher. On Sunday, November 5, 1623, he was preaching at Hunsdon House, the French ambassador's, formerly a Dominican priory, on the merciless servant, to a congregation of some three hundred persons assembled in the upper room. He enlarged 1) on man's debt to God, and the account to be rendered; 2) God's mercy in remitting the debt; 3) man's hardness of heart toward God and his brethren. After the sermon had proceeded about half an hour, the floor suddenly gave way, and the congregation was precipitated through the second floor, twenty-four feet to the ground, and lay crowded and buried beneath a mass of boards, beams, and human bodies. Nearly eighty persons perished, of high and low condition. Among the victims was Fr. Whittington, S.J., who was said to have converted 150 persons that year. The Puritans regarded the catastrophe as a judgment of God on the papist idolaters. The Catholics, on the other hand, consoled themselves with the assured hope of the salvation of the dead, who, many of them that morning, had confessed and communicated.

"Blessed are those servants whom the Lord, when He cometh, shall find watching" (Lk 12:37).

November 6

THE VOW OF RELIGIOUS

Ven. John Cornelius, S.J. to a nun

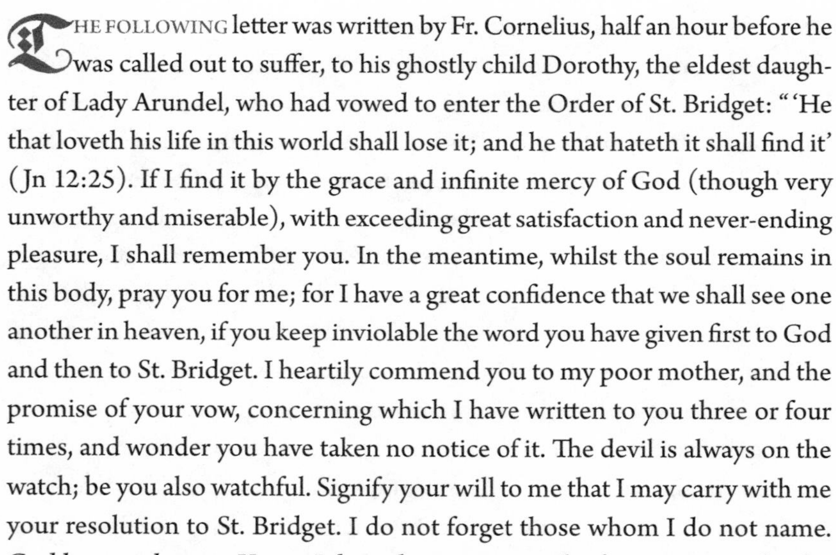

THE FOLLOWING letter was written by Fr. Cornelius, half an hour before he was called out to suffer, to his ghostly child Dorothy, the eldest daughter of Lady Arundel, who had vowed to enter the Order of St. Bridget: "'He that loveth his life in this world shall lose it; and he that hateth it shall find it' (Jn 12:25). If I find it by the grace and infinite mercy of God (though very unworthy and miserable), with exceeding great satisfaction and never-ending pleasure, I shall remember you. In the meantime, whilst the soul remains in this body, pray you for me; for I have a great confidence that we shall see one another in heaven, if you keep inviolable the word you have given first to God and then to St. Bridget. I heartily commend you to my poor mother, and the promise of your vow, concerning which I have written to you three or four times, and wonder you have taken no notice of it. The devil is always on the watch; be you also watchful. Signify your will to me that I may carry with me your resolution to St. Bridget. I do not forget those whom I do not name. God be your keeper. Yours, John, who is going to die for a moment that he may live forever."

"When thou hast made a vow to the Lord thy God, thou shalt not delay to pay it; because the Lord thy God will require it" (Dt 23:21).

EDMUND GENINGS

"Broke open the chamber door where he was celebrating"

November 7

GOD'S WAYS NOT OURS

Ven. Edmund Genings, Pr., 1591

PAGE IN the family of Mr. Sherwood, a Catholic gentleman, he was converted, ordained priest at Rheims, and, when only twenty-three years old, landed in England. His first desire was to convert his family in Lichfield, but finding that all were dead except a brother, who had gone to London, thither he went himself. After a month's fruitless search, he was about returning to the country when, walking by St. Paul's, an unaccountable fear came over him, and, looking round, seeing only a youth in a brown cloak, he went on to say Mass. On his way home, the same strange feeling returned, and finding the same youth behind him, felt sure this was his brother John. He accosted him, told him he was a kinsman, and asked him what had become of his brother Edmund, without revealing himself as a priest. The youth replied that he had gone to the pope, was become a traitor to God and his country, and if he returned would certainly be hung. Finding him hopelessly bigoted, he left him, promising on his return to confide to him an important matter. The matter was indeed important. John was converted by Edmund's martyrdom, and, as a Franciscan friar, renewed the life of his order in England.

"My thoughts are not your thoughts, nor My ways your ways, saith the Lord" (Is 55:8).

* *Genings was canonized by Pope Paul VI on 25 October 1970.*

November 8

FAITH AND LOYALTY

Bl. Edward Powell, Pr., 1540

Born in Wales, educated at Oxford, fellow of Oriel College, 1495, rector of Bleadon in the Diocese of Wells, prebendary of Salisbury Cathedral, and vicar of St. Mary's, Redcliffe, Bristol, he held a plurality of benefices by license of Leo X. He was in high repute, especially for a treatise against the heresies of Luther, and was recommended to Henry VIII, then a zealous Catholic, by the university as "a chief and brilliant gem." He was celebrated also as a preacher, notably for his sermon against Latimer and for that against the divorce, in which he declared that for a king to put away his first wife and take a second without the dispensation of the Church was an open sin infecting the people as did King David with his adultery. This was his undoing. He was cast into Dorchester jail, and so cruelly fettered that he could not lie down. Removed to the Tower, he was condemned with Bl. Fisher and others in 1534 for refusing the oath, and was executed with Bls. Abel and Fetherston and three apostate Zwinglian priests, Barnes, Gerard, and Jerome, July 30, 1540. Against Barnes, in a pamphlet still extant, he defended Catholics against the charge of disloyalty, and declared that sedition and rebellion were unknown in the ancient Faith, but were the offspring of heresy alone.

"Let every soul be subject to higher powers, for there is no power but from God" (Rom 13:1).

GEORGE NAPPIER

"They began to offer him some speeches"

November 9

THE LAST MASS

✠ Ven. George Nappier, Pr., 1610

"BEING AT supper, I [his friend, a layman] said unto him: 'Mr. Nappier, if it be God's holy will that you should suffer, I do wish that it might be tomorrow, Friday, for our Savior did eat the paschal lamb with His disciples the Thursday night and suffered Friday following.' He answered, very sweetly, 'Welcome, by God's grace; pray you all that I may be constant.' The next morning, the keeper's wife begged me to tell him that he was to die between one and two in the afternoon, for she could not bear to take the news herself. On hearing the message, he seemed much rejoiced, and asked if he might say Mass. I prepared all things, and surely methought he did celebrate that day as reverently in all his actions and with as much sweet behavior as ever I saw him. At the end, he prayed some hours and then declined my offer of some drink, for he said that, hoping to meet his Savior, he would have a sumptuous banquet shortly. Then I put him on a fair shirt which I had warmed at the fire and a white waistcoat. He then went out to suffer, and beat his breast thrice as his soul flew to God."

"With desire I have desired to eat this pasch
with you before I suffer" (Lk 22:15).

* *Nappier was beatified by Pope Pius XI on 15 December 1929.*

November 10

UNSEEN IN THE MIDST OF THEM

Ven. George Nappier, Pr., 1610

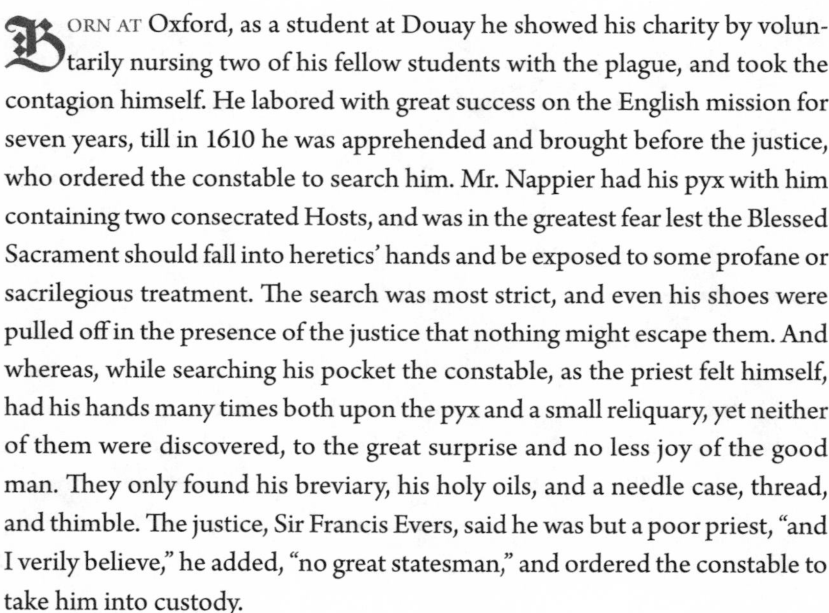

Born at Oxford, as a student at Douay he showed his charity by voluntarily nursing two of his fellow students with the plague, and took the contagion himself. He labored with great success on the English mission for seven years, till in 1610 he was apprehended and brought before the justice, who ordered the constable to search him. Mr. Nappier had his pyx with him containing two consecrated Hosts, and was in the greatest fear lest the Blessed Sacrament should fall into heretics' hands and be exposed to some profane or sacrilegious treatment. The search was most strict, and even his shoes were pulled off in the presence of the justice that nothing might escape them. And whereas, while searching his pocket the constable, as the priest felt himself, had his hands many times both upon the pyx and a small reliquary, yet neither of them were discovered, to the great surprise and no less joy of the good man. They only found his breviary, his holy oils, and a needle case, thread, and thimble. The justice, Sir Francis Evers, said he was but a poor priest, "and I verily believe," he added, "no great statesman," and ordered the constable to take him into custody.

"But He [Jesus] passing through the midst of them, went His way" (Lk 4:30).

November 11

A BLESSED LOT

Ven. Peter Wright, S. J., on the scaffold, 1651

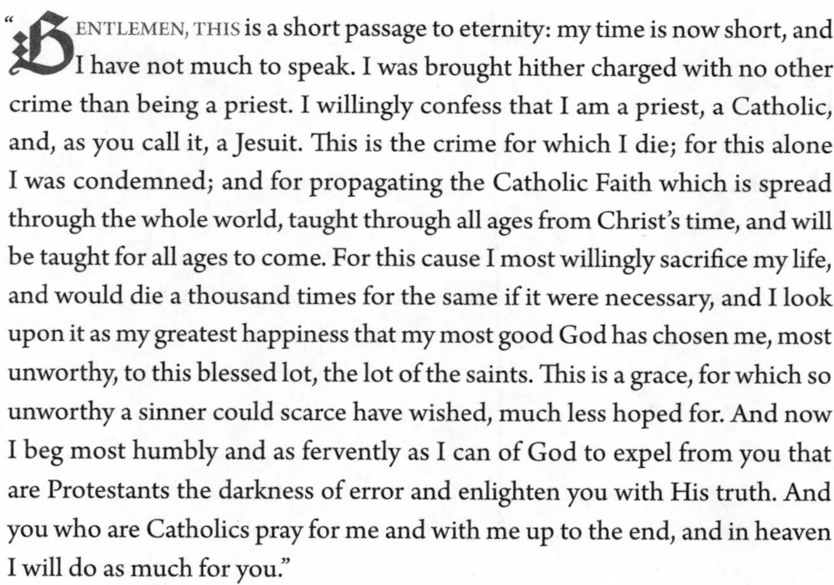

"GENTLEMEN, THIS is a short passage to eternity: my time is now short, and I have not much to speak. I was brought hither charged with no other crime than being a priest. I willingly confess that I am a priest, a Catholic, and, as you call it, a Jesuit. This is the crime for which I die; for this alone I was condemned; and for propagating the Catholic Faith which is spread through the whole world, taught through all ages from Christ's time, and will be taught for all ages to come. For this cause I most willingly sacrifice my life, and would die a thousand times for the same if it were necessary, and I look upon it as my greatest happiness that my most good God has chosen me, most unworthy, to this blessed lot, the lot of the saints. This is a grace, for which so unworthy a sinner could scarce have wished, much less hoped for. And now I beg most humbly and as fervently as I can of God to expel from you that are Protestants the darkness of error and enlighten you with His truth. And you who are Catholics pray for me and with me up to the end, and in heaven I will do as much for you."

"Giving thanks to God the Father, Who hath made us worthy to be partakers of the lot of the saints in light" (Col 1:12).

November 12

CALLED TO ACCOUNT

Bl. Edmund Campion, S. J. to Protestant Bp. Cheney

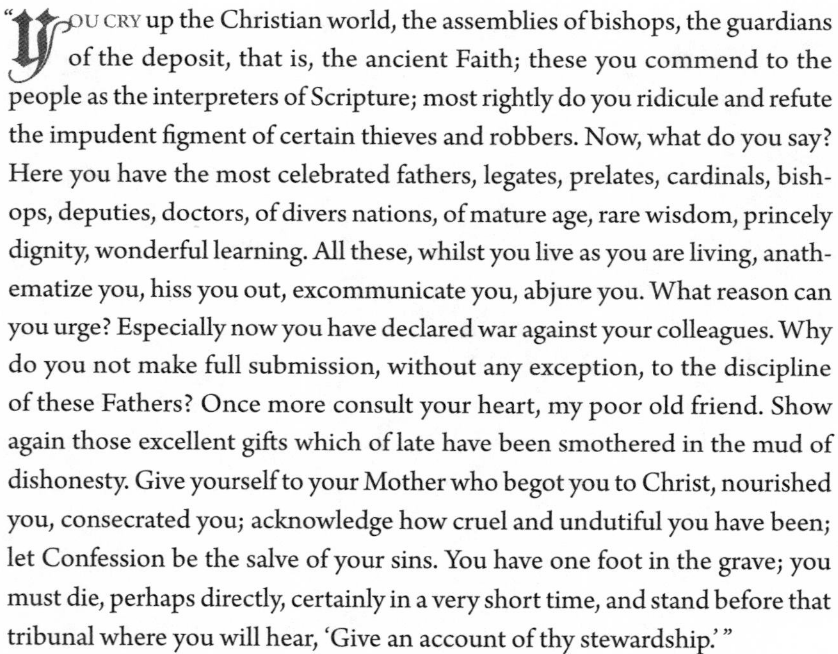

"You cry up the Christian world, the assemblies of bishops, the guardians of the deposit, that is, the ancient Faith; these you commend to the people as the interpreters of Scripture; most rightly do you ridicule and refute the impudent figment of certain thieves and robbers. Now, what do you say? Here you have the most celebrated fathers, legates, prelates, cardinals, bishops, deputies, doctors, of divers nations, of mature age, rare wisdom, princely dignity, wonderful learning. All these, whilst you live as you are living, anathematize you, hiss you out, excommunicate you, abjure you. What reason can you urge? Especially now you have declared war against your colleagues. Why do you not make full submission, without any exception, to the discipline of these Fathers? Once more consult your heart, my poor old friend. Show again those excellent gifts which of late have been smothered in the mud of dishonesty. Give yourself to your Mother who begot you to Christ, nourished you, consecrated you; acknowledge how cruel and undutiful you have been; let Confession be the salve of your sins. You have one foot in the grave; you must die, perhaps directly, certainly in a very short time, and stand before that tribunal where you will hear, 'Give an account of thy stewardship.' "

"Give an account of thy stewardship, for now thou canst be steward no longer" (Lk 16:2).

November 13

NEED OF CONTRITION

Ven. John Almond, Pr., 1612

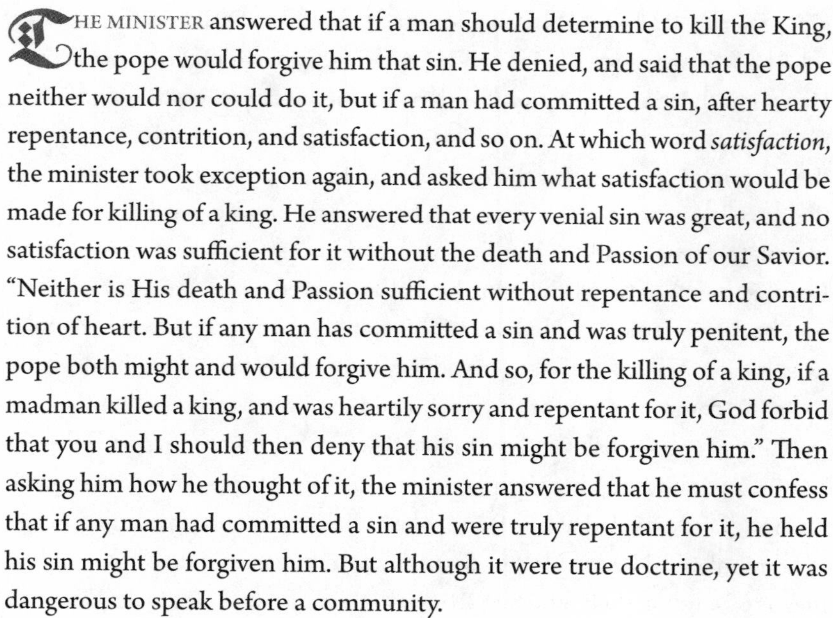

THE MINISTER answered that if a man should determine to kill the King, the pope would forgive him that sin. He denied, and said that the pope neither would nor could do it, but if a man had committed a sin, after hearty repentance, contrition, and satisfaction, and so on. At which word *satisfaction*, the minister took exception again, and asked him what satisfaction would be made for killing of a king. He answered that every venial sin was great, and no satisfaction was sufficient for it without the death and Passion of our Savior. "Neither is His death and Passion sufficient without repentance and contrition of heart. But if any man has committed a sin and was truly penitent, the pope both might and would forgive him. And so, for the killing of a king, if a madman killed a king, and was heartily sorry and repentant for it, God forbid that you and I should then deny that his sin might be forgiven him." Then asking him how he thought of it, the minister answered that he must confess that if any man had committed a sin and were truly repentant for it, he held his sin might be forgiven him. But although it were true doctrine, yet it was dangerous to speak before a community.

"A contrite and humble heart, O God, Thou wilt not despise" (Ps 50:19).

* *Almond was canonized by Pope Paul VI on 25 October 1970.*

November 14

GUARDIAN OF THE SANCTUARY

Bl. Hugh Faringdon, O. S. B., 1539

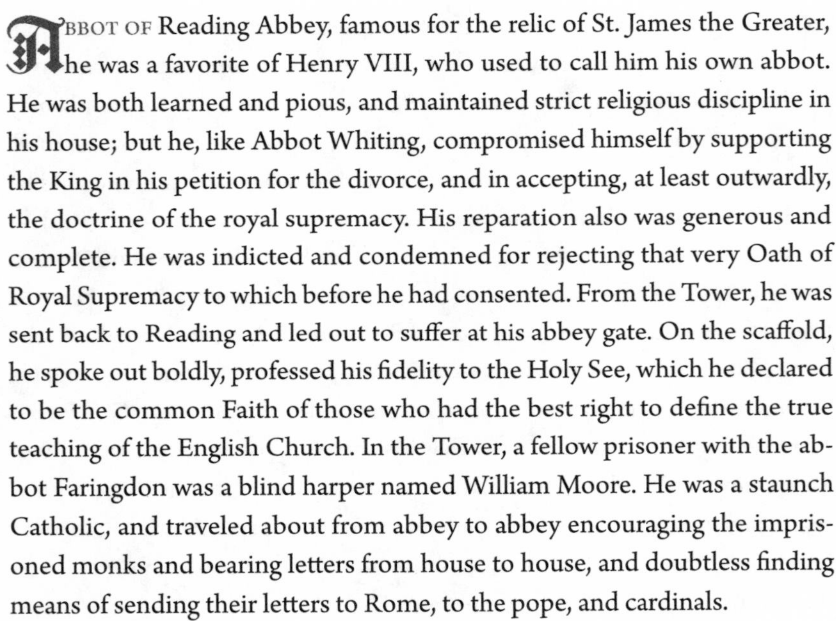

ABBOT OF Reading Abbey, famous for the relic of St. James the Greater, he was a favorite of Henry VIII, who used to call him his own abbot. He was both learned and pious, and maintained strict religious discipline in his house; but he, like Abbot Whiting, compromised himself by supporting the King in his petition for the divorce, and in accepting, at least outwardly, the doctrine of the royal supremacy. His reparation also was generous and complete. He was indicted and condemned for rejecting that very Oath of Royal Supremacy to which before he had consented. From the Tower, he was sent back to Reading and led out to suffer at his abbey gate. On the scaffold, he spoke out boldly, professed his fidelity to the Holy See, which he declared to be the common Faith of those who had the best right to define the true teaching of the English Church. In the Tower, a fellow prisoner with the abbot Faringdon was a blind harper named William Moore. He was a staunch Catholic, and traveled about from abbey to abbey encouraging the imprisoned monks and bearing letters from house to house, and doubtless finding means of sending their letters to Rome, to the pope, and cardinals.

"Our heart is sorrowful. . . . for Mount Sion, because it is destroyed. . . .
But Thou, O Lord, wilt remain forever" (Lam 5:17–19).

November 15

THE WATCHMAN ON THE WALLS

✠ Bl. Richard Whiting, O. S. B., 1539

HE WAS the sixty-first and last abbot of Glastonbury, the most ancient and famous of the great English Benedictine houses. In rank, he stood next to the abbot of St. Albans, was a peer of Parliament and lord, or rather the administrator, of vast estates. He ruled his hundred monks with singular prudence, and his large revenues were spent for the relief of the poor and works of charity. He trained some three hundred youths in a solid and Christian education, and, when the visitors of Henry VIII arrived at Glastonbury, they found only a religious house of strict observance and could discover no scandal to report. But the King's greed was set on the abbey wealth, and it was not to be withstood. The abbot at first submitted to take the Oath of Supremacy, whether with or without some saving clause is uncertain, but when he saw that the King demanded nothing less than the surrender of his abbey, he stood firm and was attaindered. He was first ordered to London, and there proving deaf to the King's persuasions, he was given leave to return home, but to his surprise was tried for high treason at Wells, and hung on Tor Hill.

> *"Upon thy walls, O Jerusalem, I have appointed watchmen all the day and all the night: they shall never hold their peace" (Is 62:6).*

November 16

DEVOTION TO ST. JEROME

✠ Ven. Edward Osbaldeston, Pr., 1594

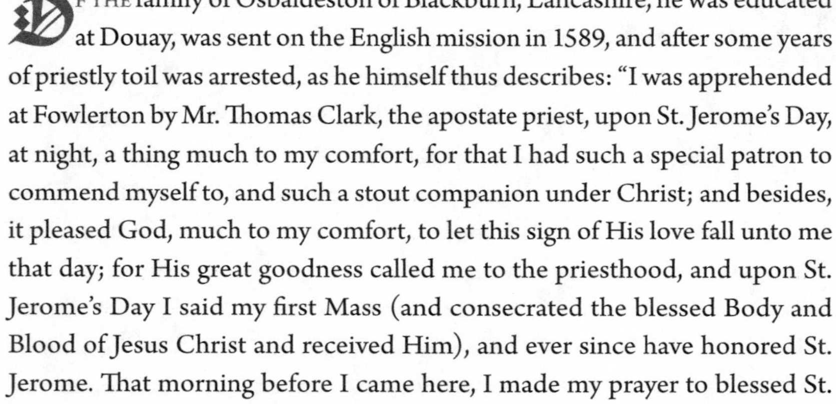

Of the family of Osbaldeston of Blackburn, Lancashire, he was educated at Douay, was sent on the English mission in 1589, and after some years of priestly toil was arrested, as he himself thus describes: "I was apprehended at Fowlerton by Mr. Thomas Clark, the apostate priest, upon St. Jerome's Day, at night, a thing much to my comfort, for that I had such a special patron to commend myself to, and such a stout companion under Christ; and besides, it pleased God, much to my comfort, to let this sign of His love fall unto me that day; for His great goodness called me to the priesthood, and upon St. Jerome's Day I said my first Mass (and consecrated the blessed Body and Blood of Jesus Christ and received Him), and ever since have honored St. Jerome. That morning before I came here, I made my prayer to blessed St. Jerome, and in his merits I offered myself to God to direct me according to His will and pleasure, that I might walk aright in my vocation, and follow St. Jerome as long as God should see it expedient for His Church; that I might never refuse to labor or murmur at any pain or travail, and that if I fell into the persecutor's hands, He would protect me to the end." He suffered at York, November 16, 1594.

"To me Thy friends are exceedingly honorable" (Ps 138:17).

* *Osbaldeston was beatified by Pope John Paul II on 22 November 1987.*

November 17

STRONG IN HOPE

Bp. Ralph Bayne of Lichfield, 1559

HE WAS born in Yorkshire, educated at Cambridge, a biblical scholar of repute, and professor of Hebrew in the University of Paris. He was of such constancy of mind, Sander writes, in his persecution that he always went with joy to any questionings, and returned still happier; but on his deposition he was sitting both sick and sorrowful in his chains when he heard a voice saying to him, "Be of good courage, for thou shalt suffer martyrdom." He related this occurrence without, however, saying what kind of martyrdom he would endure. But it was thus. He suffered such excruciating torment from the stone for six days, that to the bystanders, among whom were the bishop of Chester and the dean of St. Paul's, the pain seemed quite unbearable. Yet he did not complain, but lifting his eyes at one time to heaven and at another time resting them on the crucifix, he invoked the name of Jesus to the last moment of his life. He was deposed June 21, 1559, and died five months later, November 18, 1559. His jailer was Grindal, a virulent apostate priest, made Protestant bishop of London. But he had the consolation of receiving the last Sacraments from his fellow prisoners, the abovenamed bishop and dean.

"Arise, arise, put on thy strength, O Sion; ... for henceforth the uncircumcised and unclean shall no more pass through thee" (Is 52:1).

November 18

THE PASSION FORETOLD

Bl. Edmund Campion, S. J., 1581

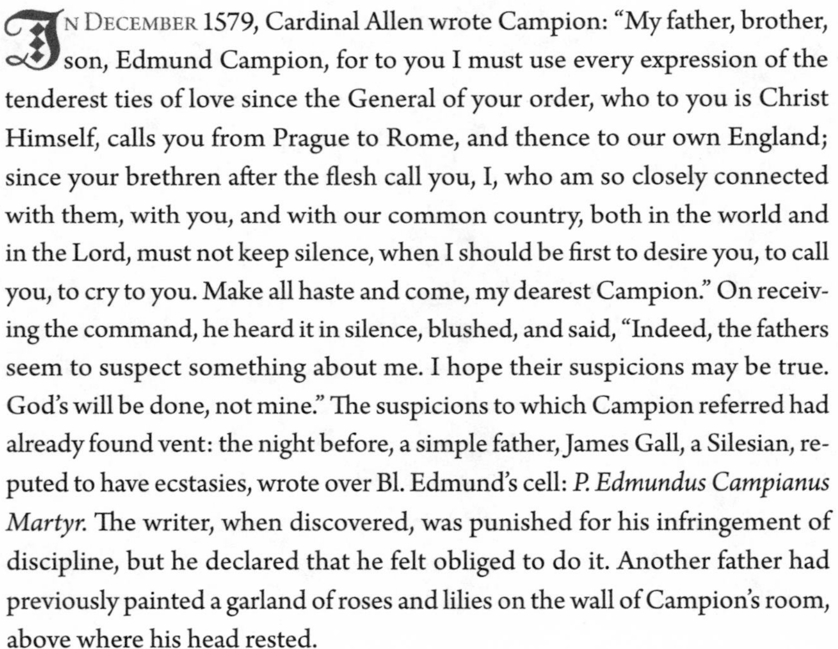

In December 1579, Cardinal Allen wrote Campion: "My father, brother, son, Edmund Campion, for to you I must use every expression of the tenderest ties of love since the General of your order, who to you is Christ Himself, calls you from Prague to Rome, and thence to our own England; since your brethren after the flesh call you, I, who am so closely connected with them, with you, and with our common country, both in the world and in the Lord, must not keep silence, when I should be first to desire you, to call you, to cry to you. Make all haste and come, my dearest Campion." On receiving the command, he heard it in silence, blushed, and said, "Indeed, the fathers seem to suspect something about me. I hope their suspicions may be true. God's will be done, not mine." The suspicions to which Campion referred had already found vent: the night before, a simple father, James Gall, a Silesian, reputed to have ecstasies, wrote over Bl. Edmund's cell: *P. Edmundus Campianus Martyr.* The writer, when discovered, was punished for his infringement of discipline, but he declared that he felt obliged to do it. Another father had previously painted a garland of roses and lilies on the wall of Campion's room, above where his head rested.

"Behold we go up to Jerusalem, and the Son of Man shall be betrayed to the chief priests and scribes: and they shall condemn Him to death" (Mt 20:18).

November 19

FALSE WITNESSES

Bl. Edmund Campion, S.J., 1581

"IN COMMON matters, we often see witnesses impeached, and if at any time their credit be little, it ought then to be less when they swear against life. Call, I pray you, to your remembrance how faintly some have deposed, how coldly others, how untruly the rest; especially two who have testified most. What truth may you expect from their mouths? The one hath confessed himself a murderer, the other well known as a detestable atheist — a profane heathen — a destroyer of two men already. On your consciences, would you believe them — they that have betrayed both God and man, nay, that have left nothing to swear by, neither religion nor honesty? Though you would believe them, can you? I know your wisdom is greater, your consciences uprighter; esteem of them as they be. Examine the other two, you shall find neither of them precisely to affirm that we, or any of us, have practiced aught that might be prejudicial to this estate or dangerous to this Commonwealth. God give you grace to weigh our causes aright, and have respect to your own consciences; and so I will keep the jury no longer. I commit the rest to God, and our convictions to your good discretions."

"Many bore false witness against Him, and their witness did not agree" (Mk 14:56).

November 20

LIFELONG REPENTANCE

Bp. Cuthbert Tunstall of Durham, 1559

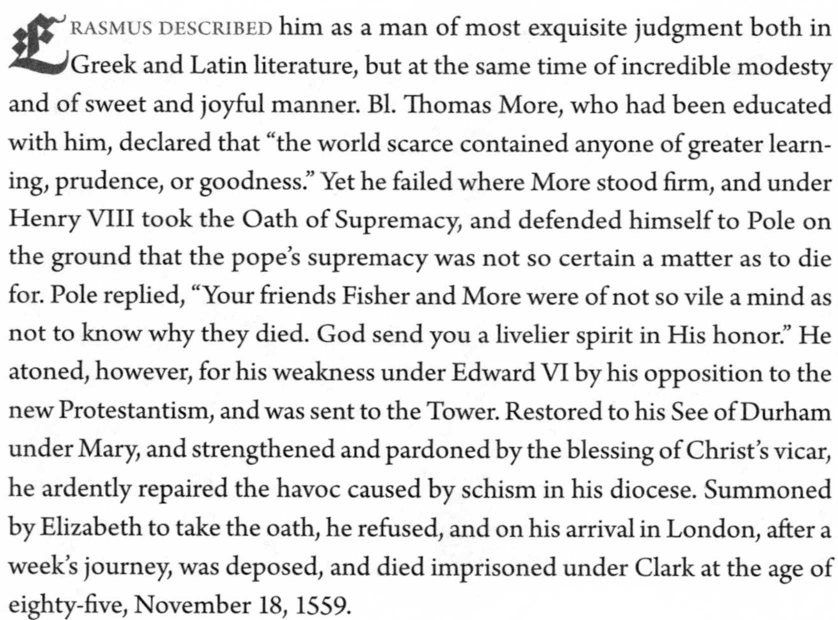

ERASMUS DESCRIBED him as a man of most exquisite judgment both in Greek and Latin literature, but at the same time of incredible modesty and of sweet and joyful manner. Bl. Thomas More, who had been educated with him, declared that "the world scarce contained anyone of greater learning, prudence, or goodness." Yet he failed where More stood firm, and under Henry VIII took the Oath of Supremacy, and defended himself to Pole on the ground that the pope's supremacy was not so certain a matter as to die for. Pole replied, "Your friends Fisher and More were of not so vile a mind as not to know why they died. God send you a livelier spirit in His honor." He atoned, however, for his weakness under Edward VI by his opposition to the new Protestantism, and was sent to the Tower. Restored to his See of Durham under Mary, and strengthened and pardoned by the blessing of Christ's vicar, he ardently repaired the havoc caused by schism in his diocese. Summoned by Elizabeth to take the oath, he refused, and on his arrival in London, after a week's journey, was deposed, and died imprisoned under Clark at the age of eighty-five, November 18, 1559.

"To depart from iniquity pleaseth the Lord, and to depart from injustice is an entreaty for sin" (Ecclus 35:5).

SHEDDING INNOCENT BLOOD

Bl. Edmund Campion, S.J., 1581

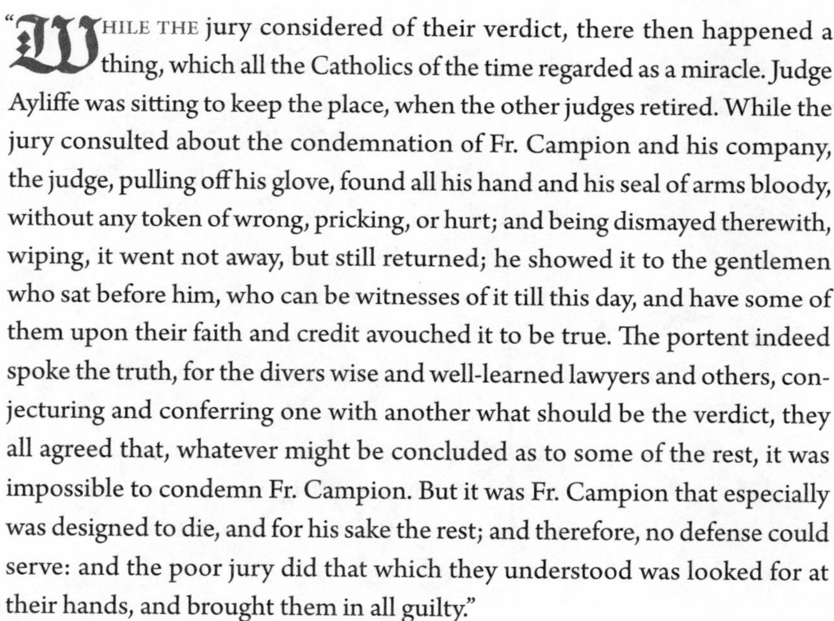

"WHILE THE jury considered of their verdict, there then happened a thing, which all the Catholics of the time regarded as a miracle. Judge Ayliffe was sitting to keep the place, when the other judges retired. While the jury consulted about the condemnation of Fr. Campion and his company, the judge, pulling off his glove, found all his hand and his seal of arms bloody, without any token of wrong, pricking, or hurt; and being dismayed therewith, wiping, it went not away, but still returned; he showed it to the gentlemen who sat before him, who can be witnesses of it till this day, and have some of them upon their faith and credit avouched it to be true. The portent indeed spoke the truth, for the divers wise and well-learned lawyers and others, conjecturing and conferring one with another what should be the verdict, they all agreed that, whatever might be concluded as to some of the rest, it was impossible to condemn Fr. Campion. But it was Fr. Campion that especially was designed to die, and for his sake the rest; and therefore, no defense could serve: and the poor jury did that which they understood was looked for at their hands, and brought them in all guilty."

"The Lord detesteth . . . hands that shed innocent blood" (Prv 6:16–17).

November 22

WILLING SACRIFICES

Ven. Robert Southwell, S.J., 1595

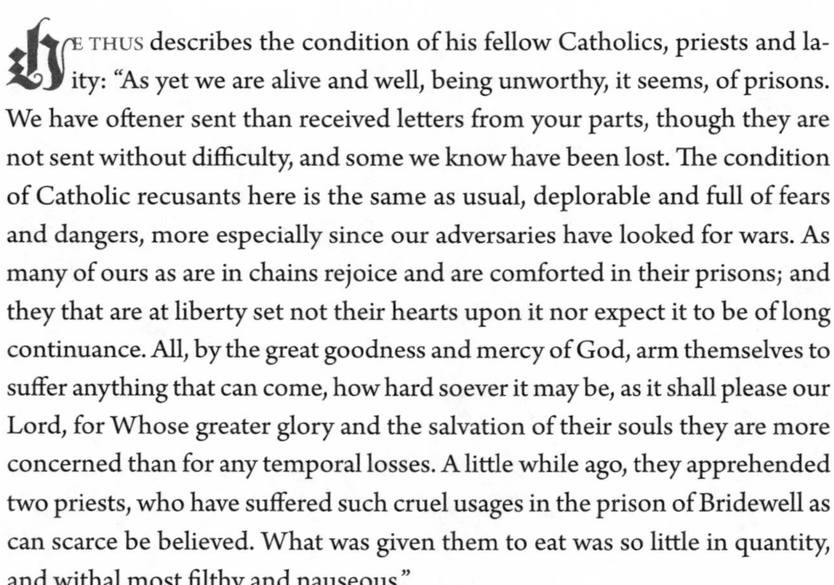

He thus describes the condition of his fellow Catholics, priests and laity: "As yet we are alive and well, being unworthy, it seems, of prisons. We have oftener sent than received letters from your parts, though they are not sent without difficulty, and some we know have been lost. The condition of Catholic recusants here is the same as usual, deplorable and full of fears and dangers, more especially since our adversaries have looked for wars. As many of ours as are in chains rejoice and are comforted in their prisons; and they that are at liberty set not their hearts upon it nor expect it to be of long continuance. All, by the great goodness and mercy of God, arm themselves to suffer anything that can come, how hard soever it may be, as it shall please our Lord, for Whose greater glory and the salvation of their souls they are more concerned than for any temporal losses. A little while ago, they apprehended two priests, who have suffered such cruel usages in the prison of Bridewell as can scarce be believed. What was given them to eat was so little in quantity, and withal most filthy and nauseous."

"Then said I, Behold I come.... to do Thy will, O my God" (Ps 39:8–9).

November 23

WASTED AWAY

✠ Bp. Richard Pate of Worcester, 1565

He was the nephew of Longland, the courtier bishop of Lincoln, confessor to Henry VIII, and was made by him canon and archdeacon of his cathedral, even before taking his degree at Corpus Christi College, Oxford. Through his uncle's influence, he was sent as ambassador to Charles V in Spain. Recalled to England in 1537, he accepted the royal supremacy, and in 1540 returned as ambassador to Charles. Though his desire to please the King led him into schism, Henry secretly mistrusted him, and recalled him to England. Pate fled to Rome, and was attaindered. In Rome, he was fully reconciled to the Church, and nominated to the See of Worcester by Paul III in 1541, and assisted as one of two English bishops at the Council of Trent. On Mary's accession, he returned to England, and took possession of his see. Under Elizabeth, he voted in the first Parliament against every anti-Catholic measure, and made reparation for his previous fall by refusing to take the oath. He was imprisoned in the Tower, and then for a year and a half placed under the custody of Jewel, September 1563, at Salisbury, and finally recommitted to the Tower, where he died of his sufferings after six years' confinement, November 23, 1565.

"Because I was silent my bones grew old, whilst I cried out all the day long.... I have acknowledged my sin to Thee" (Ps 31:3, 5).

November 24

ALONE WITH GOD

Bl. Thomas More, L., 1535

"Now when he had remained in the Tower little more than a month, my wife, longing to see her father, by her earnest suit at length got leave to go unto him. At whose coming, after the Seven Psalms and litany said (which whensoever she came unto him, ere he fell in talk of any worldly matter, he used accustomably to say with her), among other communications he said unto her, 'I believe, Meg, that they have put me here ween that they have done me a high displeasure; but I assure thee, on my faith, mine own good daughter, if it had not been for my wife and ye that be my children, I would not have failed long ere this to have closed myself in as strait a room, and straiter too. But since I have come hither without mine own desert, I trust that God of His goodness will discharge me of my care, and with His gracious help supply my lack among you. I find no cause, I thank God, Meg, to reckon myself in worse case here than at home, for methinks God maketh me a wanton, and setteth me on His lap, and dandleth me.' "

"I will allure her, and lead her into the wilderness:
and I will speak to her heart" (Os 2:14).

November 25

A DAUGHTER'S FAREWELL

Bl. Thomas More, L., 1535

HIS DAUGHTER awaited his return to the Tower on the entrance by the wharf. As soon as she saw him, after his blessing upon her knees reverently received, she, hasting toward him, without consideration or care of herself, pressing in amongst the midst of the throng and company of the guard, that with halberds and bills went round about him, hastily ran to him, and there openly, in sight of them, embraced him, took him about the neck, and kissed him. Who, well liking her most natural and dear daughterly affection toward him, gave her his fatherly blessing and many godly words of comfort besides. She was not able to say any words but, "Oh, my Father! Oh, my Father!" "Take patience, Margaret," he said, "and do not grieve; God has willed it so. For many years didst thou know the secret of my heart." From whom after she was departed, like one that had forgotten herself, being all ravished with the entire love of her father, having respect neither to herself nor to the press of people, suddenly turned back, ran to him as before, and divers times kissed him lovingly, till at last she was fain to depart, the beholding whereof made those present for very sorrow to weep and mourn.

"Going they went and wept, casting their seeds. But coming they shall come with joyfulness, carrying their sheaves" (Ps 125:6–7).

November 26

THE HOUSE OF ZACCHEUS

✠ Ven. Marmaduke Bowes, L., 1585

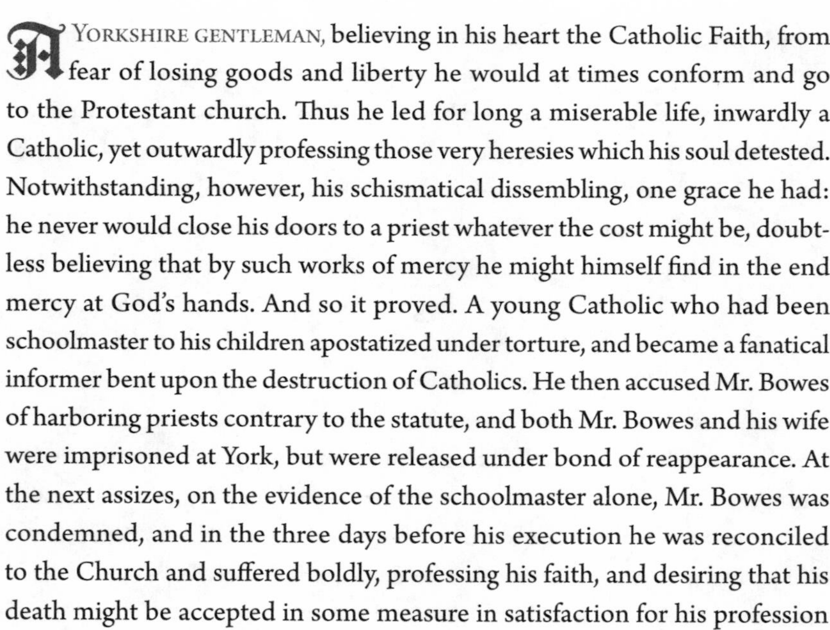

A Yorkshire gentleman, believing in his heart the Catholic Faith, from fear of losing goods and liberty he would at times conform and go to the Protestant church. Thus he led for long a miserable life, inwardly a Catholic, yet outwardly professing those very heresies which his soul detested. Notwithstanding, however, his schismatical dissembling, one grace he had: he never would close his doors to a priest whatever the cost might be, doubtless believing that by such works of mercy he might himself find in the end mercy at God's hands. And so it proved. A young Catholic who had been schoolmaster to his children apostatized under torture, and became a fanatical informer bent upon the destruction of Catholics. He then accused Mr. Bowes of harboring priests contrary to the statute, and both Mr. Bowes and his wife were imprisoned at York, but were released under bond of reappearance. At the next assizes, on the evidence of the schoolmaster alone, Mr. Bowes was condemned, and in the three days before his execution he was reconciled to the Church and suffered boldly, professing his faith, and desiring that his death might be accepted in some measure in satisfaction for his profession of schism.

"This day is salvation come to this house" (Lk 19:9).

* *Bowes was beatified by Pope John Paul II on 22 November 1987.*

November 27

WOLVES IN SHEEP'S CLOTHING

Ven. George Errington, L., and companions, 1596

George Errington, gentleman, William Knight, and William Gibson, yeomen, were in prison at York Castle for recusancy. Confined there also for some misdemeanor was a Protestant minister, who, to reinstate himself in the favor of his superiors, took the following treacherous course. He professed to the Catholic prisoners his sincere repentance for his previous life, and his desire of embracing the Catholic Faith. They believed him sincere, and directed him when he was set free to Mr. Abbott, a zealous convert, who endeavored to procure a priest to reconcile him, and took him to Squire Stapelton's house for this purpose, but in vain. The minister, having now evidence enough to bring them within the law, accused them to the magistrate, and thus displayed his zeal for the Protestant religion. They were all arraigned for high treason in persuading the minister to be reconciled to the Church of Rome. At the bar, they confessed that they had, according to their capacity, explained to the traitor the Catholic Faith, but had used no other persuasion. Upon this they were found guilty, and suffered with joy, November 29.

"Beware of false prophets, who come to you in sheep's clothing, but inwardly they are ravening wolves" (Mt 7:15).

* *Errington was beatified by Pope John Paul II on 22 November 1987.*

JAMES THOMPSON

"He there prayed for a long time"

November 28

THE MARTYRS' SHRINES

Bl. James Thompson, Pr., 1582

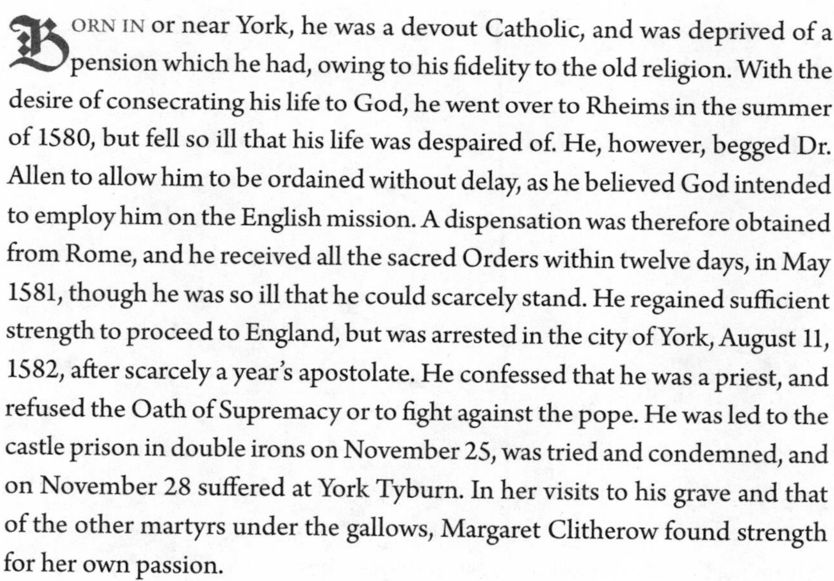

Born in or near York, he was a devout Catholic, and was deprived of a pension which he had, owing to his fidelity to the old religion. With the desire of consecrating his life to God, he went over to Rheims in the summer of 1580, but fell so ill that his life was despaired of. He, however, begged Dr. Allen to allow him to be ordained without delay, as he believed God intended to employ him on the English mission. A dispensation was therefore obtained from Rome, and he received all the sacred Orders within twelve days, in May 1581, though he was so ill that he could scarcely stand. He regained sufficient strength to proceed to England, but was arrested in the city of York, August 11, 1582, after scarcely a year's apostolate. He confessed that he was a priest, and refused the Oath of Supremacy or to fight against the pope. He was led to the castle prison in double irons on November 25, was tried and condemned, and on November 28 suffered at York Tyburn. In her visits to his grave and that of the other martyrs under the gallows, Margaret Clitherow found strength for her own passion.

"And she rendered to the just the wages of their labors and conducted them in a wonderful way, and was to them for a covert by day and for the light of the stars by night" (Ws 10:17).

November 29

FIRSTFRUITS

✠ Bl. Cuthbert Mayne, Pr., 1577

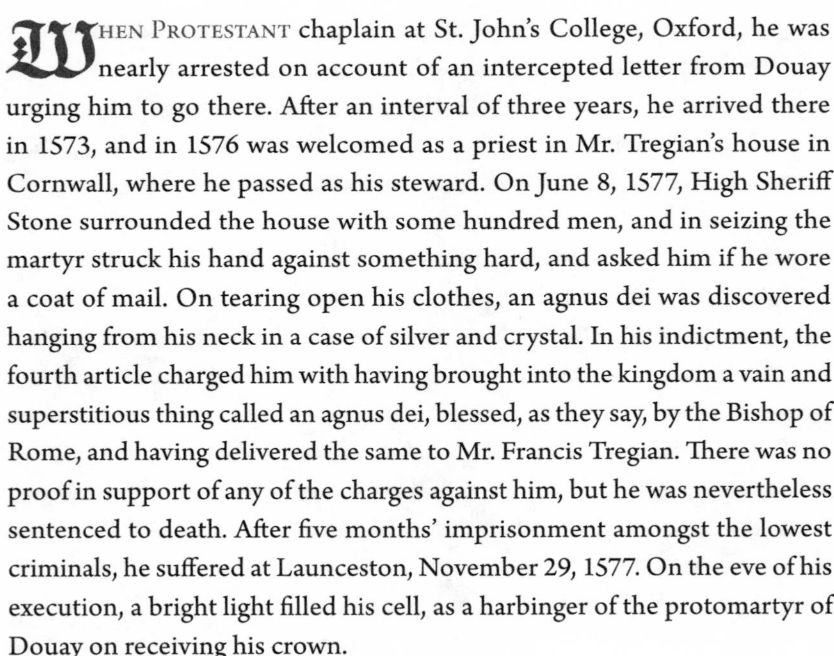

When Protestant chaplain at St. John's College, Oxford, he was nearly arrested on account of an intercepted letter from Douay urging him to go there. After an interval of three years, he arrived there in 1573, and in 1576 was welcomed as a priest in Mr. Tregian's house in Cornwall, where he passed as his steward. On June 8, 1577, High Sheriff Stone surrounded the house with some hundred men, and in seizing the martyr struck his hand against something hard, and asked him if he wore a coat of mail. On tearing open his clothes, an agnus dei was discovered hanging from his neck in a case of silver and crystal. In his indictment, the fourth article charged him with having brought into the kingdom a vain and superstitious thing called an agnus dei, blessed, as they say, by the Bishop of Rome, and having delivered the same to Mr. Francis Tregian. There was no proof in support of any of the charges against him, but he was nevertheless sentenced to death. After five months' imprisonment amongst the lowest criminals, he suffered at Launceston, November 29, 1577. On the eve of his execution, a bright light filled his cell, as a harbinger of the protomartyr of Douay on receiving his crown.

"The firstfruits to God and the Lamb" (Apoc 14:4).

* *Mayne was canonized by Pope Paul VI on 25 October 1970.*

November 30

SATAN THWARTED

✠ Ven. Alexander Crowe, Pr., 1587

A BOOTMAKER IN York, he became a servant at the seminary at Rheims, and for his virtues and diligence was admitted as a student, and finally ordained priest. He arrived on the English mission in 1584, and after nearly two years' labor was arrested at South Duffield, where he had gone to baptize a child, and sentenced at York. On the night before his execution, he was seen by a Catholic fellow prisoner who shared his cell to be wrestling, as it were, in agony with some unseen foe, whilst he prayed continuously. At length, he broke out with joy into the *Laudate Dominum,* and sank, exhausted on his plank bed. He said he had been assailed by the evil one in a monstrous form, who assured him that his soul was lost, and urged him to take his life at once and not wait for the gallows. He was in the greatest strait when our Lady and St. John the Evangelist appeared and put Satan to flight. Yet on the gallows, the evil one made a last final assault, and flung him off the ladder. Though the fall was from a great height, the martyr rose unhurt, and, smiling, remounted the ladder and won his crown, 1587.

"Thou shalt walk upon the asp and the basilisk, and tread underfoot the lion and the dragon" (Ps 90:13).

* *Crowe was beatified by Pope John Paul II on 22 November 1987.*

December

A SIGHT TO GOD AND MAN

✠ Bl. Edmund Campion, S.J., 1581

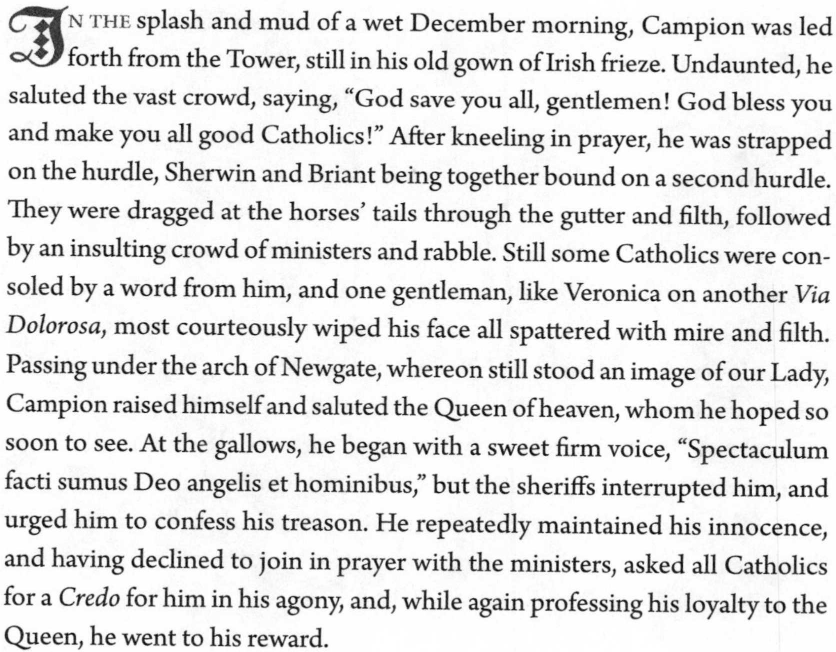

In the splash and mud of a wet December morning, Campion was led forth from the Tower, still in his old gown of Irish frieze. Undaunted, he saluted the vast crowd, saying, "God save you all, gentlemen! God bless you and make you all good Catholics!" After kneeling in prayer, he was strapped on the hurdle, Sherwin and Briant being together bound on a second hurdle. They were dragged at the horses' tails through the gutter and filth, followed by an insulting crowd of ministers and rabble. Still some Catholics were consoled by a word from him, and one gentleman, like Veronica on another *Via Dolorosa,* most courteously wiped his face all spattered with mire and filth. Passing under the arch of Newgate, whereon still stood an image of our Lady, Campion raised himself and saluted the Queen of heaven, whom he hoped so soon to see. At the gallows, he began with a sweet firm voice, "Spectaculum facti sumus Deo angelis et hominibus," but the sheriffs interrupted him, and urged him to confess his treason. He repeatedly maintained his innocence, and having declined to join in prayer with the ministers, asked all Catholics for a *Credo* for him in his agony, and, while again professing his loyalty to the Queen, he went to his reward.

"We are made a spectacle to the world, to angels and to men" (1 Cor 4:9).

December 2

KEEPER OF THE VINEYARD

Bl. John Beche, O. S. B., 1539

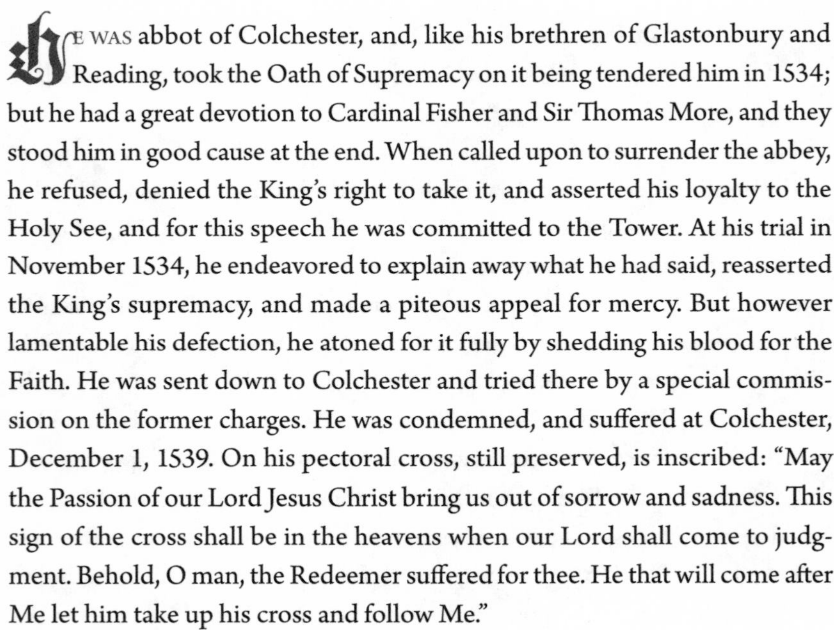

He was abbot of Colchester, and, like his brethren of Glastonbury and Reading, took the Oath of Supremacy on it being tendered him in 1534; but he had a great devotion to Cardinal Fisher and Sir Thomas More, and they stood him in good cause at the end. When called upon to surrender the abbey, he refused, denied the King's right to take it, and asserted his loyalty to the Holy See, and for this speech he was committed to the Tower. At his trial in November 1534, he endeavored to explain away what he had said, reasserted the King's supremacy, and made a piteous appeal for mercy. But however lamentable his defection, he atoned for it fully by shedding his blood for the Faith. He was sent down to Colchester and tried there by a special commission on the former charges. He was condemned, and suffered at Colchester, December 1, 1539. On his pectoral cross, still preserved, is inscribed: "May the Passion of our Lord Jesus Christ bring us out of sorrow and sadness. This sign of the cross shall be in the heavens when our Lord shall come to judgment. Behold, O man, the Redeemer suffered for thee. He that will come after Me let him take up his cross and follow Me."

"Turn again, O God of hosts, look down from heaven and see and visit this vineyard . . . which Thy right hand hath planted" (Ps 79:15–16).

December 3

THE CROSS AND THE CROWN

Bl. Alexander Briant, S. J., 1581

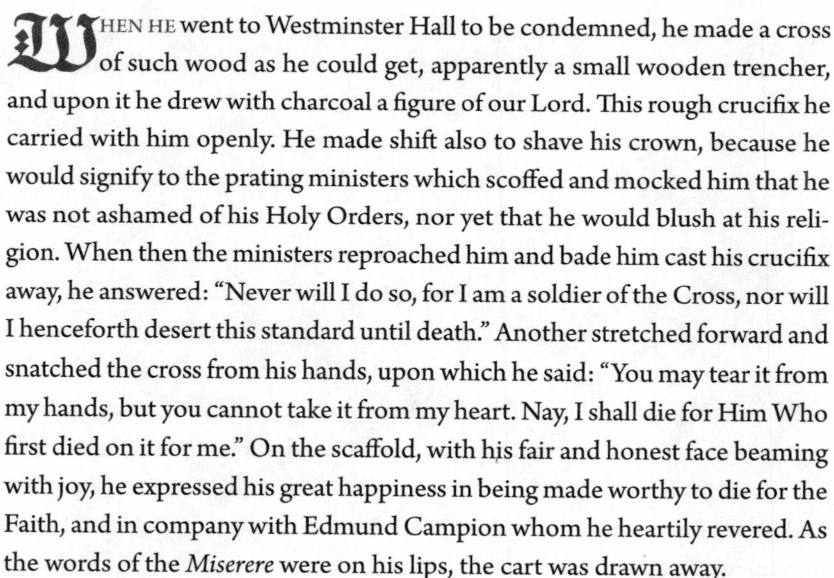

When he went to Westminster Hall to be condemned, he made a cross of such wood as he could get, apparently a small wooden trencher, and upon it he drew with charcoal a figure of our Lord. This rough crucifix he carried with him openly. He made shift also to shave his crown, because he would signify to the prating ministers which scoffed and mocked him that he was not ashamed of his Holy Orders, nor yet that he would blush at his religion. When then the ministers reproached him and bade him cast his crucifix away, he answered: "Never will I do so, for I am a soldier of the Cross, nor will I henceforth desert this standard until death." Another stretched forward and snatched the cross from his hands, upon which he said: "You may tear it from my hands, but you cannot take it from my heart. Nay, I shall die for Him Who first died on it for me." On the scaffold, with his fair and honest face beaming with joy, he expressed his great happiness in being made worthy to die for the Faith, and in company with Edmund Campion whom he heartily revered. As the words of the *Miserere* were on his lips, the cart was drawn away.

> *"God forbid that I should glory, save in the Cross of our Lord Jesus Christ: by Whom the world is crucified to me, and I to the world"* (Gal 6:14).

December 4

PAINLESS TORMENT

Bl. Alexander Briant, S.J., 1581

"Whether this that I say be miraculous or no, God knoweth. But true it is, and thereof my conscience is a witness before God. And this I say that in the end of the tortures, though my hands and feet were violently racked, and my adversaries fulfilled their wicked lust in practicing their cruel tyranny on my body, yet notwithstanding, I was without sense or feeling, well-nigh of grief and pain; and not so only, but, as it were, comforted, eased, and refreshed of grievousness of the tortures bypast. I continued still with perfect and present senses in quietness of heart and tranquility of mind; which thing, when the commissioners did see, they departed, and in going forth of the door they gave orders to rack me again the next day following after the same sort. Now when I heard them say so, it gave me, in my mind, by-and-by, and I did verily believe and trust that, with the help of God, I should be able to bear and suffer it patiently. In the meantime, (as well as I could) I did muse and meditate upon the most bitter Passion of our Savior, and how full of innumerable pains it was."

"For He woundeth and He cureth. He striketh and His hands shall heal" (Jb 5:18).

December 5

BLOOD FOR BLOOD

✠ Ven. John Almond, Pr., 1612

On the scaffold, he flung some seven or eight pounds in silver, with his beads, his points, and his discipline, for those to get them who would, and gave to the hangman an angel, not to spare him, but to treat him as he should. He had come hither, he said, to shed his blood for his Savior's sake, Who had shed His blood for his sins. In which respect he wished that every drop that he would shed might be a thousand; that he might have St. Lawrence's gridiron to be broiled on, St. Peter's cross to be hanged on, St. Stephen's stones to be stoned with, to be ript, ript, ript, and ript again. Then, being in his shirt, he kneeled down, and often repeating, *In manus tuas, Domine,* etc., "Into Thy hands, O Lord, I commend my spirit," he waited till the hangman was ready without any sign of fear; but, ever smiling, he protested he died chaste, but not through his own ability or worthiness, but by Christ's special grace, and that he ever hated those carnal sins for which the Catholic religion had been slandered. At last, the cart was drawn away, and with the words "Jesu, Jesu," his soul flew to Him for Whom he shed his blood, Tyburn, December 5, 1612.

"Jesus also, that He might sanctify the people by His own blood, suffered without the gate" (Heb 13:12).

December 6

FLORES MARTYRUM

Ven. John Almond, Pr., 1612

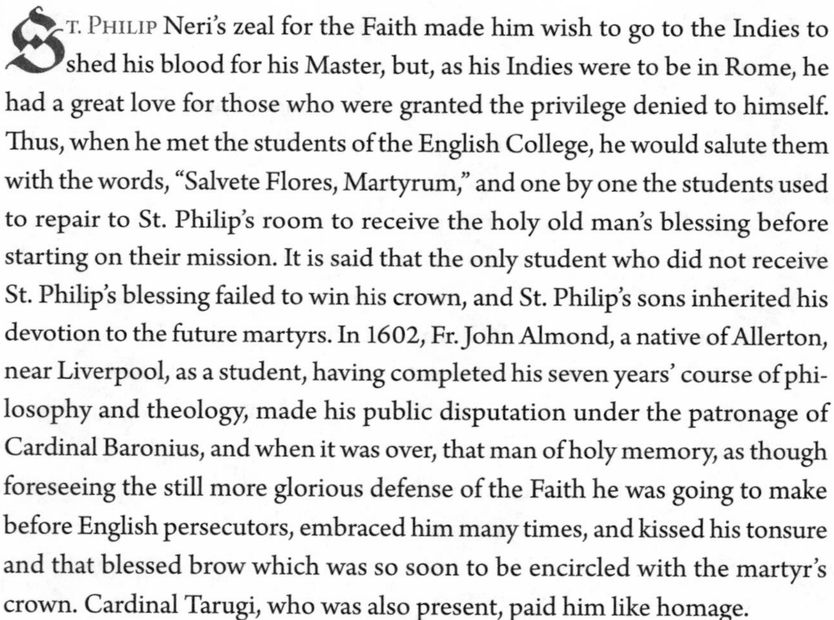

St. Philip Neri's zeal for the Faith made him wish to go to the Indies to shed his blood for his Master, but, as his Indies were to be in Rome, he had a great love for those who were granted the privilege denied to himself. Thus, when he met the students of the English College, he would salute them with the words, "Salvete Flores, Martyrum," and one by one the students used to repair to St. Philip's room to receive the holy old man's blessing before starting on their mission. It is said that the only student who did not receive St. Philip's blessing failed to win his crown, and St. Philip's sons inherited his devotion to the future martyrs. In 1602, Fr. John Almond, a native of Allerton, near Liverpool, as a student, having completed his seven years' course of philosophy and theology, made his public disputation under the patronage of Cardinal Baronius, and when it was over, that man of holy memory, as though foreseeing the still more glorious defense of the Faith he was going to make before English persecutors, embraced him many times, and kissed his tonsure and that blessed brow which was so soon to be encircled with the martyr's crown. Cardinal Tarugi, who was also present, paid him like homage.

> *"These were purchased from among men, the firstfruits to God and to the Lamb. And in their mouth there was found no lie: for they are without spot before the throne of God" (Apoc 14:4–5).*

December 7

FAITH AND WORKS

Ven. John Almond, Pr., 1612

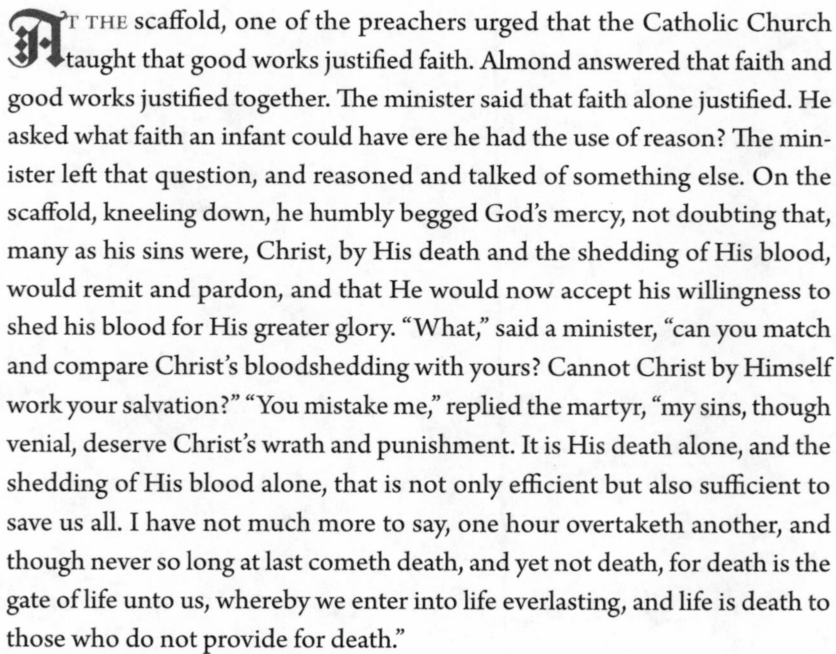

AT THE scaffold, one of the preachers urged that the Catholic Church taught that good works justified faith. Almond answered that faith and good works justified together. The minister said that faith alone justified. He asked what faith an infant could have ere he had the use of reason? The minister left that question, and reasoned and talked of something else. On the scaffold, kneeling down, he humbly begged God's mercy, not doubting that, many as his sins were, Christ, by His death and the shedding of His blood, would remit and pardon, and that He would now accept his willingness to shed his blood for His greater glory. "What," said a minister, "can you match and compare Christ's bloodshedding with yours? Cannot Christ by Himself work your salvation?" "You mistake me," replied the martyr, "my sins, though venial, deserve Christ's wrath and punishment. It is His death alone, and the shedding of His blood alone, that is not only efficient but also sufficient to save us all. I have not much more to say, one hour overtaketh another, and though never so long at last cometh death, and yet not death, for death is the gate of life unto us, whereby we enter into life everlasting, and life is death to those who do not provide for death."

"Faith without works is dead" (Jas 2:20).

December 8

THE SLEEP OF THE JUST

Bl. Ralph Sherwin, Pr., 1581

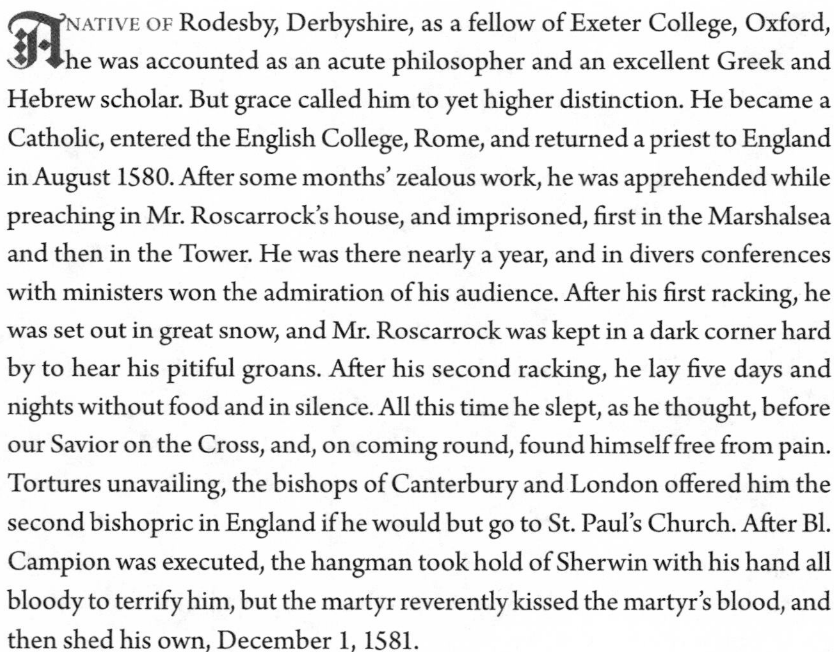

A native of Rodesby, Derbyshire, as a fellow of Exeter College, Oxford, he was accounted as an acute philosopher and an excellent Greek and Hebrew scholar. But grace called him to yet higher distinction. He became a Catholic, entered the English College, Rome, and returned a priest to England in August 1580. After some months' zealous work, he was apprehended while preaching in Mr. Roscarrock's house, and imprisoned, first in the Marshalsea and then in the Tower. He was there nearly a year, and in divers conferences with ministers won the admiration of his audience. After his first racking, he was set out in great snow, and Mr. Roscarrock was kept in a dark corner hard by to hear his pitiful groans. After his second racking, he lay five days and nights without food and in silence. All this time he slept, as he thought, before our Savior on the Cross, and, on coming round, found himself free from pain. Tortures unavailing, the bishops of Canterbury and London offered him the second bishopric in England if he would but go to St. Paul's Church. After Bl. Campion was executed, the hangman took hold of Sherwin with his hand all bloody to terrify him, but the martyr reverently kissed the martyr's blood, and then shed his own, December 1, 1581.

"When He shall give His beloved sleep" (Ps 126:2).

December 9

MALCHUS'S EAR

Ven. John Mason, L., 1591

HE HAD been servant to Mr. Owen of Oxfordshire, who was condemned at the bar as an aider and abettor of priests, and was himself first indicted for knowing and not revealing a seminary priest, but pleaded successfully that the three days allowed for such denunciations had not expired. He was then charged for abetting a priest to escape. On Topcliffe trying to enter the room where Fr. Genings was saying Mass, Mason seized him and thrust him downstairs, falling with him, and Topcliffe met with a broken head. This much the young man confessed. On this charge, Mason was condemned, and executed the morrow after. Asked if he were not sorry for the fact, he replied, "No; if it were to do again, I would resist the wicked, that they should not have God's priests, yea, although I were to be punished with twenty deaths." There suffered with him a fellow servant, Robert Sydney Hodgson, who, finding himself unpinioned, on the belief that he had recanted, boldly declared that, although he had asked Her Majesty's pardon, he would not have the judge think that he would deny his Faith, for that he would rather die twenty times first. They were suffered to hang till they were dead, and together they won their crowns. — Tyburn, December 10, 1591.

"And one of them that stood by, drawing a sword, struck a servant of the chief priest, and cut off his ear" (Mk 14:47).

* *Mason was beatified by Pope Pius XI on 15 December 1929.*

December 10

THE SWEAT OF THE PASSION

✠ Ven. Eustace White, Pr., 1591

HE WAS born at Louth, Lincolnshire, and his conversion so much offended his father, an earnest Protestant, that he laid his curse upon him; but God turned the curse to a blessing, and Eustace White became a priest and entered on the English mission, October 1588. He was apprehended at Blandford, and having confessed himself a priest, a certain minister, one Dr. Houel, a tall man, reputed of great learning, was sent for to dispute with him, but was ignominiously vanquished, as he failed to disprove a certain text which White affirmed to be in the Bible. At the Bridewell, London, he was once hung by Topcliffe in iron manacles for eight hours together; but, though the torment caused the sweat from his body to wet the ground beneath, nothing could be extracted from him of the least prejudice to Catholics. Under the extremity of his passion, he cried out, "Lord, more pain if Thou pleasest, and more patience." To his torturer he said, "I am not angry at you for all this, but shall pray to God for your welfare and salvation." Topcliffe replied in a passion that he wanted not the prayers of heretics, and would have him hung at the next session. Then said the martyr, "I will pray for you at the gallows, for you have great need of prayers." He suffered at Tyburn, December 10, 1591.

"And His sweat became as drops of blood running down to the ground" (Lk 22:44).

* *White was canonized by Pope Paul VI on 25 October 1970.*

December 11

THE OFFICE OF OUR LADY

✠ Ven. Arthur Bell, O. S. F., 1643

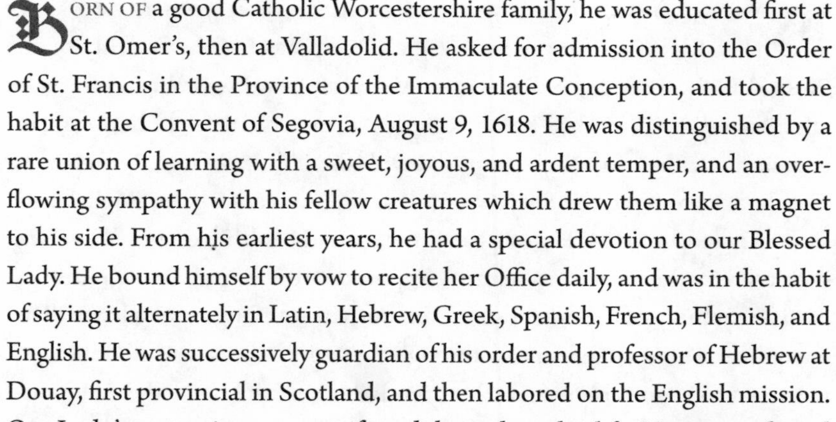

Born of a good Catholic Worcestershire family, he was educated first at St. Omer's, then at Valladolid. He asked for admission into the Order of St. Francis in the Province of the Immaculate Conception, and took the habit at the Convent of Segovia, August 9, 1618. He was distinguished by a rare union of learning with a sweet, joyous, and ardent temper, and an overflowing sympathy with his fellow creatures which drew them like a magnet to his side. From his earliest years, he had a special devotion to our Blessed Lady. He bound himself by vow to recite her Office daily, and was in the habit of saying it alternately in Latin, Hebrew, Greek, Spanish, French, Flemish, and English. He was successively guardian of his order and professor of Hebrew at Douay, first provincial in Scotland, and then labored on the English mission. Our Lady's protection was manifested throughout his life. He was professed on the feast of her Nativity, September 8, 1619. On the same feast, 1634, he was sent on the English mission, and his death sentence, for which he had prayed her twenty years, and had recited daily the Psalm 35, *Dixit injustus,* was pronounced on the feast of her Immaculate Conception, 1643.

"Blessed is the man that heareth Me, and that watcheth daily at My gates, and waiteth at the posts of My doors" (Prv 8:34).

December 12

ALL THINGS TO ALL MEN

✠ Ven. Thomas Holland, S.J., 1642

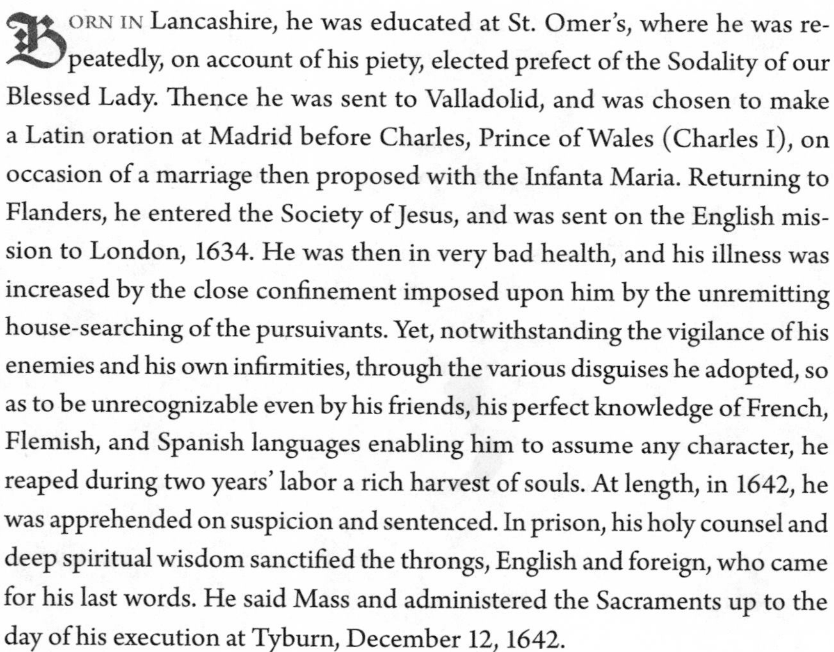

Born in Lancashire, he was educated at St. Omer's, where he was repeatedly, on account of his piety, elected prefect of the Sodality of our Blessed Lady. Thence he was sent to Valladolid, and was chosen to make a Latin oration at Madrid before Charles, Prince of Wales (Charles I), on occasion of a marriage then proposed with the Infanta Maria. Returning to Flanders, he entered the Society of Jesus, and was sent on the English mission to London, 1634. He was then in very bad health, and his illness was increased by the close confinement imposed upon him by the unremitting house-searching of the pursuivants. Yet, notwithstanding the vigilance of his enemies and his own infirmities, through the various disguises he adopted, so as to be unrecognizable even by his friends, his perfect knowledge of French, Flemish, and Spanish languages enabling him to assume any character, he reaped during two years' labor a rich harvest of souls. At length, in 1642, he was apprehended on suspicion and sentenced. In prison, his holy counsel and deep spiritual wisdom sanctified the throngs, English and foreign, who came for his last words. He said Mass and administered the Sacraments up to the day of his execution at Tyburn, December 12, 1642.

"I became all things to all men, that I might save all" (1 Cor 9:22).

* *Holland was canonized by Pope Paul VI on 25 October 1970.*

December 13

INVOCATION OF THE SAINTS

Ven. Edmund Genings, Pr., 1591

HE WAS executed with Ven. Wells opposite the latter's house in Gray's Inn, where he had said Mass. On the scaffold, in answer to Topcliffe's gibes, he professed his loyalty to his dear anointed Queen, and declared that being a priest and saying Mass in noways made him a traitor. Of these things he acknowledged himself guilty, and rejoiced in having done such good deeds, and with God's help would do them again at the risk of a thousand lives. Topcliffe, angered at this speech, bade them turn the ladder and cut the rope, so that the holy priest stood scarcely stunned on his feet, till the hangman tripped him up, and quartered him while living. After he was dismembered, he cried out in agony, "It smarts!" To which Mr. Wells replied, "Alas, sweet soul, thy pain is great, but almost past; pray for me now, most holy saint, that mine may come." After Fr. Genings was ripped up and his bowels cast into the fire, the blessed martyr, his heart being in the executioner's hands, uttered these words, "Sancte Gregori, ora pro me," at which the hangman swore a most wicked oath: "Zounds, his heart is in my hand, and yet Gregory is in his mouth. O egregious papist."

"And the smoke of the incense of the prayers of the saints ascended up before God by the hand of an angel" (Apoc 8:4).

December 14

THE FOOL'S ROBE

Ven. Edmund Genings, Pr., 1591

On December 4, 1591, Fr. Genings and his companions were brought upon their trial, and a jury was empaneled to find them all guilty, yet nothing could any prove against them but that one of them had said Mass in Mr. Well's house, and that one of them had heard the said Mass. Many bitter words and scoffs were used by the judges and others on the bench, particularly to Fr. Genings, because he was very young and had angered them with disputes. And the more to make him a scoff to the people, they vested him not now in his priestly garments (in which they had before carried him through the streets), but in a ridiculous fool's coat which they had found in Mr. Well's house. On his return to Newgate, Topcliffe, Justice Young, and others called on him and offered him life, liberty, a benefice, and promotion if he would go to church and renounce his religion. But, finding him constant and resolute, they were highly offended, and thrust him into a dark hole, where he could not even see his hands nor get up or down without risk to his neck. Here he remained in prayer and contemplation without any food till the hour of his death.

"And Herod with his army set Him at nought and mocked Him, putting on Him a white garment: and sent Him back to Pilate" (Lk 23:11).

December 15

NOT IN THE JUDGMENT HALL

Ven. Edmund Genings, Pr., 1591

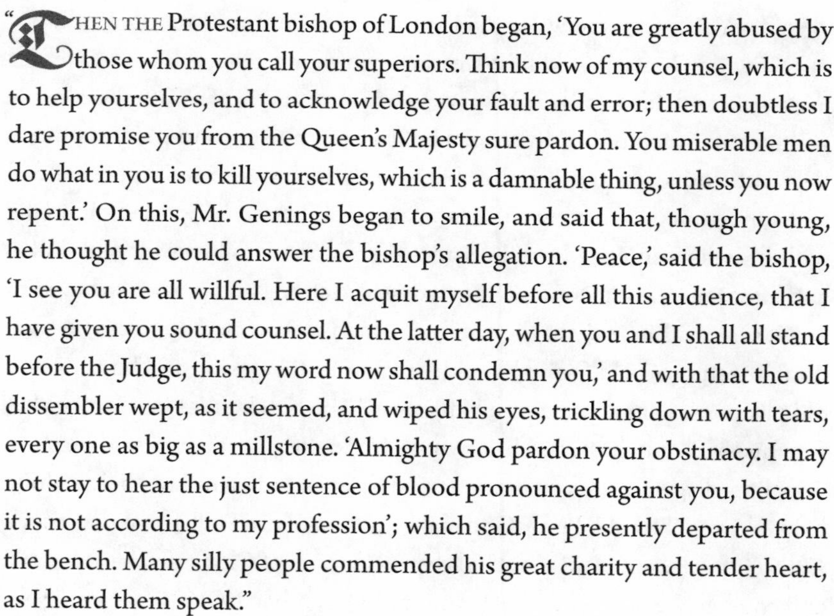

“Then the Protestant bishop of London began, ‘You are greatly abused by those whom you call your superiors. Think now of my counsel, which is to help yourselves, and to acknowledge your fault and error; then doubtless I dare promise you from the Queen’s Majesty sure pardon. You miserable men do what in you is to kill yourselves, which is a damnable thing, unless you now repent.’ On this, Mr. Genings began to smile, and said that, though young, he thought he could answer the bishop’s allegation. ‘Peace,’ said the bishop, ‘I see you are all willful. Here I acquit myself before all this audience, that I have given you sound counsel. At the latter day, when you and I shall all stand before the Judge, this my word now shall condemn you,’ and with that the old dissembler wept, as it seemed, and wiped his eyes, trickling down with tears, every one as big as a millstone. ‘Almighty God pardon your obstinacy. I may not stay to hear the just sentence of blood pronounced against you, because it is not according to my profession’; which said, he presently departed from the bench. Many silly people commended his great charity and tender heart, as I heard them speak.”

“And they went not into the hall, that they might not be defiled, but that they might eat the pasch” (Jn 18:28).

December 16

A MIGHTY HUNTER

Ven. Swithin Wells, L., 1591

His father was renowned in Hampshire as a confessor for the Faith, and Swithin himself — kindly, pleasant, courteous, generous, brave, a leader in every kind of field and manly sport — was an example of a Catholic country gentleman. Much of his diversions he gave up, however, to train youths in the Faith and learning, who thus became staunch Catholics. Apprehended and condemned for having had Mass said in his house, he was led out to die with his wife, sentenced for the same offense. She was however remanded, and after ten years in Newgate of fasting, watching, and prayer, she died in 1602. On Swithin's way to the scaffold, which was erected opposite his own door, meeting an old friend he said: "Farewell all hawking and hunting and old pastimes; I am now going a better way." The butchery of Fr. Genings before his eyes only hastened his own desire to die. "Dispatch," said he, "Mr. Topcliffe, dispatch; are you not ashamed to let an old man stand here so long in his shirt in the cold. I pray God make you of a Saul a Paul, of a persecutor a Catholic professor." And in suchlike speeches, full of Christian charity, piety, and courage, he happily ended his course, December 10, 1591.

"He began to be mighty on the earth, and he was a stout hunter before the Lord" (Gn 10:8–9).

* *Wells was canonized by Pope Paul VI on 25 October 1970.*

December 17

IN BONDS, BUT FREE

Ven. Swithin Wells, L., 1591

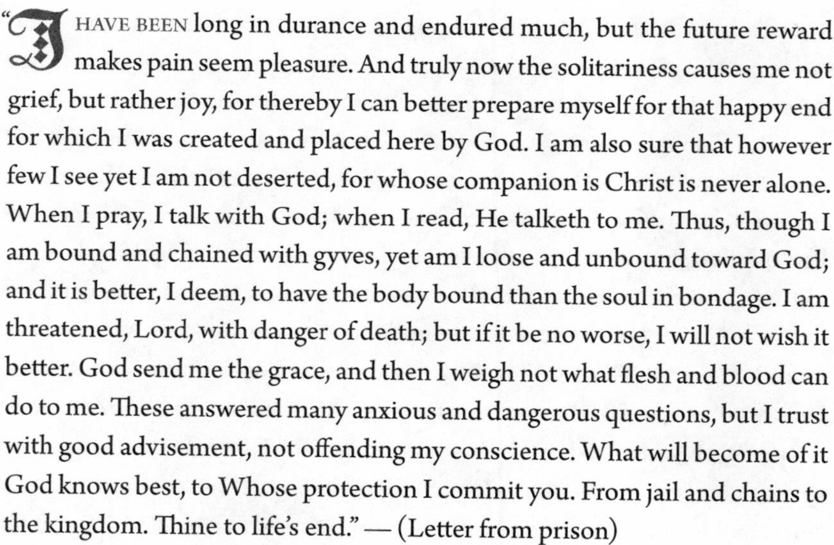

"I HAVE BEEN long in durance and endured much, but the future reward makes pain seem pleasure. And truly now the solitariness causes me not grief, but rather joy, for thereby I can better prepare myself for that happy end for which I was created and placed here by God. I am also sure that however few I see yet I am not deserted, for whose companion is Christ is never alone. When I pray, I talk with God; when I read, He talketh to me. Thus, though I am bound and chained with gyves, yet am I loose and unbound toward God; and it is better, I deem, to have the body bound than the soul in bondage. I am threatened, Lord, with danger of death; but if it be no worse, I will not wish it better. God send me the grace, and then I weigh not what flesh and blood can do to me. These answered many anxious and dangerous questions, but I trust with good advisement, not offending my conscience. What will become of it God knows best, to Whose protection I commit you. From jail and chains to the kingdom. Thine to life's end." — (Letter from prison)

"So then, brethren, we are not children of the bondwoman, but of the free: by the freedom whereby Christ has made us free" (Gal 4:31).

December 18

THE GOOD THIEF

Ven. John Roberts, O. S. B., 1610

FINDING HIMSELF about to be hung in company with eight traitors and criminals, he blessed them and spoke: "Here we are all going to die, nor have we any hope of escape; but if you die in that religion now professed and established in this country, without any doubt you will be condemned to the eternal fire of hell. For the love then of our Blessed Savior I earnestly pray you to return from the evil path, so that we may all die in one and the same true Faith, and to show this say with me the following words: 'I believe in the holy Catholic Church, and I desire to die a member of that Church. I repent and am sorry for having led so wicked a life, and that I have grievously offended my sweet and merciful Savior.' If you say these words truly and from your hearts, I will absolve you, and then my soul for yours." At these words one of the poor wretches was so affected that he burst into tears. The father then exhorted him specially and prayed silently to God for him, then again spoke to him in a low voice. In the end, the poor creature publicly professed that he died a Catholic.

"This day thou shalt be with Me in paradise" (Lk 23:43).

* *Roberts was canonized by Pope Paul VI on 25 October 1970.*

December 19

THE LAST SUPPER

Ven. John Roberts, O. S. B., 1610

Luisa de Carvajal, a noble Spanish lady, came to London to minister to Catholics suffering for the Faith. She visited the prisoners, stood by the scaffold to cheer the dying, and buried the dead — all this amid the hootings of the rabble dogging her footsteps. On one occasion, she obtained leave to prepare a supper for Frs. Roberts and Somers on the eve of their martyrdom, and for their fellow prisoners. The feast is thus described: "They then sat down to supper — twenty prisoners for conscience's sake, twenty confessors of the Faith — Luisa de Carvajal presiding at the head of the table. The meal was a devout and a joyful one — heavenly the refreshment ministered to the guests, great the fervor and spiritual delight which our Lord bestowed on His valiant soldiers, giving them that peace which passeth all understanding. Scarcely anyone thought of eating. In the course of the evening, Fr. Roberts asked her, 'Do you not think I may be causing disedification by my great glee? Would it not be better to retire into a corner and give myself up to prayer?' 'No, certainly not,' Luisa answered. 'You cannot be better employed than by letting them all see with what cheerful courage you are about to die for Christ.' "

"The Master saith to thee: Where is the guest chamber, where I may eat the pasch with My disciples?" (Lk 22:11).

December 20

THE MISSION TO TEACH

Ven. John Roberts, O. S. B., 1610

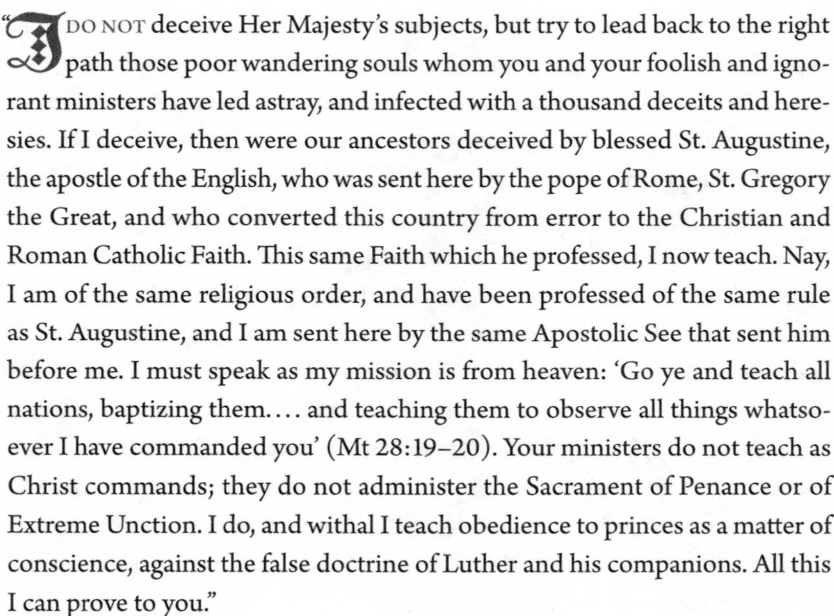

"I do not deceive Her Majesty's subjects, but try to lead back to the right path those poor wandering souls whom you and your foolish and ignorant ministers have led astray, and infected with a thousand deceits and heresies. If I deceive, then were our ancestors deceived by blessed St. Augustine, the apostle of the English, who was sent here by the pope of Rome, St. Gregory the Great, and who converted this country from error to the Christian and Roman Catholic Faith. This same Faith which he professed, I now teach. Nay, I am of the same religious order, and have been professed of the same rule as St. Augustine, and I am sent here by the same Apostolic See that sent him before me. I must speak as my mission is from heaven: 'Go ye and teach all nations, baptizing them.... and teaching them to observe all things whatsoever I have commanded you' (Mt 28:19–20). Your ministers do not teach as Christ commands; they do not administer the Sacrament of Penance or of Extreme Unction. I do, and withal I teach obedience to princes as a matter of conscience, against the false doctrine of Luther and his companions. All this I can prove to you."

"Going, therefore, teach ye all nations" (Mt 28:19).

December 21

PRIEST, NOT TRAITOR

Ven. John Roberts, O. S. B., 1610

To the Protestant bishop of London he said, "Can you name a single instance of a Catholic bishop being seated, as you are, among secular judges in a capital case? You would have done much better to remain in your place, reproving the dissolute conduct of your clergy, than to come and sit on this bench, while matters of life and death are being decided. These twelve men, who have to give a verdict in this case, are ignorant persons, unable to discern or judge of the difference between the priesthood and treason. You strive to do an impossible thing when you wish to make it appear that to be a priest is to be a traitor. That would make Christ Himself a traitor, and all His apostles, St. Augustine also, the apostle of England, and all the priests and bishops who have succeeded him to this day, would also be esteemed traitors, and you would condemn them if they were brought before you. I therefore say that it is impossible that being a priest should make me a traitor. If a priest commit treason, I am not so ignorant as not to know that the man is a traitor, but not by reason of his being a priest, or in consequence of exercising his priestly office."

"We have found this man perverting our nation and forbidding to give tribute to Caesar, and saying that He is Christ the King" (Lk 23:2).

December 22

THE RIGHTS OF THE CHURCH

Ven. John Roberts, O. S. B., 1610

"I ACKNOWLEDGED THEN, as I do now, that I am a priest and a monk of the holy Order of St. Benedict, as were also Sts. Augustine, Lawrence, Paulinus, Mellitus, and Justus; and as these monks converted our country from unbelief, so I have done what little I could to liberate it from heresy. I leave it to you, Mr. Recorder, and the rest of you to judge whether this is high treason. But suppose I had really offended against the state and were worthy of death, I ought not even then to be judged by you, nor by this court, nor by these twelve men, they not being men of my condition or quality, since it has been decreed by the councils of the Church and the popes, the Vicars of Christ on earth, that priests should not be brought before secular judges; but if their crimes are great and merit death, that they must be first examined and found guilty by the ecclesiastical judges, and be degraded by them, then they can be handed over to the secular arm to be dealt with as the laws of God and man decree. This being the case, I do not see, Mr. Recorder, that you are competent to pronounce sentence against me."

"Concerning the ministers of the house of this God,
you have no authority to impose toll or tribute,
or custom upon them" (1 Esd 7:24).

December 23

FREEMEN BORN

Ven. Edmund Genings and companions, 1591

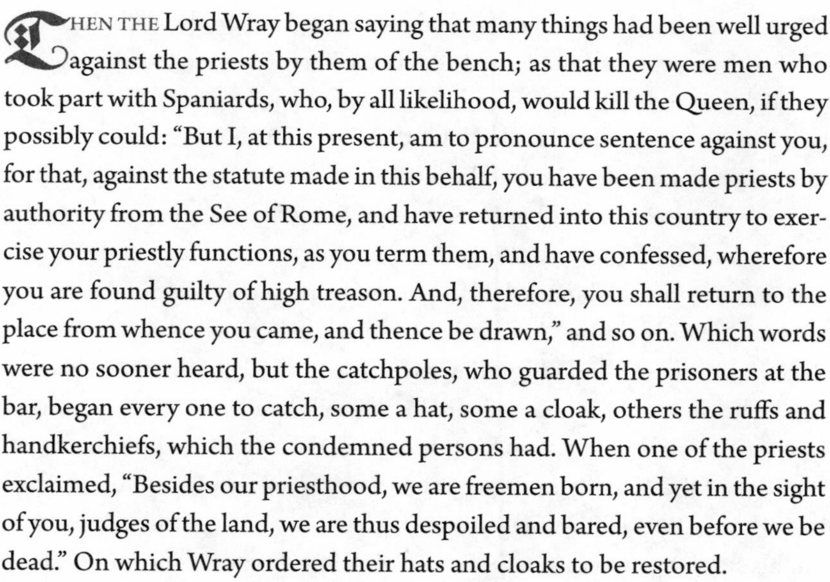

Then the Lord Wray began saying that many things had been well urged against the priests by them of the bench; as that they were men who took part with Spaniards, who, by all likelihood, would kill the Queen, if they possibly could: "But I, at this present, am to pronounce sentence against you, for that, against the statute made in this behalf, you have been made priests by authority from the See of Rome, and have returned into this country to exercise your priestly functions, as you term them, and have confessed, wherefore you are found guilty of high treason. And, therefore, you shall return to the place from whence you came, and thence be drawn," and so on. Which words were no sooner heard, but the catchpoles, who guarded the prisoners at the bar, began every one to catch, some a hat, some a cloak, others the ruffs and handkerchiefs, which the condemned persons had. When one of the priests exclaimed, "Besides our priesthood, we are freemen born, and yet in the sight of you, judges of the land, we are thus despoiled and bared, even before we be dead." On which Wray ordered their hats and cloaks to be restored.

"The tribune also was afraid after he understood that Paul was a Roman citizen, and because he had bound him" (Acts 22:29).

December 24

A PRIEST'S EPITAPH AT DOUAY

✠ George Muscot, Pr., 1645

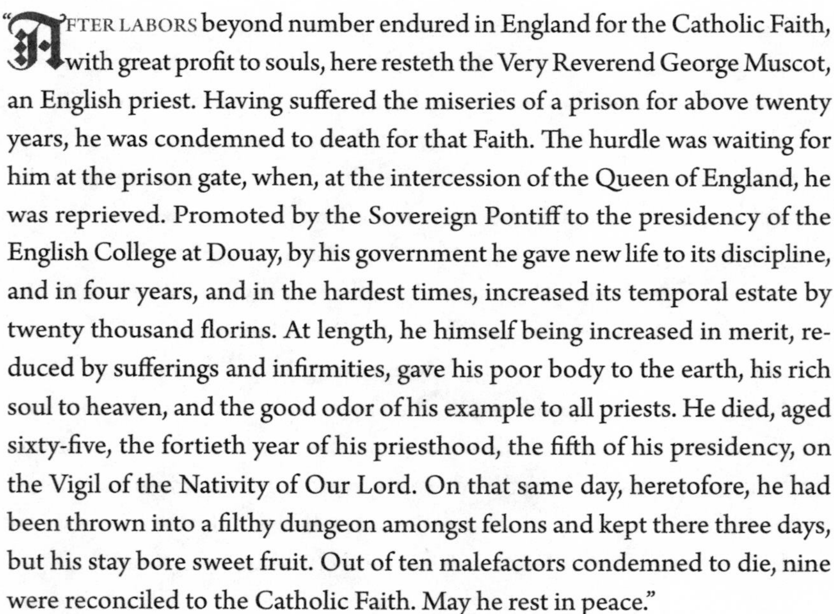

"After labors beyond number endured in England for the Catholic Faith, with great profit to souls, here resteth the Very Reverend George Muscot, an English priest. Having suffered the miseries of a prison for above twenty years, he was condemned to death for that Faith. The hurdle was waiting for him at the prison gate, when, at the intercession of the Queen of England, he was reprieved. Promoted by the Sovereign Pontiff to the presidency of the English College at Douay, by his government he gave new life to its discipline, and in four years, and in the hardest times, increased its temporal estate by twenty thousand florins. At length, he himself being increased in merit, reduced by sufferings and infirmities, gave his poor body to the earth, his rich soul to heaven, and the good odor of his example to all priests. He died, aged sixty-five, the fortieth year of his priesthood, the fifth of his presidency, on the Vigil of the Nativity of Our Lord. On that same day, heretofore, he had been thrown into a filthy dungeon amongst felons and kept there three days, but his stay bore sweet fruit. Out of ten malefactors condemned to die, nine were reconciled to the Catholic Faith. May he rest in peace."

"He chose him out of all men living to offer sacrifice to God, incense, and a good savor, for a memorial to make reconciliation for His people" (Ecclus 45:20).

December 25

THE BURNING BABE

Ven. Robert Southwell, S. J., 1595

As I in hoary winter's night stood shivering in the snow,
Surprised I was with sudden heat, which made my heart to glow;
And lifting up a fearful eye to view what fire was near,
A pretty babe all burning bright did in the air appear;
Who, scorched with excessive heat such floods of tears did shed,
As though His floods should quench His flames which with His tears were bred;
"Alas!" quoth He, "but newly born in fiery heats I fry,
Yet none approach to warm their hearts, or feel My fire, but I!
My faultless breast the furnace is; the fuel wounding thorns;
Love is the fire, and sighs the smoke, the ashes shames and scorns;
The fuel Justice layeth on, and Mercy blows the coals,
The metal in this furnace wrought are men's defiled souls;
For which, as now on fire I am to work them to their good,
So will I melt into a bath to wash them in My blood."
With this He vanished out of sight and swiftly shrank away,
And straight I called unto mind that it was Christmas Day.

December 26

FIT FOR WAR AND COMELY

Bl. Alexander Briant, S.J., 1581

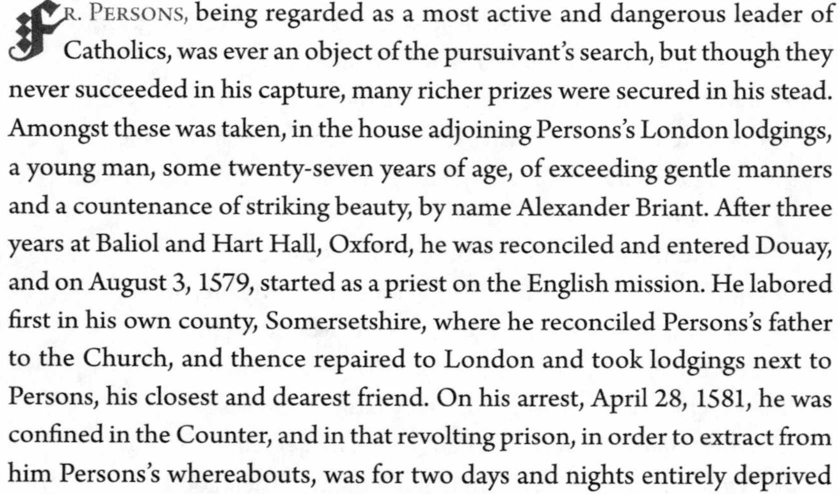

FR. PERSONS, being regarded as a most active and dangerous leader of Catholics, was ever an object of the pursuivant's search, but though they never succeeded in his capture, many richer prizes were secured in his stead. Amongst these was taken, in the house adjoining Persons's London lodgings, a young man, some twenty-seven years of age, of exceeding gentle manners and a countenance of striking beauty, by name Alexander Briant. After three years at Baliol and Hart Hall, Oxford, he was reconciled and entered Douay, and on August 3, 1579, started as a priest on the English mission. He labored first in his own county, Somersetshire, where he reconciled Persons's father to the Church, and thence repaired to London and took lodgings next to Persons, his closest and dearest friend. On his arrest, April 28, 1581, he was confined in the Counter, and in that revolting prison, in order to extract from him Persons's whereabouts, was for two days and nights entirely deprived of food and drink. He then contrived to get some hard cheese and broken bread with a pint of beer, but this caused an agonizing thirst. After six days in the Counter, nothing had been gained from him, and sharper methods were resolved on.

"With thy comeliness and beauty set out, proceed prosperously, and reign" (Ps 44:5).

December 27

BLACK BUT BEAUTIFUL

Bl. Alexander Briant, S.J., 1581

AFTER ALMOST dying of thirst at the Counter, he was transferred to the Tower, with directions to Norton, the rack-master, to put him to the tortures to wring from him by the pain and terror thereof the knowledge of such things as shall appertain. As he would neither confess where he had seen Fr. Persons, how he was maintained, where he had said Mass, or whose Confessions he had heard, needles were thrust under his nails — the torture of pricking often applied to witches. He bore them all unmoved, and with a constant mind and pleasant countenance said the psalm *Miserere,* desiring God to forgive his tormentors. Whereat Dr. Hammond stamped and stared as if beside himself, saying, "What a thing is this! If a man were not settled in his religion, this were enough to convert him." He was now removed into a pit twenty feet deep without light, whence after eight days he was drawn out and taken to the rack chamber. There he was rent and torn upon the rack till his body was disjointed, and the next day, though his body was one sore, his senses dead, and his blood congealed, he was brought to the torture again and racked yet more severely; but he resolved to die rather than hurt any living creature by word of his.

"They have dug My hands and feet, they have numbered all My bones" (Ps 21:17–18).

December 28

GRAVEN IN GOD'S HANDS

Bl. Ralph Sherwin, Pr., 1581

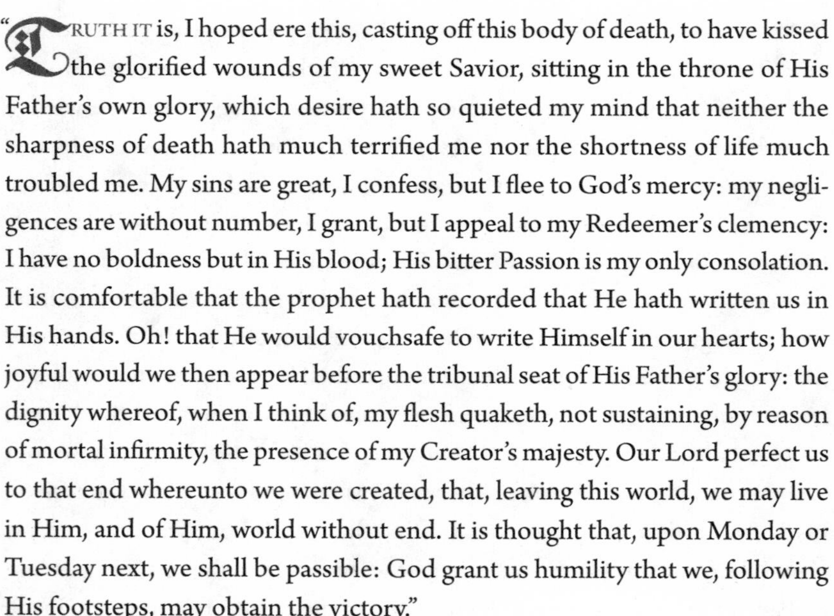

"Truth it is, I hoped ere this, casting off this body of death, to have kissed the glorified wounds of my sweet Savior, sitting in the throne of His Father's own glory, which desire hath so quieted my mind that neither the sharpness of death hath much terrified me nor the shortness of life much troubled me. My sins are great, I confess, but I flee to God's mercy: my negligences are without number, I grant, but I appeal to my Redeemer's clemency: I have no boldness but in His blood; His bitter Passion is my only consolation. It is comfortable that the prophet hath recorded that He hath written us in His hands. Oh! that He would vouchsafe to write Himself in our hearts; how joyful would we then appear before the tribunal seat of His Father's glory: the dignity whereof, when I think of, my flesh quaketh, not sustaining, by reason of mortal infirmity, the presence of my Creator's majesty. Our Lord perfect us to that end whereunto we were created, that, leaving this world, we may live in Him, and of Him, world without end. It is thought that, upon Monday or Tuesday next, we shall be passible: God grant us humility that we, following His footsteps, may obtain the victory."

"Behold, I have graven thee in My hands: thy walls are always before My eyes" (Is 49:16).

WILLIAM VISCOUNT STAFFORD
"He knelt down before the block"

December 29

THE WITNESS OF A GOOD CONSCIENCE

✠ Ven. William Howard, Viscount, 1680

THE SECOND son of Thomas, Earl of Arundel, and uncle to Thomas and Henry, Dukes of Norfolk, he married Mary, heiress to Henry, Lord Stafford, and succeeded to her title [Viscount Stafford]. During the civil war, he suffered much for his loyalty to the King, but always bore himself with the courage and constancy proper to his birth, his loyalty, and his faith. After the Restoration, he lived in peace and happiness with his wife and children till his sixty-sixth year, when he was accused by Oates as being a party to the plot. Although he heard of the impending charge, knowing his own innocency, he made no change in his manner of life, and so was arrested. After two years in the Tower, he was brought on his trial before the House of Peers. For four days the prosecuting lawyers assailed him, yet by the mere force of his integrity he exposed the falsehood of his accusers. Nevertheless, he was condemned by fifty-five peers against thirty-one. He was recommended to put on his cloak on his way to the scaffold, to which he assented, "Lest," he said, "I shake from cold, but never from fear." So proceeding he won his crown.

"For our glory is this: the testimony of our conscience, that in simplicity of heart . . . and not in carnal wisdom . . . we have conversed in this world" (2 Cor 1:12).

* *Howard was beatified by Pope Pius XI on 15 December 1929.*

December 30

A PERSECUTOR PENITENT

Ven. John Almond, Pr., 1612

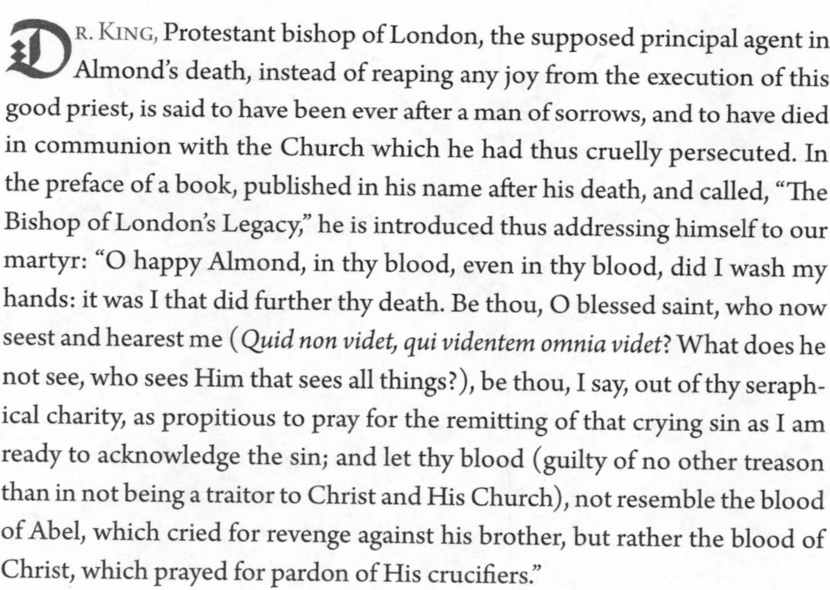

Dr. King, Protestant bishop of London, the supposed principal agent in Almond's death, instead of reaping any joy from the execution of this good priest, is said to have been ever after a man of sorrows, and to have died in communion with the Church which he had thus cruelly persecuted. In the preface of a book, published in his name after his death, and called, "The Bishop of London's Legacy," he is introduced thus addressing himself to our martyr: "O happy Almond, in thy blood, even in thy blood, did I wash my hands: it was I that did further thy death. Be thou, O blessed saint, who now seest and hearest me (*Quid non videt, qui videntem omnia videt*? What does he not see, who sees Him that sees all things?), be thou, I say, out of thy seraphical charity, as propitious to pray for the remitting of that crying sin as I am ready to acknowledge the sin; and let thy blood (guilty of no other treason than in not being a traitor to Christ and His Church), not resemble the blood of Abel, which cried for revenge against his brother, but rather the blood of Christ, which prayed for pardon of His crucifiers."

"I have sinned in betraying innocent blood" (Mt 27:4).

December 31

SORROW TO LIFE

Bp. Owen Oglethorpe of Carlisle, 1559

THE ARCHBISHOP of York, whose office it was to crown Elizabeth (the metropolitan being dead), declined to do so, and Bishop Oglethorpe at length performed the ceremony in the most solemn manner. Elizabeth then took the usual oath of Christian princes prescribed by tradition and law to defend the Catholic Faith and to guard the rights and immunities of the Church, hoping thus to secure unquestioned her possession of the throne; but throughout the function she displayed her contempt of the Faith. At the anointing, she expressed her abhorrence in her own choice language, saying, "The oil is stinking." At the Mass, she forbade the bishop to elevate the Host, and on his refusal to obey her command, her chaplain performed a mutilated rite. Although the bishop had only crowned Elizabeth in the hope of thus preventing an open schism, when he saw the ruin she brought on religion, he never ceased to bewail his act. He defended the Faith boldly in the Westminster Conference, and was fined in consequence by the council. In spite of threats and promises, he refused to take the Oath of Supremacy, and was deposed, and after months of physical suffering and heartbroken contrition, he died in prison in charge of Grindal, the Protestant bishop of London, December 31.

"Lord, my desire is before Thee, and my groaning is not hid from Thee.... For in Thee, O Lord, have I hoped" (Ps 37:10, 16).

MATTHEW FLATHERS

"A desperate cut on the head"

APPENDIX

Select Poetry of the Martyrs

The following stanzas are proprietary redactions of public domain versions of the original poems.

EULOGY FOR EDMUND CAMPION

By St. Henry Walpole

Why do I use my paper, ink, and pen?
  Or call my wits to counsel what to say?
Such memories were made for mortal men.
  I speak of saints, whose names cannot decay.
An angel's trump were meeter far to sound
  Their glorious deaths, if such on earth were found.

Pardon my wants. I offer nought but will.
  Their register remaineth safe above.
Campion exceeds the compass of my skill.
  Yet let me use the measure of my love,
And give me leave, in low and homely verse,
  His high attempt in England to rehearse.

He came by vow. The cause, to conquer sin;
  His armor, prayer; the Word, his targe and shield;
His comfort, heaven; his spoil, our souls to win;
  The devil his foe; the wicked world his field;
His triumph, joy; his wage, eternal bliss;
  His captain, Christ, Who ever during is.

From ease to pain, from honor to disgrace,
  From love to hate, to danger, being well,
From safe abroad, to fears in every place,
  Contemning death, to save our souls from hell,
Our new apostle coming to restore
  The faith, which Austin planted here before.

His native flowers were mixt with herbs of grace;
  His mild behavior tempered well with skill;
A lowly mind possess'd a learned place;
  A sugared speech; a rare and virtuous will;
A saint-like man was set in earth below,
  The food of truth in erring hearts to sow.

With tongue and pen the truth he taught and wrote,
  By force whereof they came to Christ apace;
But when it pleased God it was his lot
  He should be thrall, He lent him so much grace,
His patience there did work so much or more
  As had his heavenly speeches done before.

His fare was hard, yet mild and sweet his cheer;
  His prison close, yet free and loose his mind;
His torture great, yet scant, or none, his fear;
  His offers large, yet nothing could him blind.
O constant man! O mind, O virtue strange!
  Whom want, nor woe, nor fear, nor hope could change.

From racks in Tower they brought him to dispute —
  Bookless, alone, to answer all that came —
Yet Christ gave grace; he did them all confute,
  So sweetly there in glory of His Name,
That even the adverse part are forced to say
  That Campion's cause did bear the bell away.

This foil enraged the minds of some so far,
 They thought it best to take his life away,
Because they saw he would their matter mar,
 And leave them shortly naught at all say.
Traitor he was with many a silly sleight,
 Yet was a Jury packed, that cried guilty straight.

Religion there was treason to the queen;
 Preaching of penance war against the land;
Priests were such dangerous men as hath not been;
 Prayers and beads were fight and force of hand;
Cases of conscience bane unto the State:
 So blind is error, so false a witness hate.

And yet, behold! these lambs are drawn to die;
 Treason's proclaim'd, the queen is put in fear.
Out upon Satan! fie, malice, fie!
 Speak'st thou to them that did the guiltless hear?
Can humble souls departing now to Christ
 Protest untrue? Avaunt, foul fiend, thou liest!

My Sovereign Liege, behold your subjects' end!
 Your secret foes do misinform your grace:
Who in your cause their holy lives would spend
 As traitors die, a rare and monstrous case.
The bloody wolf condemns the harmless sheep
 Before the dog, the while the shepherds sleep.

England, look up! thy soil is stained with blood;
 Thou hast made martyrs many of thine own.
If thou hadst grace, their deaths would do thee good.
 The seed will take which in such blood is sown,
And Campion's learning, fertile so before,
 Thus watered too must needs of force be more.

Repent thee, Elliott, of thy Judas kiss,
I wish thy penance, not thy desperate end.
Let Norton think, which now in prison is,
To whom was said, he was not Cæsar's friend;
And let the Judge consider well in fear,
That Pilate wash'd his hands and was not clear.

The witness false, Sledd, Munday, and the rest,
Which had your slanders noted in your books,
Confess your fault beforehand, it were best,
Lest God do find it written, when He looks
In dreadful doom upon the souls of men.
It will be late, alas! to mend it then.

You bloody Jury, Lee and all th' eleven,
Take heed, your verdict, which was given in haste,
Do not exclude you from the joys of heaven,
And cause you rue it when the time is past,
And every one whose malice caused him say
Crucify! let him dread the terror of that day.

Fond Elderton, call in thy foolish rhyme,
Thy scurril ballads are too bad to sell.
Let good men rest, and mend thyself in time;
Confess in prose, thou hast not metered well.
Or if thy folly cannot choose but feign,
Write alehouse joys, blaspheme thou not in vain.

Remember you that would oppress the cause,
The Church is Christ's; His honor cannot die,
Though hell itself revest her grisly jaws,
And join in league with schism and heresy.
Though craft devise and cruel rage oppress,
Yet skill will write, and martyrdom confess.

You thought, perhaps, when learned Campion dies,
  His pen must cease, his sugared tongue be still;
But you forget how loud his death it cries,
  How far beyond the sound of tongue and quill.
You did not know how rare and great a good
  It was to write his precious gifts in blood.

Living, he spoke to those who present were;
  His writing took their censure of the view:
Now fame reports his learning far and near,
  And now his death confirms his doctrine true.
His virtues now are written in the skies,
  And often read with holy inward eyes.

All Europe wonders at so rare a man,
  England is filled with rumor of his end;
London must needs, for it was present then
  When constantly three saints their lives did spend.
The streets, the stones, the steps they hale them by,
  Proclaim the cause for which these martyrs die.

The Tower says the truth he did defend;
  The bar bears witness of his guiltless mind;
Tyburn doth tell he made a patient end;
  In every gate his martyrdom we find.
In vain you wrought who would obscure his name,
  For heaven and earth will still record the same.

Your sentence wrong pronounced of him here
  Exempts him from the judgment for to come:
O happy he that is not judged there!
  God grant me, too, to have an earthly doom!
Your witness false and lewdly taken in
  Doth cause he is not now accused of sin.

His prison now the city of the King;
    His rack and torture, joys and heavenly bliss:
For men's reproach with angels he doth sing
    A sacred song, which everlasting is.
For shame but short, and loss of small renown,
    He purchased hath an ever-during crown.

His quartered limbs shall join with joy again,
    And rise a body brighter than the sun.
Your bloody malice tortured him in vain,
    For every wrench some glory hath him won;
And every drop of blood which he did spend
    Hath reaped a joy which never shall have end.

Can dreary death, then, daunt our faith, or pain?
    Is't lingering life we fear to lose, or ease?
No, no, such death procureth life again.
    'Tis only God we tremble to displease,
Who kills but once, and ever since we die
    Whose whole revenge torments eternally.

We cannot fear a mortal torment, we.
    These martyrs' blood hath moistened all our hearts:
Whose parted quarters when we chance to see
    We learn to play the constant Christian parts.
His head doth speak, and heavenly precepts give
    How we that look should frame ourselves to live.

His youth instructs us how to spend our days;
    His flying bids us learn to banish sin;
His straight profession shows the narrow ways
    Which they must walk that look to enter in;
His home return by danger and distress
    Emboldeneth us our conscience to profess.

His hurdle draws us with him to the cross;
  His speeches there provoke us for to die;
His death doth say, this life is but a loss;
  His martyr'd blood from heaven to us doth cry;
His first and last and all conspire in this,
  To shew the way that leadeth us to bliss.

Blessed be God, which lent him so much grace;
  Thanked be Christ, which blest His martyr so;
Happy is he which seeth his Master's face;
  Cursed all they that thought to work him woe;
Bounden be we to give eternal praise
  To Jesus' name, which such a man did raise.

I DIE ALIVE

By St. Robert Southwell

O life! what lets thee from a quick decease?
O death! what draws thee from a present prey?
My feast is done, my soul would be at ease,
My grace is said; O death! come take away.

I live, but such a life as ever dies;
I die, but such a death as never ends;
My death to end my dying life denies,
And life my living death no whit amends.

Thus still I die, yet still I do revive;
My living death by dying life is fed;
Grace more than nature keeps my heart alive,
Whose idle hopes and vain desires are dead.

Not where I breathe, but where I love, I live;
Not where I love, but where I am, I die;
The life I wish must future glory give,
The death I feel in present dangers lie.

TRUE CHRISTIAN HEART

—From *The Song which Mr. Thulis Writ for Himself*

By Bl. John Thulis

True Christian heart cease to lament,
For grief it is in vain;
For Christ you know was well content
To suffer bitter pain.
That we may come to Heaven bliss,
There joyfully to sing,
Who doth believe, shall never miss
To have a joyful rising.

But England hear, my heart is sad,
For thy great cruelty,
And loss of faith, which once thou had,
Of Christianity.
In thee false doctrine doth appear
Abundantly to spring,
Which is the cause I greatly fear
Thou lose thy happy rising.

As for myself I am not afraid
To suffer constantly,
For why due debt must needs be paid
Unto sweet God on high.
Saint Paul he being firm of faith,
Hoping with saints to sing,
Most patiently did suffer death.
Lord send us happy rising!

O you poor prisoners dread not death,
Though you have done amiss,
But pray to God with faithful hearts
To bring you unto bliss.
Confess your sins with contrite hearts
Unto your heavenly King,
For He is merciful indeed:
Christ send us happy rising.

The saints also did suffer death,
And martyrs, as you hear,
And I myself am now at hand,
And death I do not fear.
Then have I trust of greater grace
Unto my soul will bring,
Where we shall meet both face to face
Before our heavenly King.

No hurdle hard, nor hempen rope
Can make me once afraid.
No tyrant's knife against my life
Shall maketh me dismayed.
Though flesh and bones be broke and torn
My soul I trust will sing,
Amongst the glorious company
With Christ our heavenly King.

Thus I, your friend John Thewlis,
Have made my latest end,
Desiring God when His will is
Us all to Heaven send.
Where neither strange nor damned crew
Can grief unto us bring.
And now I bid my last adieu:
Christ send us happy rising!

God grant you grace still in your hearts
False doctrine to refrain,
And hold the true Catholic faith,
Which Christ did once ordain.
All honor be to God of hosts,
All glory to His Son,
All praise be to the Holy Ghost,
Three Persons all in one.

MEDITATION UPON HEAVEN

—From *A Fourfold Meditation on the Four Last Things*

By St. Philp Howard

No eye hath seen what joys the Saints obtain,
No ear hath heard what comforts are possessed;
No heart can think in what delight they reign,
Nor pen express their happy port of rest,
Where pleasure flows, and grief is never seen,
Where good abounds, and ill is banish'd clean.

Those sacred Saints remain in perfect peace,
Which Christ confessed, and walked in His ways,
They shine in bliss, which now shall never cease,
And to His Name do sing eternal praise:
Before His throne in white they ever stand,
And carry palms of triumph in their hand.

Above them all the Virgin hath a place,
Which caused the world with comfort to abound;
The beams do shine in her unspotted face,
And with the stars her head is richly crowned:
In glory she all creatures passeth far,
The moon her shoes, the sun her garments are.

Lo! here the look which Angels do admire!
Lo! here the spring from whom all goodness flows!
Lo! here that sight which men and Saints desire!
Lo! here that stalk on which our comfort grows!
Lo! this is she whom heaven and earth embrace,
Whom God did choose, and fillèd full of grace.

Next above her, and on a higher throne,
Our Savior in His Manhood sitteth here;
From Whom proceeds all perfect joy alone,
And in Whose Face all glory doth appear:
The Saints' delight conceived cannot be
When they a Man the Lord of Angels see.

O worthy place, where such a Lord is chief!
O glorious Lord, Who princely servants keeps!
O happy Saints, which never taste of grief!
O blessed state, where malice ever sleeps!
No one is here of base or mean degree,
But all are known the sons of God to be!

JOHN FINCH

"His head beating all the way upon the stones."

INDEX OF NAMES

A

Abbot, Henry, 375
Abel, Bl. Thomas, 246, 283, 284, 355
Adams. Bl. John, 320
Allen, William Cardinal, 7, 38, 328, 329, 330, 366, 377
Almond, Ven. John, 6, 361, 385, 386, 387, 410
Amias, Fr. John, 93, 94
Anderton, Ven. Robert, 6, 140, 143, 144, 145, 258
Arrowsmith, Ven. Edmund, 276, 296, 301, 302
Aske, Sir Robert, 18
Atkins, John, 38
Atkinson, Ven. Thomas, 88

B

Baker, Ven. Charles, 273
Bamber, Ven. Edward, 250, 254, 255
Barkworth, Ven. Mark, 71, 73
Barlow, Ven. Edward, 6, 286, 294, 295, 296, 297
Barnes, Robert, 5, 246, 355
Bayne, Bishop of Lichfield, 365
Beche, Bl. John, 382
Belchiam, Ven. Thomas, 251
Bell, Ven. Arthur, 37, 251, 391
Bell, Ven. James, 135
Bellarmine, Robert, 98
Bird, Ven. James, 81, 82, 249
Blount, Richard, 38
Blundell, William (cavalier), 6, 173, 174, 188
Blundell, William (poet), 9, 10, 126–27, 128–29
Bodey, Ven. John, 348, 349
Boleyn, Anne, 40, 150, 223

Bonner, Bishop of London, 11, 285, 319
Bost, Ven. John, 239, 242
Bourne, Bishop of Bath and Wales, 290
Bowden, Henry Sebastian, 1–2
Bowes, Ven. Marmaduke, 374
Briant, Bl. Alexander, 6, 340, 341, 381, 383, 384, 406, 407
Brookby, Ven. Anthony, 234
Buckley, Ven. John, 227
Bullaker, Ven. Thomas, 48, 323, 324, 325, 326, 327

C

Cadwallador, Ven. Roger, 6, 266, 275, 310
Campion, Bl. Edmund, 3, 5, 6, 24, 25, 26, 27, 28, 29, 39, 118, 177, 179, 184, 316, 333, 360, 366, 367, 369, 381, 383, 388, 415–21
Catesby, Robert, 149
Catherick, Fr. Edmund, 125
Catherine of Aragon, Queen, 150, 159, 160, 166, 171, 223, 246
Cecil, Robert, 149
Cecil, William, 186, 195, 307
Challoner, Richard, 2, 7
Charles I, King, 5, 262, 281, 392
Charles II, King, 5, 173
Charles V, King, 116, 371
Clement, Margaret, 209
Clement IX, Pope, 215
Clement VIII, Pope, 329
Clitheroe, Bl. Margaret, 3, 103, 104, 105, 106, 107, 185, 377
Colman, Fr. Walter, 78
Copgrave, John, 158
Corby, Ven. Ralph, 288, 289, 300
Cornelius, Ven. John, 219, 350, 352
Cottam, Bl. Thomas, 5, 153, 154, 176
Cromwell, Thomas, 74, 151, 166
Crowe, Ven. Alexander, 379

, Ven. Robert, 93, 94
s, Ven. William, 233, 236
ntwater, James, Earl of, 68
e, Ven. Richard, 320
son, Ven. Roger, 222, 224, 226
Ven. Robert, 5, 70, 351
t, Ven. James, 134
t, Ven. John, 287, 288, 289, 300
e, Robert, 291

VI, King, 11, 20, 115, 183, 285, 368
h I, Queen, 4, 5, 6, 7, 11, 12, 13, 16, 17, 70, 115, 120, 135, 145, 177, 184, 187, 256, 260, 268, 274, 290, 307, 315, 333, 334, 368, 371, 412
n, Ven. George, 375
en. Philip, 237
Bl. William, 201

n, Bl. Hugh, 362
on, Richard, 246
m, Abbot, 11, 13
. John, 4, 256
n. Thomas, 4, 279
. James, 56, 57, 59
ohn, 197
, Bl. Richard, 355
William, 179
. Roger, 73
n, 428
John, 3, 23, 51, 52, 53, 74, 138, 139, 204, 205, 206, 207, 208, 230, 8, 382
atthew, 414

Ford, Bl. Thomas, 5, 175, 177, 179
Forest, Bl. John, 159, 160, 171, 246, 283, 284
Fortescue, Bl. Adrian, 223, 292, 293

G

Gardiner, Bl. German, 16, 84
Garlick, Ven. Nicholas, 238
Garnet, Henry, 149
Gavan, John, 197
Genings, Fr. John, 14, 354
Genings, Ven. Edmund, 14, 353, 354, 389, 393, 394, 395, 396, 403
Gerard, Fr. John, 120
Gervase, Ven. George, 123, 124
Gibson, William, 375
Gilbert, George, 318
Goldwell, Bishop of St. Asaph, 116
Goodman, Ven. John, 281, 307
Gray, Fr. John, 187
Green, Ven. Hugh, 262, 263, 264, 267
Gregory XIII, Pope, 5, 16, 87, 318
Grissold, Bl. Robert, 232
Grove, Ven. John, 33, 155

H

Haile, Bl. John, 150
Hambley, Ven. John, 102
Hanse, Bl. Everard, 5, 247, 304
Hanse, William, 247
Harcourt, Bl. William, 191, 197
Harpsfield, Nicholas, 158
Hart, Bl. William, 6, 85, 86, 87, 88, 89, 90, 92, 95, 107, 108, 109, 164, 321
Hartley, Ven. William, 5, 317
Haydock, Ven. George, 54, 55, 59
Heath, Archbishop of York, 115

en. Henry, 5, 83, 98, 110, 121, 122, 130, 131, 132, 133, 342, 344
rd, Thomas, 59
I, King, 23
II, King, 3, 4, 6, 16, 35, 40, 79, 91, 115, 150, 151, 157, 166, 183, 187,
3, 226, 234, 251, 285, 307, 315, 355, 362, 363, 368, 371
Richard, 277, 298, 299
H . John, 80, 317
H obert Sydney, 389
H Thomas, 265
Ho Thomas, 392
Ho Nicholas, 3, 66, 80
Ho . John, 148, 151
Ho Philip, 3, 331, 332, 333, 334, 426–27
Hun Lawrence, 34
Hutto , 164

I

Ingleby, Ven. Francis, 185
Ingram, Ven. John, 240, 242
Ireland, Bl. John, 84
Ireland, Ven. William, 33, 155

J

James I, King, 17, 70
James II, King, 173
Jessop, John, 100
Johnson, Bl. Robert, 168, 169

K

Kemble, Ven. John, 271
Kirby, Bl. Luke, 6, 163, 176, 180
Kirkman, Bl. Richard, 291, 321
Knight, William, 375
Knox, Ronald, 1

L

Lacy, Bl. William, 270, 321
Langhorne, Ven. Richard, 229
Larke, Bl. John, 84
Lawrence, Bl. Robert, 151
Line, Ven. Anne, 72, 73, 143
Lloyd, Fr. John, 237
Lloyd, Ven. William, 22
Lockwood, Ven. John, 6, 125
Lowe, Bl. John, 320
Ludlam, Ven. Robert, 238
Luisa de Carvajal, 399

M

Marsden, Ven. William, 140, 144
Mary, Queen of Scots, 165, 315
Mary I, Queen, 3, 4, 5, 11, 13, 20, 25, 115, 116, 166, 183, 187, 260, 285, 307, 328, 371
Mason, Ven. John, 3, 389
Maxfield, Ven. Thomas, 217, 218
Maxwell, Ven. Thomas, 113
Mayne, Bl. Cuthbert, 50, 114, 378
Middlemore, Bl. Humphrey, 201
Milner, Ven. Ralph, 3, 222, 224, 226
More, Bl. Thomas, 3, 6, 35, 63, 64, 69, 79, 84, 91, 151, 183, 190, 208, 209, 221, 225, 230, 259, 282, 314, 368, 372, 373, 382
Morgan, Ven. Edward, 141
Morgan, William, 38
Morse, Ven. Henry, 43, 44, 60, 61
Munden, Ven. John, 5, 59
Muscot, Fr. George, 98, 404

N

Nappier, Ven. George, 356, 357, 358

Nelson, Bl. John, 45, 46, 47
Newdigate, Bl. Sebastian, 201
Newman, John Henry Cardinal, 1
Newport, Bl. Richard, 156
Nichols, Ven. George, 220
Nutter, Ven. John, 58, 59

O

Oates, Titus, 33, 155, 173, 193, 229, 410
Oglethorpe, Bishop of Carlisle, 410
Oldcorne, Ven. Edward, 120, 149
Osbaldestone, Ven. Edward, 364
Owen, John, 38
Owen, Walter, 38

P

Page, Ven. Francis, 73, 142, 143
Palasor, Ven. Thomas, 257
Pate, Bishop of Worcester, 371
Pattenson, Ven. William, 31
Paul III, Pope, 371
Payne, Bl. John, 114
Percy, Bl. Thomas, 19, 259, 260, 261, 268, 269
Persons, Fr. Robert, 39, 291, 318, 406, 407
Peto, Fr. William, 40
Philip II, King, 70, 116
Pibush, Ven. John, 62
Pickering, Bl. Thomas, 155, 253
Pickering, John, 19
Pikes, Ven. William, 101
Pilchard, Ven. Thomas, 5, 99, 100, 101
Pius V, Pope St., 177, 256, 259, 279
Plessington, Ven. William, 6, 235
Plumtree, Bl. Thomas, 12, 268

Plunket, Ven. Oliver, 3, 215, 305, 306
Pole, Bl. Margaret, 3, 166
Pole, Reginald Cardinal, 116, 152, 166, 368
Poole, Bishop of Peterborough, 186
Postgate, Ven. Nicholas, 252, 253
Pounde, Thomas, 17
Powell, Bl. Edward, 5, 246, 355
Powell, Margaret, 48
Powell, Ven. Philip, 212, 315
Price, Fr. Ignatius, 273

R

Rawlins, Fr. Alexander, 119
Reding, Fr., 250
Reynolds, Bl. Richard, 147, 152
Reynolds, Ven. Thomas, 30
Richardson, Bl. Lawrence, 5, 172, 176
Rigby, Bl. John, 196, 203
Roberts, Ven. John, 6, 398, 399, 400, 401, 402
Robinson, Ven. John, 313
Rochester, Bl. John, 157
Roe, Ven. Bartholomew, 30
Roper, William, 35
Rowsam, Ven. Stephen, 77

S

Scot, Ven. William, 156, 170
Scott, Ven. Monford, 216
Shert, Bl. John, 5, 175
Sherwin, Bl. Ralph, 5, 6, 39, 381, 388, 408
Sherwood, Bl. Thomas, 49, 50
Sixtus V, Pope, 328
Slade, Ven. John, 343, 349
Somers, Thomas, 399

Southwell, Ven. Robert, 3, 6, 65, 66, 67, 194, 211, 318, 335, 336, 337, 338, 347, 370, 405, 422
Southworth, Ven. John, 198, 199, 200, 210, 276
Spenser, Ven. William, 309
Stafford, William Viscount, 409, 410
Stone, Bl. John, 158
Storey, Bl. John, 4, 183, 184
Stransham, Ven. Edward, 38
Sugar, Ven. John, 231, 232
Sutton, Ven. Robert, 5, 243, 317
Swallowell, Ven George, 241, 242
Sympson, Ven. Richard, 238

T

Thirkell, Bl. Richard, 161, 162, 164, 178, 189, 321, 322, 339
Thirlby, Bishop of Ely, 274
Thomas, John, 249
Thompson, Bl. James, 73, 321, 376, 377
Thomson, Fr. Gerard, 143
Thulis, Ven. John, 96, 97, 423–25
Tichborne, Ven. Thomas, 136
Tunstall, Bishop of Durham, 16, 368
Tunstall, Ven. Thomas, 228
Turner, Ven. Antony, 197

W

Wall, Ven. John, 272, 303
Walpole, Ven. Henry, v, 117, 118, 119, 415–21
Walsingham, Francis, 59
Walworth, Bl. John, 157
Ward, Ven. Margaret, 6, 278
Ward, Ven. William, 244, 245, 324
Waterson, Ven. Edward, 15
Watkinson, Ven. Robert, 137

Watson, Bishop of Lincoln, 307
Webster, Bl. Augustine, 151
Wells, Ven. Swithin, 3, 393, 394, 396, 397
Whitaker, Ven. Thomas, 250
White, Bishop of Winchester, 20, 21
White, Ven. Eustace, 390
Whitebread, Ven. Thomas, 192, 193, 197, 202
Whiting, Bl. Richard, 362, 363
Wilde, Oscar, 1
Wolsey, Cardinal, 35
Woodcock, Ven. John, 250, 254, 258, 308
Woodfen, Ven. Nicholas, 32
Woodhouse, Bl. Thomas, 4, 195
Wrenno, Ven. Roger, 96, 97
Wright, Ven. Peter, 167, 359

Y

Yaxley, Ven. Richard, 220

Sophia Institute

Sophia Institute is a nonprofit institution that seeks to nurture the spiritual, moral, and cultural life of souls and to spread the gospel of Christ in conformity with the authentic teachings of the Roman Catholic Church.

Sophia Institute Press fulfills this mission by offering translations, reprints, and new publications that afford readers a rich source of the enduring wisdom of mankind.

Sophia Institute also operates the popular online resource CatholicExchange.com. *Catholic Exchange* provides world news from a Catholic perspective as well as daily devotionals and articles that will help readers to grow in holiness and live a life consistent with the teachings of the Church.

In 2013, Sophia Institute launched Sophia Institute for Teachers to renew and rebuild Catholic culture through service to Catholic education. With the goal of nurturing the spiritual, moral, and cultural life of souls, and an abiding respect for the role and work of teachers, we strive to provide materials and programs that are at once enlightening to the mind and ennobling to the heart; faithful and complete, as well as useful and practical.

Sophia Institute gratefully recognizes the Solidarity Association for preserving and encouraging the growth of our apostolate over the course of many years. Without their generous and timely support, this book would not be in your hands.

www.SophiaInstitute.com
www.CatholicExchange.com
www.SophiaInstituteforTeachers.org

Sophia Institute Press is a registered trademark of Sophia Institute.
Sophia Institute is a tax-exempt institution as defined by the Internal Revenue Code, Section 501(c)(3). Tax ID 22-2548708.